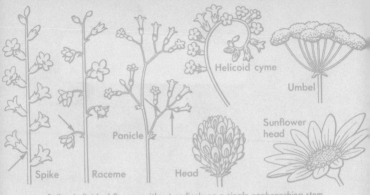

Spike: Individual flowers *without* pedicels on a *single nonbranching* stem.
Raceme: Individual flowers *with* a pedicel on a *single nonbranching* stem.
Panicle: Flowers with a pedicel and on a *branched* raceme.
Helicoid cyme: A coiled branching stem with youngest flowers at tip.
Umbel: All flowers have pedicels attached at same point.
Head: A dense cluster of flowers without pedicels on a single stem.

FLOWER ARRANGEMENTS ON STEM (INFLORESCENCES)

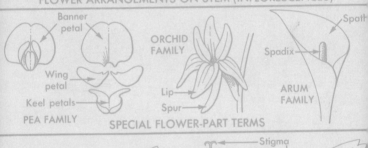

SPECIAL FLOWER-PART TERMS

SPECIAL SUNFLOWER FAMILY TERMS

THE PETERSON FIELD GUIDE SERIES

A Field Guide to Southwestern and Texas Wildflowers

Text by

Theodore F. Niehaus

Illustrations by

Charles L. Ripper

Virginia Savage

*Sponsored by
the National Audubon Society,
the National Wildlife Federation, and
the Texas Parks and Wildlife Department*

HOUGHTON MIFFLIN COMPANY · BOSTON

Library of Congress Cataloging in Publication Data

Niehaus, Theodore F.
A field guide to southwestern and Texas wildflowers.

(The Peterson field guide series; 31)
Includes index.
1. Wild flowers — Southwest, New — Identification.
2. Wild flowers — Texas — Identification. I. Ripper,
Charles L. II. Savage, Virginia. III. Title.
IV. Series.
QK142.N54 1984   582.13′0979   84 8926
ISBN 0-395-32876-4
ISBN 0-395-36640-2 (pbk.)

Printed in the United States of America

V 10 9 8 7 6 5 4 3 2

Contents

Editor's Note

Our Southwest, basically dry, becomes a flower garden after the rains. The deserts of Arizona and New Mexico become especially colorful in those years when seeds, long dormant, are brought to life. The open prairies, fields, and roadsides of Texas are always a spectacular show in the spring. Later in the season the high meadows of the mountains attract hummingbirds of several sorts. The botanist or flower lover need never run out of new finds to delight the eye.

An intensive amount of field work by Dr. Theodore Niehaus has gone into the preparation of this field guide. It has involved four growing seasons during which he visited each plant community from January until late fall, revisiting them periodically to catch the various species when they came into bloom. Equally demanding has been the task faced by Charles Ripper, who executed the line drawings, and Virginia Savage, who painted the color plates except for three done by Allianora Rosse. More than 1500 species are described and illustrated. The work of this skilled team demands our admiration.

Like the other volumes in the Field Guide Series, this book is based on a visual system, with species likely to be confused placed near each other for quick comparison and their key characters or "field marks" indicated by little arrows on the illustrations. Taken as a whole it is, in a sense, a pictorial key, consistent with the fundamental philosophy of the other Peterson Field Guides, which is based on readily noticed visual impressions rather than technical or phylogenetic features. This flower guide is patterned similarly to its counterparts, *A Field Guide to Pacific States Wildflowers* by Dr. Niehaus, and *A Field Guide to Wildflowers of Northeastern and North-central North America* by Margaret McKenny and myself. All three guides stress (1) color, (2) general shape or structure, and (3) distinctions between similar species — the field marks. The text is placed opposite the pictures; thus all pertinent information about a plant is confined within one double-page spread, eliminating the need for time-consuming cross-references. Like *A Field Guide to Pacific States Wildflowers,* this book gives an introduction to the plant regions of its area: in this case the vast region extending through Arizona, Colorado, New Mexico, and Texas, to adjacent Louisiana. There is also a key to the families, which presents the family symbols that are used throughout the book.

The Southwest, because of its wide variety of environments — mountains, valleys, plains, deserts, coastal marshes, and barrier beaches — has a great diversity of wildflowers. Even though this pocket guide describes and illustrates more than 1500 species, it cannot cover them all. However, it presents those you are most likely to find during your travels in the Southwest.

Roger Tory Peterson

Introduction

The Southwest and Texas area, as considered here, consists of Arizona, New Mexico, Colorado, and Texas. You will find this book quite useful in adjacent states—eastern California, southern Utah, Oklahoma, Louisiana, and northern Mexico—but should remember that the farther from the main area you go, the fewer species will be represented in this guide. As an aid to let you know if a species is present in adjacent areas, the abbreviations R. Mts. (Rocky Mountains), Pl. Sts. (Plains States), and S.E. (Southeastern States) are used in the appropriate species descriptions.

For our purposes, wildflowers are plants that have a main above-ground growth and die at the end of one growing season. Wildflowers generally lack a woody stem, although a very few (*Penstemon, Eriogonum,* and so on) have a low above-ground stem that is woody. Except for cacti, which are considered to be shrubs but are thoroughly covered in this Field Guide, shrubs and trees are not included due to lack of space.

All known cactus species of the area are illustrated in this guide, something that very few other books have done. All cactus species were observed as live plants in their natural habitat, not just as preserved specimens. Cacti are primarily identified by the number and arrangement of *main (central)* and *radial* spines of each cluster, color and shape of seed capsules, and overall plant shape. Flower shape and color are often the least useful identification features for cacti. Since a great deal of variation exists within most cactus species, a large number of species names have been proposed for variants that represent what is often but a single species. Before arriving at the species listed in this guide, I studied all known named species of cacti, including species that I later concluded did not merit species status.

The most representative species from each geographical plant community and its microhabitats are included in this guide. (The plant communities within the region covered by this guide are discussed in detail in the next chapter.) Selection of the wildflowers to be covered was a complex process; every known flowering plant species in the area was given careful consideration. As the field work and technical research progressed, I found that some species considered uncommon by various sources were in fact common and widespread, and added them to this *Field Guide*.

Intensive field study was conducted over four growing seasons. I visited each plant community and all of its microhabitats from

January until late fall, and revisited each area every two or three weeks to see each species come into flower. Of the 1505 species in this guide, 1498 were observed in the living state. Each species was photographed in color as a whole plant; the small parts were then recorded as close-ups. No one photograph can show all the important identifying features of most plants, but photographs can be of great value to an artist. My able partner, Charles Ripper, prepared all the black-and-white line illustrations to precise scale by projecting the plant images. (Note the scale at the lower right-hand corner of each illustration page.) The color plates were beautifully painted by Virginia Savage, who did 29 plates, and Allianora Rosse, who did 3.

This guide includes 1511 illustrations representing the common species in 86 different plant families. All families with wildflowers that users of this guide are likely to encounter are covered.

Each species description in the text provides the common and scientific name for the species, a brief description of its identifying characters and the region where it is found, and its flowering time.

Plant Names. Common names are sometimes debatable, since no system for common plant names exists. Some species have 15 to 20 different local names; on the other hand, 5 or 6 totally unrelated plants may have the same name. The genus name may be used as a common name for only one species in the genus, with the rest remaining unnamed, so that many species have never been given an individual common name. Every source for common names was consulted, including all popular and scientific books for the United States and many European sources. The common names given here are the ones most widely used or judged to be most appropriate to the species; of necessity, some new names were also coined.

The scientific name for each species represents the latest information available from all sources. Where controversy exists, the best solution for this guide has been used.

Descriptive Text. The preparation of each species description required extensive study of many sources. These included floras, scientific papers, consultation with scientists specializing in certain species or groups, study of thousands of museum specimens, and direct field study of living plants. Many new field observations are included here. Visual features most useful for species identification are italicized.

Region Where Found. The geographic regions are shown on the map on p. x and described on pp. ix–xiv.

Flowering Times. These are intended as a general guide; earlier times are for lower elevations and the southernmost areas.

Measurements. The measurements given for a species represent *the length of the stem* (which is not always the height of the plant). Measurements are given in metric units. For convenience, a rule showing U.S./metric equivalents is provided on the back cover (cloth edition) or inside back cover (paperback edition).

Wildflower Identification Methods

This guide provides two approaches to wildflower identification: 1) picture matching, using color and general shape, and 2) a key to plant families that will guide you to the appropriate section of the book where picture matching takes over.

Picture Matching. Field marks — the exact distinctions between similar species — are emphasized both by arrows in the illustration and by italics in the text description opposite the plate. A few species that may give a slight impression of being different are very hard to distinguish visually, since the critical differences are microscopic or otherwise do not lend themselves to illustration.

Breakdown by flower color is used in many scientific keys. Some species have more than one color phase, so illustrations for these are repeated in different sections of the book whenever possible. Text pages include cross references to sections where similar but differently colored specimens are found. Borderline colors are often difficult to categorize, especially in the lavender-red and violet-blue areas. The terms red-purple and blue-purple used here will help the reader make color interpretations; most of the plants in this ambiguous category are red-purple. If a flower has two main colors, look in both color sections. Remember that all plant species are as variable as the human species; an individual with a different number of petals or one that is an albino is not necessarily a new species, but rather an example of extreme variation.

Key to Families. The system of keys beginning on p. 408 will lead you to the family of the wildflower in question. The pages where that plant family is covered in the main text are then used for visual matching. The key will also prove useful to those who teach field courses in plant identification.

Plant families are presented on the basis of identifying features (field marks); as in the species descriptions, the most useful features for quick visual recognition are italicized. Many of these family field marks are also used for text page headings (*e.g.,* Pealike Flowers—Pea Family). The page headings in the family key (pp. 408–426) can also help narrow down the families under consideration to a very few. Once you have learned to recognize families, you can go anywhere in the world and use any wildflower book, since the world's number of plant families is only about 280, and the organization of families in other books may be nearly the same as in this Field Guide. The plant family symbols represent a condensed visual summary of the important field marks for each family.

Acknowledgments

Many friends, professional colleagues, and institutions have helped to produce this book; space permits me to acknowledge only a few directly. To Clayton Gilman and Brom and Joisie Wilkin, whose knowledge of Texas and the Southwest proved invaluable in researching this book, a special thanks. Institutions in the following states gave permission for me to use their specimens, libraries, and picture collections extensively. *Arizona:* University of Arizona, Tucson; Arizona State University, Tempe; Desert Botanical Garden, Phoenix; Southwest Research Station, Portal; Northern Arizona University and Museum of Northern Arizona, both at Flagstaff. *New Mexico:* University of New Mexico, Albuquerque; Western New Mexico University, Silver City; New Mexico Zoological-Botanical State Park, Carlsbad. *Texas:* Texas Parks and Wildlife Dept.; University of Texas at Austin; Sul Ross State University, Alpine; Texas A & M University, College Station; Southern Methodist University, Dallas; Rob and Bessie Welder Wildlife Foundation, Sinton; Stephen F. Austin State University, Nacogdoches; Sam Houston State University, Huntsville. *Colorado:* University of Colorado, Boulder. *California:* Jepson Herbarium and the University Herbarium at the University of California, Berkeley; California Academy of Sciences, San Francisco; Rancho Santa Ana Botanic Garden, Claremont. Among those who helped me with special problems, particularly the cacti, are Ed Gay, Dale and Allan Zimmerman, W. Hubert Earle, Pierre Fischer, Del Weniger, Barton Warnock, William Martin, J.J. Sperry, and a host of others. The careful work and constructive criticisms by my partner Charles Ripper, Roger Tory Peterson, and James Thompson and others at Houghton Mifflin Company were also a great help. The plant family symbols, with a few additions for the Southwest and Texas region, are from *A Field Guide to Wildflowers* (Eastern), by permission of Roger Tory Peterson, or from *A Field Guide to Pacific States Wildflowers*, by permission of Theodore F. Niehaus and Charles L. Ripper.

Plant Geography of the Southwest and Texas

The Southwest and Texas area contains a large number of flowering plant species in many kinds of desert, forest, and grassland communities. The Southwest is the crossroads of many flowering plant communities that have species also found thousands of miles outside our area. For example, some species from the Tundra and Northern Forest plant communities in the higher mountains of Arizona and New Mexico are also found in northern Canada and Alaska; some of the Plains Grassland communities species in Texas and New Mexico occur in grasslands extending all the way to Canada; and the Oak and Piney Woods species in eastern Texas are found in similar habitats extending eastward to Florida and Maine.

Throughout the Southwest and western Texas are many small to large mountain ranges that often rise well above the desert elevations. Biologically, these are "Sky Islands" surrounded by dry oceans of desert. The plants found on these Sky Islands differ considerably from south to north within our area. The southern mountains of Arizona, New Mexico, and the Big Bend region of Texas have many species that are primarily found southward to Central America. Central Arizona and southwestern New Mexico mountains (Mogollon Rim region) have a unique mixture of Central American, Rocky Mountain, and endemic species found only in that region. The mountains of northern Arizona and northern New Mexico have species that are peculiar to the Rocky Mountains, including some found in Canada and Alaska.

The map on the next page shows the most basic plant vegetation types found within the area covered by this guide. Each of these generalized vegetation types includes several specific plant communities. Each plant community has many additional smaller microhabitats — areas that are marshy, dry, steep, flat, sunny, and in deep shade. With practice, the observer can use this information about vegetation type, community type, and microhabitat to find many species in a relatively small area. Knowledge of the basic wet and dry seasons for the area, observation of different kinds of soil and rock, and visits to the same place at different times of year will yield even more different wildflower species.

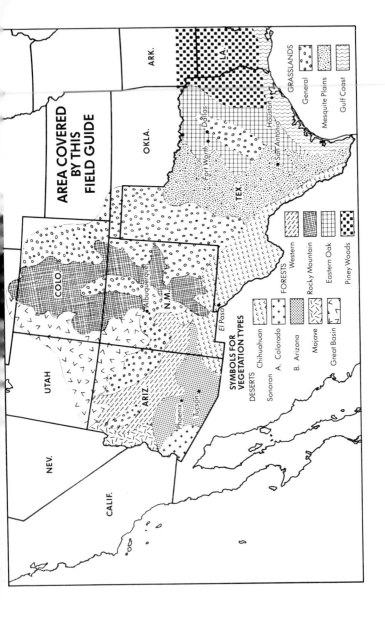

Desert Types

1. Chihuahuan Desert-Big Bend Region. Big Bend National Park in southwestern Texas has all of the various Chihuahuan subcommunities, from low-elevation desert zones to high-mountain cloud forests, and is highly recommended for wildflower observation from March through October. The portion of the Chihuahuan Desert within the U.S. occurs south of a line running from the southeast corner of Arizona to Silver City, New Mexico, and from El Paso, Texas, to Carlsbad, New Mexico, and thence southeasterly 50 to 100 miles north of the Rio Grande to Brownsville, Texas. The main rainy season is from July to October, with immense quantities of rain falling during the first two months. The winter and spring months are the dry season, with occasional moisture arriving on dying Pacific Coast storms. In some years a good, entirely separate group of spring wildflowers (not seen in the summer season) blooms in tremendous displays in March and April.

The Chihuahuan Desert is best known for its great number of cacti species, with the main group flowering in March and April. A second, smaller group of cacti flowers in July and August. All known cacti species of the area are illustrated in this guide. The months from late July to October are the peak of the main flowering season in the mountains.

2. Sonoran Desert. Two distinct subtypes of this plant community are known: the Colorado Desert subtype and the Arizona Desert subtype. The **Colorado Desert** subtype occurs in the southwestern corner of Arizona including Organ Pipe Cactus National Monument and extends south into Sonora, Mexico. This is an area of low elevation with large, plainlike areas and tremendous sand dunes. In some years heavy rainfall from Gulf of California hurricanes *(chubascos)* that come inland during September and October produces fantastic wildflower displays the following spring, starting in late February in the Yuma area through April, in Organ Pipe Cactus National Monument. One such special spring bloom occurred during research for this book; many wildflower species were observed at Organ Pipe Cactus National Monument for the first time.

The **Arizona Desert** subtype is found over the southern third of Arizona; the Giant Saguaro Cactus is a characteristic species of this subtype. This desert gets quite cold during the winter and receives only small amounts of rain from Pacific Coast winter storms. In March, the profusion of the main wildflower season at Organ Pipe Cactus National Monument (in the Colorado Desert subtype) contrasts sharply with the complete lack of flowers as one enters the Arizona Desert subtype on the short drive east to Tucson. In April and May, however, a substantial color display occurs; most of the cacti flower during this period. The main wet season in the Arizona Desert is July and August, when torrential thunderstorms (with flash floods a common feature) occur. During late July and early August, the tremendous golden carpets of "Summer Poppy" between Tucson and Nogales are a special display not to be missed. Most of the wildflowers in the Arizona Desert bloom from late July through September. June is impossibly hot with zero humidity; many Arizonans vacation out-of-state to escape the ovenlike heat.

3. Mojave Desert. This is primarily a cold desert, with the Joshua Tree one of the common species. Many cacti species are specific only to this desert. Northwestern Arizona (Wickenburg and northwest) and the depths of the Grand Canyon (but not the rim plateaus) belong to this desert type. Many of the valley-floor wildflowers at Zion National Park are also of this desert type. Rainfall is low, with a part coming from Pacific Coast winter storms and another part from July to September thunderstorms. The main flowering season is early March through May.

4. Great Basin Desert. The southeastern portion of the Great Basin Desert region is within our area and is often named the Navajoian subtype. This area extends across the top of Arizona and northwestern New Mexico into adjacent parts of Utah and western Colorado. The shrub, sagebrush, is the main indicator species of this desert type, with the Juniper Woodland Forest community (see below) present at the upper elevations. Many rare, tiny, button-sized cacti species are known only from this area. There are two wildflower seasons: a spring (April and May) bloom produced by Pacific Coast winter storms—with lower Zion National Park and Arches National Monument good at this time—and a mid- to late-summer bloom from torrential summer thunderstorms.

Forest Types

1. Juniper Forest. This is usually a narrow zone, like a bathtub ring, around nearly every mid-elevation mountain throughout the Southwest and Texas. The juniper species (called "cedars" in Texas) vary from area to area and are often associated with pinyon pines. The Claret Cup Cactus is almost always found in this forest type, although it also occurs in other vegetation types. Flowering seasons are April to early June and July to September.

2. Mogollon Ponderosa Pine Forest. The Mogollon Region is an oblong-shaped range of mountains extending at a southeasterly slant from Flagstaff, Arizona, to the Gila Wilderness of southwestern New Mexico. A sharp rim or cliff runs along the crest of the southern side. The plant communities are Ponderosa Pine Forest, Aspen Forest, Spruce-Fir Forest, and occasional large meadows resembling golf courses (named "parks" in the Southwest and

Rocky Mountains). Many wildflower species are known only from the Mogollon area. Considerable snow is common during the winter months. Wildflowers bloom in two waves: from late May to June, after the snowmelt; and in a heavy bloom from late July to early September, after torrential summer thunderstorms.

3. Oak Woodland Forests. The Southwest and Texas have an exceptionally large number of oak species. The oak forests of the western portion of the Southwest often are associated with a separate band of chaparral (low shrub community). In the eastern third of New Mexico and western Texas, and to the north on the plains are Dwarf Oak Forests (1 to 3 meters tall). In eastern Texas oak forests, oaks are mixed with other deciduous tree species from the eastern U.S. These eastern oak forests often extend as long, narrow fingers (cross timbers) through the prairies of central and eastern Texas.

4. Rocky Mountain Forest. The Rocky Mountains are botanically and physically composed of three distinct sections. The southern section is a series of narrow, very high mountains that run north-south in New Mexico from an area near El Paso, Texas through Colorado and from northeastern Arizona. A small amount of moisture from Pacific Coast winter storms is deposited in this area as snow. Summer thunderstorms deposit huge quantities of moisture from the Gulf of Mexico. Various narrow plant-community zones of Ponderosa Pine Forest, Mixed Spruce and Fir Forest, Aspen Forest, Subalpine Meadows (parks), and Alpine Tundra occur, each with its special group of wildflower species. June to August is the main flowering season. The first week of July is the best time to see the maximum tundra wildflower display.

5. Piney Woods. The mixture of pines in the Loblolly, Shortleaf, and Longleaf Pine Forest with hardwood trees in eastern Texas is often called the Piney Woods. Rainfall occurs throughout the year, making a very long flowering season possible, from February to November. The smallest change in habitat—even from bottomland to the nearest mound—means that different wildflower species are to be found. Two special subcommunities within the Piney Woods are the Pitcher Plant Bog and the Beech Forest. Many wildflower species that grew along streams at low elevations have become extinct in this area as many new reservoirs have covered nearly all of this habitat.

Prairie and Plains Grassland Types

1. General. Although many people (especially visitors from other parts of the U.S.) tend to think of the Southwest as predominantly a desert area, more than half of the land within the area covered by this Field Guide consists of grasslands of various types.

The wide variety of different grassland communities makes it impossible to name and describe them here. Each kind of grassland community is usually named for certain characteristic grass species (such as Blue Grama) that grow there. Some grassland communities are composed entirely of grasses and herbs; others typically have shrubs as well. Texas has more species of grasses than any other state. Some rain falls during the winter and spring months, but the great bulk falls over the summer. The wildflower season is from late spring through late summer.

2. Mesquite Plains. A broad area of plains runs through the center of Texas from Brownsville and vicinity to the northern border. These woodlands are characterized by spiny mesquite and catclaw shrubs. Open areas of prairie are common, and this vegetation type is considered part of the plains grassland. There are two periods of heavy rainfall; the first in spring, with March and April the peak months for wildflowers, and the second in late summer, following Gulf hurricanes.

3. Gulf Coast Prairies and Dunes. An area of flat woodlands, prairies, bayous, fresh and saltwater marshes, and beach dunes forms a narrow belt along the Texas Gulf Coast. Rainfall occurs throughout the year in this area, with some storms dumping enormous amounts in a few minutes. Wildflowers bloom from early spring through late summer, but most can be seen in the spring. Plant species found here usually range far down the Mexican coast and eastward to Florida.

White or
Whitish Flowers

A large category in which most species are clearly white, but also including flowers that are mostly white or that give a whitish impression (such as those spotted or tinted with yellow, red, blue, or green). If your flower is not in this section, check under the other colors. When possible, the group characteristics given in the text page titles are repeated in each color section, and in the same order. Where the flowers on a page look nearly the same but your sample does not fit, use the cross references given for other colors.

TREELIKE AND SHRUBLIKE CACTI

Cactus Family (Cactaceae)
See also pp. W 2–4; Y 126–142; R 252–270.

SAGUARO CACTUS *Carnegiea gigantea*
Gigantic, treelike stem with 12–24 prominent ribs. Flowers creamy white, opening at night and lasting into the morning hours. Fruit red-purple, edible. 6–15 m. Rocky slopes and well-drained flats. Southeastern quarter of Ariz. APRIL–MAY

GEARSTEM CACTUS *Cereus striatus*
Note the gray-green, sticklike stems with 6–9 barely distinguishable *broad, flat ribs, gearlike* in cross-section. Downward-projecting spine clusters with 2 main spines. 1–2 m. Grows among other shrubs for support. Sw. Ariz. near Organ Pipe Cactus National Monument. JUNE

QUEEN OF THE NIGHT *Cereus greggii*
The sticklike, branching, *rasplike stems* have 4–6 *sharply raised ribs* with many *small clusters of downward-projecting, blackish spines*. Large, funnel-like white flowers (10–20 cm) open only at night. Large, edible roots look like sweet potatoes. A lavender color form near Organ, N.M. 50 cm–2 m. Usually grows among acacias or creosote bushes for support. S. Ariz. to sw. Tex. JUNE

BARBWIRE CACTUS *Cereus pentagonus*
Large, sprawling (1–2 m) stems with 3 prominent ribs; stem triangular in cross-section. Each barbed-wirelike spine cluster has 7–8 gray radial spines and 1–3 central spines. Large (7–10 cm) white flowers. 1–2 m. Grows in thickets for support. Along Rio Grande from Laredo to Brownsville, Tex. APRIL

ORGANPIPE CACTUS *Cereus thurberi*
Large, upright, organ-pipelike stems, all growing from a central base at ground level. Large (5–10 cm), greenish white flowers (sometimes pale pink) near stem tips. Flowers open at night, wilt at dawn. 3–7 m. Sw. Ariz. at Organ Pipe Cactus National Monument; also Sonora and Baja, Mexico. MAY–JULY

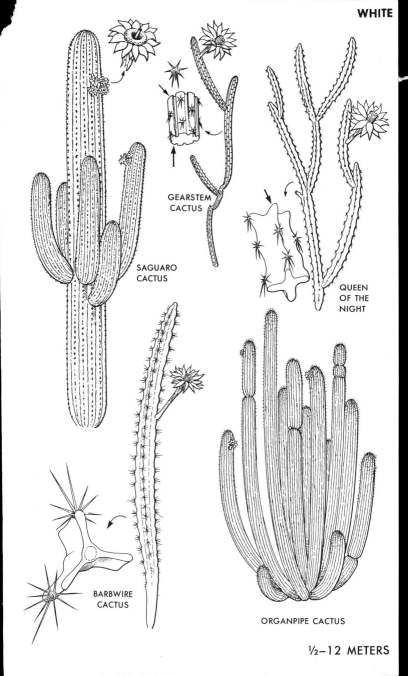

GEARSTEM
CACTUS

SAGUARO
CACTUS

QUEEN
OF THE
NIGHT

BARBWIRE
CACTUS

ORGANPIPE CACTUS

½–12 METERS

SMALL, ROUND OR CYLINDRICAL CACTI

Cactus Family (Cactaceae)
See also pp. W 2–4; Y 126–142; R 252–270.

PANCAKE CACTUS *Mammillaria gummifera*
Stem a low tussock with a *wide, flat pancake top* and numerous nipples, each with a cluster of brown spines of which *only 1 is erect*. Flowers white or yellowish, or pale pink. *Milky sap.* Highly variable. Rocky plains. Tucson, Ariz. to cen. and s. Tex.
MARCH–MAY

PAPERSPINE CACTUS *Pediocactus papyracanthus*
In each spine cluster 1 *long, broad, twisted, brown-paperlike spine* arises from a *ring of white radial spines* below. Flowers white. Fruits green. Cylindrical stem, 5–8 cm. Grows *within grama grass rings*. Grassland plains. Cen. N.M. to e. Ariz.
MAY–JUNE

NAVAJO CACTUS *Pediocactus peeblesianus*
Note the 1–4 *stout, wormlike central spines* curved (subspecies *fickeiseniae*) or flattened into a Maltese cross (subspecies *peeblesianus*). Each set of spines arises from a nipple tipped by a wad of cottony hairs and a ring of smaller spines. Flowers cream to coppery. Fruit green. Golfball-like stem. 2–5 cm. Plains, juniper woodlands. N. Ariz.
MARCH–APRIL

BRADY'S CACTUS *Pediocactus bradyi*
Golfball-like stem has *flattened, silverfishlike spine* clusters with a spineless center. Cream to pale yellow *urnlike flowers.* 1–5 cm. Plateaus. N. Ariz.
MARCH–APRIL

SILVERHAIR CACTUS *Pediocactus paradinei*
Silvery, hairlike spine clusters on rounded nipples, *nearly concealing* the golfball-sized stem. Petals white with pink midribs. 2–5 cm. Juniper woods. N. Ariz.
APRIL–MAY

WOVEN PINEAPPLE CACTUS *Echinomastus intertextus*
Note the *woven pattern of flattened, chalky blue to brown* spine clusters in *spiraling rows* of low nipples. *Green stem surface visible.* Each cluster has 2 *very long, pinkish* central spines pointing upward and *1 or few shorter ones* pointing downward, and a whorl of stout radial spines below. Flowers white to pink. Football-like stems. 5–20 cm. Grasslands in limestone areas. Se. Ariz. to Big Bend region of Tex.
MARCH–APRIL

MESA VERDE CACTUS *Sclerocactus mesae-verdae*
Small cylindrical stem has spiraling rows of stout, *silverfishlike* spine clusters, often with *1 erect central spine*. Flowers cream to yellowish with a *bright green throat.* 5–10 cm. Four Corners area, Ariz., N.M., Ut., Colo.
APRIL–MAY

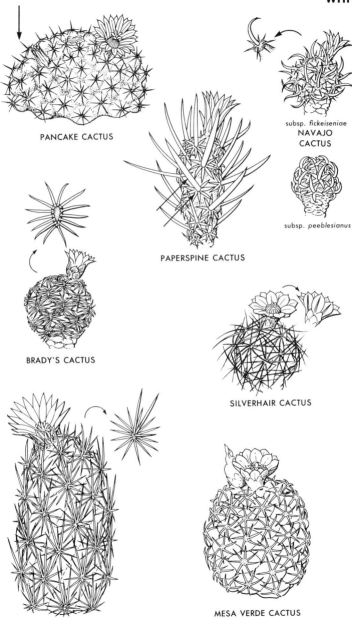

PANCAKE CACTUS

subsp. *fickeiseniae*
NAVAJO
CACTUS

subsp. *peeblesianus*

PAPERSPINE CACTUS

BRADY'S CACTUS

SILVERHAIR CACTUS

WOVEN PINEAPPLE CACTUS

MESA VERDE CACTUS

X ½

3 PETALS; POND OR MARSH PLANTS

Water Plantain Family (Alismataceae)

COMMON WATER PLANTAIN *Alisma plantago-aquatica*
Petals *smooth-edged.* Flowers in umbels along a leafless flower stem and with an overall pyramid shape. Seed capsule button-like. Leaves oblong to oval. 50 cm–1 m. Pond edges. S.W., n. Tex., R. Mts., Pl. Sts. JUNE–SEPT.

DUCK POTATO *Sagittaria latifolia*
The *arrow-shaped,* parallel-veined leaves vary in width. The 3-petaled flowers are in whorls of 3 along a leafless flower stem. 30 cm–1.2 m. Pond edges. S.W., Tex., R. Mts., Pl. Sts., S.E.
MAY–AUG.

GRASSLEAF ARROWHEAD *Sagittaria graminea*
Note the *lancelike* or *grasslike* leaves. Each flower has 3 large, oval to round petals. 30–60 cm. Grows in shallow water in ditches, ponds, marshes. Eastern third of Tex., Pl. Sts.
APRIL–NOV.

Bur-reed Family (Sparganiaceae)

BUR REED *Sparganium simplex*
Note the *round balls* of flowers along a usually floating stem. The linear, grasslike leaves usually float gracefully in the same direction. 30 cm–1 m. Shallow ponds. S.W., Tex., R. Mts.
APRIL–AUG.

Lizard-tail Family (Saururaceae)

YERBA MANSA *Anemopsis californica*
Many small flowers in a *tall cone* above a *circle* of petal-like *white bracts.* Leaf blades oblong to oval. 10–50 cm. Alkali and salt marshes. S.W., western quarter of Tex., R. Mts.
MAY–AUG.

LIZARD'S-TAIL *Saururus cernuus*
Note the *nodding tip* of the *lizardlike tail* of minute flowers and the large, dark green, *heart-shaped* leaves. 30–90 cm. Shallow water. Eastern quarter of Tex., Pl. Sts., S.E.
MAY–AUG.

Water Lily Family (Nymphaeaceae)
See also Y 186; B 344; G 406.

FRAGRANT WATER LILY Alien *Nymphaea odorata*
The large, floating flowers are white and fragrant. Large float-ing leaves. Ponds, lakes. S.W., Tex. MARCH–OCT.

Sedge Family (Cyperaceae)

WHITETOP *Dichromena colorata*
Note the large *umbrella* of broad, *white, leafy bracts* at the top of a *naked, triangular stem.* 30–60 cm. Wet ditches. Eastern third of Tex., S.E. APRIL–OCT.

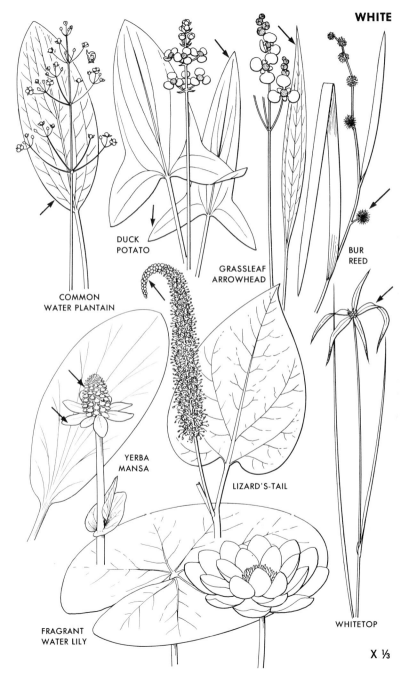

WHITE

COMMON
WATER PLANTAIN

DUCK
POTATO

GRASSLEAF
ARROWHEAD

BUR
REED

YERBA
MANSA

LIZARD'S-TAIL

WHITETOP

FRAGRANT
WATER LILY

X ⅓

3 OR 6 PETALS; LILYLIKE FLOWERS

Lily Family (Liliaceae)
See also pp. W 8–14; Y 114; O & R 226;
R 272; B 338; G 390.

SEGO LILY   *Calochortus nuttallii*
Note the *yellow, rounded spot* and the *red-purple horseshoe
mark* above it at the base of the white petals. Hairs at petal
base *unbranched*. Utah state flower. 20–40 cm. Open places.
Northern S.W., R. Mts.   MAY–JULY

ARIZONA MARIPOSA TULIP   *Calochortus ambiguus*
Note the *narrow, halfmoon band of dark purple* (sometimes
absent) above a broad band of numerous long, *branched,* yellow hairs that are enlarged at tips. Below the yellow hair band
is a *feltlike semicircle mat* of pale purple, plus a bare, darker
purple, *thumbnail-like semicircle* below the mat. Petal color
varies: white to bluish purple. 10–60 cm. Rocky open slopes and
woods. Ariz.   APRIL–AUG.

WHITE TROUT LILY   *Erythronium albidum*
Note the usually *single, nodding, bell-like flower* on a long leafless stem above a pair of broad, linear leaves. Leaves sometimes
have fawnlike purple mottling. 5–20 cm. Moist hardwood
slopes. N.-cen. and e. Tex., Pl. Sts., S.E.   FEB.–MARCH

TEXAS TRILLIUM   *Trillium texanum*
Note the 3 *large, white, triangular* petals of the upright flowers
and the 3 green, *lancelike* sepals, which are longer. Flowers are
on a stem above a single whorl of 3 lancelike leaves. 10–30 cm.
Low, moist hardwood forests along mossy streambanks. Rare.
Ne. Tex.   MARCH–APRIL

ALP LILY   *Lloydia serotina*
Note the *drooping,* creamy white sepals and petals; both are
veined outside, with a yellow or purplish hue. Stems have narrow, grasslike leaves. 5–20 cm. Moist alpine meadows. Sangre de
Cristo Mts., N.M.; R. Mts.   JUNE–AUG.

GREENSTRIPE LILY   *Eremocrinum albomarginatum*
Note the *lancelike* white petals, each with 3 *parallel green
veins.* Many narrow grasslike leaves. 10–50 cm. Deep sand
dunes. N. Ariz., s. Ut.   APRIL–JUNE

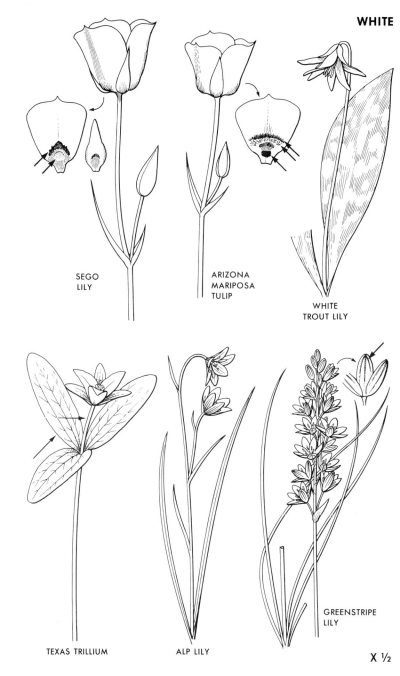

SEGO
LILY

ARIZONA
MARIPOSA
TULIP

WHITE
TROUT LILY

TEXAS TRILLIUM

ALP LILY

GREENSTRIPE
LILY

X ½

3 OR 6 LINEAR PETALS
YELLOW-GREEN GLAND AT PETAL BASES

Lily Family (Liliaceae)
See also pp. W 8–14; Y 114; O & R 226;
R 272; B 338; G 390.

ELEGANT CAMAS *Zigadenus elegans*
Note the *yoke-shaped gland* on each petal base. Stamens same length as petals. Flowers in racemes. Mountains of S.W., w. Tex., R. Mts. JUNE–SEPT.

FRILLYBELL CAMAS *Zigadenus virescens*
Note the *small, strongly bell-like,* white to greenish flowers, widely spaced on long pedicels. Petal edges *frilly;* gland at base of each petal rounded, dark yellow-green. Stubby stamens *shorter than petals.* 10–60 cm. High mountain slopes. S. Ariz. to Central America. JULY–SEPT.

BRANCHED CAMAS *Zigadenus paniculatus*
Thick, brushlike flower inflorescence, *branched along lower portion.* Yellow-green gland on each petal vaguely rounded to slightly bilobed. Stamens *longer than petals.* 30–60 cm. Open woods. Northern S.W., R. Mts. MAY–JUNE

NUTTALL'S CAMAS *Zigadenus nuttallii*
Inflorescence of numerous white to pale yellow flowers. Each petal has an *elongated base* and a *rounded* yellow gland spot. Stamen *filaments wider at base.* Stamens as long as or slightly shorter than petals. 30–90 cm. Pastures, rocky hillsides. Eastern third of Tex., Pl. Sts. MARCH–MAY

DEATH CAMAS *Zigadenus venenosus*
Numerous flowers in a thick spike. Stamens longer than petals. Petal tips rounded. Yellow gland on each petal base rounded. Linear leaves. *Bulb coat black.* Poisonous to livestock. 30–60 cm. Moist places. Plains, foothills. Northern S.W., R. Mts. MARCH–JUNE

BUNCHFLOWER *Melanthium virginicum*
Numerous flowers, creamy white at first, later dull green to purplish. Petal *narrow at base* with a *bilobed gland spot.* Long, *rough, linear* leaves (2 cm wide). 60 cm–1.2 m. Meadows, bogs, thickets. Eastern quarter of Tex. MAY–JULY

CALIFORNIA CORN LILY *Veratrum californicum*
Tall, *cornstalklike stem* with large, *parallel-veined leaves* in alternate arrangement. Flowers in a terminal panicle. 6 smooth-edged petals, each with a green V-*shaped spot* at the base. 1–2 m. Mountain meadows. S.W., R. Mts. JUNE–AUG.

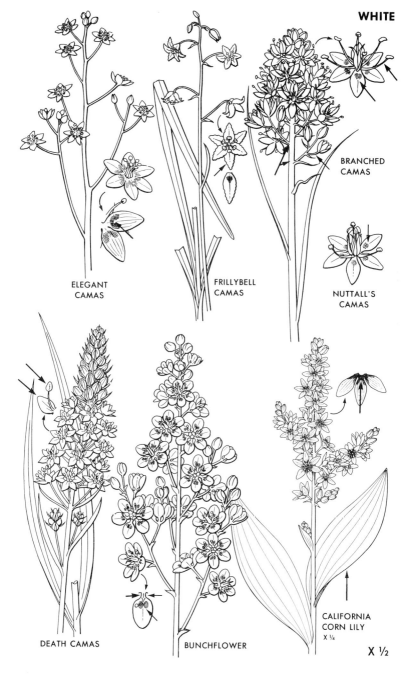

WHITE

ELEGANT CAMAS

FRILLYBELL CAMAS

BRANCHED CAMAS

NUTTALL'S CAMAS

DEATH CAMAS

BUNCHFLOWER

CALIFORNIA CORN LILY
X 1/4

X 1/2

3 OR 6 PETALS IN STARS OR TUBES

Lily Family (Liliaceae)
See also pp. W 8–14; Y 114; O & R 226;
R 272; B 338; G 390.

HOOKER'S FAIRYBELL   *Disporum hookeri*
Hanging, funnel-like flowers. Stigma *headlike.* The oval leaves
are attached to the stem by their clasping bases. 30–90 cm.
Shady woods in mountains. S.W., R. Mts.   MAY–JUNE

CLASPING TWISTED STALK   *Streptopus amplexifolius*
Note the sharply twisted, *right-angled pedicel* from which
hangs a *single bell-like* flower under each leaf. The parallel-
veined leaves are oval, with bases clasping the well-branched
stem. Flowers white or tinted greenish. 30–90 cm. Moist, shady
woods in mountains. S.W., R. Mts.   JULY–AUG.

BRANCHED SOLOMON'S SEAL   *Smilacina racemosa*
Numerous starlike flowers on a *well-branched* raceme. Many
parallel-veined leaves alternate on the arching stem. Berries red
with occasional purple spots. 30–90 cm. Shady woods in mountains. S.W., R. Mts.   MAY–JULY

STAR SOLOMON'S SEAL   *Smilacina stellata*
Similar to Branched Solomon's Seal. 3–15 flowers on an *unbranched* raceme. Berries red-purple, becoming black. 30–
60 cm. Damp woods in mountains. S.W., R. Mts.

MAY–JUNE

GREAT SOLOMON'S SEAL   *Polygonatum biflorum*
Note the *tubular, paired,* or 3 creamy white to pale yellow-
green flowers that *dangle below* the alternate, petioleless leaves
on *arching stems.* Berries blue-black. 30–60 cm. Moist hardwood slopes. Eastern quarter of Tex., S.E.   MARCH–MAY

SOUTHWEST SOLOMON'S SEAL
(not shown)   *Polygonatum cobrense*
Very similar to Great Solomon's Seal. Grows under trees in
mountains. W. Tex. to e. Ariz.   APRIL–JUNE

WESTERN TOFIELDIA   *Tofieldia glutinosa*
Small white flowers in a *terminal cluster.* Leafless flower stem
covered with minute, *reddish, glandular hairs.* Linear basal
leaves. 30–90 cm. Wet meadows, bogs. Northern S.W., R. Mts.
JUNE–JULY

SOUTHERN TOFIELDIA   *Tofieldia racemosa*
Small white to pale yellow flowers on an *open and spreading*
raceme. Each flower has *widely separated,* linear petals. The
tall leafless stem has *white glandular hairs.* Grasslike leaves in
a basal tuft. 30–60 cm. Wet pine savannahs, pitcher-plant bogs.
Eastern quarter of Tex., S.E.   JUNE–SEPT.

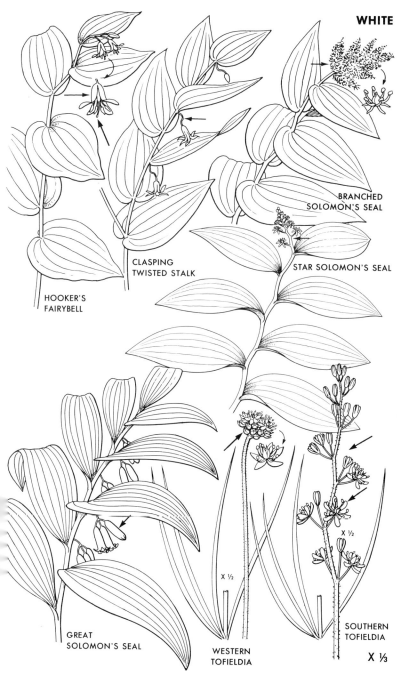

HOOKER'S
FAIRYBELL

CLASPING
TWISTED STALK

BRANCHED
SOLOMON'S SEAL

STAR SOLOMON'S SEAL

GREAT
SOLOMON'S SEAL

WESTERN
TOFIELDIA

X ½

SOUTHERN
TOFIELDIA

X ½

X ⅓

3 OR 6 PETALS; UMBEL ON LEAFLESS STEM OR LILY FLOWERS ON UPRIGHT SPIKE

Amaryllis Family (Amaryllidaceae)
See also pp. W 14–16; Y 116; R 274; B 338.

SOUTHERN SWAMP LILY *Crinium americanum*
The corolla tube is *twice as long* as any of the 6 *long, narrow petal lobes*. 2–6 large (5–10 cm) fragrant flowers in an umbel. Large, straplike leaves. 50–80 cm. Edges of swamps, lakes. Se. and coastal Tex., S.E. MAY–NOV.

SPRING SPIDER LILY *Hymenocallis liriosme*
Note the *inner white cup* between 6 *narrow upright petals*. Flowers in an umbel on a leafless stem. *Not fragrant*. Straplike leaves. Very similar is the **Sweet Spiderlily** (*H. caroliniana*) with fragrant flowers that bloom in spring. **Summer Spiderlily** (*H. eulae*) is fragrant and flowers during the summer. 50–80 cm. Common in marshy places. Eastern third of Tex. MARCH–MAY

MEXICAN STAR *Milla biflora*
Note the large, *starlike circle* of 6 white sepals and petals. Each flower has a long, slender, purplish brown *striped corolla tube*. Flowers in umbels. 30–60 cm. Open oak woodlands, plains. S. Ariz. to Big Bend area of Tex. AUG.–SEPT.

TRAUB'S RAIN LILY *Cooperia traubii*
Single, delicate, *very long* (10–15 cm), *narrow* corolla tube. Inner 3 petals *strongly rolled along margins*. Strong, sweet fragrance. Flower opens in evening hours. 30–60 cm. Heavy soils of Coastal Bend region, Tex. SEPT.–OCT.

DRUMMOND'S RAIN LILY *Cooperia drummondii*
Single, *short* (2–10 cm), *somewhat stout-tubed*, trumpetlike flower on a leafless stem. Inner 3 petals *flat or slightly rolled*. Variable fragrance. Blooms after heavy rain; flowers open in the evening. 10–30 cm. Extremely common. Eastern N.M., Tex., Pl. Sts., S.E. MAY–SEPT.

Lily Family (Liliaceae)
See also pp. W 8–14; Y 114; O & R 226;
R 272; B 338; G 390.

DESERT LILY *Hesperocallis undulata*
Flowers trumpetlike. Leaves with *wavy margins*. Tall, spikelike stem. 30 cm–1 m. Sandy flats, deserts. W. Ariz. FEB.–MAY

SAND LILY *Leucocrinum montanum*
Flowers *starlike* with long tubes, *tufted* among linear leaves. Fragrant. 5–15 cm. Sandy flats. Northern S.W.
MARCH–JUNE

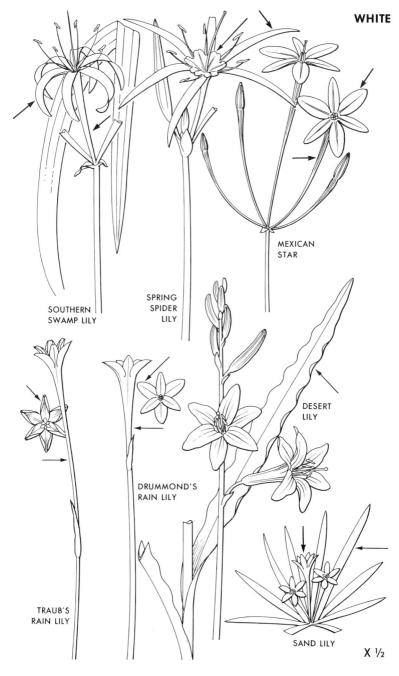

WHITE

MEXICAN
STAR

SOUTHERN
SWAMP LILY

SPRING
SPIDER
LILY

DESERT
LILY

DRUMMOND'S
RAIN LILY

TRAUB'S
RAIN LILY

SAND LILY

X ½

6 PETALS; UMBEL ON LEAFLESS STEM
DISTINCT ONION ODOR: WILD ONIONS

Amaryllis Family (Amaryllidaceae)
See also pp. W 14–16; Y 116; R 274; B 338.

CANADA GARLIC   *Allium canadense*
Note the *3–7 pink veins in each papery bract* at base of umbel
of flower pedicels. Umbel is at top of leafless stem. Petals
broadly oval. A variable species with *none, some, or all* flowers
replaced by *tiny bulblets*. Flowers white to pale pink. Ovary
walls smooth. Onion odor. 30–60 cm. Very common. Eastern
third of Tex., Pl. Sts., S.E.   MARCH–MAY

DRUMMOND'S ONION   *Allium drummondii*
Note the 1 *central pink vein* in each papery bract at the base of
the flower umbel. Ovary wall smooth. (In some areas, flowers
replaced by bulblets.) Flowers white to pink or red. Onion odor.
10–30 cm. Plains, prairies. Tex., N.M., Pl. Sts.   MARCH–MAY

PLUMMER'S ONION   *Allium plummerae*
Petal tips taper evenly to sharp points. Ovary walls have 6 *jagged crests*. Papery umbel bracts with *3–5 veins*. Flowers white
to pink. 10–30 cm. Mountains. Southern S.W.   JULY–AUG.

TEXTILE ONION   *Allium textile*
The usually white flowers (rarely pinkish) are urnlike, with the
tips of the 3 inner petals reflexed but *not constricted below* as in
Geyer's Onion (below). The back of each petal has a reddish
brown midrib. Bracts at base of umbel have 3–7 veins. Leaves 2.
Bulbs covered by a netlike textile coat. Dry plains. Northern
N.M., R. Mts.   APRIL–MAY

ARIZONA ONION   *Allium macropetalum*
The urnlike flower is *constricted at upper center* with the *petal
tip gently spreading*. 6 *rounded and flattened crests* near ovary
top. Usually 2 leaves. Flower white or pale pink with a dark
red-brown stripe on each lancelike petal. Distinct onion odor.
5–25 cm. Open desert flats and slopes. Extremely common.
S.W. to w. Tex., R. Mts.   MARCH–JUNE

GEYER'S ONION   *Allium geyeri*
Flowers white to pink with a distinct *constriction* immediately
below the *reflexed, tiny, sharply triangular* petals. A thick rib
on each petal back. In some areas flowers replaced by *small
bulblets*. 3 or more leaves. 10–90 cm. Damp mountain meadows.
S.W., R. Mts.   JUNE–AUG.

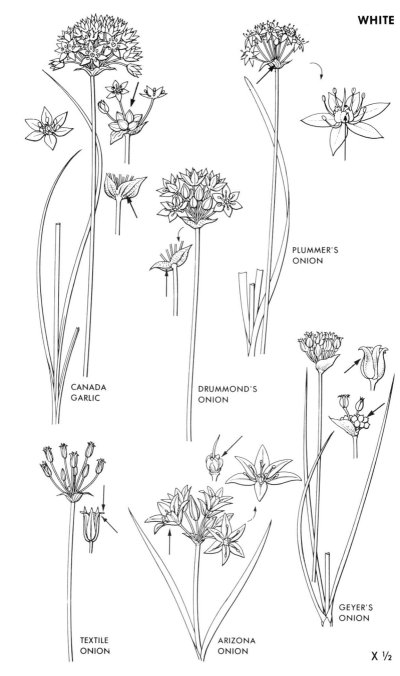

CANADA
GARLIC

PLUMMER'S
ONION

DRUMMOND'S
ONION

TEXTILE
ONION

ARIZONA
ONION

GEYER'S
ONION

X ½

3 UNEQUAL PETALS; ORCHIDS

Species of Arizona to West Texas
Orchid Family (Orchidaceae)
See also pp. W 18–20; Y 114; O & R 228–230; BG 390–394.

BOG CANDLES   *Habenaria dilatata*
Flowers with a curving spur *shorter* than the lip petal are subspecies *albiflora* — **Bog Candles** — or, if spur is *longer* than lip petal, subspecies *leucostachys* — **Sierra Crane Orchid.** Numerous flowers in a long spike. 10–60 cm. Wet places, mountains. Northern S.W., R. Mts.   MAY–AUG.

WESTERN LADIES' TRESSES   *Spiranthes porrifolia*
Similar to Hooded Ladies' Tresses (below). The lip petal is *triangular to oval* with 2 prominent *protuberances* at the base. 10–60 cm. Wet springy places. Northern S.W., R. Mts.

                                           MAY–AUG.

HOODED LADIES' TRESSES   *Spiranthes romanzoffiana*
Lip petal *constricted near tip.* Flower spike a dense spiral, much like a single braid of hair. 10–50 cm. Wet streambanks, meadows in mountains. S.W., R. Mts.   JULY–OCT.

REDSPOT LADIES' TRESSES   *Spiranthes parasitica*
Basal half of lip petal *rectangular.* Spongy, *deep orange-red spot* hidden deep inside throat of flower. A basal cluster of 2–3 dark green, *oval leaves* and a thin, leafless stem with very few, small, scattered, creamy to pale yellow flowers. 5–20 cm. Deep Douglas Fir humus on deeply shaded north slopes in mountains. S.W. to sw. Tex.   JULY–AUG.

MENZIES' RATTLESNAKE   *Goodyera oblongifolia*
ORCHID
The *skin pattern of a rattlesnake* is simulated by a central strip of mottled white on the dark green oblong leaves. Leaves in a basal rosette. A few white to greenish tubular flowers on a *naked stem.* 30–90 cm. Dry shady woods in mountains. E. Ariz. to w. N.M., R. Mts.   JULY–SEPT.

MICHOACÁN LADIES'   *Spiranthes michuacana*
TRESSES
The stout flower stem and bracts are *conspicuously long-haired.* Flower leaf bracts *extra long.* Flowers cream to pale yellow-green. Petal *edges* with conspicuous long hairs. All petals except lip petal have *dark green lines.* 30–60 cm. Near water-washed boulders in mountains. Southern S.W. to sw. Tex.

                                         SEPT.–OCT.

DWARF RATTLESNAKE ORCHID   *Goodyera repens*
Leaves dark green with *white zones* along principal veins, giving a *checkered appearance.* Leaves *loosely scattered up lower portion* of flower stem. Flowers small, white to greenish. 10–30 cm. Mountains. Northern S.W., R. Mts.   JULY–SEPT.

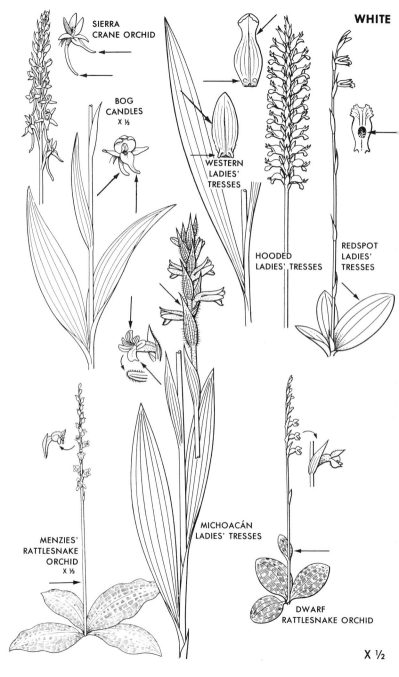

SIERRA CRANE ORCHID

BOG CANDLES X ⅓

WESTERN LADIES' TRESSES

WHITE

HOODED LADIES' TRESSES

REDSPOT LADIES' TRESSES

MENZIES' RATTLESNAKE ORCHID X ⅓

MICHOACÁN LADIES' TRESSES

DWARF RATTLESNAKE ORCHID

X ½

3 UNEQUAL PETALS; ORCHIDS

Species of Central and East Texas
Orchid Family (Orchidaceae)
See also pp. W 18–20; Y 114; O 228–230; G 390–394.

NODDING LADIES' TRESSES *Spiranthes cernua*
Flowers in a *double spiral, arching downward.* Flowers white
with a yellowish center and downy, white hair. Leaves basal, slender, narrower toward base. 30–50 cm. Seepage slopes,
swamps. Eastern quarter of Tex., Pl. Sts., R. Mts.

JULY–DEC.

GREENSPOT LADIES' TRESSES *Spiranthes gracilis*
Note the *bright green spot* on the lip petal. The very slender
stem has a single *corkscrewlike* spiral of flowers. 30–60 cm.
Woodlands, open fields. Eastern third of Tex. JULY–OCT.

LITTLE PEARL TWIST *Spiranthes grayi*
Stem very thin, with a slender spiral of *tiny, pure white* flowers.
Each petal 5 mm long. 15–40 cm. Well-drained hardwood forest
slopes. Eastern quarter of Tex. JUNE–AUG.

GREENVEIN LADIES' TRESSES *Spiranthes praecox*
Note the thin, *parallel green veins* with lateral branches,
within the *oblong* lip petal, which is *broadest at its lower end*
(5–15 mm long). Flowers in a single spiral. 60–70 cm. Wet,
grassy pine woods, coastal marshes. Eastern quarter of Tex.

MARCH–JUNE

SPRING LADIES' TRESSES *Spiranthes vernalis*
Note the *reddish brown hairs on ovary.* Other parts of flower,
bracts, and stem also have dense, downy hair, but it is often
nearly white. Flowers in a *long, single* spiral. 30–60 cm. Common in wet ditches, dunes, coastal marshes. Eastern third of
Tex., S.E. APRIL–JULY

EGGHEAD LADIES' TRESSES *Spiranthes ovalis*
Stem slender, with several tight, *multi-rowed spirals* of tiny
flowers in a *dense, egglike cylinder* that tapers at both ends.
10–40 cm. Moist shady woods. Eastern quarter of Tex.

AUG.–OCT.

SNOWY ORCHID *Habenaria nivea*
Note that the lip petal of this snowy-white orchid is *on top.* The
spur is *long and horizontal.* 30–90 cm. Wet savannahs, bogs.
Se. Tex., S.E. MAY–AUG.

WHITE FRINGED ORCHID *Habenaria blephariglottis*
Note the *long, deeply fringed lip petal* (2–3 cm). Stems stout.
15–75 cm. Marshes, wet prairies. Se. Tex. JUNE–SEPT.

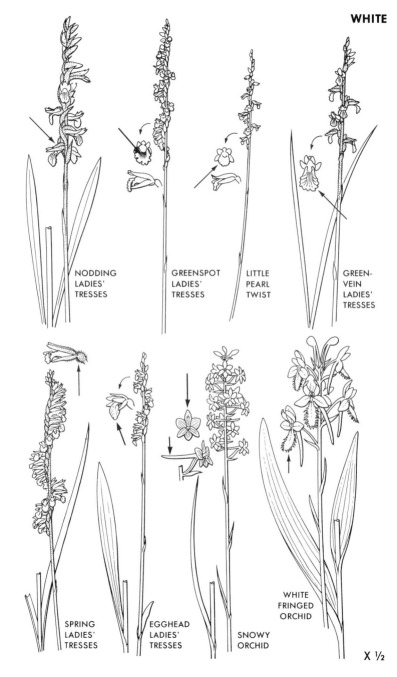

WHITE

NODDING
LADIES'
TRESSES

GREENSPOT
LADIES'
TRESSES

LITTLE
PEARL
TWIST

GREEN-
VEIN
LADIES'
TRESSES

SPRING
LADIES'
TRESSES

EGGHEAD
LADIES'
TRESSES

SNOWY
ORCHID

WHITE
FRINGED
ORCHID

X ½

6 SHOWY PETALS; MILKY SAP
NUMEROUS BUSHY STAMENS; POPPIES

Poppy Family (Papaveraceae) See also pp. Y 122; O-R 232.

CREAM CUPS *Platystemon californicus*
The 6 creamy petals have bright yellow basal spots. Flower stems have conspicuous *long hairs*. Leaves linear, in a basal cluster. Milky sap. 10–30 cm. Open fields. Ariz. MARCH–MAY

FATBUD PRICKLY POPPY *Argemone munita*
Many *small prickles between the veins* on the undersides of the leaves. Longer prickles on leaf veins, margins, and stem. Leaves usually *lobed for half of width or less*. Pale yellow, milky sap. Prickles on the *fat, rounded flower buds* are at right angles. 30 cm–1.5 m. Western half of Ariz., Ut. MAY–SEPT.

DEEPLOBE PRICKLY POPPY *Argemone squarrosa*
Similar to Fatbud Prickly Poppy, with prickles between veins. Leaves *lobed for more than half of width*. 30–60 cm. Plains country. W. Tex., e. N.M., Pl. Sts., R. Mts. APRIL–SEPT.

ARIZONA PRICKLY POPPY *Argemone pleiacantha*
(not shown)
Similar to Fatbud Prickly Poppy, but area between veins on leaf undersides *bare*. 50 cm–1 m. Common in Ariz., w. N.M.
APRIL–NOV.

TEXAS PRICKLY POPPY *Argemone albiflora*
Prickles on flower buds *point upward*. Prickles *absent between veins* on undersides of deeply lobed leaves. Tex.
MARCH–JUNE

BROADLEAF PRICKLY POPPY *Argemone polyanthemos*
Similar to Texas Prickly Poppy, but *leaf blades broad,* only *slightly lobed*. Plains. Cen. and n. Tex., N.M. APRIL–NOV.

RED PRICKLY POPPY *Argemone sanguinea*
Prickles at *right angles* on flower buds. *No prickles between veins* on undersides of leaves. Stamen filaments lemon yellow to dark red. Petals white, deep pink, or blood red. Leaves deeply lobed. 50 cm–1 m. S. Tex. FEB.–APRIL

CHISOS PRICKLY POPPY *Argemone chisosensis*
(not shown)
Very similar to Red Prickly Poppy. Petals white to deep pink. 50 cm–1 m. Big Bend region, Tex. MARCH–JUNE

BLOODROOT *Sanguinaria canadensis*
Large, round, shiny green leaf blades with *rounded lobes*. Large white flowers have 8 or more *narrow petals*. Numerous stamens. Red-orange, *bloodlike sap*. 15–30 cm. Edges of well-drained hardwood slopes. E. Tex., Pl. Sts. FEB.–MARCH

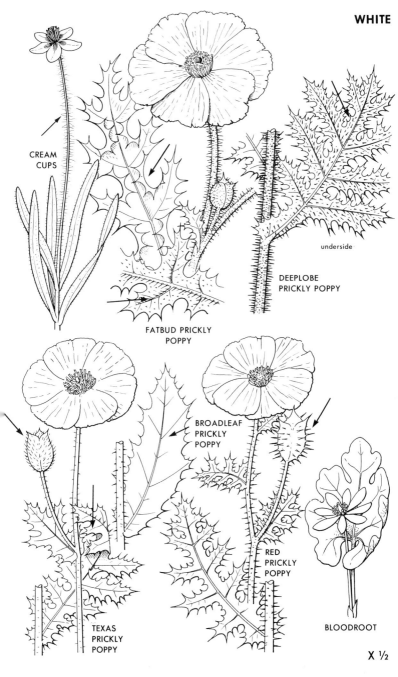

WHITE

CREAM CUPS

FATBUD PRICKLY POPPY

DEEPLOBE PRICKLY POPPY

underside

BROADLEAF PRICKLY POPPY

TEXAS PRICKLY POPPY

RED PRICKLY POPPY

BLOODROOT

X ½

4 OR 6–9 PETALS

Bedstraw or Madder Family (Rubiaceae)
See also p. R 280.

NORTHERN BEDSTRAW *Galium boreale*
Stem leaves in *whorls of 4, each with 3 prominent veins*. Numerous flowers in *thick panicles*. Stem and leaves *nearly smooth*. 30–60 cm. Common. Mountain woods, meadows. Northern S.W., R. Mts. JULY–SEPT.

FENDLER'S BEDSTRAW (not shown) *Galium fendleri*
Similar to Northern Bedstraw, but leaves have *1 central vein*. 10–30 cm. High mountains. S.W. JULY–AUG.

PRAIRIE BLUETS *Hedyotis nigricans*
Petal *tips sharply pointed* in a 4-petaled Maltese cross. Leaves *linear, in opposite pairs*. Flowers white, pink, or purplish. Stem square. 5–50 cm. Very common. S.W., Tex., Pl. Sts.
APRIL–NOV.

COMMON BEDSTRAW *Galium aparine*
4-angled *spiny* stems have *whorls* of 6–8 leaves. Tiny flowers with 4 petals. *Spiny twin seeds*. 30 cm–1 m. Moist places. S.W., Tex., Pl. Sts., R. Mts. MARCH–MAY

PARTRIDGEBERRY *Mitchella repens*
Note the white or pink, fragrant flowers with 4 petals in *twinlike union* at the end of creeping stems. Petal surface has *velvety hairs*. Small rounded leaves in pairs. Fruit a red berry with *2 eyespots*. Shady woods. Eastern quarter of Tex., Pl. Sts., S.E. APRIL–JULY

Barberry Family (Berberidaceae)

MAY APPLE or MANDRAKE *Podophyllum peltatum*
Note the *single, nodding, waxy* flower with 6–9 petals in the crotch below 2 very large, deeply divided, umbrella-like leaves. Fruit a large, lemonlike berry, edible. 30–40 cm. Often in large colonies in semishaded woodland openings. A pink-flowered form occurs in ne. Tex. Woods. E. Tex., Pl. Sts., S.E.
MARCH–APRIL

Dogwood Family (Cornaceae)

BUNCHBERRY *Cornus canadensis*
Umbrella-like leaf whorl with a large, 4-petaled flower. Red berries. 5–20 cm. Mountains. Northern S.W., R. Mts.
MAY–JULY

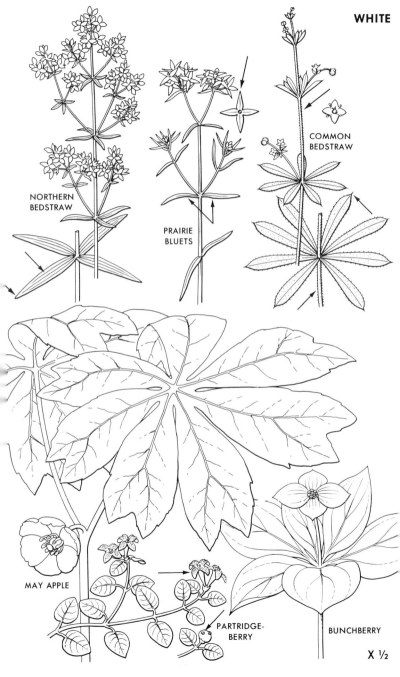

WHITE

NORTHERN
BEDSTRAW

PRAIRIE
BLUETS

COMMON
BEDSTRAW

MAY APPLE

PARTRIDGE-
BERRY

BUNCHBERRY

X ½

4-PETALED MALTESE CROSS; SMALL OVAL SEEDPODS

Mustard Family (Cruciferae)
See also pp. W 26–32; Y 144–152; O 232; R 276.

CALIFORNIA SPECTACLE POD *Dithyrea californica*
Note the 2 *eyeglass-shaped pods,* somewhat thickened and with a *corky margin;* they are held *horizontally.* Numerous pods crowded together. Leaves basal. 10–30 cm. Common in sandy places. W. Ariz. MARCH–MAY

TOURIST PLANT *Dimorphocarpa wislizenii*
Note the *sunglass-shaped seedpod* that contains 1 seed in each of the 2 rounded "lenses." Each seedpod is *held upright* in a *loose, scattered* arrangement. Leaves lancelike with shallow, scattered teeth. 10–60 cm. Common in sandy places. S.W. to w. Tex., Pl. Sts. MARCH–JUNE

WEDGELEAF DRABA *Draba cuneifolia*
A low cluster of *wedge-shaped leaves* with toothed margins, below a number of leafless flower stems. Small flowers in cylindrical columns, becoming *flat, banana-shaped seedpods.* 10–30 cm. Very common. S.W., Tex. FEB.–MAY

SHEPHERD'S PURSE Alien *Capsella bursa-pastoris*
Note the flat, *heart-shaped seedpods.* If inverted they resemble a *shepherd's purse.* Flowers tiny. Basal leaves dandelionlike. 10–60 cm. Common. S.W., Tex., R. Mts. FEB.–MAY

LACE POD *Thysanocarpus curvipes*
Note the *flattened, lacy-margined, round,* single-seeded pods hanging from a curved pedicel. Leaves slender, arrow-shaped. Plant covered with tiny hairs. One of the first spring plants. 10–90 cm. Grassy places. N. Ariz., R. Mts. JAN.–MAY

SWEET ALYSSUM Alien *Lobularia maritima*
Note the numerous small white flowers in *thick, thumblike* branches; entire plant a small, cushiony mass. Seedpods oval; leaves linear. 2–25 cm. Occasional. Tex., R. Mts. JAN.–MAY

HOARY CRESS Alien *Cardaria draba*
Seedpods kidney-shaped in outline. Flowers light gray. Oval gray leaves, *petioled* at stem base, but becoming arrow-shaped and *clasping* on upper stem. 30–60 cm. Disturbed places. S.W., w. Tex., R. Mts. FEB.–AUG.

McVAUGH'S BLADDERPOD *Lesquerella mcvaughiana*
Low, central cluster of *silvery gray, spatula-like leaves.* White to pale purplish flowers in terminal clusters. Round, *pealike* seedpods. 10–40 cm. Big Bend region. Tex. MARCH–APRIL

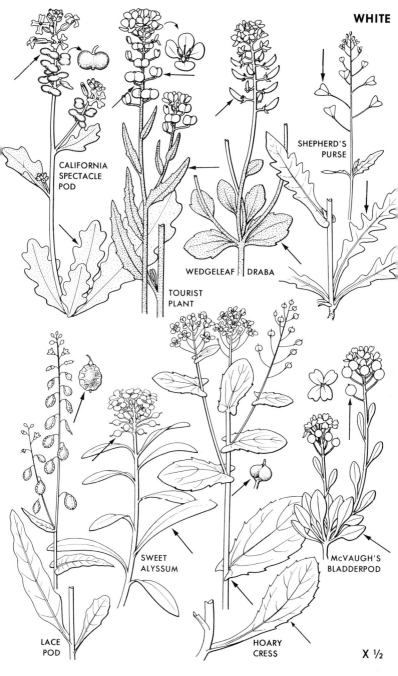

WHITE

CALIFORNIA
SPECTACLE
POD

TOURIST
PLANT

WEDGELEAF   DRABA

SHEPHERD'S
PURSE

LACE
POD

SWEET
ALYSSUM

HOARY
CRESS

McVAUGH'S
BLADDERPOD

X ½

4-PETALED MALTESE CROSS; SMALL OVAL SEEDPODS

Mustard Family (Cruciferae)
See also pp. W 26–32; Y 144–152; O 232; R 276.

FREMONT'S PEPPERGRASS   *Lepidium fremontii*
Large, rounded, *bushlike* plant with numerous flowering branches. Leaves linear, or divided into a few linear lobes. Base of *stem somewhat woody.* Seedpod flattened into 2 *winglike* portions. 10–60 cm. Common. W. Ariz.   MARCH–MAY

POORMAN'S PEPPERGRASS   *Lepidium campestre*
Alien
Basal leaves *tonguelike;* upper leaves arrow-shaped. Seedpods oval with a notch. 10–60 cm. Disturbed places. Northern S.W., R. Mts.   MARCH–AUG.

LONGPETAL PEPPERGRASS   *Lepidium medium*
The large petals are *longer than* the sepals. Lower stem leaves *pinnate* with a long, central strap and *linear lobes.* Upper stem leaves straplike with 2 or 3 sharp lobes. Round, flattened seedpods have a tiny terminal *notch.* 10–60 cm. Common. S.W., Tex., R. Mts.   FEB.–AUG.

THURBER'S PEPPERGRASS   *Lepidium thurberi*
Note the *lacy, pointed,* pinnate lobes of each leaf. Stem has *many long hairs.* Leaves nearly hairless. Seedpod oval to oblong. Flowers relatively large for a peppergrass. 30–60 cm. Common on flats. Cen. and s. Ariz. to sw. N.M.   FEB.–NOV.

HAIRY PEPPERGRASS   *Lepidium lasiocarpum*
Note the *lacy, rounded lobes* of the pinnate lobes of each leaf. *Both* leaves and stem have many *short, stiff, white hairs.* Seedpods oval. 10–30 cm. Sandy plains. S.W., western half of Tex., R. Mts.   FEB.–JULY

FIELD PENNYCRESS Alien   *Thlaspi arvense*
Note the round, *penny-sized* seedpods. Stem leaves narrow and lancelike. 10–60 cm. Northern S.W., Tex., R. Mts., Pl. Sts.
    MARCH–JUNE

FENDLER'S PENNYCRESS   *Thlaspi fendleri*
Flowers in dense, *headlike clusters.* Seedpods *triangular.* Stem leaves *arrow-shaped* with a dense cluster of spoon-shaped basal leaves. 10–60 cm. Pine woods in mountains. S.W., to w. Tex., R. Mts.   FEB.–AUG.

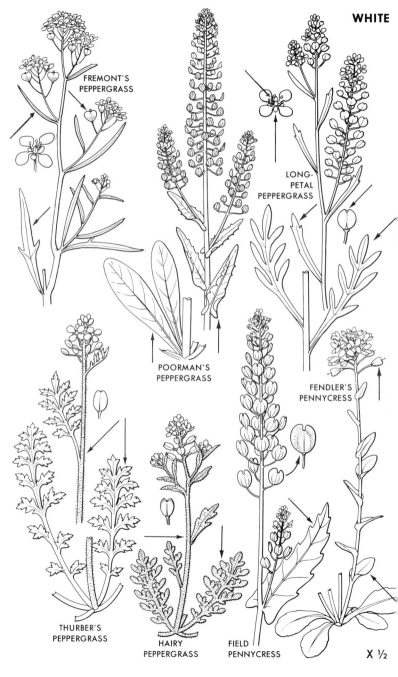

WHITE

FREMONT'S
PEPPERGRASS

LONG-
PETAL
PEPPERGRASS

POORMAN'S
PEPPERGRASS

FENDLER'S
PENNYCRESS

THURBER'S
PEPPERGRASS

HAIRY
PEPPERGRASS

FIELD
PENNYCRESS

X ½

4-PETALED MALTESE CROSS;
LINEAR SEEDPODS

Mustard Family (Cruciferae)
See also pp. W 26–32; Y 144–152; O 232; R 276.

BICOLOR MUSTARD *Nerisyrenia camporum*
Note the *broad, frosty, semi-maplelike leaves* with *thick petioles*. Curved, flattened, *banana-shaped* seedpods. Petals white, or with some pale lavender. 30–60 cm. W. Tex., e. N.M.
JAN.–NOV.

WHITE SANDS MUSTARD *Nerisyrenia linearifolia*
Note the *greenish, rounded, fleshy, linear* leaves. 10–30 cm. Gypsum flats and dunes. White Sands and Carlsbad, N.M., south into sw. Tex.
APRIL–AUG.

GARDEN ROCKET Alien *Brassica eruca*
Note the *dark-veined, windmill-like,* white or palest yellow petals. Leaves pinnate-lobed. Seedpods linear and *closely pressed* against the stem. 30–60 cm. Frequent on sandy roadsides. Sw. Ariz.
FEB.–MARCH

WILD RADISH Alien *Raphanus sativus*
Seedpod a *fat cylinder with constrictions* between each seed. Flowers pale white to various shades of pink and yellow. All colors usually found at the same location. Broad pinnate leaves along stem. 30 cm–1 m. Common in disturbed places. Tex., R. Mts.
FEB.–SEPT.

DRUMMOND'S ROCK CRESS *Arabis drummondii*
Seedpods *crowded and erect*. Flowers white to pinkish. Basal leaves lancelike, with a narrowing basal portion. Leaves become slim arrowheads clasping the upper stem. Hairless to sparsely haired. 30–60 cm. Open mountain slopes. Northern S.W., R. Mts.
MAY–SEPT.

WHITE WATERCRESS *Rorippa nasturtium-aquaticum*
Alien
Sprawling, succulent stems with pinnate leaves, each leaf consisting of 3–9 *oval leaflets*. Tiny flowers in terminal clusters. Pungent taste. 30–90 cm. Common in quiet running water. Low to high elevations. S.W., Tex., R. Mts., Pl. Sts., S.E.
MARCH–MAY

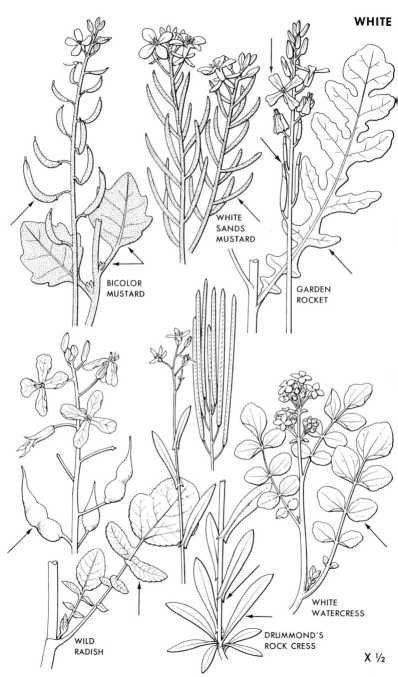

WHITE

BICOLOR MUSTARD

WHITE SANDS MUSTARD

GARDEN ROCKET

WILD RADISH

DRUMMOND'S ROCK CRESS

WHITE WATERCRESS

X ½

4-PETALED MALTESE CROSS;
LINEAR SEEDPODS

Mustard Family (Cruciferae)
See also pp. W 26–32; Y 144–152; O 232; R 276.

WHOLELEAF MUSTARD   *Thelypodium integrifolium*
Numerous long, narrow seedpods give a *brushlike* appearance.
White to pale blue or pink flowers in terminal clusters. *Large, oblong leaves* in a basal rosette. Stem leaves short and linear.
1–2 m. Northern S.W., R. Mts.   JULY–AUG.

CALIFORNIA MUSTARD   *Thelypodium lasiophyllum*
The *broad,* elongated leaves are *sharply lobed.* Seedpods *whiskerlike,* hanging downward. The white to pale yellow flowers are in terminal spikes on well-branched stems. 20 cm–1 m.
Common in low deserts. Ariz.   FEB.–APRIL

TEXAS MUSTARD   *Thelypodium texanum*
Leaves *pinnate, ladderlike.* Flowers and *long,* linear seedpods in a thick terminal brush. 30–60 cm. Clay bottoms, bare hillsides. Big Bend region, Tex.   FEB.–APRIL

WRIGHT'S MUSTARD   *Thelypodium wrightii*
Leaves *lancelike* with *sharp, sawtoothed margins.* Plant widely branched. 50 cm–1.5 m. Among pines, chaparral, junipers. S.W. to w. Tex., R. Mts., Pl. Sts.   MARCH–OCT.

LYALL'S BITTERCRESS   *Cardamine lyallii*
Leaves *rounded to kidney-shaped,* scattered along the erect stem. Dense terminal racemes of flowers, becoming elongated as the linear seedpods develop. 10–60 cm. Mountain meadows and streambanks. S.W., R. Mts.   JULY–AUG.

CUTLEAF TOOTHWORT   *Dentaria laciniata*
Note the *whorl of 3 leaves,* each divided into 3 *narrow, sharply lacerated segments.* Flowers white to pale red-purple. 10–40 cm. Rich, moist hardwood forests. E. Tex., Pl. Sts., S.E.
                                                      FEB.–APRIL

Caper Family (Capparidaceae). See also pp. Y 152; R 236.

REDWHISKER CLAMMYWEED   *Polanisia dodecandra*
Numerous flowers crowded together, each with all 4 slender petals *bent upward above the long, red, whiskerlike* stamens.
Each leaf has 3 leaflets. Seedpods *bananalike* with a *thin, tapering base* attached to a long, threadlike pedicel. 30–60 cm.
Numerous habitats. S.W., Tex., R. Mts.   MARCH–NOV.

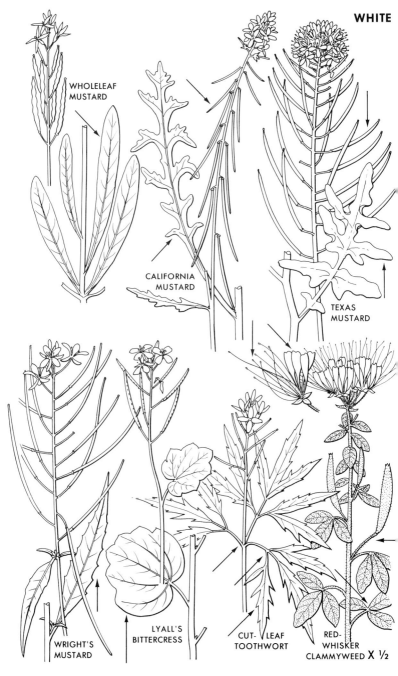

WHITE

WHOLELEAF MUSTARD

CALIFORNIA MUSTARD

TEXAS MUSTARD

WRIGHT'S MUSTARD

LYALL'S BITTERCRESS

CUT-LEAF TOOTHWORT

RED-WHISKER CLAMMYWEED X ½

4 SHOWY PETALS ON TOP OF OVARY

Evening Primrose Family (Onagraceae)
See also pp. W 34–36; Y 154–158; R 278–280.

SAWTOOTH EVENING PRIMROSE *Oenothera pallida*
Large white flowers aging pink on *erect white stems; 30–60 cm*
Sawtooth Evening Primrose (subspecies *runcinata*) has *strongly sawtoothed* linear leaves and is most common in our area, on dry plains and sand dunes. Leaves are *linear* in **Whitepole Evening Primrose** (subspecies *pallida*), which is relatively uncommon in the S.W. and rare in the N.W. S.W., w. Tex., R. Mts.   APRIL–SEPT.

PRAIRIE EVENING PRIMROSE   *Oenothera albicaulis*
Erect stem. Stem leaves *completely pinnate;* basal leaves *broad, undivided,* spoonlike. Large white flowers become pink with age. 10–40 cm. Lower elevations on sandy flats. S.W. to w. Tex., Pl. Sts.   MARCH–JUNE

KUNTH'S EVENING PRIMROSE   *Oenothera kunthiana*
Erect stem. Note the *broad, triangular* portion of the terminal leaf blade and 1 or more pairs of linear *lobes* below. To 40 cm. Cen. and s. Tex.   FEB.–MAY

BIRDCAGE EVENING PRIMROSE   *Oenothera deltoides*
Flat, spokelike stems at flowering time later curve upward to form a "birdcage." Stems have a *peeling skin.* Leaves *spatula-shaped* on a short, erect stem. Large white petals. Blooms in the evening. 5–30 cm. Sandy places in lower deserts. W. Ariz.
                           FEB.–APRIL

TUFTED EVENING PRIMROSE   *Oenothera caespitosa*
Low, flat rosette of linear leaves with *lobed margins.* Stem skin *smooth.* Large white flowers age to pink. 1–20 cm. Dry, rocky slopes. S.W., to w. Tex., R. Mts.   APRIL–AUG.

CALIFORNIA   *Oenothera californica*
EVENING PRIMROSE
Tall, erect stem. Leaves have *wavy margins.* Stem skin *not peeling.* Large white flowers turn pink with age. 10–60 cm. Washes, plains on lower deserts. W. Ariz.   FEB.–JUNE

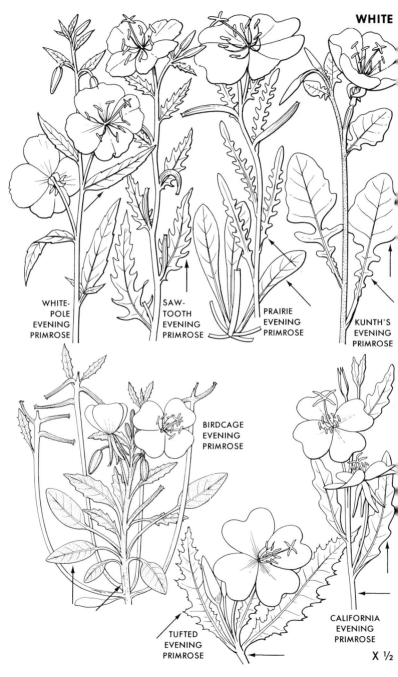

WHITE

WHITE-POLE EVENING PRIMROSE

SAW-TOOTH EVENING PRIMROSE

PRAIRIE EVENING PRIMROSE

KUNTH'S EVENING PRIMROSE

BIRDCAGE EVENING PRIMROSE

TUFTED EVENING PRIMROSE

CALIFORNIA EVENING PRIMROSE

X ½

4 SHOWY PETALS ON TOP OF OVARY

Evening Primrose Family (Onagraceae)
See also pp. W 34–36; Y 154–158; R 278–280.

Note: *Gaura* species have white petals that later turn reddish.

WILLOWLEAF BEEBLOSSOM *Gaura filiformis*
A single, erect stem branching at mid-level is clothed with numerous *green, petioleless, willowlike leaves.* Stem nearly *smooth.* Flowers in summer and fall. 30–90 cm. Open fields. Cen. and s. Tex., Pl. Sts. JUNE–DEC.

KISSES *Gaura suffulta*
Note the *petioled, green* leaves with broad, lancelike blades whose margins vary from wavy to occasionally sawtoothed lobes. Stem often has *many stiff hairs.* 10 cm–1 m. Common in open fields. N.M., Tex. MARCH–JUNE

WOOLLY BEEBLOSSOM *Gaura villosa*
Note the numerous *grayish,* lancelike leaves with undulating margins. Leaves and stem *gray with velvety or woolly surfaces.* 50 cm–2 m. Eastern N.M., western third of Tex., Pl. Sts.

APRIL–OCT.

MIDGET BEEBLOSSOM *Gaura parviflora*
Tiny flowers, *nearly hidden* among large, green, elliptical leaves. 30 cm–1 m. S.W., Tex., Pl. Sts. MARCH–NOV.

BOOTH'S EVENING PRIMROSE *Camissonia boothii*
Note the *bright green* leaves *spotted with red* that form a basal cluster. Smallish flowers in a *compact, spikelike cluster.* Stem skin *peeling or shredding.* 5–30 cm. Cinders. Nw. Ariz.

JULY–SEPT.

BROWN EYES *Camissonia clavaeformis*
Brown, eyelike spot often present at the petal base. Flowers with rounded petals in a cluster above the basal rosette of oval, *strongly toothed* leaves. Flower buds in a *nodding cluster.* Seed capsules club-shaped with a definite pedicel. 10–20 cm. Sandy washes. Lower deserts. Ariz. FEB.–APRIL

NUTTALL'S GAYOPHYTUM *Gayophytum nuttallii*
Note the fine, *threadlike* stems and leaves. Often well-branched, with minute white flowers that dry pink or red. 10–60 cm. Common in dry pine forests. S.W., R. Mts.

JULY–SEPT.

STICKY FIREWEED *Epilobium glandulosum*
Many small flowers (less than 10 mm) on long ovaries. Flowers vary from white to pink. Stem has tiny *sticky hairs.* Opposite, lancelike leaves with minutely *sawtoothed* margins. 30 cm–1 m. Moist places in mountains. Northern S.W., R. Mts.

JUNE–AUG.

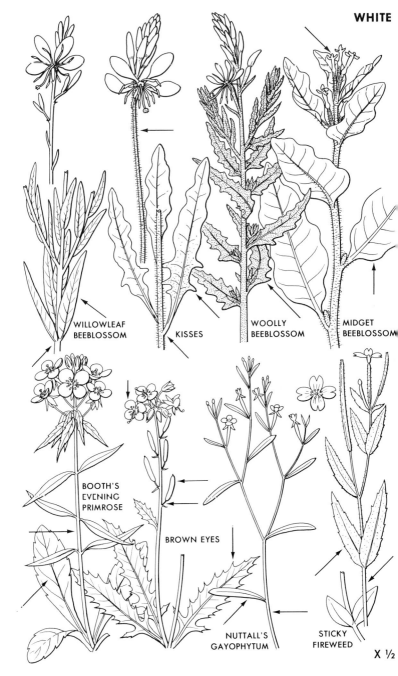

WILLOWLEAF
BEEBLOSSOM

KISSES

WOOLLY
BEEBLOSSOM

MIDGET
BEEBLOSSOM

BOOTH'S
EVENING
PRIMROSE

BROWN EYES

NUTTALL'S
GAYOPHYTUM

STICKY
FIREWEED

X ½

4 OR 5 PETALS; TINY TUBULAR FLOWERS IN CLUSTERS

Buckwheat Family (Polygonaceae)
See also pp. W 38–40; Y 158–160; R 282–284.

WESTERN BISTORT *Polygonum bistortoides*
Note the *rounded ball* of small flowers on a *wiry, leafless stem,* well above the leaves. Basal leaves broad, lancelike, and petioled. 10–60 cm. Common in wet mountain meadows. S.W., R. Mts. JUNE–SEPT.

WILLOWLEAF SMARTWEED *Polygonum lapthifolium*
Note the rounded, *smooth-edged, papery bracts* that surround the stem immediately above the point where each leaf is attached. Leaves willowlike. Flowers white to pale pink in dense, spikelike clusters. 50 cm–1 m. Moist places. S.W., Tex., R. Mts., Pl. Sts., S.E. APRIL–DEC.

LADY'S THUMB *Polygonum persicaria*
Similar to Willowleaf Smartweed, but the papery stem bracts are *fringed.* White to pink flowers, in somewhat *thumblike clusters.* 30 cm–1 m. Common in moist places. S.W., Tex., R. Mts., Pl. Sts., S.E. JULY–SEPT.

YARD KNOTWEED Alien *Polygonum aviculare*
The prostrate, small, sprawling, wiry stems have many *tiny, blue-green,* lancelike leaves with *silvery bracts* at their bases. Tiny white, pale green, or pink flowers. 30–60 cm. Very common in yards, roadsides. S.W., Tex., R. Mts., Pl. Sts., S.E.
APRIL–NOV.

DOUGLAS' KNOTWEED *Polygonum douglasii*
Stems *erect. Narrow, linear leaves* with papery basal bracts. Flowers white to greenish or reddish in loosely flowered racemes. 10–50 cm. Dry mountain meadows, plains. S.W., R. Mts., Pl. Sts. JUNE–SEPT.

Amaranth Family (Amaranthaceae) See also pp. G 402.

SNAKE COTTON *Froelichia floridiana*
Note the *cottony,* 5-lobed, tubular flowers in a *dense, spikelike cluster* on very tall (50 cm–1 m), *wandlike stems.* Lancelike leaves few, in *opposite pairs.* Open fields. S.W., Tex., Pl. Sts., S.E. MAY–NOV.

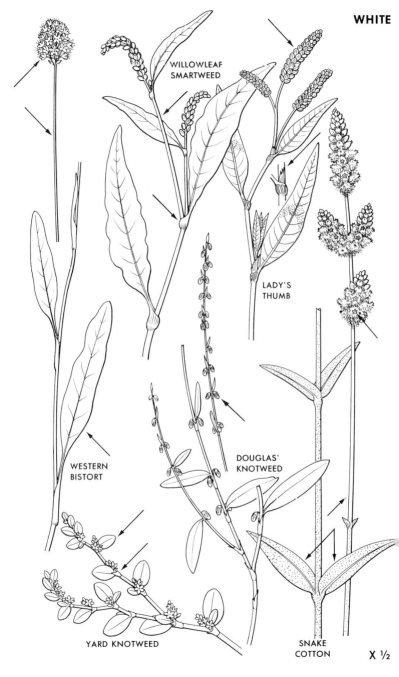

WHITE

WILLOWLEAF
SMARTWEED

LADY'S
THUMB

WESTERN
BISTORT

DOUGLAS'
KNOTWEED

YARD KNOTWEED

SNAKE
COTTON

X ½

4 OR 6 PETALS; TINY TUBULAR FLOWERS IN CLUSTERS

Buckwheat Family (Polygonaceae)
See also pp. W 38–40; Y 158–160; R 282–284.

BRITTLE SPINEFLOWER *Chorizanthe brevicornu*
Flowers within a *narrowly elongated cylinder* with ribs and 6 curved spines at the top. Linear leaves. 5–20 cm. Gravelly slopes of low deserts. Ariz. MARCH–MAY

THURBER'S SPINEFLOWER *Chorizanthe thurberi*
Cylindrical flowers with 3 *inflated, buttresslike sacs at base.* 5 short teeth at top, a small horn on each sac. Spatula-like leaves. 5–20 cm. Common in lower deserts. Ariz. MARCH–MAY

ROUNDLEAF SPINEFLOWER *Oxytheca perfoliata*
Stem leaves *rounded.* Flowers 4-lobed halfway down the corolla. 5–30 cm. Lower deserts. W. Ariz. MARCH–APRIL

NODDING ERIOGONUM *Eriogonum cernuum*
Flowers *nodding* or pendulous, tinted with white or rose. Petals rectangular with wavy margins. Rounded leaves. 10–30 cm. Northern S.W., R. Mts. JULY–OCT.

ANGLESTEM ERIOGONUM *Eriogonum angulosum*
The erect, *angled stem* has whitish hairs. Basal leaves broadly *lancelike with wavy margins.* A few linear leaves along the open-branched stems. Flower clusters in a broad bowl of rounded bracts. Each flower white and rose. 10–30 cm. Joshua Tree, juniper woodlands. W. Ariz. APRIL–NOV.

ANTELOPE SAGE *Eriogonum jamesii*
Gray-green, *lancelike* leaf blades on a long, *tapering* petiole form a basal rosette and whorls of leaves on the flowering stems. Ball-like flower clusters with small lancelike *leaves* at the *base* of each cluster. 10–30 cm. Plains, lower mountains. S.W., Tex., R. Mts., Pl. Sts. JUNE–OCT.

ROUNDLEAF ERIOGONUM *Eriogonum rotundifolium*
Note the *round, bright green* leaf blades on long petioles. Leaves only in basal rosettes. Few white flowers per cluster on *limp-looking,* leafless flower stems. 30 cm. Frequent in open sandy places. E. Ariz. to w. Tex. MARCH–NOV.

YERBA COLORADO *Eriogonum annuum*
Broad, branching sprays of flowers on a tall, gray, erect, leafless stem. Many *cottony, lancelike* leaves on lower stem. 5–15 cm. Open grasslands. N.M., Tex., Pl. Sts. APRIL–NOV.

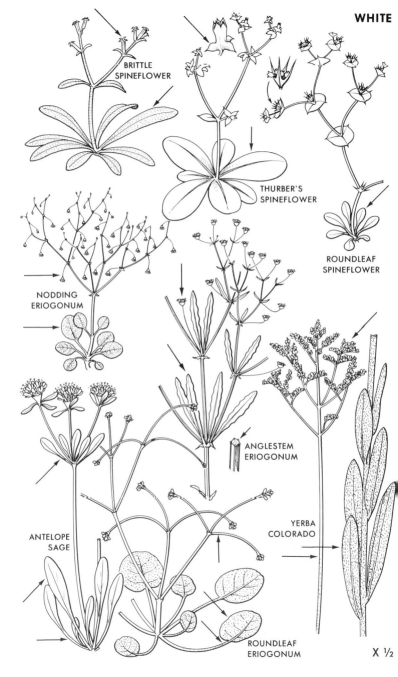

WHITE

BRITTLE
SPINEFLOWER

THURBER'S
SPINEFLOWER

ROUNDLEAF
SPINEFLOWER

NODDING
ERIOGONUM

ANGLESTEM
ERIOGONUM

YERBA
COLORADO

ANTELOPE
SAGE

ROUNDLEAF
ERIOGONUM

X ½

5 TO MANY PETALS; NUMEROUS STAMENS

Buttercup Family (Ranunculaceae)
See also pp. W 42–44; Y 162–164;
R 236, 286; B 344, 356–358; G 396, 406.

MARSH MARIGOLD *Caltha leptosepala*
Note the fleshy, *round to kidney-shaped* leaves. Large, solitary flowers on leafless stems well above the leaves. 10–30 cm. Wet mountain meadows. S.W., R. Mts. JUNE–SEPT.

AMERICAN GLOBEFLOWER *Trollius laxus*
Solitary flowers on a *leafy stem*. Leaves divided into usually 5 fingerlike lobes, each lobe of 3 smaller segments. 10–40 cm. Wet mountain meadows. Northern S.W., R. Mts. JUNE–JULY

WESTERN BANEBERRY *Actaea rubra*
Leaves pinnate; each lateral leaflet narrow, toothed, and *maplelike. Small* flowers in terminal *clusters*. Shiny red or white berries. 30–90 cm. Moist mountain forests, streambanks. S.W., R. Mts. MAY–JULY

WATER BUTTERCUP *Ranunculus aquatilis*
Submerged leaves, divided into many *threadlike filaments*. Flowers 5-petaled. Submerged floating stems. Ponds and slow streams. S.W., R. Mts. MARCH–AUG.

CANADIAN ANEMONE *Anemone canadensis*
Note that each leaf is divided into many *straplike* segments, tipped by sharp, pointed lobes. Large white flower. *Seedhead round.* 10–30 cm. Wet streambanks in mountains. N.M., R. Mts. JULY–AUG.

BASKET ANEMONE *Anemone heterophylla*
Each leaf divided into *short, diverging lobes*. Open, *basketlike flower* of linear, white or deep blue petals around an *elongated dome* of ovaries. Seedhead *cylindrical*. 10–30 cm. Frequent in open woods. Tex., Pl. Sts. FEB.–APRIL

WESTERN VIRGIN'S BOWER *Clematis ligusticifolia*
Vines with bright green, pinnate leaves, each of 5–7 lancelike, sharply toothed leaflets. The large white male flowers have numerous bushy stamens. Female flowers less showy, but later become *nests of long, silky-haired seeds*. S.W., R. Mts.
APRIL–SEPT.

OLD MAN'S BEARD *Clematis drummondii*
Similar to Western Virgin's Bower. *Grayish* pinnate leaflets, cleft or pointed. Climbing over shrubs. 1–5 m. Southernmost S.W. to cen. Tex. APRIL–SEPT.

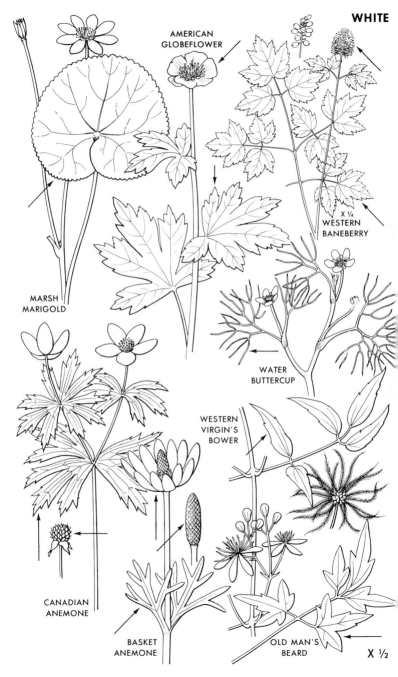

WHITE

AMERICAN
GLOBEFLOWER

x ¼
WESTERN
BANEBERRY

MARSH
MARIGOLD

WATER
BUTTERCUP

WESTERN
VIRGIN'S
BOWER

CANADIAN
ANEMONE

BASKET
ANEMONE

OLD MAN'S
BEARD

X ½

5 TO MANY PETALS; NUMEROUS STAMENS

Buttercup Family (Ranunculaceae)
See also pp. W 42–44; Y 162–164;
R 236, 286; B 344, 356–358; G 396, 406.

COLORADO COLUMBINE *Aquilegia caerulea*
White, 5-spurred flowers *point upward*. This is a white form of a usually blue-flowered species (see p. 344). Each blue-green leaf is doubly tripinnate and smooth (hairless). Stamens barely protruding. 30–60 cm. Rocky areas near aspen and spruce groves. N. Ariz., Ut. JUNE–JULY

MINIATURE COLUMBINE *Aquilegia micrantha*
Flowers tiny (2–4 cm), *short-spurred,* usually *horizontal or nodding.* Stamens strongly protruding. Leaflets and petioles small, *sticky-haired.* A variable species — flowers white, pale blue, or pale pink. 30–60 cm. Wet, weeping wall ledges. N. Ariz., R. Mts. JUNE–SEPT.

PLAINS DELPHINIUM *Delphinium virescens*
White to faintest blue flowers. *Leaf segments forked,* narrow, daggerlike, including those of the lowermost leaves. *Very thin,* long, blackish hair covers *lower inner petals.* 1–1.5 m. Common in grassy places. Se. Ariz. to southern and eastern N.M., Tex., Pl. Sts. APRIL–JULY

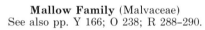

Mallow Family (Malvaceae)
See also pp. Y 166; O 238; R 288–290.

WHITE CHECKERMALLOW *Sidalcea candida*
Flower petals straplike with *semi-squared tips.* Flowers in terminal racemes along a slender stem with *rounded* basal leaves. Upper stem leaves divided into a whorl of *lancelike leaflets.* Central fused stamen column. 30 cm–1 m. Damp woods along streams. Mountains. N.M., R. Mts. JUNE–JULY

WOOLLY HIBISCUS *Hibiscus lasiocarpos*
Very large, white flowers with a *red throat.* Stamens combined into an elongated central shaft. Woolly, gray-green leaves, oval to oval-lancelike on long petioles. 1–2 m. Moist to wet bottomlands. E. Tex., Pl. Sts. JUNE–SEPT.

ALKALI MALLOW *Sida hederacea*
Note the *round to kidney-shaped* leaves along the *prostrate stem,* all short with velvety hairs. Creamy, bowl-shaped flowers with stamens fused into a central column. 10–40 cm. Dry places. S.W., w. Tex., R. Mts., Pl. Sts. MARCH–OCT.

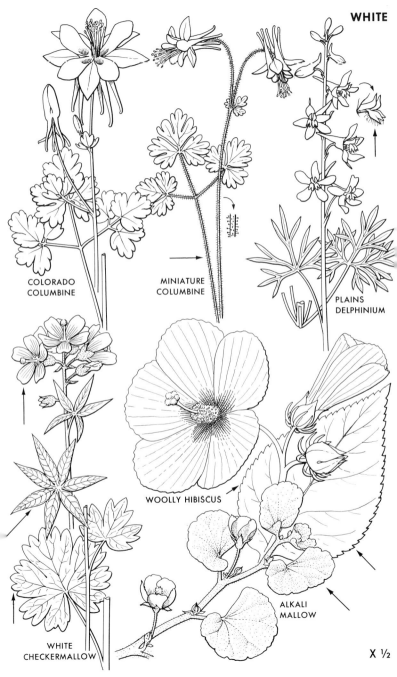

WHITE

COLORADO
COLUMBINE

MINIATURE
COLUMBINE

PLAINS
DELPHINIUM

WOOLLY HIBISCUS

ALKALI
MALLOW

WHITE
CHECKERMALLOW

X ½

5 DEEPLY CLEFT PETALS; SEPALS FREE

Pink Family (Caryophyllaceae)
See also pp. W 46–48; Y 158–160; R 296.

LARGE MOUSE-EAR Alien   *Cerastium vulgatum*
Oval leaves hairy, *stalkless*. Stems with sticky hairs. Petals
broadly notched. Sepals and petals of *equal length.* 10–40 cm.
Lawns, etc. S.W., Tex., R. Mts., Pl. Sts.   APRIL–SEPT.

STICKY MOUSE-EAR Alien   *Cerastium glomeratum*
Sepals *sharply pointed* with long sticky hairs. Petals notched,
often *shorter than* the sepals. Leaves oval. Stem erect, sticky-
haired. 10–30 cm. N.M., R. Mts., Pl. Sts.   APRIL–OCT.

MEADOW CHICKWEED   *Cerastium arvense*
Leaves *linear.* Petals *broad,* sharply notched, *longer than
sepals.* 10–30 cm. Wet mountain meadows. Northern S.W.,
R. Mts.   JUNE–JULY

ALPINE MOUSE-EAR   *Cerastium beeringianum*
Petals *narrow, straplike,* deeply notched at tip. Petals *much
longer* than sepals. Leaves oblong. Stems matted. 5–20 cm. Alpine meadows. N. Ariz., northern N.M., R. Mts.   JULY–AUG.

LLOVISNA   *Stellaria prostrata*
Broad, dark green, elliptical leaves in opposite pairs. Several to
many *tubular* flowers. Petals *much longer* than sepals. Stem
completely haired. 10–20 cm. Moist, sandy soils. Cen. and s.
Tex.   MARCH–JULY

STICKY STARWORT   *Stellaria jamesiana*
Petals triangular in outline with the tips squared and with a
short V-shaped notch. *Long, linear* leaf pairs. Sticky stems. 10–
30 cm. Mountain forests. S.W., R. Mts.   APRIL–JULY

COMMON CHICKWEED Alien   *Stellaria media*
Note the *single line of hairs* running down *one side* of stem.
Leaves oval. Petals with 2 parts, *shorter* than sepals. 10–40 cm.
Common. Ariz., eastern third of Tex., R. Mts.   MARCH–AUG.

LONGSTALK STARWORT   *Stellaria longipes*
Stems erect with *lancelike linear leaves.* Single flowers on *long
pedicels.* Petals with 2 parts. Sepals *same length* as petals. 10–
30 cm. Mountain meadows, forests. S.W., R. Mts.

MAY–JULY

UMBRELLA CHICKWEED   *Stellaria umbellata*
Small flowers on *long pedicels* form a loose *umbrella.* Petals
minute or absent. Stems sprawling. Northern S.W.

JULY–AUG.

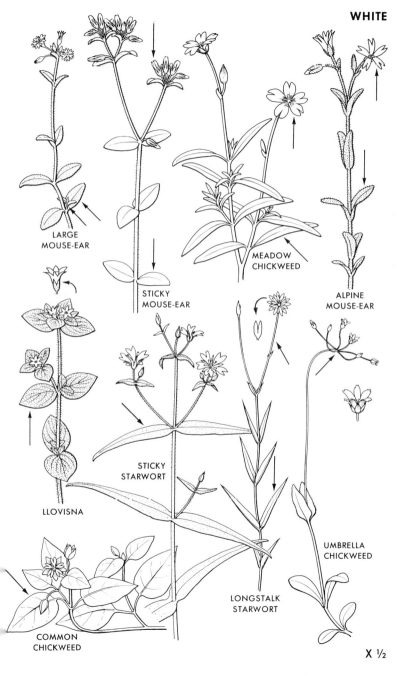

WHITE

LARGE
MOUSE-EAR

STICKY
MOUSE-EAR

MEADOW
CHICKWEED

ALPINE
MOUSE-EAR

LLOVISNA

STICKY
STARWORT

UMBRELLA
CHICKWEED

LONGSTALK
STARWORT

COMMON
CHICKWEED

X ½

5 LINEAR OR CLEFT PETALS; SEPALS FREE OR UNITED AS A TUBE

Pink Family (Caryophyllaceae)
See also pp. W 46–48; Y 158–160; R 296.

MOJAVE SANDWORT *Arenaria macradenia*
Sepal backs *bulge* at base. Plants tall with long leaves. 10–50 cm. Rocky ledges, slopes. Nw. Ariz., Ut. APRIL–JULY

NEEDLELEAF SANDWORT *Arenaria aculeata*
Petals *narrowly bilobed.* Sepals triangular, each with *3 lines close to each other* on the back. 10–30 cm. Sandy places. Nw. N.M. APRIL–AUG.

ALPINE SANDWORT *Arenaria obtusiloba*
Sepals *oval,* but with rounded tips that end in *purplish spinelike points.* Each sepal has 3 lines on the back. Petals bilobed and longer than sepals. 2–8 cm. Alpine rocky places. Northern S.W., R. Mts. JULY–AUG.

RUBY SANDWORT *Arenaria rubella*
Similar to Alpine Sandwort. Each sepal *oval* but *round-tipped,* with 3 lines on its back. Petals rounded and *shorter than sepals* (or same length). 2–10 cm. Dry alpine slopes. Northern S.W., R. Mts. JULY–AUG.

RYDBERG'S SANDWORT *Arenaria confusa*
Leaves *short, but broad.* Sepals triangular, each with *1 line* on the back. Petals narrow. 10–30 cm. Mountain pine forests. S.W., R. Mts. JULY–SEPT.

MENZIES' CATCHFLY *Silene menziesii*
Flowers white. Each petal has 2 broad, *diverging and rounded lobes.* Inner "teeth" on each petal small or absent. 5–20 cm. Openings in damp mountain woods. Northern S.W., R. Mts. JUNE–JULY

COMMON CATCHFLY Alien *Silene gallica*
Flowers white or tinted with pink. Petal tips *rounded,* with *2 inner "teeth."* Calyx tube long-haired, with 10 *purplish ribs.* 10–50 cm. Common at lower elevations. Ariz., eastern third of Tex. APRIL–MAY

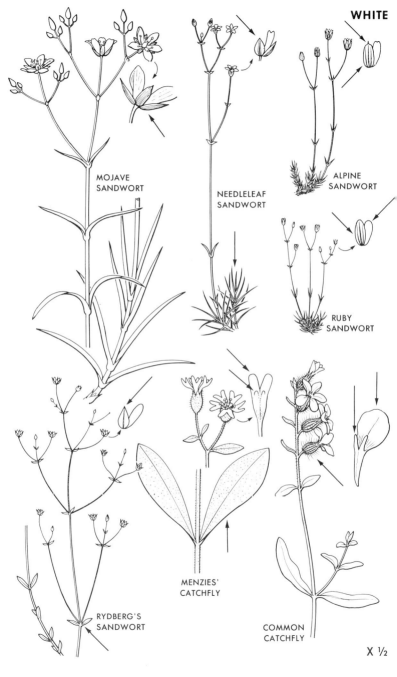

WHITE

MOJAVE SANDWORT

NEEDLELEAF SANDWORT

ALPINE SANDWORT

RUBY SANDWORT

RYDBERG'S SANDWORT

MENZIES' CATCHFLY

COMMON CATCHFLY

X ½

5 TO 8 PETALS; ROSELIKE FLOWERS, GERANIUMS, AND IRREGULAR-SHAPED VIOLETS

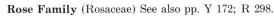

Rose Family (Rosaceae) See also pp. Y 172; R 298.

STICKY CINQUEFOIL   *Potentilla glandulosa*
Pinnate leaves, each with 5–9 *strongly toothed leaflets*. Flowers creamy white to pale yellow. *Sticky stems*. 30 cm–1 m. Wet meadows. S.W., R. Mts.   MAY–JULY

VIRGINIA STRAWBERRY   *Frageria virginiana*
Note the 3 broadly oblong leaflets with *no teeth at base*. Leaves *blue-green*. Delicious, edible strawberries. A variable species with many named entities; all are now included in this one species. 2–30 cm. Open woods, mountain meadows. S.W., R. Mts., Pl. Sts.   MARCH–SEPT.

EIGHTPETAL DRYAS   *Dryas octopetala*
This low mat plant has 8-petaled, roselike flowers. Leaf blade linear with *scalloped edges;* base of petiole has *2 tail-like stipules.* Alpine tundra. 2–10 cm. N.M., R. Mts.   JULY–AUG.

Violet Family (Violaceae) See also pp. Y 170; B 378.

CANADA VIOLET   *Viola canadensis*
Note the *broadly triangular lip petal.* Two upper petals *widely separated, not* reflexed backward; middle pair of petals upright. Petal bases yellow, the lower 3 petals with some purple speckles. All petals purple-tinted on the back. Flowers long-stemmed. Leaves *heart-shaped.* 10–40 cm. Common in mountains. S.W., R. Mts.   APRIL–SEPT.

PRIMROSE VIOLET   *Viola primulifolia*
Petals in a nearly *square arrangement.* Lip petal pointed, veined with red-purple or blue. Leaf blades *heart-shaped.* 2–10 cm. Common as masses in low marshy places. E. Tex., Pl. Sts.   MARCH–MAY

Geranium Family (Geraniaceae) See also p. R 292.

RICHARDSON'S GERANIUM   *Geranium richardsonii*
Stem hairs tipped with *red glands.* Large rounded petals, white to pale pink with purple veins. Each leaf has 5–7 narrow lobes with pointed tips. 30–90 cm. Very common. Moist mountain meadows, forests. S.W., R. Mts.   APRIL–OCT.

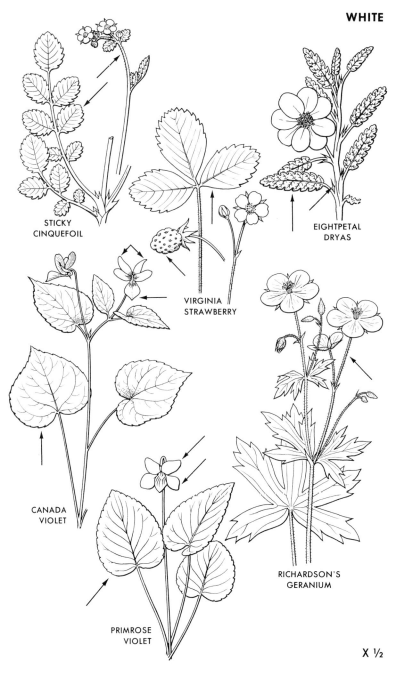

STICKY
CINQUEFOIL

EIGHTPETAL
DRYAS

VIRGINIA
STRAWBERRY

CANADA
VIOLET

PRIMROSE
VIOLET

RICHARDSON'S
GERANIUM

X ½

5 DAINTY PETALS; 2 HORNLIKE STYLES

Saxifrage Family (Saxifragaceae)
See also pp. W 52–54; Y 170; R 236; G 404.

OREGON SAXIFRAGE   *Saxifraga oregana*
Flowers in clusters above a basal rosette of *oblong leaves* (2–15 cm long). *Petals oval.* 30–90 cm. Moist rocky slopes in mountains. N.M., R. Mts.   JUNE–AUG.

TUFTED SAXIFRAGE   *Saxifraga caespitosa*
Note the small, *narrow, trilobed leaves* in tiny basal tufts. The white to palest yellow flowers are somewhat bowl-shaped, with *rounded petals.* 5–30 cm. Rocky crevices in high mountains. S.W., R. Mts.   JULY–AUG.

SPOTTED SAXIFRAGE   *Saxifraga bronchialis*
Oval petals with *numerous yellow and orange spots.* Tiny, lancelike leaves with short bristles along margins. 5–30 cm. Wet rocky places in mountains. N.M., R. Mts.   JULY–AUG.

BROOK SAXIFRAGE   *Saxifraga punctata*
Note the *kidney-shaped to rounded leaves* with triangular-toothed margins. Each petal has 2 yellow dots. 10–50 cm. Mountain streambanks. E. Ariz., N.M., R. Mts.   JULY–AUG.

DIAMONDLEAF SAXIFRAGE   *Saxifraga rhomboidea*
Leaf blades somewhat *diamond-shaped,* with slightly *sawtoothed edges* at tips. Leaves in a basal rosette. Stem stout, leafless, with small clusters of flowers at the top. *5 linear petals.* 2–30 cm. Foothills to alpine. Northern S.W., R. Mts.
APRIL–AUG.

REDFUZZ SAXIFRAGE   *Saxifraga eriophora*
Elliptical leaves with *rounded, scalloped margins* form a basal rosette. Undersides of leaves, stem, and calyx have *long reddish hairs.* 5 rounded petals. 10–30 cm. Mountain slopes. S. Ariz. and N.M.   APRIL–MAY

PYGMY SAXIFRAGE   *Saxifraga debilis*
Each leaf has *5 rounded to pointed lobes.* Most of leaves basal. Small white flowers. 10–15 cm. Alpine rocky places. S.W., R. Mts.   JULY–AUG.

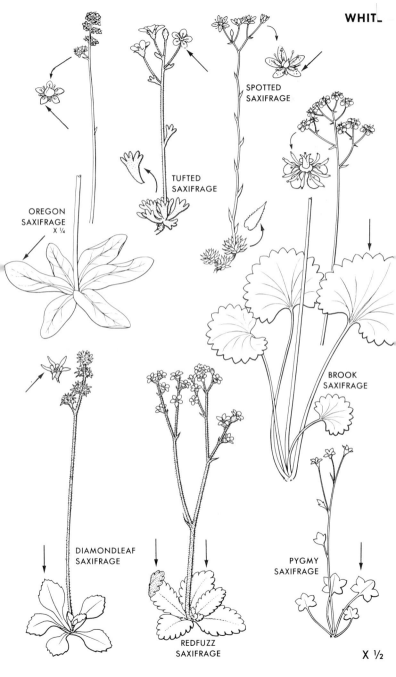

SPOTTED SAXIFRAGE

TUFTED SAXIFRAGE

OREGON
SAXIFRAGE
X ¼

BROOK
SAXIFRAGE

DIAMONDLEAF
SAXIFRAGE

REDFUZZ
SAXIFRAGE

PYGMY
SAXIFRAGE

X ½

5 DAINTY PETALS; 2 HORNLIKE STYLES

Saxifrage Family (Saxifragaceae)
See also pp. W 52–54; Y 170; R 236; G 404.

FRINGED PARNASSUS *Parnassia fimbriata*
Petals oval, with *fringed edges* at base. Leaves *kidney-shaped*.
Gland at base of each petal has *stubby lobes*. 30–60 cm. Wet
places in mountains. Northern N.M., R. Mts.   JULY–SEPT.

ARCTIC PARNASSUS *Parnassia parviflora*
Petals oval, with *smooth margins*. Gland at petal base has a
fringe of smaller, threadlike glands with globular tips. Dark
green, *oval leaves* on long petioles. 10–20 cm. Wet places in
mountains. N.M., R. Mts.   JUNE–AUG.

COMMON ALUMROOT *Heuchera parvifolia*
Note the yellow-green, *broadly triangular sepals* between the
slightly smaller white petals. Basal rosette of *maplelike leaves*
on long petioles. 30–60 cm. Mountains. S.W., R. Mts.
     JUNE–JULY

JACK O' THE ROCKS *Heuchera rubescens*
Note the *straight margin at the base* of each maplelike leaf
blade. Numerous *tiny, white to pale pink flowers* in loose
racemes on leafless stems. 10–30 cm. Dry rocky slopes. N. Ariz.,
w. Tex., R. Mts.   MAY–SEPT.

SOUTHWESTERN STAR *Lithophragma tenellum*
Starlike flowers on a tall stem that is usually leafless or has
occasional *highly reduced* leaves on upper flower stem. Each
petal has a *broad central lobe* and *2 pairs* of smaller lateral
lobes. Basal rosette of divided leaves. Shape of main leaf divisions tends to duplicate shape of petal lobes. All vegetative
parts hairy. 10–30 cm. Open pine woods. Northern S.W.,
R. Mts.   APRIL–JUNE

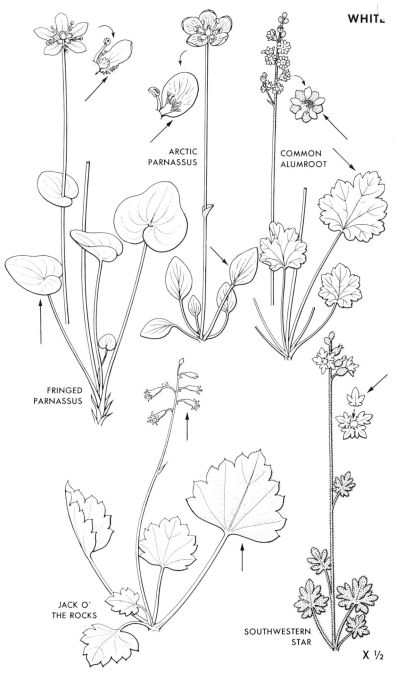

ARCTIC
PARNASSUS

COMMON
ALUMROOT

FRINGED
PARNASSUS

JACK O'
THE ROCKS

SOUTHWESTERN
STAR

X ½

5-PETALED STARS; VINES, TINY MELONS

Cucumber Family (Cucurbitaceae) See also p. Y 124.

BRANDEGEA *Brandegea bigelovii*
Each leaf has 3–5 simple, *triangular lobes.* The *tiny* (5–10 mm), *spiny melon is narrowly oblong.* Small, flat, starlike flowers. Long vines. Desert washes. W. Ariz. JAN.–MAY

GILA MANROOT *Marah gilensis*
Note the large (3–5 cm), *round, spiny* melons. Leaf lobes *pointed to rounded.* Long vines. Immense underground tuber (not shown). Lower elevations. Ariz., w. N.M. MARCH–APRIL

COCKLEBUR MELON *Cyclanthera dissecta*
Leaves highly *divided,* with a *narrow, petiolelike* base for each main lobe. Melon a small (2–3 cm), *elongated, spiny cockle-bur.* Vine. S. Ariz. and N.M., western two-thirds of Tex.
AUG.–OCT.

WRIGHT'S MELON *Echinopepon wrightii*
Broad, *undivided,* roundish leaves with kidney-shaped basal lobes. Tiny (1 cm), *spiny, elongated melon.* Vines. Along streams in mountains. S. Ariz., sw. N.M. AUG.–OCT.

NEW MEXICO PEAMELON *Sicyos ampelophyllus*
Each leaf has 5 sharp, pointed main lobes; *upper lobe longest.* Leaf base *a deep, narrow* V. Spiny, pealike melons. Vines. Mountains. Southern half of N.M., sw. Tex. JULY–SEPT.

MAPLELEAF PEAMELON *Sicyos angulatus*
Note the evenly lobed, large, *maplelike* leaves, each with a deep V at the base. Spiny, pealike, pale yellow melons. Vines. Streams, rivers. Eastern half of Tex. MAY–SEPT.

RIO GRANDE GLOBEBERRY *Ibervillea tripartita*
Male flowers (not shown) *flat, bowl-like.* Leaf lobes *narrowly parallel.* Vines with round red melons. S. Tex. APRIL–OCT.

ARIZONA PEAMELON *Sicyos laciniatus*
Broad triangular leaves with *roughly toothed margins* and a *broad, oblong basal notch.* Pealike melons. Mountains. Ariz.
AUG.–SEPT.

LINDHEIMER'S GLOBEBERRY *Ibervillea lindheimeri*
Leaf blade divided into 3–5 lobes, which are usually broad but can be narrow in some areas. Male flowers *tubular. Round, smooth, globelike red* melons. Vines. Cen. Tex. APRIL–JULY

DEER APPLES *Ibervillea tenuisecta*
Leaf blade has 5 *highly divided, slender lobes.* Male flowers *tubular.* Vines with red melons. Se. Ariz. to sw. Tex.
SUMMER

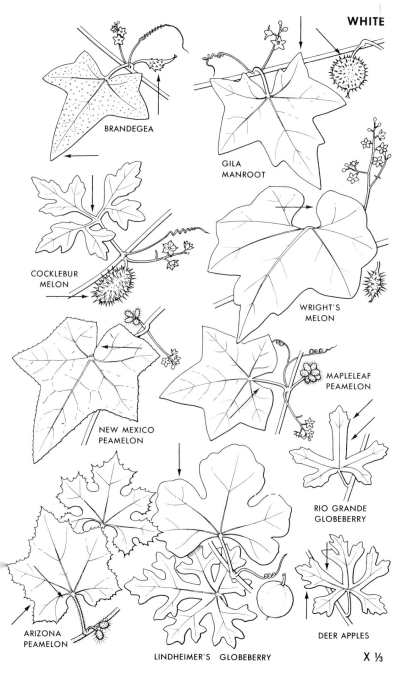

BRANDEGEA

GILA
MANROOT

COCKLEBUR
MELON

WRIGHT'S
MELON

NEW MEXICO
PEAMELON

MAPLELEAF
PEAMELON

RIO GRANDE
GLOBEBERRY

ARIZONA
PEAMELON

LINDHEIMER'S GLOBEBERRY

DEER APPLES

X 1/3

5 TINY PETALS; FLOWERS IN UMBEL
STOUT STEMS, HUGE PLANTS

Ginseng Family (Araliaceae)

AMERICAN SPIKENARD *Aralia racemosa*
Ball-like umbels of flowers in branching racemes at the top of *stout, fleshy stems* (1–2 m long). Each huge, compound pinnate leaf is divided 2–3 times into *oval leaflets*. Fruit a black berry. 2–3 m. Moist, shady places along streams in mountain canyons. S.W., w. Tex. JULY–SEPT.

Carrot Family (Umbelliferae)
See also p. W 58–62; Y 176; R 286.

POISON HEMLOCK Alien *Conium maculatum*
A single towering stem, *spotted with purple*. Leaves fernlike. *Very poisonous*. 30 cm–3 m. Disturbed places. S.W., southern half of Tex., R. Mts. JUNE–SEPT.

SPOTTED WATER HEMLOCK *Cicuta maculata*
Stem smooth, *streaked with purple*. Each compound pinnate leaf is divided 2–3 times into coarsely toothed, lancelike leaflets. Compare with Poison Hemlock (above). *Very poisonous*. 50 cm–2 m. Along streams, marshes. Eastern two-thirds of Tex., Pl. Sts., S.E. MAY–SEPT.

PORTER'S LOVAGE *Ligusticum porteri*
Note the large, pinnate leaves with *numerous small,* lancelike leaflets. Broad, nearly flat umbel of flowers. Stout stem. 1–2 m. Wet areas in mountains. S.W., R. Mts. JUNE–AUG.

DOUGLAS' WATER HEMLOCK *Cicuta douglasii*
Stout, hollow stems with long, pinnate leaves, each divided 1–3 times. Each leaflet narrow, lancelike, with *sawtoothed edges*. Flowers in a flat-topped umbel. Fruit round with low, corky ribs; ribs broader than intervals. *Poisonous*. 50 cm–2 m. Mountain marshes. N. Ariz., N.M. JULY–AUG.

WATER PARSNIP *Sium suave*
Each simple pinnate leaf is divided into 3–7 pairs of long, *lancelike* leaflets with *sawtoothed edges*. Leaf *veins end at leaflet tips*. Stems strongly ridged. 50 cm–2 m. Marshes. Occasional in S.W., more frequent in Tex., R. Mts. MAY–SEPT.

COW PARSNIP *Heracleum lanatum*
Huge leaves divided into maplelike leaflets, 30–60 cm across. Flower umbel 20–40 cm wide on tall, stout, hollow stem. 1–2 m. Moist thickets. S.W., R. Mts. JULY–AUG.

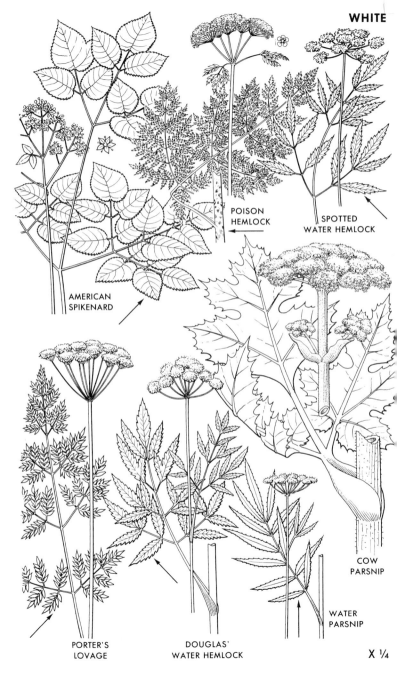

POISON
HEMLOCK

SPOTTED
WATER HEMLOCK

AMERICAN
SPIKENARD

COW
PARSNIP

WATER
PARSNIP

PORTER'S
LOVAGE

DOUGLAS'
WATER HEMLOCK

X ¼

5 TINY PETALS; FLOWERS IN UMBEL
SMALL PLANTS (30–90 cm)

Carrot Family (Umbelliferae)
See also pp. W 58–62; Y 176; R 286.

QUEEN ANNE'S LACE Alien — *Daucus carota*
Flowers in a *flat umbel;* older flower clusters *cuplike,* resembling *bird's nests.* Immediately below the umbel are stiff, *3-forked bracts.* Leaves finely subdivided. Strong carrotlike odor. 30–90 cm. Open places. S.W., R. Mts., Pl. Sts.   APRIL–JULY

AMERICAN CARROT — *Daucus pusillus*
Note the *long, delicately lacy bracts* immediately below the *small flower umbel.* Lower stem leaves also have short, lacy, linear lobes. 10–70 cm. Disturbed soils. S.W., Tex., Pl. Sts.

MARCH–JUNE

SHEPHERD'S NEEDLE Alien — *Scandix pecten-veneris*
Note the many *long, needlelike fruits* that appear soon after the small white flowers. Leaves compound pinnate, each divided 2–3 times into *fine, linear* leaflets. 10–30 cm. Disturbed places. Occasional. S.W.   APRIL–AUG.

TAINTURIER'S CHERVIL — *Chaerophyllum tainturieri*
Pinnate leaves, *triangular* in *general outline;* each with *tiny, lancelike leaflets.* Umbels with few flowers; seeds *long, linear.* 10 cm–1 m. Common in many habitats. Eastern half of Tex., occasional in Ariz., Pl. Sts.   MARCH–MAY

THREADLEAF — *Ptilimnium capillaceum*
Threadlike leaves, each divided 2–4 times. Flower umbels compound (divided twice). Seeds globelike. 10 cm–1 m. Frequent in masses. Eastern half of Tex., Pl. Sts., S.E.   APRIL–AUG.

CELERY Alien — *Apium graveolens*
Compound pinnate leaves, each divided into 3 *toothed leaflets.* Flowers in a rounded cluster. Fruits *oblong* with 5–15 narrow, slightly raised ribs. Strong celery odor. 50 cm–1 m. Occasional in wet places. S.W., w. Tex.   MAY–OCT.

KNOTTED HEDGE PARSLEY — *Torilis nodosa*
Many tiny, *spiny, cockleburlike seeds* are clustered near the *base* of each leaf. Leaves compound pinnate, with *fernlike leaflets.* 30–60 cm. Moist places. A pest in lawns. Occasional in S.W., frequent in eastern half of Tex., Pl. Sts.   APRIL–JUNE

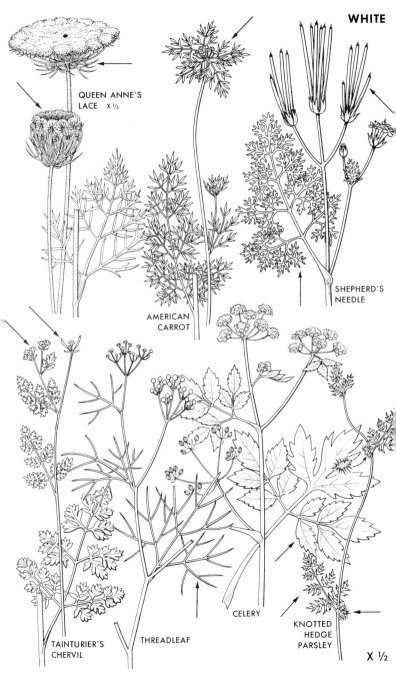

WHITE

QUEEN ANNE'S
LACE X ⅓

AMERICAN
CARROT

SHEPHERD'S
NEEDLE

TAINTURIER'S
CHERVIL

THREADLEAF

CELERY

KNOTTED
HEDGE
PARSLEY

X ½

5 TINY PETALS; FLOWERS IN UMBEL

Carrot Family (Umbelliferae)
See also pp. W 58–62; Y 176; R 286.

YUCCALEAF SNAKEROOT *Eryngium yuccifolium*
Note the long, *spiny, parallel-veined leaves,* similar to yucca
leaves. Flower bracts similar to leaves but with *large streaks of
white.* Spiny, *buttonlike* flowerheads in umbels. 20–90 cm. Open
areas, prairies, pine woodlands. Eastern half of Tex., Pl. Sts.,
S.E.   MAY–AUG.

MEXICAN THISTLE *Eryngium heterophyllum*
Buttonlike flowerhead surrounded by a large, *white-striped
sunburst* of spiny bracts. 30–60 cm. Flats and open slopes.
Western to s. Tex.   JULY–SEPT.

NEVADA LOMATIUM *Lomatium nevadense*
Note the broad, *triangular outline* of the ground-hugging, silvery gray, pinnate leaves. Thick, white umbel of flowers appears to be *speckled with pepper* because of the black anthers.
Flower stem *shiny, red-brown.* 5–10 cm. Open slopes at middle
and lower elevations. Ariz., w. N.M., R. Mts.   MARCH–MAY

WHORLED PENNYWORT *Hydrocotyle verticillata*
Note the *umbrella-like leaf blade* with nearly *smooth margins.*
Starlike flowers in umbels, stem usually leafless. 0.5–25 cm. Fre-
quently grows in masses in low, wet places, both inland and
along coastal beaches. S.W., Tex., Pl. Sts., S.E.
                                                      MOST OF YEAR

FLOATING PENNYWORT *Hydrocotyle ranunculoides*
Leaf blade umbrella-like, but margins *partly divided,* like the
leaf of a buttercup or a maple. Flowers in umbels. Floating
or creeping stem. 5–25 cm. Wet or damp places. S.W., Tex.,
Pl. Sts., S.E.   APRIL–JULY

PARISH'S YAMPAH *Perideridia parishii*
Leaves very simple, usually of 1 leaflet but occasionally with up
to 3 leaflets. Roots (shown) are *elongated tapers.* The roots of
all yampahs are edible and were an important Indian food. 30–
90 cm. Mountain meadows. N. Ariz.   JULY–SEPT.

GAIRDNER'S YAMPAH *Perideridia gairdneri*
Stems slender, with pinnate leaves divided 1 or 2 times into
similar linear divisions. Fruits *rounded.* 30 cm–1 m. Mountain meadows, at lower to middle elevations. Northern S.W.,
R. Mts.   JUNE–SEPT.

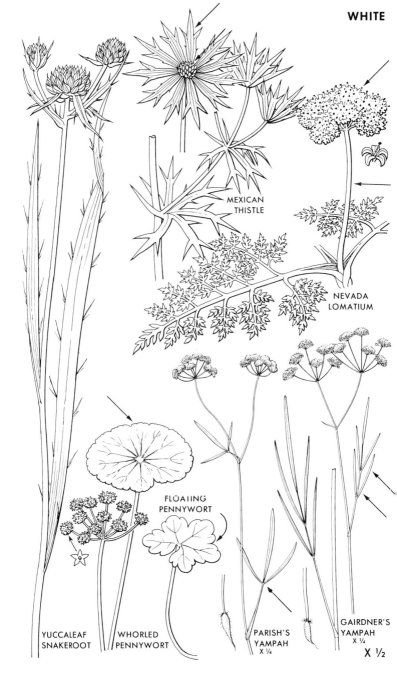

MEXICAN
THISTLE

NEVADA
LOMATIUM

FLOATING
PENNYWORT

YUCCALEAF
SNAKEROOT

WHORLED
PENNYWORT

PARISH'S
YAMPAH
X ¼

GAIRDNER'S
YAMPAH
X ¼

X ½

3–5 PETALS; TUBULAR FLOWERS
IN UMBELS WITH LARGE BRACTS

Four O'Clock Family (Nyctaginaceae) See also p. R 306.

SWEET FOUR O'CLOCK *Mirabilis longiflora*
Note the *very long* (7–20 cm), *gland-haired, trumpetlike* flowers and the *large, oval to heart-shaped leaves*. White to pale pink flowers open in late afternoon and wilt by early morning. 30–90 cm. *Near boulder bases.* Hills of s. Ariz. to w. Tex.
AUG.–SEPT.

ANGEL TRUMPETS *Acleisanthes longiflora*
Note the *very long* (7–20 cm), *trumpetlike flowers* and the *small, wrinkled, arrow-shaped leaves*. White to pale pink flowers open in midafternoon and wilt the following midmorning. Fragrant. Stem prostrate, sprawling. 30–90 cm. Open areas at low elevations. Ariz. to s. Tex.
MARCH–OCT.

DESERT WISHBONE BUSH *Mirabilis bigelovii*
Flowers white or tinted pink with *bilobed petal tips.* *Oval to kidney-shaped leaves* on weak, sticky stems. 30–60 cm. Rocky slopes and canyons on lower deserts. Ariz.
MARCH–OCT.

SNOWBALL SAND VERBENA *Abronia fragrans*
Note the *large, snowball-like umbel* of numerous trumpetlike flowers on a usually *erect stem.* Fragrant. Thick, fleshy leaves, oval to heart-shaped. Flowers open at dusk, close at midmorning. 10–90 cm. Sandy plains. N. Ariz., all of N.M., to w. Tex., R. Mts., Pl. Sts.
MARCH–SEPT.

DWARF SAND VERBENA *Abronia nana*
Note the oval to lancelike leaf blades on *long petioles* in a *central, stemless rosette*. One or more umbels of white or rarely pink flowers. 10–20 cm. N. Ariz., Ut.
APRIL–AUG.

RUNNING SAND VERBENA *Abronia elliptica*
Umbel *bracts cover nearly half* the length of the numerous small flowers. *Running stem* nearly prostrate. Leaves lancelike. 10–40 cm. Sandy plains. Northern S.W.
APRIL–NOV.

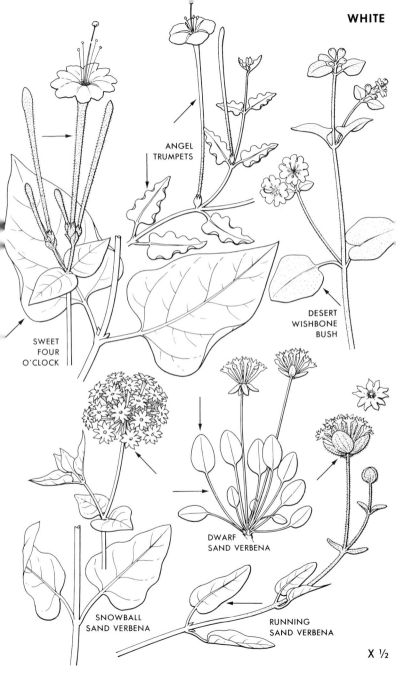

ANGEL
TRUMPETS

SWEET
FOUR
O'CLOCK

DESERT
WISHBONE
BUSH

DWARF
SAND VERBENA

SNOWBALL
SAND VERBENA

RUNNING
SAND VERBENA

X ½

5 PETALS; FLOWERS IN UMBEL CLUSTER; MILKY SAP; THREAD-LEAVED MILKWEEDS

Milkweed Family (Asclepiadaceae)
See also pp. W 66–72; Y 178; O 234; R 302–304; G 404.

Flowers of this family have a unique structure. The *tiny sepals* are hidden under the downswept, *sepal-like petals. Above the petals is a pedestal* that supports 5 *inflated hoods* with *horns* around a broad *central column* containing stamens and pistil.

PLAINS MILKWEED   *Asclepias pumila*
Leaves in whorls, each with 3–5 semi-linear, upward-pointing leaves. White petals reflexed, faintly tinted with rose or yellow-green. Short, greenish white pedestal. Hoods broadly oval and *slightly longer* than central column, with horns curving over the central column. 50 cm–1 m. Mesquite prairies, plains. Nw. Tex., e. N.M., Pl. Sts.   JUNE–SEPT.

HORSETAIL MILKWEED   *Asclepias subverticillata*
3–5 *whorled* linear leaves with *short petioles.* The white flowers have broad, rounded hoods that are *shorter* than the elongated column. Long, curving horns. 20 cm–1 m. Plains. S.W., w. Tex., R. Mts., Pl. Sts.   MAY–SEPT.

WHORLED MILKWEED   *Asclepias verticillata*
3–4 *threadlike leaves* in each whorl. Flower small (5–10 mm). Petals white to greenish, tinted with purple. *Slender pedestal.* Hoods rounded, greenish white, *shorter* than central column, but with long horns curving over the central column. 10–70 cm. S.W., Tex.   APRIL–AUG.

PINE-NEEDLE MILKWEED   *Asclepias linaria*
Single, threadlike leaves crowded together in a *spiral* arrangement. Flowers greenish white with a rose tint. Hoods scooplike; the open end *extends above* the central column. Horns not visible. 30 cm–1.5 m. S. Ariz.   FEB.–OCT.

RUSH MILKWEED   *Asclepias subulata*
Note the *narrow,* cream to pale yellow, *teethlike hoods.* Flower clusters on *whitish, rushlike stems* with *no leaves.* 30 cm–2 m. Lower deserts. W. Ariz.   APRIL–OCT.

SMOOTH MILKVINE   *Sarcostemma hirtellum*
Twining vine with umbrellalike clusters of flowers that have *no hairs on the petal edges.* Leaves linear, with tiny silvery hairs. Flowers white to greenish yellow. 1–2 m. Common in washes on lowest deserts. Ariz., s. N.M.   MARCH–OCT.

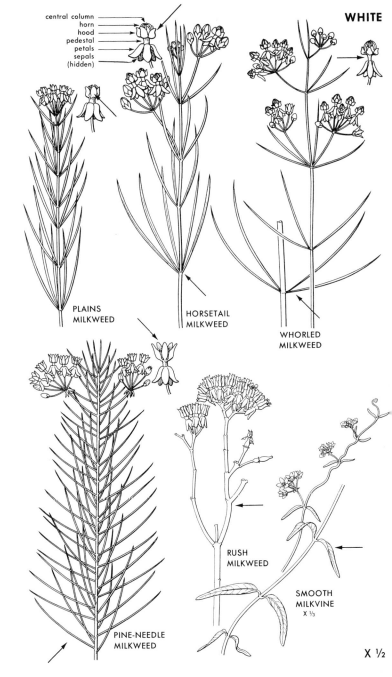

WHITE

central column
horn
hood
pedestal
petals
sepals
(hidden)

PLAINS
MILKWEED

HORSETAIL
MILKWEED

WHORLED
MILKWEED

PINE-NEEDLE
MILKWEED

RUSH
MILKWEED

SMOOTH
MILKVINE
X ⅓

X ½

5 PETALS; FLOWERS IN UMBEL CLUSTER; MILKY SAP; STRAP-LEAVED MILKWEEDS

Milkweed Family (Asclepiadaceae)
See also pp. W 66–72; Y 178; O 234; R 302–304; G 404.
See p. 66 for explanation of special flower parts.

SQUAT MILKWEED   *Asclepias linearis*
Note the 2 (rarely 3) long, *narrow, straplike leaves* in *opposite pairs.* Flower somewhat *squat.* Hoods and protruding horns bright white, on an elongated column above reflexed cream to tawny petals. 10–40 cm. Dry prairies. S.-cen. Tex. (including Padre I.), Pl. Sts.   MAY–SEPT.

SLENDER MILKWEED   *Asclepias angustifolia*
White flowers with *long,* narrow, *spreading, sharply pointed* hoods above a narrow pedestal and protruding, curving horns. Both hoods and horns are as long as or longer than central column. Leaves *narrow, lancelike, with a short petiole.* 10–60 cm. Stream bottoms, canyons. S. Ariz.   JUNE–JULY

NARROWLEAF MILKWEED   *Asclepias fascicularis*
Long, *lancelike leaves in whorls* of 3–6, usually hairless and folded upward. Flowers white to greenish or purple-tinted; hoods cupped. 50 cm–1 m. Damp places in mountains. Ariz.
JUNE–SEPT.

LONGLEAF MILKWEED   *Asclepias longifolia*
Note the *long, linear* leaves in *irregular pairs.* Flower parts greenish white with *portions* tinted purple. Hoods *shorter than* central column and *without horns. 30*–60 cm. Bottoms, swamps, pine savannahs. E. Tex.   APRIL–JULY

ENGELMANN'S MILKWEED   *Asclepias engelmanniana*
Long (12–18 cm), linear, *drooping leaves,* arranged alternately on stem. Numerous flower umbels, crowded together. Small flowers with reflexed, pale greenish white petals, tinged with purple. *No pedestal.* Hoods broad, saclike, closely upright next to central column. *Horns absent.* 50 cm–1 m. Prairies, draws, stream bottoms. Southern S.W., Tex., Pl. Sts.   JULY–SEPT.

BILOBE MILKWEED   *Asclepias stenophylla*
Linear leaves *point upward,* arranged irregularly. Flowers greenish white to creamy yellow. Petals spread *at right angles* to pedicel. No pedestal. Hoods linear, saclike, *hugging* the central column. Horns protrude between *notched (bilobed) hood tips,* giving a *3-pointed appearance.* 20–60 cm. Prairies. Cen. Tex., Pl. Sts.   JUNE–AUG.

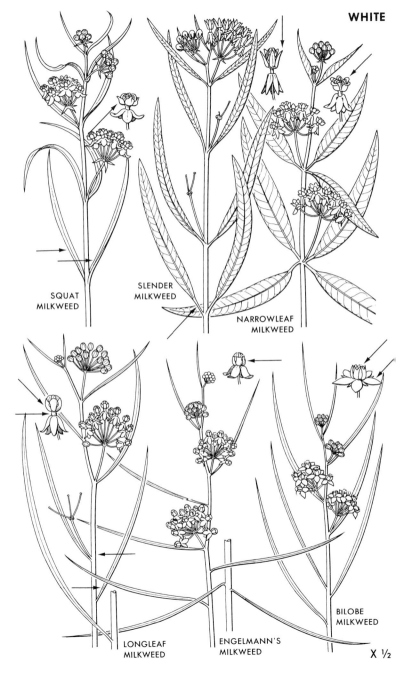

WHITE

SQUAT MILKWEED

SLENDER MILKWEED

NARROWLEAF MILKWEED

LONGLEAF MILKWEED

ENGELMANN'S MILKWEED

BILOBE MILKWEED

X ½

5 PETALS; FLOWERS IN UMBEL CLUSTERS; MILKY SAP; BROAD-LEAVED MILKWEEDS

Milkweed Family (Asclepiadaceae)
See also pp. W 66–72; Y 178; O 234; R 302–304; G 404.

NODDING MILKWEED *Asclepias alata*
Note the *extra long, erect flower stalk* with a *nodding umbel* of flowers. Broad, *blue-green,* oval leaves. Pale greenish yellow petals, partly reflexed. No pedestal. Hoods *inflated at base.* 30 cm–1 m. Rocky canyon slopes. S. Ariz. to sw. Tex.

CORN-KERNEL MILKWEED *Asclepias latifolia*
Very broad, *waxy blue,* oval leaves. Reflexed greenish yellow petals. Note the short, *broad pedestal* below the pale yellow and white *corn-kernel-like hoods.* Horns protrude over the white central column. 30 cm–1 m. Plains. S.W., Tex.

MAY–SEPT.

SAND MILKWEED *Asclepias arenaria*
Extra large, pale green to whitish flowers have reflexed petals, a *short pedestal* above the petals, and *broad, 2-lobed hoods with hollow "cheeks"* on each side. Broad oblong leaves with *petioles.* 50 cm–1 m. Sandy places. N.M., n. Tex., Pl. Sts.

MAY–AUG.

REDRING MILKWEED *Asclepias variegata*
Compact, *hemispherical* flower umbels. Large, *showy* white flowers with a broad, *red-purple ring* around the pedestal. Hoods broad, inflated, with *stout, peglike horns that curve inward at a tight right angle.* Broad, dark green leaves with long petioles. 30–90 cm. Open woods. E. Tex., S.E. APRIL–JULY

HIERBA DE ZIZOTES *Asclepias oenotheroides*
Greenish white to pale yellow hoods are *tall, narrow, and toothlike;* each hood is *bilobed* at tip, and twice as long as the central column. Petals reflexed sharply downward. Leaves broadly *lancelike.* 50 cm–1 m. Common. S. Ariz. to cen. and s. Tex.

ALL YEAR

EMORY'S COMET MILKWEED *Asclepias emoryi*
Each *cometlike white flower* has a *blunt "nose"* and a *trailing tail* of greenish yellow, reflexed petals with *thin white margins.* Slender, tawny yellow hoods with white enlarged tips project inward over the central column. Lancelike leaves with *wavy margins, fuzzy hairs,* and petioles. 10–30 cm. Plains. Southern half of Tex.

MARCH–OCT.

GREEN COMET MILKWEED *Asclepias viridiflora*
Rounded, stiff, pincushionlike flower umbels. Broad, shiny green, oblong leaves with wavy margins. Each *cometlike white flower* has a *tapered "nose"* and a trailing tail of yellow-green petals. *Tapered, sausagelike hoods, shorter than the white-tipped central column.* 10 cm–1 m. Plains. S.W., Tex.

APRIL–AUG.

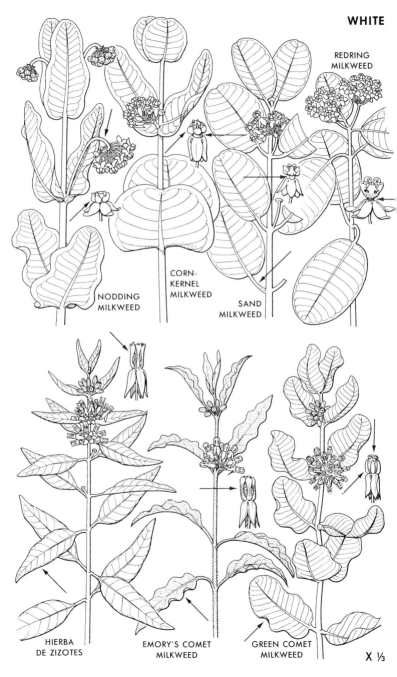

WHITE

REDRING
MILKWEED

NODDING
MILKWEED

CORN-
KERNEL
MILKWEED

SAND
MILKWEED

HIERBA
DE ZIZOTES

EMORY'S COMET
MILKWEED

GREEN COMET
MILKWEED

X ⅓

5 PETALS; FLOWERS IN UMBEL CLUSTERS OR PANICLES; MILKY SAP

Milkweed Family (Asclepiadaceae)
See also pp. W 66–72; Y 178; O 234; R 302–304; G 404.
See p. 66 for explanation of special flower parts.

TEXAS MILKWEED *Asclepias texana*
Flowers bright white; some parts may have a rosy tint. Petals sharply reflexed, below an *elongated pedestal. Long, curving horns arch* over the central column. Lancelike leaves on long petioles, many in opposite pairs. Each *seedpod erect,* on *an erect pedicel.* Seeds *hairy.* 10–40 cm. Canyons, hills. Cen. and Big Bend areas of Tex. MAY–AUG.

MARSH MILKWEED *Asclepias perennis*
Flower and leaves similar to Texas Milkweed, but *seedpod droops.* Seeds *without hairs.* 10–40 cm. *Low, swampy places.* Coastal Bend and se. Tex., S.E. APRIL–SEPT.

Dogbane Family (Apocynaceae). See also pp. R 314; B 356.

ROCK TRUMPET *Macrosiphonia macrosiphon*
Flowers with *propellerlike petals* and a *long, trumpetlike base.* Stem prostrate, with elliptical leaves. Milky sap. Flowers open in evening and morning hours. 10–30 cm. Open, rocky slopes. S. Ariz. to sw. Tex. and along Rio Grande to Brownsville, Tex. MAY–SEPT.

BEARDED SWALLOWWORT *Cynanchum barbigerum*
Twining vines with numerous *tiny, urnlike,* star-lobed flowers. Inner petal surface has *velvetlike hairs.* Leaves dark green, elliptical. Vines climb over shrubs. Lower Rio Grande Valley of s. Tex. to sw. Tex. MARCH–JULY

TUBULAR SLIMPOD *Amsonia longiflora*
Many *long, slender, trumpetlike* creamy flowers in *each cluster. Grasslike,* linear leaves. 30–60 cm. Open hills and flats. Southern N.M., sw. Tex. MARCH–JUNE

INDIAN HEMP *Apocynum cannabinum*
Erect stems with *ascending* pairs of long, broad, lancelike leaves. Small, white to pinkish, bell-like flowers in scattered cymes along the stem. 20 cm–1 m. Damp places near streams. S.W., Tex., R. Mts., Pl. Sts. APRIL–SEPT.

SPREADING DOGBANE *Apocynum androsaemifolium*
Drooping pairs of oval leaves. Terminal cymes of small, white to pinkish, bell-shaped flowers. 10–60 cm. Frequent on mountain slopes. S.W., w. Tex., R. Mts. APRIL–SEPT.

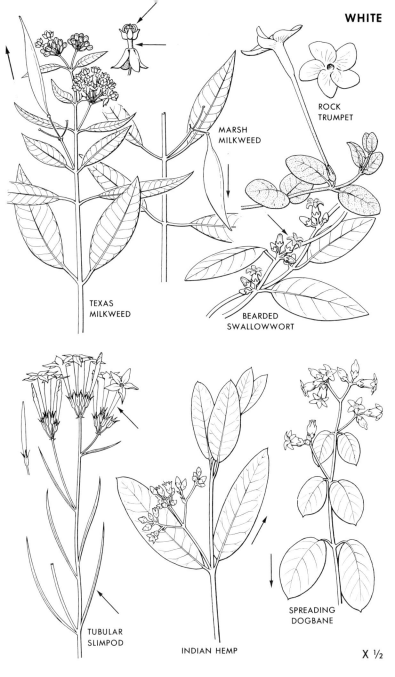

ROCK
TRUMPET

MARSH
MILKWEED

TEXAS
MILKWEED

BEARDED
SWALLOWWORT

TUBULAR
SLIMPOD

INDIAN HEMP

SPREADING
DOGBANE

X ½

5 PETALS; PINWHEELS; MILKY SAP

Spurge Family (Euphorbiaceae) See also pp. R 314; G 398.

TEXAS MALA MUJER *Cnidoscolus texanus*
Long, tubular, trumpetlike, fragrant male flowers with *stamens barely showing.* Separate female (pistillate) flowers usually hidden in lower part of inflorescence. Leaves *deeply divided* into 5 lobes. Stems and leaves covered by numerous *stinging hairs. Do not touch* — sting is severe and lasts for many hours. 10 cm–1 m. Tex.   APRIL–NOV.

ARIZONA MALA MUJER *Cnidoscolus angustidens*
Short, trumpetlike male flowers with *protruding stamens.* Separate female flowers are *round, spiny, berrylike.* The broad, shiny green leaves are only slightly lobed. Scattered *stinging hairs* have enlarged white bases. *Do not touch* — sting lasts for hours. 10 cm–3 m. Rocky foothill slopes. S. Ariz.   MAY–SEPT.

SNOW-ON-THE-PRAIRIE *Euphorbia bicolor*
Tall, slender plants with *linear* floral leaves that have *white margins.* Small, *fanlike* male flowers nearly hidden. Stem leaves green, hairy, *broadly lancelike.* 50 cm–1 m. Eastern half of Tex., Pl. Sts., S.E.   JULY–OCT.

SNOW-ON-THE-MOUNTAIN *Euphorbia marginata*
Similar to Snow-on-the-prairie, but leaves *broadly oval.* Oval floral leaves have *white margins,* but stem leaves do not. 20 cm–1 m. Plains, open fields. Eastern half of N.M., Tex., Pl. Sts., S.E.   MAY–OCT.

GREEN POINSETTIA *Euphorbia dentata*
Note the *white bases* of the *green, poinsettia-like floral* leaves around greenish flowers. Commercial poinsettias are related species of *Euphorbia.* 10–30 cm. Often in masses after spring and fall rains. Cen. Ariz. to Tex., Pl. Sts., S.E.

MARCH–MAY; AUG.–OCT.

THYMELEAF SPURGE *Euphorbia serpyllifolia*
The white flower glands look like *small white eyes.* Thymelike leaves have minutely toothed tips. Milky sap. 2–30 cm. Disturbed places. S.W., western half of Tex., Pl. Sts.

MAY–NOV.

CANDELILLA *Euphorbia antisyphilitica*
Note the *round, erect, rushlike,* leafless stems in *dense clusters.* White flowers near tips of stems have reddish centers. Stems once an important source of carnauba wax. 30–60 cm. Frequent on deserts of sw. Tex.   MAY–OCT.

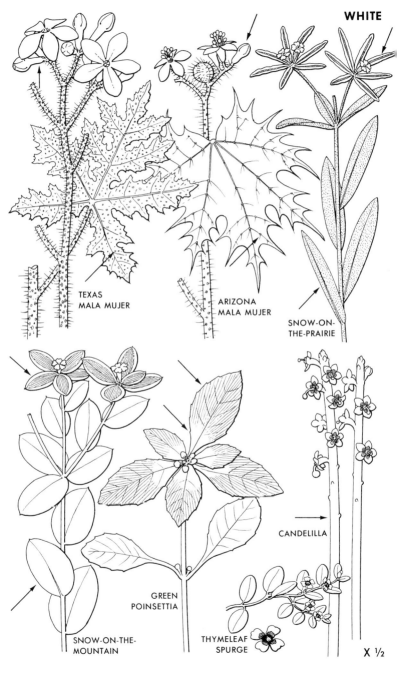

TEXAS
MALA MUJER

ARIZONA
MALA MUJER

SNOW-ON-
THE-PRAIRIE

SNOW-ON-THE-
MOUNTAIN

GREEN
POINSETTIA

THYMELEAF
SPURGE

CANDELILLA

X ½

5-PETALED, WAXY, NODDING FLOWERS, URNLIKE OR CROWNLIKE

Wintergreen Family (Pyrolaceae) See also p. R 314.

WHITEVEIN WINTERGREEN — *Pyrola picta*
Note the *white-veined* elliptical leaves. Waxy-white flowers have *styles bent to one side*. 10–20 cm. Dry, shady mountain forests. S.W., R. Mts. JULY–AUG.

SIDEBELLS — *Pyrola secunda*
White to greenish flowers *arranged along 1 side* of the erect to drooping flower stem. Oval leaves shiny, green. 10–20 cm. Dry mountain forests. N.M., R. Mts. JULY–AUG.

INDIAN PIPE — *Monotropa uniflora*
Translucent, waxy-white stems with a *single nodding,* bell-like flower. White to pink flowers turn black with age. Leaves small, colorless scales. A saprophyte, using decaying leaves for food. 10–30 cm. Dark, moist woods. E. Tex., possibly northern S.W., R. Mts. APRIL–JULY

AMERICAN PINESAP — *Monotropa hypopithys*
Several nodding, waxy-white to yellowish (or bright red) bell-like flowers. Stem and flowers either waxy-white or bright red. A saprophyte in dark conifer and aspen forests in high mountains. 5–20 cm. S.W., sw. Tex., ne. Tex., R. Mts.

APRIL–NOV.

LONGLEAF WINTERGREEN — *Pyrola elliptica*
The large style of the flower is *bent to one side.* Green, elliptical leaf blades *longer than the petiole.* 10–20 cm. Conifer forests, mountains. S.W., R. Mts. JULY–AUG.

SHORTLEAF WINTERGREEN — *Pyrola virens*
(not shown)
Similar to Longleaf Wintergreen, but leaf blade the *same length* as or *shorter than* the petiole. 5–30 cm. Conifer forests. S.W., R. Mts. JULY–AUG.

WOOD NYMPH — *Moneses uniflora*
Note the *single* nodding, waxy-white to pale pink flower on a short, leafless stem. Oval leaves with small, sharp teeth at margin. 5–12 cm. Rotting wood humus of cool, shady conifer forests in high mountains. S.W., R. Mts. JULY–AUG.

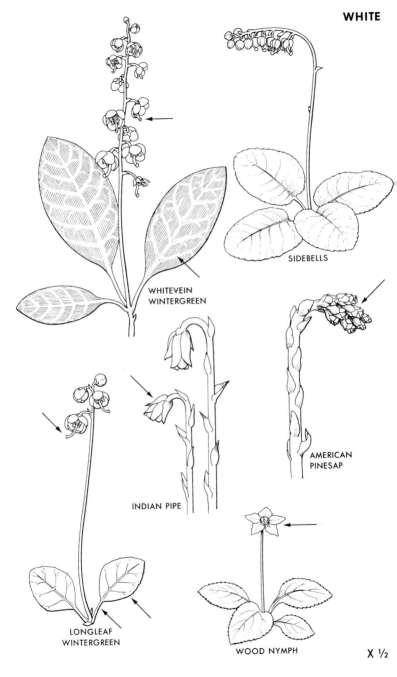

WHITEVEIN
WINTERGREEN

SIDEBELLS

AMERICAN
PINESAP

INDIAN PIPE

LONGLEAF
WINTERGREEN

WOOD NYMPH

X ½

5-PETALED PINWHEELS, URNS, STARS

Primrose Family (Primulaceae) See also pp. Y 170; R 300.

WHITE SHOOTING STAR   *Dodecatheon dentatum*
Leaves *sharp-edged,* with *jagged teeth* along margins. Creamy white petals with yellow bands, *swept backward* like a shooting star. Anthers deep red. 10–40 cm. High mountains. E. Ariz., N.M., R. Mts.   JUNE–AUG.

EASTERN SHOOTING STAR   *Dodecatheon meadia*
Leaves have a *central, dark red vein.* Leaf blade *broad, tonguelike, smooth-edged.* Flowers white or pink. 10–50 cm. Open slopes, moist woods. Eastern third of Tex., Pl. Sts.
    MARCH–MAY

COAST BROOKWEED   *Samolus ebracteatus*
Spatula-like leaves in a basal rosette; *bare red stems.* Small, urnlike corolla tube below the *wheel-like* petal lobes. 30–60 cm. Tex. coast.   APRIL–OCT.

ALPINE ROCK JASMINE   *Androsace chamaejasme*
White, pinwheel-like flowers have a *yellow "eye" that turns pink* with age. Tiny, basal, tightly clustered oval leaves, with *hairy fringes.* 5–15 cm. Common in alpine tundra. N.M., R. Mts.   JULY–AUG.

UMBRELLA ROCK JASMINE   *Androsace septentrionalis*
Tiny, white, pinwheel-like flowers with a *yellow "eye"* in *loose umbels on tall, leafless stems.* Oval, *hairless* leaves in a basal rosette, often dried up at flowering time. 5–30 cm. Rocky places in mountains. S.W., R. Mts.   APRIL–SEPT.

Gentian Family (Gentianaceae)
See also pp. Y 174; R 242; B 342; G 400.

BUCKBEAN   *Menyanthes trifoliata*
Starlike petals have *dense, velvety hair.* Each leaf has *3 leaflets.* 10–30 cm. Mountain bogs. Northern S.W., R. Mts.
    JUNE–AUG.

ARCTIC GENTIAN   *Gentianopsis algida*
Whitish, tubular flowers *speckled* with blackish purple; *nestled* among dense clusters of yellow-green, linear leaves. 5–20 cm. Alpine tundra. N.M., R. Mts.   AUG.–SEPT.

Sedum Family (Crassulaceae) See also pp. Y 180; R 286.

WRIGHT'S SEDUM   *Sedum wrightii*
Crowded, succulent leaves that are *round in cross-section.* Small, white to pale pinkish, starlike flowers. 5–20 cm. Ledges, boulder bases in mountains. Sw. Tex., N.M.   JULY–OCT.

COCKERELL'S SEDUM   *Sedum cockerellii*
Scattered, succulent leaves that are *flattened in cross-section.* Numerous small white to pale pink, starlike flowers. 5–25 cm. Rocky foothills, mountains. S.W.   JUNE–OCT.

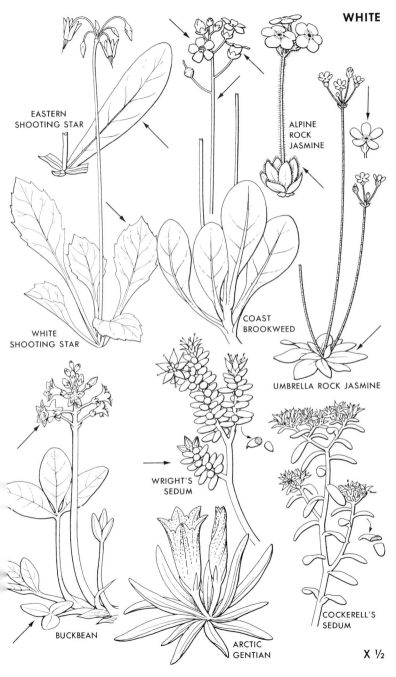

WHITE

EASTERN
SHOOTING STAR

ALPINE
ROCK
JASMINE

WHITE
SHOOTING STAR

COAST
BROOKWEED

UMBRELLA ROCK JASMINE

BUCKBEAN

WRIGHT'S
SEDUM

ARCTIC
GENTIAN

COCKERELL'S
SEDUM

X ½

5-PETALED, SHOWY TRUMPETS ON VINES

Morning Glory Family (Convolvulaceae)
See also pp. R 240; B 362.

Note: Any species with some red coloration is on p. 240.

FIELD BINDWEED Alien   *Convolvulus arvensis*
Note the arrow-shaped leaf blade with *sharp, pointed lobes.*
Small, white or pink-tinted flowers (10–40 cm wide) on trailing
stems. Disturbed places. Common. S.W., Tex., R. Mts., Pl. Sts.,
S.E.   APRIL–SEPT.

BEACH MORNING GLORY   *Ipomoea stolonifera*
Note the *thick, succulent, shiny,* oblong to heart-shaped leaves
and large white flowers with *yellow centers.* Vines in mats. Sand
dunes, beaches, Tex. Gulf Coast.   APRIL–NOV.

ZIG-ZAG MORNING GLORY   *Evolvulus nuttallianus*
Stems *erect,* or spreading on ground with alternate, "zigzag,"
silvery-haired linear leaves. Flowers white. 30–60 cm. Open
places. Eastern half of Tex.   APRIL–SEPT.

HEDGE MORNING GLORY   *Calystegia sepium*
Arrow-shaped leaves with *blunt lobes* on long, twining vines.
Flowers white to pinkish. Marshes. N. Ariz., N.M.; rare in Tex.,
R. Mts., Pl. Sts.   MAY–OCT.

SPIDERLEAF   *Ipomoea tenuiloba*
Note the 5 *threadlike leaflets* of each leaf and the long (5–
12 cm) tubelike flowers. Calyx surface *warty.* Flowers pure
white with a pale yellowish inner tube. Climbing vines. Se. Ariz.
to Big Bend region of Tex.   JULY–SEPT.

SILVER MORNING GLORY   *Evolvulus sericeus*
Short, prostrate stems crowded with *silvery, linear* leaves that
are strongly *folded together.* Flowers all white or all blue. 5–
30 cm. Open places. S.W., s. Tex.   APRIL–OCT.

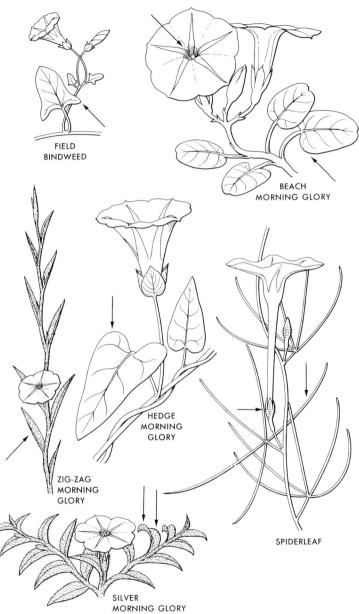

FIELD
BINDWEED

BEACH
MORNING GLORY

HEDGE
MORNING
GLORY

ZIG-ZAG
MORNING
GLORY

SPIDERLEAF

SILVER
MORNING GLORY

X ½

5 UNITED PETALS IN BOWLS OR BELLS; FLOWERS IN COILED CLUSTERS

Waterleaf Family (Hydrophyllaceae)
See also pp. Y 182; R 312; B 364.

COMMON EUCRYPTA   *Eucrypta chrysanthemifolia*
Small, *open,* bell-like flowers, white to yellowish or bluish, in a loosely coiled cluster. *Lacy* pinnate leaves. Sticky stems. Pleasant scent. 10–60 cm. Common in shady places. Lower-elevation deserts. Ariz.   FEB.–APRIL

FENDLER'S WATERLEAF   *Hydrophyllum fendleri*
Pinnate leaves, each with 7–9 leaflets. Each lateral leaflet tends to be *bilobed.* 10–60 cm. Open to shady woods, common. N.M., R. Mts.   MAY–JULY

BRITTLE PHACELIA   *Phacelia neglecta*
A low plant with thick, *succulent, shieldlike leaves* that are *very brittle* when handled. Flowers white. 5–10 cm. Frequent on stony desert pavement on low-elevation deserts. W. Ariz.
      FEB.–MARCH

DWARF WESTERN CENTAUR   *Hesperochiron pumilus*
White, *bowl-shaped* flowers *nestled* in a *low tuft* of narrow, oblong leaves. 2–5 cm. N. Ariz.   APRIL–MAY

VARILEAF PHACELIA   *Phacelia heterophylla*
1–5 grayish green leaflets per leaf. Flowers white to greenish yellow on a single, erect, *columnlike stem.* 30 cm–1 m. Common in rocky meadows. N.M., R. Mts.   MAY–JULY

TIGHT PHACELIA   *Phacelia congesta*
Note the *broad, terminal leaf blade* and *1 or 2 pairs* of leaflets below. Numerous white or bluish flowers in a *congested* coiled cyme. 5–30 cm. Open sandy or rocky places. Se. Ariz. to western two-thirds of Tex.   MARCH–JUNE

NEW MEXICO PHACELIA   *Phacelia neomexicana*
Tall, erect stem with *lacy, pinnate leaves.* Each white to pale blue petal margin has a *toothlike fringe.* 10–70 cm. Open fields, mountain foothills. Northern S.W., R. Mts.   MAY–AUG.

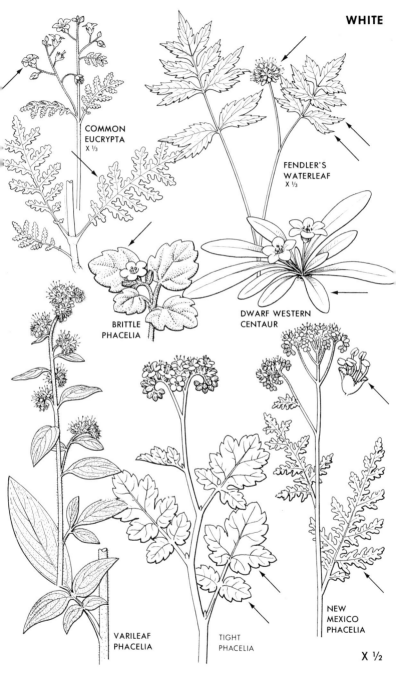

WHITE

COMMON
EUCRYPTA
X ⅓

FENDLER'S
WATERLEAF
X ⅓

BRITTLE
PHACELIA

DWARF WESTERN
CENTAUR

VARILEAF
PHACELIA

TIGHT
PHACELIA

NEW
MEXICO
PHACELIA

X ½

5-PETALED PINWHEELS IN COILED CLUSTERS; 4 NUTLIKE SEEDS

Forget-me-not Family (Boraginaceae)
See also pp. Y 182; O 234; R 314; B 344, 366.

BINDWEED   *Heliotropium convolvulaceum*
HELIOTROPE
Large, white, *morning-glorylike* flowers have *yellow throats* and grayish stems. Stems and leaves have *yellowish hairs.* Fragrant. Open in late afternoon. 10–50 cm. Very common. Sandy plains, dunes. N. Ariz. to w. Tex., Pl. Sts.   JUNE–OCT.

JAMES' POPCORN   *Cryptantha jamesii*
Small, flat, *wheel-like* flowers in thick coils that eventually spread apart. Many erect stems in 1 cluster. 10–30 cm. Near oak, juniper; in pine woodlands, sandy plains. S.W., western two-thirds of Tex., Pl. Sts.   APRIL–SEPT.

SALT HELIOTROPE   *Heliotropium curassavicum*
Tiny flowers in *long, curved sprays,* white to pale blue. Low, matlike, fleshy stems are smooth and covered with a bluish wax. 10–50 cm. Very common. Drying alkaline floodplains, salt marshes. S.W., Tex., Pl. Sts.   ALL YEAR

WHITEBRISTLE STICKSEED   *Lappula redowskii*
Numerous *white spines* on sepals surround tiny, *half-open* flowers. Stem erect with spatula-shaped leaves. Each fruit has 4 hook-spined nutlets. 10–60 cm. Frequent in open places; many habitats. S.W., western two-thirds of Tex., R. Mts., Pl. Sts.
    MARCH–SEPT.

BRISTLY PECTOCARYA   *Pectocarya setosa*
Note the 4 divergent, *rounded* seeds with many short-hooked hairs and a few longer spines below. Tiny, insignificant flowers. 5–20 cm. Sandy places on lower deserts. Ariz.   MARCH–JUNE

SLENDER PECTOCARYA   *Pectocarya linearis*
Tiny flowers soon develop into *4 linear, twisted,* spiny seeds that diverge from each other. 10–30 cm. Open places. Western S.W.   MARCH–JUNE

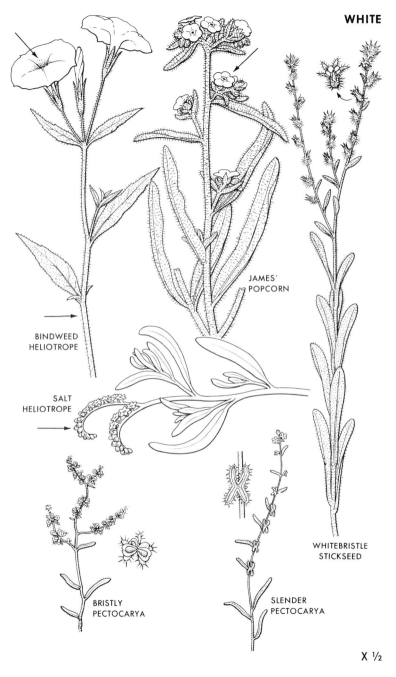

WHITE

BINDWEED
HELIOTROPE

JAMES'
POPCORN

SALT
HELIOTROPE

WHITEBRISTLE
STICKSEED

BRISTLY
PECTOCARYA

SLENDER
PECTOCARYA

X ½

5 UNITED PETALS; LARGE TRUMPETS OR FLAT, STARLIKE FLOWERS

Nightshade Family (Solanaceae)
See also pp. Y 184; R 312; B 368.

WHITE NIGHTSHADE Alien *Solanum nodiflorum*
Note the *yellow beak* of stamens projecting from the starlike, white to purple-tinted petals. Leaves triangular. Fruit a shiny black berry. Plant *not spiny*. 30–60 cm. Disturbed places. Ariz.
MAY–SEPT.

WRIGHT'S GROUND CHERRY *Physalis acutifolia*
Flowers white, disklike, with an *inner ring of yellow*. Calyx becomes an inflated papery bladder covering the seed capsule. Leaves lancelike, with wavy edges. 30 cm–1 m. Disturbed places. S.W.
JUNE–SEPT.

CAROLINA NIGHTSHADE *Solanum carolinense*
Note the *yellow spines* along the underside and petiole of each broad leaf with sawtoothed margins. White to pale blue, starlike flowers. Fruit a rounded yellow berry. 10–30 cm. Open fields, roadsides. Eastern third of Tex., Pl. Sts., S.E.
APRIL–OCT.

JIMSONWEED *Datura meteloides*
Very large (10–20 cm), trumpetlike flowers, which may be white or various shades of pale purple. Calyx tubular. Leaves grayish. Spiny seed capsule. *Poisonous*. 30 cm–1.5 m. Dry open places. S.W., Tex., R. Mts., Pl. Sts.
MAY–OCT.

COYOTE TOBACCO *Nicotiana attenuata*
Long, slender, trumpetlike flowers with *short petal lobes*. Leaves lancelike to oval with a *definite petiole*. Sticky-haired and bad-smelling. 20 cm–2 m. Common along washes. Ariz., Tex., R. Mts.
MAY–OCT.

DESERT TOBACCO *Nicotiana trigonophylla*
Each white to greenish, trumpetlike flower has a *short tube*. Note that the oval leaves have 2 *earlike basal lobes* which clasp the stem. Plants sticky-haired. 20 cm–1 m. Grows around the drip line of rocks, sandy washes. S.W., Tex.
ALL YEAR

FIDDLELEAF TOBACCO *Nicotiana repanda*
Note the *extremely long* (12–20 cm), *slender,* pure white corolla tube. *Fiddle-shaped leaves* with broad, clasping basal lobes. Flowers open from evening to midmorning. 50 cm–1 m. Frequent. Roadsides, thickets, flats. Southern and se. Tex.
FEB.–JULY

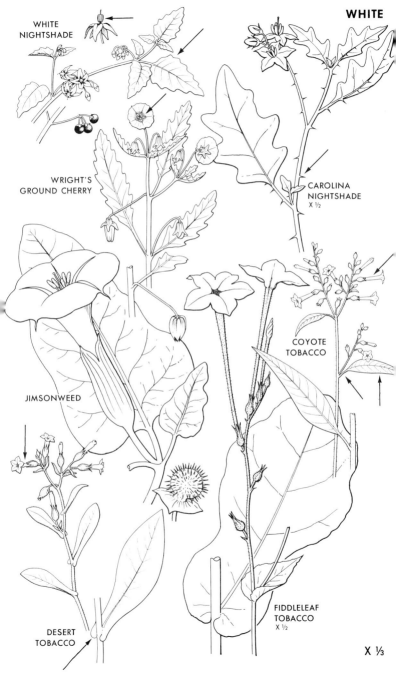

WHITE
NIGHTSHADE

WRIGHT'S
GROUND CHERRY

CAROLINA
NIGHTSHADE
X ½

JIMSONWEED

COYOTE
TOBACCO

DESERT
TOBACCO

FIDDLELEAF
TOBACCO
X ½

X ⅓

5 UNITED PETALS; ROUND PINWHEELS; 2-LIPPED, TUBULAR FLOWERS

Phlox Family (Polemoniaceae)
See also pp. Y 180; O 234; R 308–312; B 360–362.

EVENING SNOW *Linanthus dichotomus*
Large, snowy white flowers *without pedicels*. Sepals joined by translucent membranes except at the *tips, which are free*. Flowers open at dusk, making fields look snow-covered. 5–20 cm. Cen. Ariz. MARCH–MAY

NUTTALL'S LINANTHUS *Linanthus nuttallii*
Flowers funnel-shaped with a yellow tube. *No membrane* between the sepals. 10–20 cm. Pine forests. Ariz., w. N.M., R. Mts. JULY–NOV.

HOOD'S PHLOX *Phlox hoodii*
A low, cushionlike plant with *tiny, spine-tipped leaves* and white to lilac flowers. Rocky places. Northern S.W., R. Mts. APRIL–JUNE

VINE PHLOX *Phlox tenuifolia*
Large, white flowers with yellow inner tubes on long, vinelike stems. Flowers usually appear at the tops of unrelated shrubs which this species uses for support. Linear leaves, in *opposite pairs*. 50 cm–1 m. Rocky slopes. Ariz. MARCH–MAY

Snapdragon Family (Scrophulariaceae)
See also pp. Y 118–122; R 244–250; B 350–354.

REDLINE PENSTEMON *Penstemon albidus*
Upper and lower petal lobes stiffly erect, at right angles to the *slightly inflated* corolla tube. Upper petals *as long as* the lower ones. *Red lines* in corolla tube. Bright green, broadly lancelike leaves without petioles. 10–40 cm. High plains. Cen. Tex. to Panhandle and ne. N.M.; Pl. Sts. MARCH–JUNE

BUCKLEY'S PENSTEMON *Penstemon buckleyi*
Upper petals *shorter than* the lower ones. Flower white to cream, *without* other color marks. Stem leaves broadly oval, without petioles. Basal leaves narrow, lancelike. 30–60 cm. Plains country. W. Tex., N.M., Pl. Sts. APRIL–MAY

PLAINS PENSTEMON *Penstemon ambiguus*
Note the large, *mothlike petal lobes* that *curve along* the long, pinkish corolla tube. Petal lobes white or pale pink; corolla tube pale pink. A large, rounded plant with *linear, grasslike leaves*. 30 cm–1 m. Common on plains. N. Ariz., N.M., w. Tex., Pl. Sts. MAY–AUG.

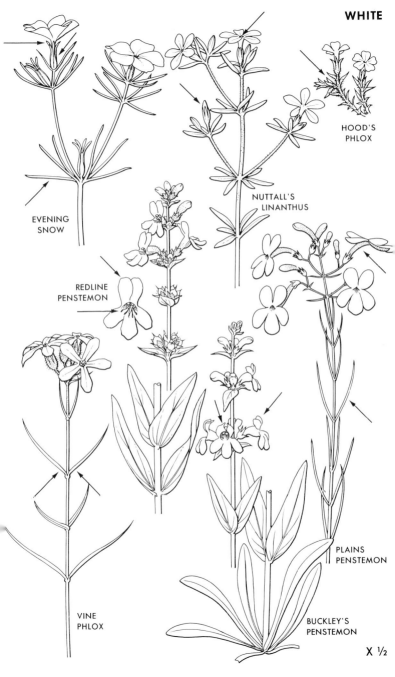

WHITE

HOOD'S
PHLOX

EVENING
SNOW

NUTTALL'S
LINANTHUS

REDLINE
PENSTEMON

PLAINS
PENSTEMON

VINE
PHLOX

BUCKLEY'S
PENSTEMON

X ½

5 PETALS; 2-LIPPED, TUBULAR FLOWERS; SQUARE STEMS; MINTLIKE ODOR

Mint Family (Labiatae)
See also pp. Y 188; R 318; B 374–376.

HOREHOUND Alien · · · · · · · · · · · · · · · · *Marrubium vulgare*
Numerous tiny flowers in *doughnutlike circles* around the square stem. Note the opposite pairs of gray, oval leaves with *crinkly* surfaces. Stem white, woolly. 30 cm–1 m. Very common in disturbed places. S.W., Tex., R. Mts., Pl. Sts.   ALL YEAR

AFRICAN SAGE Alien · · · · · · · · · · · · · · · · · *Salvia aethiopis*
Note the large, *hooked* upper corolla lip of each flower. White to pale yellow flowers in whorls surrounded by *large, cuplike bracts.* Stems branch in pairs, with each succeeding pair at right angles to the previous set, giving the plant a pyramid shape. Leaves gray-haired, mostly basal. Strong, disagreeable mintlike odor. 20 cm–1 m. Northern half of Ariz., R. Mts.
MAY–AUG.

LEMON BEEBALM · · · · · · · · · · · · · · · · *Monarda citriodora*
Pagoda-like whorls of pale yellow or pinkish floral leaves with numerous gaping, white-lipped flowers above each whorl. Calyx has numerous *spiny hairs.* Flower corolla white or pink and often pink-dotted. *Lip petal square-lobed.* 10–40 cm. Very common. Tex., se. N.M., Pl. Sts.   APRIL–OCT.

PLAINS BEEBALM · · · · · · · · · · · · · · · *Monarda pectinata*
Pagodalike whorls of *green floral leaves* below numerous gaping, white or pink flowers with pink dots. *Lip petal rounded.* Calyx has many spiny hairs. 10–30 cm. Sandy plains, pastures. Cen. Ariz. to w. Tex., Pl. Sts.   MAY–SEPT.

LACY GERMANDER · · · · · · · · · · · · · · · *Tecurium laciniatum*
Note the large, *tonguelike* lower lip petal with pink-purple lines and 2 pairs of side lobes. *Lacy,* pinnate leaves with linear lobes. Low, tufted stems. 5–15 cm. Eastern third of N.M., western two-thirds of Tex., Pl. Sts.   MAY–SEPT.

BEARDED GERMANDER · · · · · · · · · · *Tecurium glandulosum*
Tonguelike lower lip petal *bearded on underside.* Petals unmarked. Leaves *entire and lancelike or trilobed.* Often single-stemmed. 10–30 cm. Arroyos. W. Ariz.   FEB.–MARCH

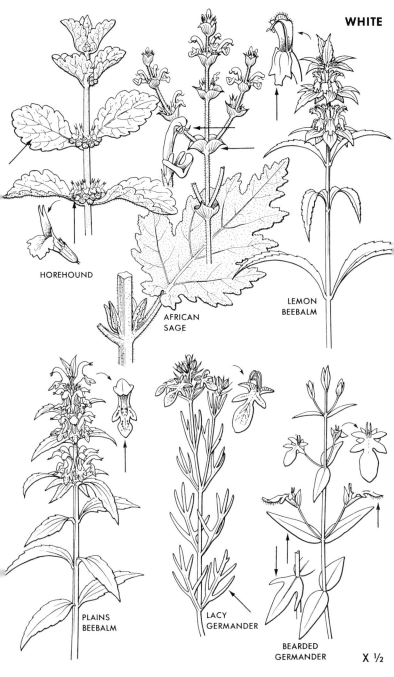

WHITE

HOREHOUND

AFRICAN SAGE

LEMON BEEBALM

PLAINS BEEBALM

LACY GERMANDER

BEARDED GERMANDER

X ½

5 UNITED, TUBULAR, 2-LIPPED FLOWERS

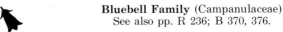

Bluebell Family (Campanulaceae)
See also pp. R 236; B 370, 376.

FOLDED-EAR LOBELIA　　　　*Lobelia flaccidifolia*
Flower 2-lipped; the 3 lower lip petals project nearly parallel to the corolla tube, while the *upper 2 fold backward. Broad, lancelike,* alternate leaves *without* petioles. A tall, spikelike plant. 30 cm–1 m. Piney woods. E. Tex.　　　JUNE–JULY

THREAD PLANT　　　　*Nemacladus glanduliferus*
The 2-lipped flower has 2 *long lower* lobes. The 3 shorter upper lobes are *tipped with red-brown.* Flowers on long, *wiry pedicels.* A bushy cluster of *zigzag* stems with a few narrow leaves near ground level. 10–30 cm. Frequent in open sandy deserts. Western half of Ariz., s. Ut.　　　FEB.–MAY

Milkwort Family (Polygalaceae)

WHITE MILKWORT　　　　*Polygala alba*
Note the *thick, pencil-sized spike* of white flowers. Long, wiry stems with only a few pairs of *linear* leaves. 30 cm–1 m. Rocky plains. S.W., Tex., Pl. Sts.　　　MARCH–OCT.

Valerian Family (Valerianaceae)
See also p. R 316.

WESTERN VALERIAN　　　　*Valeriana occidentalis*
Leaves pinnate with many *short* side leaflets and a *broader* terminal leaflet. Numerous tubular flowers with a *fat unequal lobe* on the lower side; in a dense terminal panicle. 10–60 cm. Moist mountain meadows. S.W., R. Mts.　　　MAY–JULY

EDIBLE VALERIAN　　　　*Valeriana edulis*
The *very tall stem* (1 m) has pinnate leaves with equal-sized lobes. *Tiny cuplike* flowers with an unequal lobe on underside; in tight panicles. Root *poisonous;* edible only if properly prepared. 30 cm–1 m. Open mountain meadows. S.W., R. Mts.
　　　JULY–SEPT.

HEADED VALERIAN　　　　*Valeriana capitata*
White or pink flowers in a *rounded, headlike cluster.* Leaves oval to spatula-like and *not divided.* 10–40 cm. Moist meadows, forests in mountains. S.W., R. Mts.　　　MAY–JULY

Bladderwort Family (Lentibulariaceae).
See also pp. Y 188; R 298.

SMALL BUTTERWORT　　　　*Pinguicula pumila*
Note the *single, spurred,* white or pale pink flower on a *leafless stem* above a low basal cluster of fleshy, yellow-green, elliptical leaves. 10–25 cm. Wet pine savannahs, pitcher-plant bogs. E. Tex., S.E.　　　MARCH–OCT.

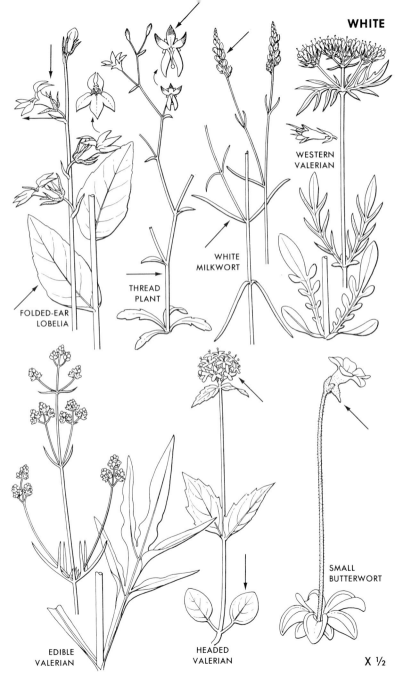

WESTERN
VALERIAN

FOLDED-EAR
LOBELIA

THREAD
PLANT

WHITE
MILKWORT

EDIBLE
VALERIAN

HEADED
VALERIAN

SMALL
BUTTERWORT

X ½

PEALIKE FLOWERS; PINNATE LEAVES

Pea Family (Leguminosae)
See also pp. W 94–96; Y 190–196; R 320–328;
B 346–348, 380–382.

WHITE LAWN CLOVER Alien   *Trifolium repens*
3 leaflets of each leaf *oval,* larger at tip end. Calyx teeth *short.*
Flowers in a head with no papery bracts underneath it. 10–
30 cm. Lawns, meadows, etc. S.W., Tex., R. Mts.   ALL YEAR

LONGSTALK CLOVER   *Trifolium longipes*
Leaflets *long and narrow* with toothed edges. Flowers in a
dense head. Calyx teeth *long, with hairy margins.* No bracts
below the flowerhead. 5–40 cm. Meadows. Northern N.M.,
R. Mts.   MAY–SEPT.

AMERICAN LICORICE   *Glycyrrhiza lepidota*
Note the oblong seed capsule with *hooked hairs.* Numerous
white to pale yellow flowers in an erect, *brushlike head.* Leaflets lancelike. 30 cm–1 m. Disturbed places. S.W., Pl. Sts.
                                          MAY–JULY

WHITE SWEET CLOVER   *Melilotus albus*
Numerous small pealike flowers in *spikelike racemes.* Each leaf
has 3 leaflets. Strong sweet odor. 50 cm–2 m. Disturbed places.
S.W., Tex., Pl. Sts.   MARCH–JULY

SCRUFFY PRAIRIE CLOVER   *Dalea albiflora*
Pinnate leaves with *numerous short, hairy,* linear lobes. Leaves
and stems with hairs. Numerous tiny pealike flowers in an *elongated spike.* 30–60 cm. Many habitats. Ariz. and southwestern
half of N.M.   APRIL–OCT.

WHITE PRAIRIE CLOVER   *Dalea candida*
Tiny pealike flowers in a *cylindrical spike.* Leaves pinnate, with
3–9 *lancelike leaflets.* 30 cm–1 m. Flats, openings in woods.
S.W., Tex., Pl. Sts.   MAY–SEPT.

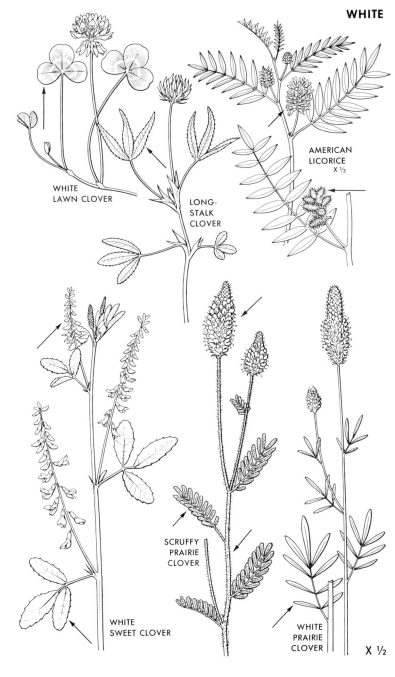

WHITE
LAWN CLOVER

LONG-
STALK
CLOVER

AMERICAN
LICORICE
X ⅓

WHITE
SWEET CLOVER

SCRUFFY
PRAIRIE
CLOVER

WHITE
PRAIRIE
CLOVER

X ½

PEALIKE FLOWERS; PINNATE LEAVES

Pea Family (Leguminosae)
See also pp. W 94; Y 190–196; R 320–328;
B 346–348, 380–382.

WHITE DWARF LOCOWEED *Astragalus didymocarpus*
The pinnate leaves have 7–17 *square-tipped* leaflets, each with
a *notch*. Flowers in dense, oblong to oval heads. Seedpods small,
rounded, *wrinkled sacs*. 5–30 cm. S. Ariz.   FEB.–APRIL

MOTTLED LOCOWEED   *Astragalus lentiginosus*
Seedpod a strongly *inflated sausage* with a *flattened triangular
tip* that curves upward. 11–19 oval leaflets, nearly hairless.
Flowers vary from creamy white or yellow to red-purple.
A highly variable and widespread species. 10–60 cm. S.W.,
R. Mts.   FEB.–JUNE

SHOWY VETCH   *Vicia pulchella*
Note the numerous, densely flowered racemes and *narrow, linear leaflets*. Tendrils at tips. Flowers creamy white or with purple veins. 50 cm–1 m. In mats. Common in mountains. S.W.
                                                JUNE–SEPT.

PALE VETCH   *Vicia caroliniana*
Banner and wing petals white, keel petals pale blue. 9–20
loosely arranged pealike flowers on a flower stem as long as a
complete leaf. Tendril-tipped, pinnate leaves have *broad,* flat,
linear leaflets. 50 cm–1 m. Shady hardwood forests. E. Tex.,
Pl. Sts., S.E.   APRIL–JUNE

ARIZONA SWEET PEA   *Lathyrus arizonicus*
The *low stem* has pinnate leaves, each with 2–6 *long, broad,*
linear leaflets. Each leaf pinnate, but *no tendril at tip. Few*
(2–4) *white flowers* with a few faint reddish lines on a stem
shorter than the leaves. 10–40 cm. Shady conifer forests.
Mountains. S.W., R. Mts.   MAY–OCT.

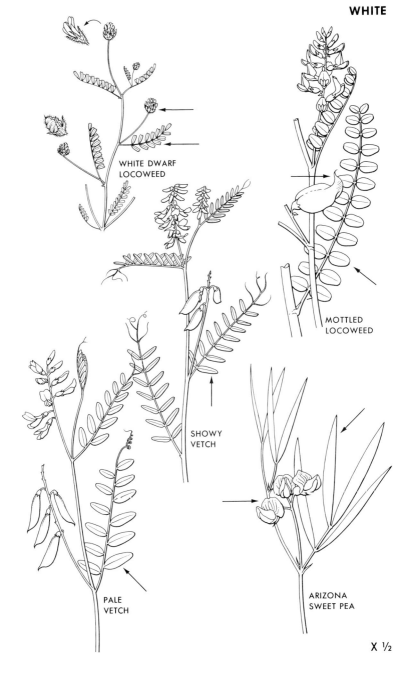

WHITE DWARF
LOCOWEED

MOTTLED
LOCOWEED

SHOWY
VETCH

PALE
VETCH

ARIZONA
SWEET PEA

X ½

TRUE SUNFLOWERS AND TARWEEDS

Sunflower Family (Compositae)

Sunflower Tribe: Heliantheae
See also pp. W 98–110; Y 198–222;
O 234; R 330–334; B 384–386; G 402.

FROSTWEED   *Verbesina virginica*
Note the *winglike margins* on both the leaf petiole and stem.
Black, pepperlike stamens in the central disk flowers. Large,
egg-shaped leaves. 30 cm–1.5 m. Common. Eastern two-thirds
of Tex., Pl. Sts., S.E.   AUG.–OCT.

HOARY BLACKFOOT   *Melampodium cinereum*
Note the *alternate sawtoothed* lobes on the *bright green,* linear
leaves in opposite pairs. Each ray flower petal *bilobed.* Flowerheads on long, naked stems. 10–60 cm. Common. S. Ariz. to
western half of Tex., Pl. Sts.   MARCH–NOV.

ASH-GRAY BLACKFOOT   *Melampodium leucanthum*
Ash gray *leaves, linear-straplike* with *smooth* margins. Each
ray flower petal bilobed. Flowerheads on long, naked stems.
10–30 cm. Rio Grande plains of s. Tex. to cen. Tex., Pl. Sts.
                                                       JAN.–DEC.

SPINYLEAF ZINNIA   *Zinnia acerosa*
Note the *semi-drooping,* oval to rounded, white to palest yellow
ray-flower petals around a small *dark center* of disk flowers.
Large *scalelike flowerbuds.* Short, grayish linear leaves. 10–
30 cm. Open mesas, plains. Cen. and s. Ariz.   APRIL–OCT.

WHITE COMPASS PLANT   *Silphium albiflorum*
Each *giant* leaf irregular, deeply divided into stiff lobes with a
rough, rasplike surface. Flowers above leaves on a *stout,
rodlike stem.* 30 cm–1 m. Open prairies, woodlands. Eastern
half of Tex., Pl. Sts., S.E.   JUNE–SEPT.

CROWDED RAYWEED   *Parthenium confertum*
Note the *buttonlike* flowerhead and *tiny, cuplike or hornlike*
ray flowers around the outer margin. Alternate pinnate leaves.
30 cm–1 m. Common. Western and s. Tex.   APRIL–OCT.

Tarweed Tribe: Madiineae

WHITE LAYIA   *Layia glandulosa*
Basal leaves linear with 1–4 pairs of *short lobes.* Stem leaves
entire. Ray-flower petal tip has 3 equal teeth. All parts covered
with tiny, sticky hairs. 10–60 cm. Common at lower elevations.
Ariz., sw. N.M.   MARCH–JUNE

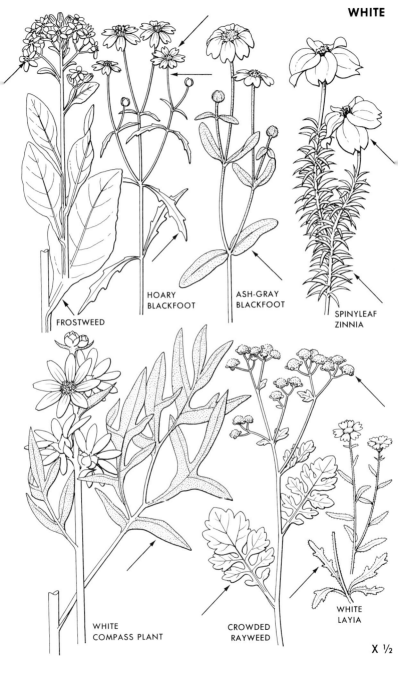

FROSTWEED

HOARY
BLACKFOOT

ASH-GRAY
BLACKFOOT

SPINYLEAF
ZINNIA

WHITE
COMPASS PLANT

CROWDED
RAYWEED

WHITE
LAYIA

X ½

WOOLLY SUNFLOWERS AND PINCUSHIONLIKE HEADS

Sunflower Family (Compositae)

Woolly Sunflower Tribe: Helenieae
See also pp. W 08 110; Y 198–222;
O 234; R 330–334; B 384–386; G 402.

WHITE WOOLLY DAISY   *Antheropeas lanosum*
Flowerheads 1–5 cm in diameter. The white ray flowers often have *red veins*. Achene (seed) with *long, pointed* pappus, alternating with *half-sized, rounded* pappus. Linear leaves *white, woolly*. 2–15 cm. Sandy places on lower deserts. Ariz.

FEB.–MAY

EMORY'S ROCK DAISY   *Perityle emoryi*
Note the *broadly triangular* leaves with *deeply toothed margins*. 5–30 cm. Common in rocky places on lower deserts. Sw. Ariz.

FEB.–OCT.

FREMONT'S PINCUSHION   *Chaenactis fremontii*
Green leaves divided into linear lobes. Pincushionlike disk flowerheads. Each achene (seed) topped by 4 *lancelike bristles*. 10–40 cm. Common on sandy slopes in lower deserts. W. Ariz.

MARCH–JUNE

OLD PLAINSMAN   *Hymenopappus scabiosaeus*
Note the *large, white, papery flowerhead bracts* around the *loosely* arranged, white to pinkish disk flowers. Stem and leaves white, woolly-haired. Pinnate leaves divided twice, the terminal lobes rounded. 40 cm–1 m. Eastern half of Tex., Pl. Sts., S.E.

MARCH–JULY

PEBBLE PINCUSHION   *Chaenactis carphoclinia*
Achene (seed) topped by *spine-tipped bristles*. Lacy pinnate leaves. 5–40 cm. Common on hot desert pavements on lower deserts. Ariz., Ut.

FEB.–MAY

DUSTY MAIDEN   *Chaenactis douglasii*
Cottony, *lacy, pinnate leaves* below the white or pink-tinted, pincushionlike flowers. Each achene (seed) topped by about 10 *oblong bristles* (not shown). 10–50 cm. Dry mountain slopes. Northern S.W., R. Mts.

MAY–SEPT.

ESTEVE'S PINCUSHION   *Chaenactis stevioides*
Grayish leaves divided twice into *numerous short, thick segments*. Achene (seed) topped by 4 flattened bristles with *short, triangular tips*. 5–25 cm. Sandy places at middle and lower elevations. S.W., R. Mts.

FEB.–MAY

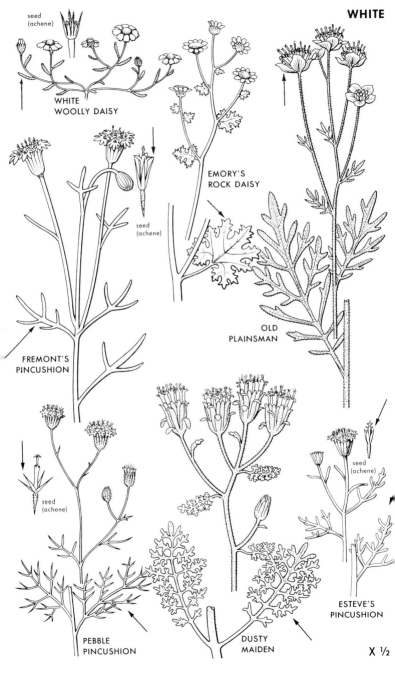

WHITE

seed (achene)

WHITE
WOOLLY DAISY

EMORY'S
ROCK DAISY

seed (achene)

FREMONT'S
PINCUSHION

OLD
PLAINSMAN

seed (achene)

PEBBLE
PINCUSHION

DUSTY
MAIDEN

ESTEVE'S
PINCUSHION

seed (achene)

X ½

DAISIES

Sunflower Family (Compositae)

Aster Tribe: Astereae
See also pp. W 98–110; Y 198–222; O 234;
R 330–334; B 384–386; G 402.

ELEGANT DAISY   *Erigeron concinnus*
Note the many *scattered, stiff hairs* on the stem and leaves.
Gray-green leaves, *narrowly* spatula-like, scattered *up the stem.*
Numerous narrow, white ray flowers in the flowerhead. Disk
flowers yellow. 10–50 cm. Ariz., northern N.M., R. Mts.

APRIL–OCT.

PLAINS DAISY   *Erigeron modestus*
Similar to Elegant Daisy, but hairs *shorter and thicker, velvety*
on the gray-green leaves and stems. Flower buds *nodding.* 10–
30 cm. Common on open plains, woodlands. S.W., western half
of Tex., R. Mts.   MARCH–JULY

WHIPLASH DAISY   *Erigeron flagellaris*
Very similar to Plains Daisy, but hairs on stem and gray-green
leaves curve inward. Long, *trailing,* whiplike lateral stems grow
from the stem base. 5–60 cm. Meadows, woods. S.W., w. Tex.,
R. Mts., Pl. Sts.   APRIL–SEPT.

CUTLEAF DAISY   *Erigeron compositus*
A low plant with *fan-shaped, pinnate leaves.* 0.5–25 cm. Rocky
alpine ridges. Northern S.W., R. Mts.   MAY–AUG.

EATON'S DAISY   *Erigeron eatonni*
Disk flowers form a *raised crown.* Leaves linear. 10–30 cm.
Mountains. N. Ariz., nw. N.M., R. Mts.   MAY–JULY

COULTER'S DAISY   *Erigeron coulteri*
Broad, lancelike leaves with *clasping bases.* 30 cm–1 m. Mountain streambanks, meadows. Northern N.M., R. Mts.

JUNE–AUG.

PHILADELPHIA DAISY   *Erigeron philadelphicus*
Each flowerhead has *hundreds of fine filamentlike* ray flowers.
Spatula-like leaves are *clasping.* Disk flowers yellow. 30 cm–
1 m. Common in moist, open fields. N.M., Tex., Pl. Sts., S.E.

MARCH–JULY

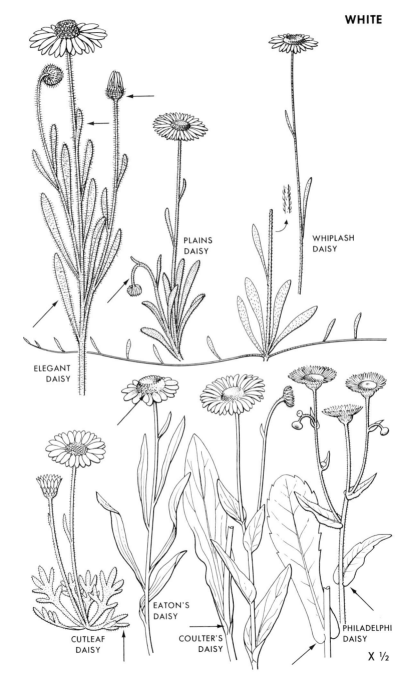

PLAINS
DAISY

WHIPLASH
DAISY

ELEGANT
DAISY

EATON'S
DAISY

CUTLEAF
DAISY

COULTER'S
DAISY

PHILADELPHI
DAISY

X ½

DAISY AND ASTERLIKE FLOWERS

Sunflower Family (Compositae)

Aster Tribe: Astereae
See also pp. W 98–110; Y 198–222;
O 234; R 330–334; B 384–386; G 402.

MOJAVE DESERT STAR   *Monoptilon bellioides*
Note the *tiny mounds* of white or blue, asterlike flowers above *linear* leaves. 1–10 cm. Common on sandy lower deserts. W. Ariz.   FEB.–APRIL

EASTER DAISY   *Townsendia exscapa*
Note the low, *ground-level cluster* of large (2–7 cm), white or pale pink flowerheads nestled among narrow, spatula-like leaves. Usually one of the first spring flowers. 2–5 cm tall. S.W., w. Tex. and occasionally to cen. Tex.   APRIL–AUG.

SAND ASTER   *Leucelene ericoides*
Note the *tiny spine on the tip* of each linear, grayish-haired leaf. Flowerhead of broad, white, straplike ray flowers and a *projecting* central area of yellow disk flowers. Flowerhead bracts in an *elongated cylinder.* Each bract *lancelike* with white papery margins and a green midrib, tips reddish tinted. 10–20 cm. Common in open plains, woodlands. S.W., w. Tex., R. Mts., Pl. Sts.   APRIL–OCT.

TOWER DAISY   *Townsendia formosa*
Note the *single,* large, daisylike flowerhead on a *tall unbranched stem* covered with small linear leaves. Large, spatula-like leaves in a basal rosette. 30–50 cm. Open mountain meadows. White Mts., Ariz., N.M.   JUNE–SEPT.

RIDDELL'S DOZE DAISY   *Aphanostephus riddellii*
Straplike to spatula-like stem leaves. Basal rosette leaves *deeply lobed* and ladderlike. 10–50 cm. Open plains. Tex., N.M.   MARCH–JUNE

HEATH ASTER   *Aster ericoides*
Note the *pink center* made of disk flowers within the bright white outer ray flowers of each flowerhead. Tall, well-branched stems. Leaves lancelike with *serrated margins.* Many smaller leaves on flowering branches. 70 cm–1 m. Common. S.W., Tex., R. Mts.   AUG.–OCT.

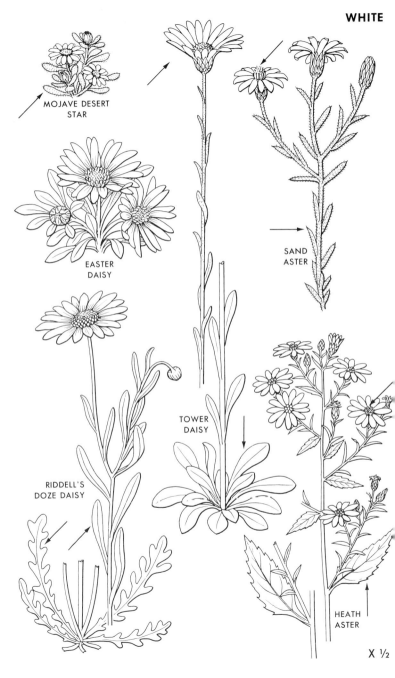

WHITE

MOJAVE DESERT
STAR

EASTER
DAISY

SAND
ASTER

RIDDELL'S
DOZE DAISY

TOWER
DAISY

HEATH
ASTER

X ½

DANDELIONLIKE FLOWERS; MILKY SAP
RAY FLOWERS ONLY IN FLOWERHEAD

Sunflower Family (Compositae)

Chicory Tribe: Cichorieae
See also pp. W 98–110; Y 198–222;
O 234; R 330–334; B 384–386; G 402.

NEW MEXICO PLUMESEED   *Rafinesquia neomexicana*
Dandelion-like leaves. Each seed topped by a *beak* and plumelike pappus (not shown). *Ray flowers only.* Milky sap. 50 cm–1.5 m. Very common on lower deserts. Ariz.

FEB.–JULY

TOBACCO WEED   *Atrichoseris platyphylla*
Spotted leaves in a flat basal rosette. Seeds awnless (not shown). Fragrant. 30 cm–2 m. Sandy washes, stony mesas in lower deserts. W. Ariz., Ut.

MARCH–APRIL

WHITE TACKSTEM   *Calycoseris wrightii*
Note the prominent *tacklike glands* on the blue-green stems and flowerhead bracts. Blue-green, pinnate leaves with *thin, linear lobes.* Flowerhead all white. 5–30 cm. Common on low desert plains, mesas. S.W., w. Tex., Ut.

MARCH–MAY

TWIGGY WREATH PLANT   *Stephanomeria exigua*
The flowerhead consists of 4–15 reddish-backed, white ray flowers; no disk flowers. Highly branched, leafless stems. 50 cm–1.5 m. Common on plains, hillsides. S.W., R. Mts.

APRIL–SEPT.

WHITE HAWKWEED   *Hieracium albiflorum*
White ray-flowered heads have bracts that are *sparsely-haired.* Heads well-separated by open-branching pedicels. Leaves conspicuously *long-haired.* 30–60 cm. Forest openings. Northern S.W., R. Mts.

JUNE–AUG.

TELEGRAPH LETTUCE   *Lactuca floridana*
Note the *deeply lobed, sharply angular leaflets* of each dark green leaf. Numerous leaves on a usually single, *stout, telegraph-polelike stem.* Flowerhead of many white or pale bluish ray flowers. 1–2 m. Very common. Eastern half of Tex., Pl. Sts., S.E.

MAY–OCT.

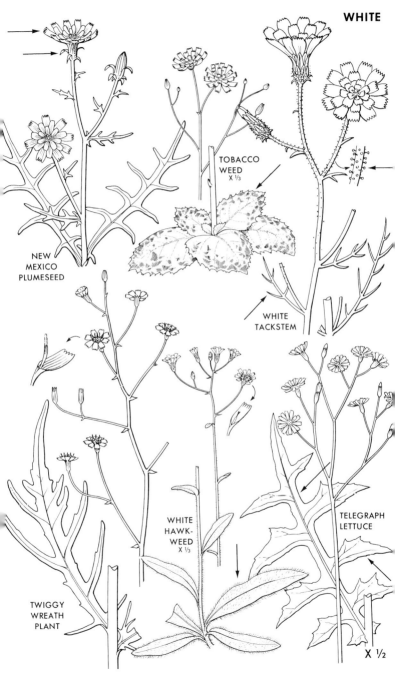

WHITE

NEW MEXICO PLUMESEED

TOBACCO WEED
X 1/3

WHITE TACKSTEM

TWIGGY WREATH PLANT

WHITE HAWK-WEED
X 1/3

TELEGRAPH LETTUCE

X 1/2

SMELLY MAYWEEDS, THISTLES

Sunflower Family (Compositae)
See also pp. W 98–110; Y 198–222;
O 234; R 330–334; B 384–386; G 402.

Mayweed Tribe: Anthemidae

OXEYE DAISY Alien   *Chrysanthemum leucanthemum*
Large *daisylike* flowers. Lower stem leaves spoon-shaped with a *toothed margin* around the spoon's "bowl." 30 cm–1 m. Disturbed places. Northern third of Ariz., occasional in N.M., R. Mts., Pl. Sts.   JUNE–SEPT.

DOG FENNEL Alien   *Anthemis cotula*
Lacy leaves divided 2–3 times into narrow segments. Many flowers at the top of a well-branched stem. Strong bad smell if handled. 10 cm–1 m. Disturbed places. S.W., Tex., R. Mts.

MARCH–JULY

COMMON YARROW   *Achillea millefolium*
Leaves linear with numerous, very short, *highly divided leaflets*. Flowers in *flat-topped* clusters. Stem covered with white, cottony hairs. Strong unpleasant odor. 30 cm–1 m. Mid- to highest mountains. S.W., northern half of Tex., R. Mts., Pl. Sts.

JUNE–SEPT.

WILD COSMOS   *Leucampyx newberryi*
Each *flat-ended, buttonlike* flowerhead has 6–9 *broad, oblong to rounded* ray flowers, and is on a *long, leafless, white, cottony stem*. Most of the twice-pinnate leaves are in a basal cluster. 30 cm–1 m. Common on low and midmountain slopes. Northern N.M., sw. Colo.   JUNE–AUG.

Thistle Tribe: Cynareae

DRUMMOND'S THISTLE   *Cirsium drummondii*
Spiny, white to pinkish *flowerheads, nestled in a flat* rosette of spiny leaves. 5–25 cm. Open places in mountains. Northern S.W., R. Mts.   JULY–SEPT.

NEW MEXICO THISTLE   *Cirsium neomexicanum*
Tall whitish stems with *shiny, green, straplike* leaf blades that are *completely divided (or nearly so) into leaflets*. Flowerheads white, pale pink, or lavender. 50 cm–1.5 m. Frequent on plains. S.W., R. Mts.   MARCH–SEPT.

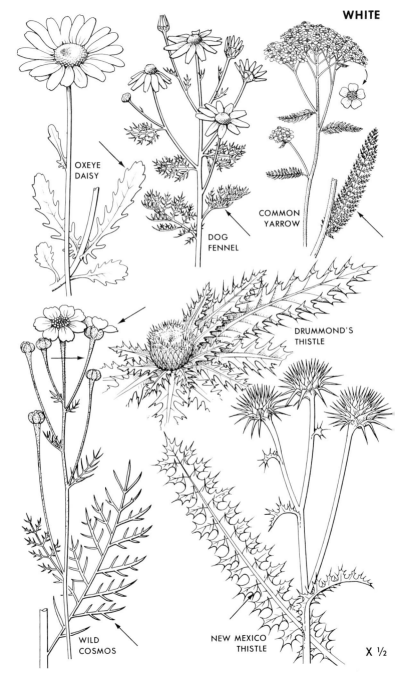

WHITE

OXEYE DAISY

DOG FENNEL

COMMON YARROW

DRUMMOND'S THISTLE

WILD COSMOS

NEW MEXICO THISTLE

X ½

FLOWERHEADS WITH DISK FLOWERS ONLY

Sunflower Family (Compositae)
See also pp. W 98–110; Y 198–222;
O 234; R 330–334; B 384–386; G 402.

Senecio Tribe: Senecioneae

FINNED INDIAN PLANTAIN *Cacalia plantaginea*
Note the long, *greenish white flowerhead bases with thin fins.*
Flowerhead consists of disk flowers only. *Broad,* bright green,
elliptical leaf blades are mostly basal. 50 cm–1.5 m. Common in
open places. Eastern half of Tex., Pl. Sts. APRIL–NOV.

LANCELEAF INDIAN PLANTAIN *Cacalia lanceolata*
Leaves *narrow, lancelike.* Flowerhead bracts *smooth (without
fins).* 50 cm–1.5 m Eastern third of Tex., S.E. JULY–OCT.

Everlasting Tribe: Inuleae

ALPINE EVERLASTING *Antennaria alpina*
Gray leaves in *tufted mats.* Papery, *round* flowerheads on
naked stems. 5–15 cm. Alpine. Northern S.W., R. Mts.
JULY–SEPT.

MOUNTAIN PUSSYTOES *Antennaria parvifolia*
Long, *cylindrical* flowerheads on nearly leafless stems, above
basal rosettes of gray, *spatula-like leaves.* Forms silvery gray
mats. 5–15 cm. Common in mountains. S.W., R. Mts.
MAY–AUG.

PEARLY EVERLASTING *Anaphalis margaritacea*
Note the terminal cluster of numerous oval flowerheads consisting mostly of *broad, white, papery bracts* around a few inconspicuous yellow disk flowers. Leaves linear, alternately arranged. 10 cm–1 m. Woods. Northern S.W., R. Mts.
JULY–SEPT.

WHITE CUDWEED *Gnaphalium leucocephalum*
Numerous linear leaves with *margins curled under.* Undersides
of leaves white, cottony; upper sides green, *without hairs.*
Rounded, papery flowerheads with yellow centers. Pleasant
lemon fragrance. 30–60 cm. Se. Ariz. to Big Bend region of
Tex. AUG.–OCT.

WESTERN CUDWEED *Gnaphalium chilense*
(not shown)
Similar to White Cudweed, but *both sides* of leaves covered
with *woolly gray hairs.* 30–60 cm. Mountains. S.W., R. Mts.
MAY–OCT.

Eupatory Tribe: Eupatorieae

YANKEE WEED *Eupatorium compositifolium*
Numerous long, *dirty white* flowerheads with long, protruding,
feathery stamens. Tall, highly-branched stems have linear
upper leaves; lower leaves pinnate. 50 cm–2.5 m. Occurs as
masses in open fields. Eastern third of Tex. SEPT.–NOV.

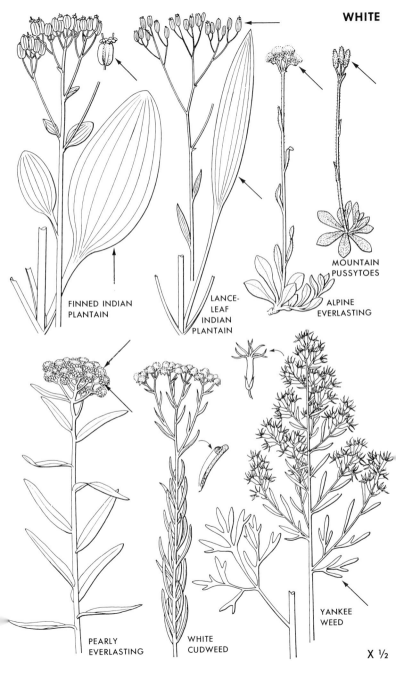

WHITE

FINNED INDIAN PLANTAIN

LANCE-LEAF INDIAN PLANTAIN

MOUNTAIN PUSSYTOES

ALPINE EVERLASTING

PEARLY EVERLASTING

WHITE CUDWEED

YANKEE WEED

X ½

Yellow
Flowers

Yellow flowers separate out fairly easily. Pale yellow, cream, or greenish yellow flowers merge into the whites or greens; if in doubt, look here and also in the White or Green sections. When possible, the group characteristics given in the text page titles are repeated in each color section, and in the same order. Where the flowers on a page look nearly the same but your sample does not fit, use the cross references given for other colors.

3 PETALS; LILIES AND ORCHIDS

Lily Family (Liliaceae)
See also pp. W 8–14; O & R 226; R 272; B 338; G 390.

YELLOW FAWN LILY   *Erythronium grandiflorum*
Large, bright yellow, *nodding, starlike flowers* on a leafless stem.
Bright green, spotless leaves. 10–30 cm. Subalpine slopes. Northern
N.M., R. Mts.   JUNE–JULY

YELLOW TROUT LILY   *Erythronium rostratum*
Similar to Yellow Fawn Lily, but leaves have *brownish, fawnlike
spots.* 8–20 cm. Low woods. E. Tex., Pl. Sts.   FEB.–MARCH

YELLOW BELLS   *Fritillaria pudica*
1–3 strongly *nodding, yellow, bell-like flowers* above linear leaves.
5–30 cm. Open places. Nw. S.W., R. Mts.   MARCH–JUNE

LEMON LILY   *Lilium parryi*
1–25 translucent, *lemon yellow, trumpetlike* flowers with occasional
maroon spots. Fragrant. 50 cm–1 m. Wet places in higher mountains. S. Ariz.   MAY–JULY

GOLDEN MARIPOSA TULIP   *Calochortus aureus*
Flower petals golden-yellow with a *rounded yellow basal spot* and a
red-purple horseshoe mark above it. Petal hairs unbranched. 20–
40 cm. N. Ariz., s. Ut.   MAY–JULY

GUNNISON'S MARIPOSA TULIP   *Calochortus gunnisonii*
Petals yellow, pink or purple. Lower half of petal has a *broad band
of numerous long, branching yellow hairs* above a *squarish outline*
of short, thick hairs; note the *smooth, shiny, purplish area* below
hairs at petal base. 10–50 cm. Mountain meadows. N.M., R. Mts.
                                                          JULY–AUG.

KENNEDY'S MARIPOSA TULIP   *Calochortus kennedyi*
Bright, dark yellow or orange petals with a *dark, red-brown area* at
the petal base. Note the flat, thumbnail-shaped central gland with a
few short, scattered hairs above it. 10–20 cm. Flats, mesas. S.W.,
southern R. Mts.   APRIL–JUNE

GOLDEN MILLER'S MAID   *Aletris aurea*
Note the *rough,* dark yellow flowers with *swollen bases,* loosely
arranged as a spike on a long, leafless flower stem. Yellow-green,
lancelike leaves in a basal cluster. 30–60 cm. Bogs, damp places.
E. Tex., Pl. Sts., S.E.   MAY–OCT.

WOOD CANDLE   *Schoenolirion croceum*
Flat, starlike flowers with *long pedicels* on a leafless stem. Long,
narrow, straplike leaves in a basal cluster, 10–30 cm. Wet slopes,
bogs. E. Tex., S.E.   MARCH–MAY

Orchid Family (Orchidaceae)
See also pp. W 18–20; O & R 228–230; G 390–394.

YELLOW LADY'S-SLIPPER   *Cypripedium calceolus*
Usually a single flower with a *bright yellow, slipperlike lip petal;*
other petals green to brownish. Several alternate, oval leaves. 30–
60 cm. Variable habitat. S.W., Tex., R. Mts., Pl. Sts.

                                                          APRIL–JULY

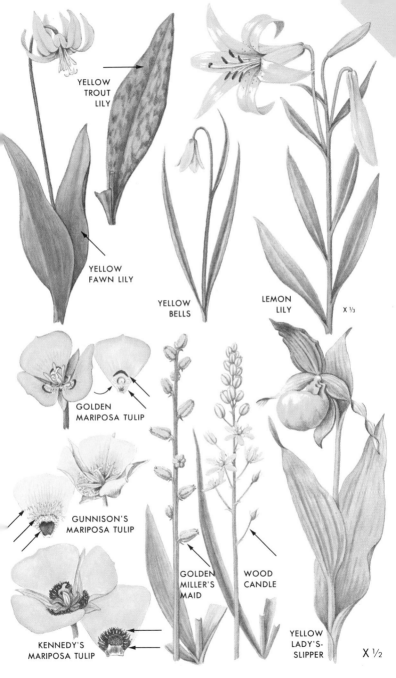

YELLOW
TROUT
LILY

YELLOW
FAWN LILY

YELLOW
BELLS

LEMON
LILY

X ⅓

GOLDEN
MARIPOSA TULIP

GUNNISON'S
MARIPOSA TULIP

KENNEDY'S
MARIPOSA TULIP

GOLDEN
MILLER'S
MAID

WOOD
CANDLE

YELLOW
LADY'S-
SLIPPER

X ½

3 OR 6 PETALS; STARS, IRISES

Amaryllis Family (Amaryllidaceae)
See also pp. W 14–16; R 274; B 338.

FALSE GARLIC or CROW POISON *Nothoscordum bivalve*
Note the 6 *pale yellow* petal lobes, *free to their bases.* Petal bases
white, stamens and ovary *dark yellow.* Plant parts odorless. 10–
60 cm. Common. Tex., Pl. Sts.   MOST OF YEAR

CORY'S YELLOW ONION   *Allium coryi*
Bright yellow, elliptical petals, free to their bases. Flowers in a
broad, rounded umbel. Plant parts with an onionlike odor. 10–
30 cm. Rocky slopes. Big Bend region of Tex.   APRIL–MAY

WESTERN ZEPHYR LILY   *Zephranthes longifolia*
The single tuliplike, buttercup-yellow flower has a greenish tinge
and is on a short, leafless stem. Leaves narrow. Blooms 1–4 days
after the first summer rainstorm. 10–20 cm. S. Ariz. to Big Bend
area of Tex.   JUNE–JULY

SOUTHERN ZEPHYR LILY   *Zephranthes pulchella*
(not shown)
Similar to Western Zephyr Lily, but grows in s. Tex.   MAY–OCT.

COPPER LILY   *Habranthus texanus*
Note the *coppery red* tints on the yellow to yellow-orange petals.
The single flower has spreading petal lobes and is on a *long pedicel.*
20–30 cm. Eastern two-thirds of Tex., Pl. Sts.   JULY–OCT.

LEMMON'S STAR   *Triteleia lemmonae*
Egg-shaped, shiny yellow petal lobes, *fused at bases* into a *short
tube.* Stamen filaments linear. Odorless. 10–60 cm. Mountains near
Flagstaff and Mogollon Rim, Ariz.   MAY–AUG.

Iris Family (Iridaceae) See also pp. R 272; B 340

WOOLLY STARGRASS   *Hypoxis hirsuta*
Note the *many long hairs* on the grasslike, linear leaves and flower
stem. Flattened, starlike flower. 10–20 cm. Open woods, pastures.
Eastern third of Tex., Pl. Sts., S.E.   MARCH–SEPT.

YELLOW IRIS Alien   *Iris pseudacorus*
The only yellow iris likely to be encountered in wild or semi-wild
places. 50 cm–1 m. Ponds, marshes. Se. Tex.   APRIL–MAY

LONGSTALK STAR IRIS   *Sisyrinchium longipes*
Yellow-orange flowers on a *tall, unbranched stem. Ovary elongated.* Iris-like leaves. 10–30 cm. Mountains. Ariz.   JULY–SEPT.

FAIRY STARS   *Sisyrinchium exile*
A *tiny plant* with flattened, iris-like leaves. Flowers arise from *several flattened leaves at the top* of the flower stem. Shiny yellow
petals with a *red-brown ring of spots* just above the urnlike base.
Ovary round. 5–15 cm. Sandy woods. Se. Tex.   MARCH–MAY

Yellow-eyed Grass Family (Xyridaceae)

YELLOW-EYED GRASS   *Xyris iridifolia*
Conelike head of *leathery scales* with small, 3-petaled flowers. Flat,
swordlike leaves. 30 cm–1 m. Bogs. E. Tex.   MAY–OCT.

116

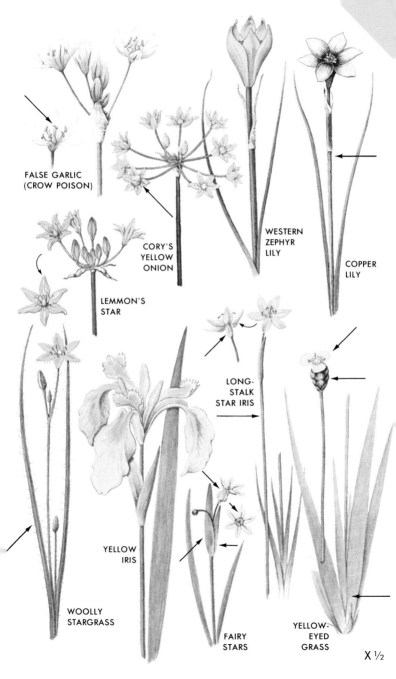

FALSE GARLIC
(CROW POISON)

CORY'S
YELLOW
ONION

WESTERN
ZEPHYR
LILY

COPPER
LILY

LEMMON'S
STAR

LONG-
STALK
STAR IRIS

YELLOW
IRIS

WOOLLY
STARGRASS

FAIRY
STARS

YELLOW-
EYED
GRASS

X ½

5 PETALS; 2-LIPPED, TUBULAR COROLLAS

Snapdragon Family (Scrophulariaceae)
See also pp. W 88; Y 118–122; R 244–250; B 350–354.

SEEP-SPRING MONKEY FLOWER *Mimulus guttatus*
Fleshy stem with *smooth leaves*. Flowers in racemes, with
pedicels shorter than the corolla. 5–80 cm. Springy places,
streamsides. S.W., R. Mts. MARCH–SEPT.

FREMONT'S MONKEY FLOWER *Mimulus glabratus*
Similar to Seep-spring Monkey Flower (above), but *pedicels
longer* than the corolla. 10–70 cm. Wet or muddy places. Western half of Tex., Pl. Sts. MOST OF YEAR

CLAMMY MONKEY FLOWER *Mimulus floribundus*
Flower and pedicel *together longer* than the adjacent petiole
and triangular leaf blade combined. Feels cold, wet. 10–60 cm.
Moist places, mountains. Ariz., w. N.M., R. Mts.

APRIL–SEPT.

PRIMROSE MONKEY FLOWER *Mimulus primuloides*
The *long, threadlike pedicel* holds the single flower well above a
basal rosette of oval leaves. 2–10 cm. Wet mountain meadows.
White Mts., Ariz.; R. Mts. JULY–AUG.

TWINING SNAPDRAGON *Antirrhinum filipes*
Note the nearly naked, *twining pedicels and main stem* with
bright yellow snapdragon flowers. Leaves linear. Tangled vines
(20 cm–1 m) over low surrounding plants. Lower deserts. W.
Ariz. FEB.–MAY

DALMATIAN TOADFLAX Alien *Linaria dalmatica*
Erect spikes of large, *snapdragonlike* flowers, each with a
pointed spur. Stem leaves *oval, blue-green*. 50 cm–1 m. Disturbed places. S.W., R. Mts. MARCH–SEPT.

COMMON TOADFLAX Alien *Linaria vulgaris*
Similar to Dalmatian Toadflax, but flower smaller (2 cm).
Numerous *pale green, narrowly straplike* leaves. 50 cm–1 m.
Disturbed places. Northern S.W., n. Tex., R. Mts.

MARCH–SEPT.

GHOST FLOWER *Mohavea confertiflora*
Pale yellowish, *cuplike flowers* with purple dots. 10–30 cm.
Sandy flats, washes. Lower deserts. W. Ariz. FEB.–APRIL

MOUNTAIN FIGWORT *Scrophularia lanceolata*
Short, pale yellow-green flowers with 2 *projecting upper petals*.
Coarse stems and large, dark green, *oval* leaf blades with sharp,
sawtoothed margins. 30–90 cm. Northern S.W., R. Mts.

JUNE–AUG.

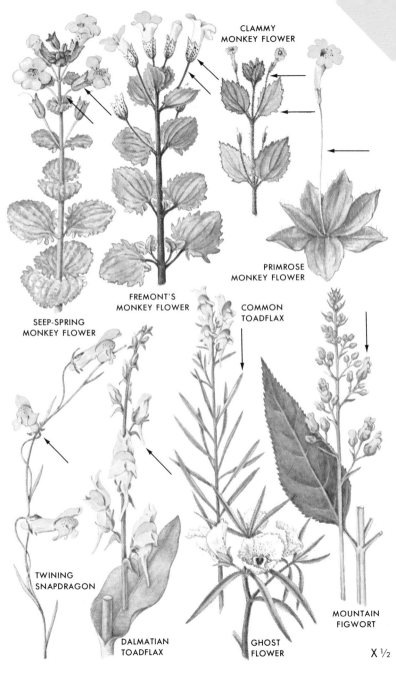

CLAMMY
MONKEY FLOWER

PRIMROSE
MONKEY FLOWER

FREMONT'S
MONKEY FLOWER

SEEP-SPRING
MONKEY FLOWER

COMMON
TOADFLAX

TWINING
SNAPDRAGON

DALMATIAN
TOADFLAX

GHOST
FLOWER

MOUNTAIN
FIGWORT

X ½

5 PETALS; 2-LIPPED, SPOUTLIKE FLOWERS

Snapdragon Family (Scrophulariaceae)
See also pp. W 88; Y 118–122; R 244–250; B 350–354.

LEMON PAINTBRUSH *Castilleja purpurea*
Subspecies *citrina* (shown here) has lemon-colored flower bracts with a *long pair* of lower side lobes, a *short upper pair,* and a central lobe. Green, spoutlike corolla protrudes from the *deeply lobed, lemon yellow calyx.* Lower leaves with 3 lobes, upper with 5. 10–30 cm. Prairies. N. Tex.   APRIL–MAY

LONGBILL PAINTBRUSH *Castilleja sessiliflora*
Each yellow or pink flower bract has *3 equally long lobes.* Corolla tube *conspicuously long, protruding.* Calyx lobes *long, linear.* Leaves divided, lobes twisted and cupped. 10–30 cm. Plains. Se. Ariz. to western half of Tex., Pl. Sts.

MARCH–MAY

LINEARLOBE PAINTBRUSH *Castilleja lineata*
Each greenish to yellowish flower bract has *3–4 pairs of side lobes;* bracts felt-haired. Corolla tube *hidden within* square-tipped calyx. Calyx *half as long* as flower bracts. 10–40 cm. High mountains. E. Ariz., N.M., R. Mts.   JULY–SEPT.

SULPHUR PAINTBRUSH *Castilleja sulphurea*
Flowers in a *short, torchlike* terminal cluster of light sulphur yellow, *broadly oval* flower bracts and *nearly hidden,* short, tubular flowers. The colored flower bracts have smooth edges *or* 1–2 tiny terminal lobe pairs. Stem leaves *lancelike.* 10–50 cm. Moist alpine meadows. N.M., R. Mts.   JULY–AUG.

CANADA LOUSEWORT *Pedicularis canadensis*
Long-beaked, yellowish to reddish flowers in a *congested, irregular* arrangement. Pinnate leaves divided into numerous *broad* leaflets, almost to base of petiole. 10–30 cm. Mountains. N.M., R. Mts., e. Tex., Pl. Sts.   MARCH–JULY

GRAY'S LOUSEWORT *Pedicularis grayi*
Short-beaked flowers with many *red-brown lines.* Large, compound pinnate, *fernlike leaves on tall stems.* 50 cm–1 m. Mountain glades. E. Ariz., N.M., R. Mts.   JULY–AUG.

PARRY'S LOUSEWORT *Pedicularis parryi*
Long-beaked flowers in a distinct *twisted whorl.* Simple pinnate leaves divided into *narrow leaflets* on upper half of petiole. 10–50 cm. Alpine meadows. S.W., R. Mts.   JUNE–SEPT.

BUTTERED OWL'S-CLOVER *Orthocarpus luteus*
Note the 3 *lower pouches and tiny upper beak* of the deep buttery yellow flowers. Each green flower bract is *sharply trilobed.* 10–40 cm. Mountain woods. S.W., R. Mts.   JULY–SEPT.

YELLOW RATTLE *Rhinanthus crista-galli*
Large, inflated calyx with a *tiny flower* emerging from it. Flower has 3 lower sacs and a short, curved beak petal above. Sawtoothed, triangular leaves. 10–50 cm. Moist mountain meadows. E. Ariz., northern N.M., R. Mts.   AUG.–SEPT.

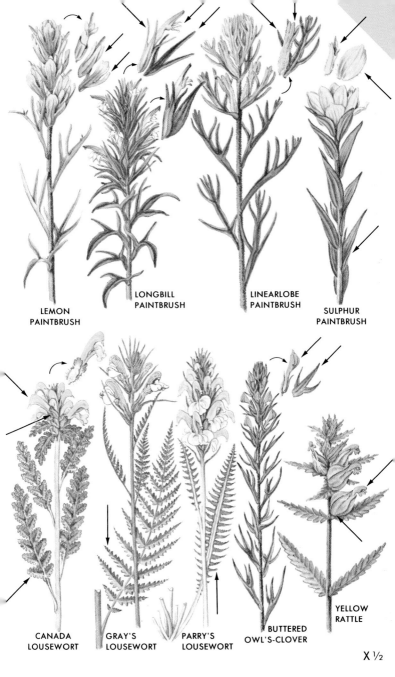

LEMON
PAINTBRUSH

LONGBILL
PAINTBRUSH

LINEARLOBE
PAINTBRUSH

SULPHUR
PAINTBRUSH

CANADA
LOUSEWORT

GRAY'S
LOUSEWORT

PARRY'S
LOUSEWORT

BUTTERED
OWL'S-CLOVER

YELLOW
RATTLE

X ½

4-6 PETALS; BOWL-LIKE,
2-LIPPED FLOWERS

Poppy Family (Papaveraceae) See also p. W 22; O & R 232.

ARCTIC POPPY *Papaver radicatum*
Small, yellow, 4-petaled flowers on leafless, *hairy stems* well above
the basal cluster of *lacy, pinnate leaves.* 5–14 cm. Alpine ridges.
Northern N.M., R. Mts. JULY

GOLDEN PRICKLY POPPY *Argemone aenea*
Large (7–12 cm wide), bright yellow, golden or bronze poppylike
flowers with 6 petals, numerous stamens. Prickly stems and leaves.
Bright yellow milky sap. 30 cm–1 m. Plains. Western and s. Tex.,
Pl. Sts. FEB.–APRIL

Devil's-claw Family (Martyniaceae) See also p. R 316.

GOLDEN DEVIL'S-CLAW *Proboscidea althaefolia*
Note the large, *bright yellow, 2-lipped* flower with yellow and
coppery lines and dots inside the throat. Leaves *longer than wide.*
Large seedpod *crested on both sides;* when dry, pod has *2 long,
sharp, curved "devil's claws."* 30–60 cm. Deserts, plains. S.W.,
Tex., Pl. Sts. JUNE–SEPT.

PALE DEVIL'S-CLAW *Proboscidea louisianica*
Large, 2-lipped flower, *pale yellow or cream with pink to purplish
dots* and yellow stripes in the throat. Leaves *equally* long and wide.
Seedpod *crested on 1 side.* 30–60 cm. Sandy open places. S.W.,
northern half of Tex., Pl. Sts. MAY–SEPT.

Snapdragon Family (Scrophulariaceae)
See also pp. W 88; Y 118–122; R 244–250; B 350–354.

WOOLLY MULLEIN Alien *Verbascum thapsus*
Large, soft, white, woolly leaves extending up a single, *coarse,
towerlike stem.* Terminal spike of many small, slightly bilateral-
shaped yellow flowers. 10 cm–1 m. Common in disturbed places.
S.W., Tex., R. Mts., Pl. Sts. MARCH–NOV.

MOTH MULLEIN Alien *Verbascum blattaria*
The large, flat, slightly bilateral-shaped flowers are bright yellow or
all white, on tall spikes. Straplike leaves are *bright green.* 30 cm–
1 m. Disturbed places. E. Tex., R. Mts., Pl. Sts. MARCH–AUG.

Flax Family (Linaceae) See also p. B 356.

BOWL FLAX *Linum rigidum*
Bowl-like flowers; yellowish, yellow-orange, or pinkish red, with *red
and white inner rings.* Wiry stem with short leaves; stem and leaves
bright green. 10–40 cm. Common. S.W., Tex., Pl. Sts.
APRIL–SEPT.

PLAINS FLAX *Linum puberulum*
Similar to Bowl Flax, but stem and leaves *gray.* S.W., Tex.
MAY–SEPT.

SAUCER FLAX *Linum alatum*
Flowers resemble *flattened saucers.* Petals entirely bright lemon
yellow, or with a red base. Leaves bright green. 10–40 cm. Eastern
N.M. to s. Tex. MARCH–JULY

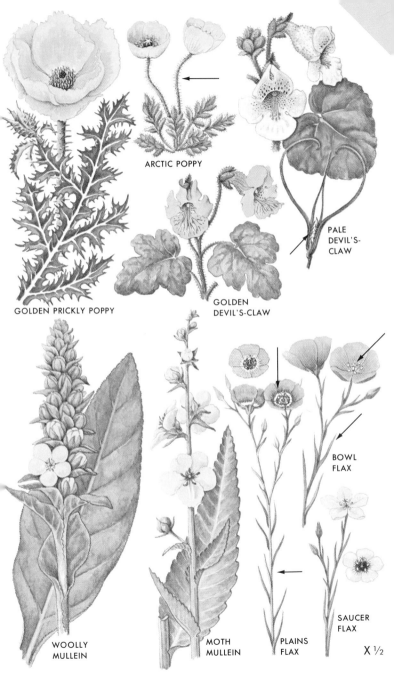

ARCTIC POPPY

PALE DEVIL'S-CLAW

GOLDEN PRICKLY POPPY

GOLDEN DEVIL'S-CLAW

BOWL FLAX

WOOLLY MULLEIN

MOTH MULLEIN

PLAINS FLAX

SAUCER FLAX

X 1/2

5 PETALS; VINES

Cucumber Family (Cucurbitaceae) See also p. W 56.

STINKING GOURD   *Cucurbita foetidissima*
Leaves *triangular*. Male flowers large (10–12 cm long), resembling upright bells. Female flowers shorter; some become rounded, dull green gourds (5–10 cm) with white stripes. Long, coarse trailing vines. Bad smell. Common in sandy places. S.W., Tex.   MAY–AUG.

FINGERLEAF GOURD   *Cucurbita digitata*
Note the *narrow, 5-fingered leaf* with a central white stripe. Flowers and gourds similar to those of Stinking Gourd. Trailing vines. Sandy places on lower deserts. Ariz., sw. N.M.
JUNE–OCT.

COYOTE GOURD   *Cucurbita palmata*
Flowers and gourds as in Fingerleaf Gourd (above), but note the *palmate, 5-lobed leaves*. Dry sandy flats. W. Ariz.
APRIL–SEPT.

MELONETTE   *Melothria pendula*
Note the *miniature, white-spotted, watermelonlike fruit*. Leaves with 5 sharp-pointed lobes. Tiny yellow flowers. Long twining vines climb over shrubs, fences, etc. S. Tex. and La., along Gulf Coast to Fla., Pl. Sts., S.E.   MARCH–OCT.

MELONLOCO   *Apodanthera undulata*
Starlike flowers with completely *free* petal lobes. Oblong, melonlike fruits have *raised lengthwise ribs*. Leaves *rounded* in outline. Sprawling clusters of vines on gravelly or sandy flats. S. Ariz. to w. Tex.   MAY–SEPT.

Caltrop Family (Zygophyllaceae) See also p. O 232.

PUNCTURE VINE Alien   *Tribulus terrestris*
Leaves *pinnate,* in opposite pairs along a weak, sprawling stem. Flowers yellow-orange, becoming *starlike, spiny seedpods*. Disturbed places. S.W., Tex., Pl. Sts.   MARCH–NOV.

CALIFORNIA CARPETWEED   *Kallstroemia californica*
Similar to Puncture Vine, but seedpods are *spineless* and have a *hairless beak*. Flat, carpetlike stems. Common. S. Ariz. to cen. and s. Tex.   MARCH–NOV.

HAIRY CARPETWEED   *Kallstroemia hirsutissima*
Similar to California Carpetweed, but beak on seed capsule *covered with short hairs*. Common. Se. Ariz. to Tex., Pl. Sts.
JUNE–NOV.

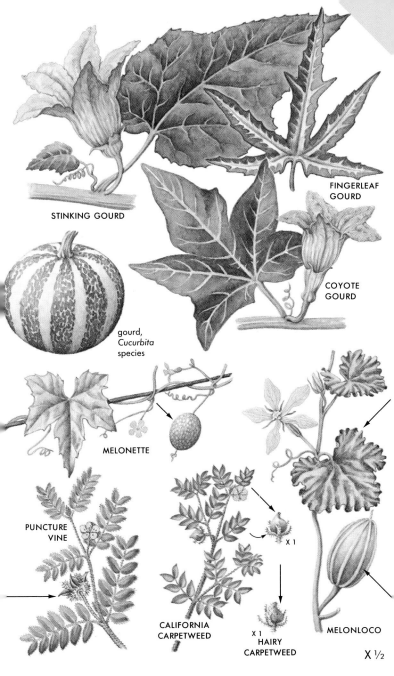

STINKING GOURD

FINGERLEAF GOURD

COYOTE GOURD

gourd, *Cucurbita* species

MELONETTE

PUNCTURE VINE

CALIFORNIA CARPETWEED

x 1

x 1 HAIRY CARPETWEED

MELONLOCO

X ½

CACTI; CYLINDRICAL STEMS

Cactus Family (Cactaceae)
See also pp. W 2–4; Y 126–142; R 252–270.

RAINBOW CACTUS *Echinocereus pectinatus*
Large, thick, cylindrical stems have *rainbowlike, alternating horizontal rows* of darker pinkish red spine clusters and lighter grayish, *comblike* spine clusters. Each spine cluster *vertically elongate* with a flattened circle of leglike spines and 0–9 *vertical* spines along the teardrop-shaped base. Immense, funnel-like flowers — yellow, orange, pink, or dark magenta. 10–30 cm. Grasslands, brushy scrub on limestone soil. Southeastern quarter of Ariz. in a southerly band to Del Rio, Tex.
MARCH–MAY

PICKLE CACTUS *Echinocereus blanckii*
Note the strongly raised, *wartlike bumps* on the pickle-shaped, globular (5–15 cm) stem joints. Large, funnel-like flowers, yellow with dark red basal stripes or completely rose red. Stems prostrate, in clumps under shrubs. 30–60 cm. Mesquite brushlands. Cen. and s. Tex.
FEB.–MARCH

BEEHIVE NIPPLE CACTUS *Coryphantha vivipara*
Grayish brown, baseball-sized or larger stems, usually in *beehivelike mounds.* Nipplelike stem bumps *completely obscured* by terminal clusters of 3–5 central, erect spines and 10–20 smaller ones in a flattened, circular pattern. Flowers yellow, pink, or red. 10–20 cm. Very common in woodlands, plains. S.W., w. Tex., R. Mts., Pl. Sts.
MAY–JULY

PLAINS NIPPLE CACTUS *Coryphantha missouriensis*
Tennis-ball-sized stem has *prominent nipples,* each with a *flattened, white-centered, spiny star.* Spine clusters usually *lack* central upright spines (or rarely have 1–2). Petals yellow or streaked with pink. 2–5 cm. E. Ariz. to n. Tex., Pl. Sts.
MAY–AUG.

RHINOCEROS CACTUS *Coryphantha cornifera*
Note the straight, white, *thick, rhinoceros-hornlike* central spine (or 2–3 spines) projecting from a *flat circle* of 20–30 radial spines. Stems round, sea-urchinlike. Flower yellow. 5–10 cm. Limestone areas. Big Bend region, Tex.
APRIL–MAY

NEEDLE MULEE *Coryphantha scheeri*
Fist-sized (10–15 cm) stem has *prominent nipplelike bumps* with 1 to usually *several long, curving,* thick-based, brownish central spines and 10–15 widely spaced, pinkish radial spines. Flowers yellow or streaked with red. *Long, fingerlike, green fruit.* 10–20 cm. Deep soil. Se. Ariz. to Big Bend region of Tex.
JULY–AUG.

FINGER CACTUS *Coryphantha sulcata*
Long, nipplelike bumps, highly visible. Usually *1 main* erect, thick-based central spine and *very few (5–9) short,* widely-spaced radial spines. Central spine *often missing* (falls off early). Yellow flowers with *red bases.* Stems form clumps. 7–15 cm. Cen. Tex.
MARCH–JUNE

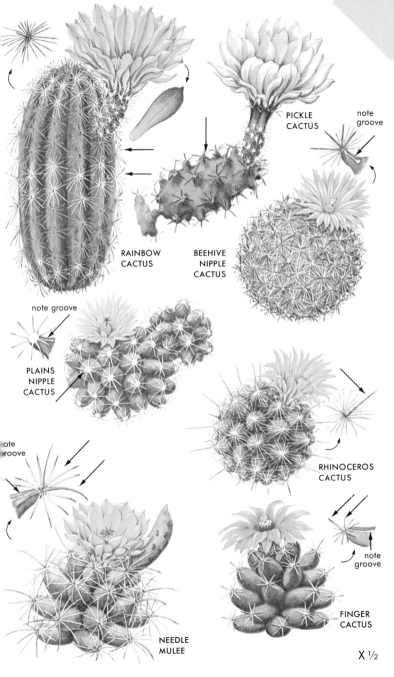

RAINBOW CACTUS

PICKLE CACTUS

note groove

BEEHIVE NIPPLE CACTUS

note groove

PLAINS NIPPLE CACTUS

note groove

RHINOCEROS CACTUS

NEEDLE MULEE

FINGER CACTUS

note groove

X ½

PRICKLY PEAR CACTI

Cactus Family (Cactaceae)
See also pp. W 2–4; Y 126–142; R 252–270.

TEXAS PRICKLY PEAR *Opuntia lindheimeri*
Large, oval to elliptical pads; usually with 1–2 *yellowish* to red-brown main spines per spine cluster, spreading at right angles. Sometimes nearly spineless. Spines *flattened* near bases. Stems in massive, sprawling, right-angled chains. Petals usually a *translucent lemon yellow,* sometimes orangish, or red. *Ovary barrel or cone-shaped.* A highly variable species. See p. 130 for Cowtongue Cactus (form 'linguiformis') and Engelmann's Prickly Pear, *O. phaeacantha,* both part of this species complex. 20 cm–2 m. Eastern four-fifths of Tex. FEB.–JUNE

BIG BEND PRICKLY PEAR *Opuntia phaeacantha*
Note the *extra long,* 1–3 blackish brown spines growing from the upper margins of yellow-green, egg-shaped pads. Middle and lower spine clusters have 3 main spines that are *bent downward.* This subspecies (*spinosibacca*) may be an intermediate hybrid between Texas Prickly Pear (above) and Redeye Prickly Pear (below), seen only when both parents are in the immediate area. 50 cm–1.5 m. Hills along Rio Grande in Big Bend National Park, Tex. MARCH–MAY

REDEYE PRICKLY PEAR *Opuntia violacea*
This is subspecies *macrocentra.* Note the 1 or more *very long (7–18 cm), black or brownish spines* in each spine cluster along the *upper margins* of the egg-shaped pads. *Pad margins reddish or purplish.* Other spine clusters *lack long spines.* Flowers yellow with *"red eye" centers.* Stems sprawling. 50 cm–1.5 m. Gravelly slopes. In a narrow band from s. Ariz. to Del Rio, Tex. MARCH–MAY

PURPLE PRICKLY PEAR *Opuntia violacea*
This is subspecies *santa-rita.* Note the *purple to reddish, round pads* and the spine clusters *without* long spines, but with *elongated tufts* of spinelets. Ovary short, barrel-like, with *clusters of short spinelets.* Flowers lemon yellow, sometimes with red bases. *Pads deep red-purple* during drought periods and winter. Stems erect. 50 cm–1.5 m. Southern third of S.W., Big Bend area of Tex. APRIL–MAY

PORCUPINE PRICKLY PEAR *Opuntia erinacea*
Long (1–3 cm), oblong or elliptical, green or blue-green pads with *numerous long (2–10 cm), white or gray, whiskerlike* spines. The longer spines are slightly twisted, with *flattened bases.* Flowers red, pink, or yellow at any one locality. Stems in low, sprawling clumps. In **Porcupine Prickly Pear** (subspecies *erinacea*), pads have moderately thick, *straight spines.* **Grizzly Bear Prickly Pear** (subspecies *ursina*) has *very long, curving, threadlike spines* that densely cover the pads in a tangled mass. 30–60 cm. Northern S.W., sw. R. Mts. APRIL–JULY

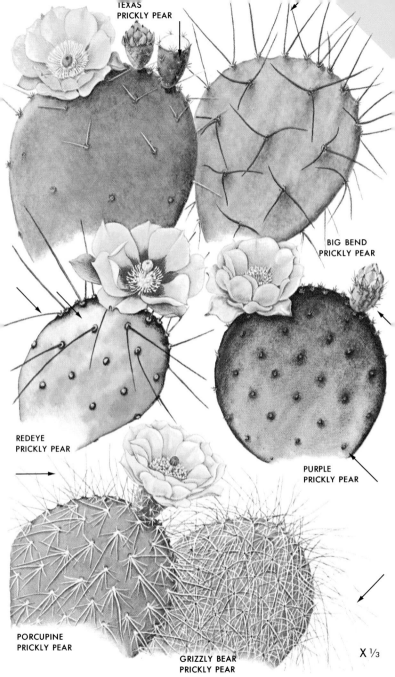

TEXAS
PRICKLY PEAR

BIG BEND
PRICKLY PEAR

REDEYE
PRICKLY PEAR

PURPLE
PRICKLY PEAR

PORCUPINE
PRICKLY PEAR

GRIZZLY BEAR
PRICKLY PEAR

X 1/3

SPINY PRICKLY PEAR CACTI

Cactus Family (Cactaceae)
See also pp. W 2–4; Y 126–142; R 252–270.

ENGELMANN'S PRICKLY PEAR   *Opuntia phaeacantha*
Usually 3 *reddish brown* to grayish main spines per cluster, *spreading at right angles.* Spines *flattened* near bases. Fruit and ovary cone-shaped or barrel-like. Stem pads round to oblong, in *sprawling, right-angled chains.* Flowers dark yellow-orange to red. 30 cm–1 m. Common. S.W. to w. Tex., Pl. Sts. See also Texas Prickly Pear, p. 128.   APRIL–JUNE

COWTONGUE PRICKLY PEAR   *Opuntia lindheimeri*
This is form 'linguiformis.' Note the *elongate pads,* which resemble a *cow's tongue.* 1–3 spines per cluster, spreading at right angles. Pads heavily spined to nearly naked. Ovary *conelike or barrel-like.* A popular garden plant; mostly extinct in the wild. 1–2 m. S.W., Tex.   FEB.–MAY

PLAINS PRICKLY PEAR   *Opuntia polyacantha*
Each main spine is mostly *round at base.* A *circle of gray, woolly hair* surrounds each cluster of 5–11 spines. Flat, oblong stem pads (5–15 cm). Forms broad, low mats. 10–30 cm high. Northern S.W., n. Tex., Pl. Sts.   MAY–JUNE

CHAIN PRICKLY PEAR   *Opuntia macrorhiza*
Chains of round pads with *long, needlelike spines* run along the ground. Spines *round* in cross-section. Flowers yellow or tinted with red at bases. Pads 5–10 cm long and broad. Plains. S.W., n. Tex., Pl. Sts.   APRIL–JUNE

PANCAKE PRICKLY PEAR   *Opuntia chlorotica*
Erect, *treelike stem* has large, yellow-green, *pancakelike* pads. Each spine cluster has 3–6 *all-yellow main spines* that bend down to one side (2–3 cm long). Each spine cluster is surrounded by a *round fringe of very tiny spinelets.* 50 cm–2 m. Rocky walls, mesas. W. Ariz.   APRIL–JUNE

BEARDED PRICKLY PEAR   *Opuntia strigil*
Numerous distinctive, downward-slanting, *double sets* of *long, pinlike spines* and *shorter, hairlike* spines in each cluster. Spines yellowish with red-brown bases. Ovary a *short barrel, or marblelike.* Pads round or egg-shaped. 50 cm–1 m. West of Del Rio, Tex.   APRIL–MAY

MARTIN'S PRICKLY PEAR   *Opuntia littoralis*
This is subspecies *martiniana.* Long (3–8 cm), *needlelike spines* on round or pear-shaped pads, several sections or more *above the ground.* Main spines *round* in cross-section. Each spine cluster of 1–16 spines has 1 erect central spine and 2 side spines that *bend downward.* Flowers yellow or with reddish bases, rarely all red. 50 cm–1 m. Northwestern quarter of Ariz., Ut.   APRIL–JUNE

PEST PEAR Alien   *Opuntia stricta*
Similar to Texas Prickly Pear (p. 128). Fruit *clublike* with a *smaller, handlelike lower portion.* 4–5 flat, *twisted* spines per cluster in a spreading, irregular pattern. Stems erect or sprawling. Tex. Gulf Coast.   APRIL–MAY

YELLOW

COWTONGUE PRICKLY PEAR

ENGELMANN'S PRICKLY PEAR

PLAINS PRICKLY PEAR

CHAIN PRICKLY PEAR

PANCAKE PRICKLY PEAR

MARTIN'S PRICKLY PEAR

BEARDED PRICKLY PEAR

PEST PEAR

X ¼

SPINELESS PRICKLY PEAR CACTI

Cactus Family (Cactaceae)
See also pp. W 2–4; Y 126–142; R 252–270.

PURPLE PRICKLY PEAR   *Opuntia violacea*
This is subspecies *santa-rita. Naked, purple to reddish,* round
pads with only short, elongated tufts of spinelets (no long
spines). Flowers lemon yellow, sometimes with red bases. Pads
turn deep purple during drought periods and winter. Stems
erect. 50 cm–1.2 m. Southern third of S.W. to Big Bend region
of Tex.   APRIL–MAY

BLIND PRICKLY PEAR   *Opuntia rufida*
Pads *round, gray-green.* Eyespots on pads look like flat buttons
and are formed by clusters of *tiny, red-brown spinelets* that fly
into the air when the plant is disturbed. Spinelets can blind
cattle that attempt to eat plant. Tapering, *funnel-like ovary*
with clusters of short spinelets. Fruit red. Upright stems.
50 cm–1.2 m. Rocky hillsides along Rio Grande, Big Bend area
of Tex.   MARCH–MAY

CLIFF PRICKLY PEAR   *Opuntia phaeacantha*
This is subspecies *laevis.* Pads *elongate* — egg-shaped or
pearlike. Spots of *tiny spinelets without* larger spines, or with
1–3 *small, hairlike* main spines that *bend downward.* Pad margins may have some longer spines. Ovary *short,* funnel-shaped,
with clusters of tiny spinelets. Sprawling or erect stems. 50 cm–
1.5 m. Restricted to desert cliffs and ledges; rarely found elsewhere. S. Ariz.   APRIL–MAY

YELLOW BEAVERTAIL   *Opuntia basilaris*
This is subspecies *aurea.* Blue-green or yellow-green pads are
flat, like beaver tails, and have small *eyespots* that are filled
with tufts of tiny spinelets. Stems in clumps of a few pads,
either erect or prostrate. Pads turn leaden blue during the winter. Flowers yellow in this subspecies. 30–60 cm. Sagebrush,
juniper-pinyon woodlands. Nw. Ariz., Ut.   MAY–JUNE

EASTERN PRICKLY PEAR   *Opuntia compressa*
Stems *prostrate* along ground or nearly so. *Swollen* stem pads,
oblong (5–12 cm) *or globular,* shiny green and spineless (sometimes with 1 short spine). Ovary a short funnel or urnlike, and
spineless. Stem pads become wrinkled and reddish purple during winter and drought periods. Stems in sprawling clumps.
Shady woods, brushlands. Eastern third of Tex., Pl. Sts., S.E.
     MARCH–JUNE

INDIAN FIG   *Opuntia ficus-indica*
Huge (2–4 m), *treelike* plant with giant, *green,* oblong pads
(30–60 cm wide). Pads usually spineless, but sometimes with a
few spines. Frequent garden plant, but may escape and hybrid-
ize with native species, and thus become somewhat spiny. 2–
4 m. Usually near or in towns. Grown for cattle feed. S.W.,
Tex.   MOST OF YEAR

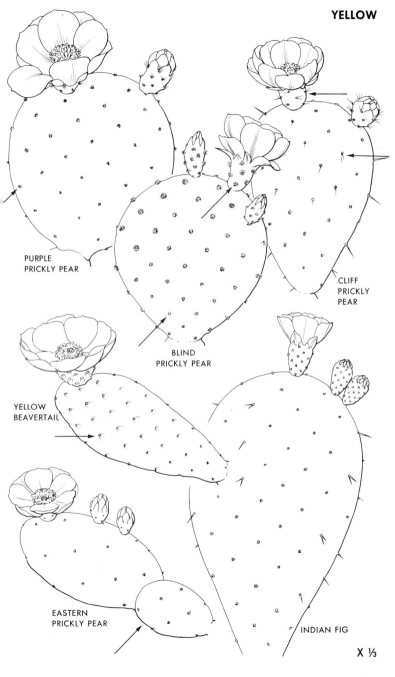

YELLOW

PURPLE PRICKLY PEAR

BLIND PRICKLY PEAR

CLIFF PRICKLY PEAR

YELLOW BEAVERTAIL

EASTERN PRICKLY PEAR

INDIAN FIG

X ⅓

MINIATURE CLUBLIKE, OR PENCIL-LIKE PRICKLY PEAR CACTI

Cactus Family (Cactaceae)
See also pp. W 2–4; Y 126–142; R 252–270.

PYGMY PRICKLY PEAR   *Opuntia fragilis*
Tiny (1–5 cm), dark green, *globular stem pads.* Each round stem bump has 1–5 slender, white to brown spines (5–25 mm long). Flowers yellow-green, or rarely reddish. 5–15 cm. Northern S.W., Tex. Panhandle, Pl. Sts.   JUNE–JULY

EL PASO PRICKLY PEAR   *Opuntia arenaria*
Small (5–8 cm), shaggy, pear-shaped pads with many prominent spine clusters. 1 or more very long, downward-pointing white spines, an underlayer of short spines, and a *tuft of brown spinelets at the top* of each cluster. Flowers yellow. Matlike clumps. Rare; protection badly needed. 15–20 cm. Sand dunes near El Paso, Tex.
MAY–NOV.

SCHOTT'S DWARF CHOLLA   *Opuntia schottii*
Finger-sized (5–8 cm), club-shaped stem joints have long, *sharply raised ridges* and a *"top hat" of long black spines.* Flowers yellow. Stem joints easily detached. Forms large mats. 10–14 cm. Along Rio Grande, Tex.   MARCH–JULY

CLUBBED CHOLLA   *Opuntia clavata*
Note the *broad, daggerlike main spine* of each cluster, which has lengthwise *ridges and grooves.* Stem joints shaped like *fat clubs* or blackjacks. Flowers yellow. Forms clumps. 10–15 cm. Ne. Ariz. to cen. N.M.   MAY–JUNE

DEVIL'S CHOLLA   *Opuntia stanlyi*
Narrow, daggerlike main spines with *cross-grained, wavy grooves.* Stem pads *slender, clublike.* Flower yellow or with a red tint, rarely all red. Low mats. 2–10 cm. Lower deserts. Ariz., sw. N.M.
MAY–JUNE

ARIZONA PENCIL CHOLLA   *Opuntia arbuscula*
Note the *smooth,* pencil-sized (5–15 cm) stem joints and the usually 2–3 medium-sized (3 cm), yellow-green spines on each stem bump. Flowers yellow, orangish, or reddish, all on one plant. Bushlike. 50 cm–2 m. Southern two-thirds of Ariz.   MAY–JUNE

CHRISTMAS CHOLLA   *Opuntia leptocaulis*
Note the single, huge (5 cm), *brownish yellow, needlelike spine* on each stem bump. Long, thin, cablelike stems with a *wrinkled surface* and *occasional short side branches.* Flowers yellow-green or with a reddish tint. *Bright red cylindrical fruits* last through the Christmas season. Erect stems. 50 cm–1 m. Southern two-thirds of Ariz. to western two-thirds of Tex.   MAY–JUNE

DIAMOND CHOLLA   *Opuntia ramosissima*
Note the *diamondlike* surface pattern on the thin, pencil-like, cylindrical stem pads. *Long, solitary, yellow spines.* Flowers yellow-green, orangish, or tinted red. Bushlike. 30 cm–1.3 m. Sandy soil. Western third of Ariz.   MAY–SEPT.

134

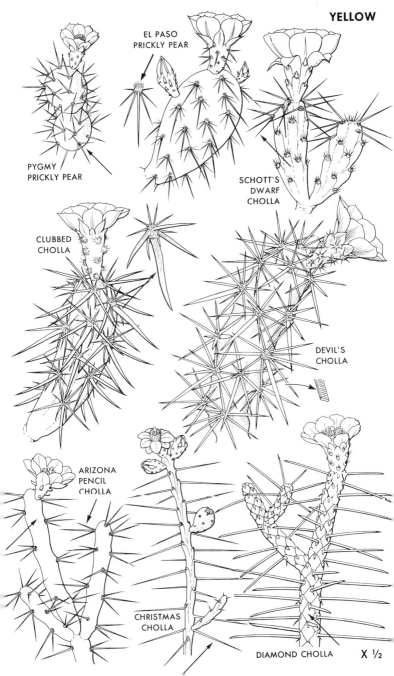

YELLOW

PYGMY
PRICKLY PEAR

EL PASO
PRICKLY PEAR

SCHOTT'S
DWARF
CHOLLA

CLUBBED
CHOLLA

DEVIL'S
CHOLLA

ARIZONA
PENCIL
CHOLLA

CHRISTMAS
CHOLLA

DIAMOND CHOLLA

X ½

CYLINDRICAL-STEMMED CHOLLA CACTI

Cactus Family (Cactaceae)
See also pp. W 2–4; Y 126–142; R 252–270.

TEDDY BEAR CHOLLA *Opuntia bigelovii*
Single, erect, treelike trunk with many *thick, "teddy-bear" arms* clustered at the top. Stem joints *densely packed with porcupine-like* white to pale yellow spines. Flowers yellow to pale green. Each joint loosely attached, "jumps" if touched. 50 cm–1.5 m. Drained slopes. Ariz. APRIL–MAY

THISTLE CHOLLA *Opuntia tunicata*
Thin cylindrical stem joints, *densely covered* with clusters of 6–10 white to pale yellow spines. *Widely branched, bushy stems* without a lower treelike trunk. Flowers yellow-green or tinted red. Ovary and fruit spiny. Stem joints easily detached and thus may "jump." 30 cm–1 m. Deep soil of lower hillsides. Big Bend region of Tex.
APRIL–JUNE

SILVER CHOLLA *Opuntia echinocarpa*
Each *short, round* stem bump (5–15 mm long, 25 mm wide) holds clusters of 3–10 long spines with *silvery or golden, papery sheaths.* Stem pads slender; 10–20 cm long, 2 cm wide. Yellow-green flowers streaked with red. Erect stems. 50 cm–1.3 m. W. Ariz., Ut.
MARCH–MAY

STAGHORN CHOLLA *Opuntia versicolor*
Note the long (15–30 cm), narrow, *sticklike stem joints* with *elongated bumps* (2 cm long, 1 cm wide); each bump has 6–9 short, spreading spines. The greenish *fruits* are *spineless,* with a shallow cup. Some fruit lasts several years, with new flowers growing from its sides, forming *short chains.* Flowers yellow, bronze, red, or dark purple. A treelike shrub. 50 cm–3 m. S.-cen. Ariz. APRIL–JUNE

BUCKHORN CHOLLA *Opuntia acanthocarpa*
Stem joints *slender cylinders* (30 cm long) *with elongated bumps* (3 cm long, 1 cm wide). Each spine cluster has 10–12 stout (3–4 cm), straw-colored spines. Flowers yellow or red. Open shrubs. 1–2 m. Dry slopes. Ariz. APRIL–JUNE

WHIPPLE'S CHOLLA *Opuntia whipplei*
Each short (5 mm), raised stem bump has a prominent, *slanted spine cluster* with a *white, eyelike base.* Each spine cluster has 5–9 *white spines,* 1 of which is extra long and slants downward. *Stem joints short.* Flowers lemon or yellow-green. Fruit spineless. Compact, erect stems. 30 cm–2 m. Grasslands, woodlands. Northern half of Ariz., nw. N.M., Ut. MAY–JUNE

HANDLEGRIP CHOLLA *Opuntia spinosior*
Note the *closely-packed, short,* sharply-raised stem bumps (2 cm or less long, 5 mm or less wide) that *resemble handlegrips.* Widely radiating clusters of 8–20 short (5 mm or less) spines; *5 rows* (from side to side) usually visible. Ovary and fruit spineless. Flowers yellow or red. Spreading, erect shrubs. 1–3 m. Common. Southeastern quarter of Ariz., southern N.M. APRIL–JUNE

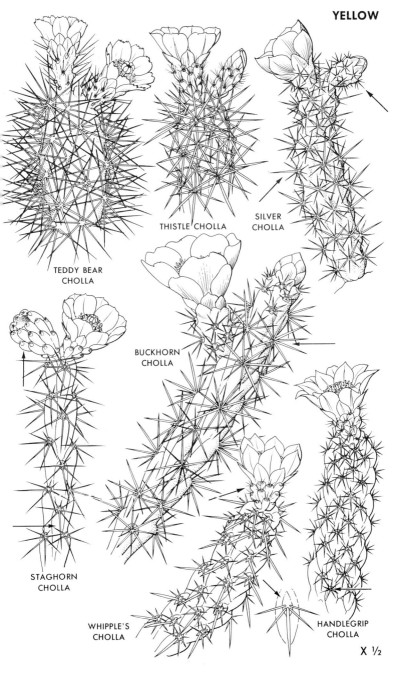

YELLOW

TEDDY BEAR
CHOLLA

THISTLE CHOLLA

SILVER
CHOLLA

BUCKHORN
CHOLLA

STAGHORN
CHOLLA

WHIPPLE'S
CHOLLA

HANDLEGRIP
CHOLLA

X ½

BARREL CACTI, LARGE AND SMALL

Cactus Family (Cactaceae)
See also pp. W 2–4; Y 126–142; R 252–270.

ARIZONA BARREL CACTUS   *Ferocactus wislizenii*
Many *slender, hairlike, radial spines* below the 4 large main spines. Spines flattened, cross-ribbed; main spine often hooked. Flowers yellow, yellow-orange, or red; all colors often found in one place. Blooms in mid- to late summer, after the rainy season starts. Stem shaped like a barrel or tall column; often leans toward the southeast, and thus given the name "compass barrel," but other species also lean this way, keeping most of the stem shaded. 30 cm–2 m. Southern half of Ariz. to El Paso, Tex.   JULY–SEPT.

COVILLE'S BARREL CACTUS   *Ferocactus covillei*
Similar to Arizona Barrel Cactus, but note that the *lower radial spines* and *all but one* of the central spines *look alike,* and are *round with thick bases.* Main central spine *flattened,* the tip curved to hooked. Round or columnlike stem. Flowers yellow, or more commonly red-purple. Blooms in summer. 50 cm–2 m. Lower deserts. Mostly sw. Ariz., but occasionally to Phoenix area.   JUNE–AUG.

RED BARREL CACTUS   *Ferocactus acanthodes*
Single stem large, elongated, red, barrel-like. 4 central spines and smaller radial spines below are all reddish. Blooms in the spring. 30 cm–1.5 m. Western two-thirds of Ariz.
                                          APRIL–JUNE

MOJAVE MOUND CACTUS   *Ferocactus polycephalus*
Stems in clumps; 10–20 watermelon-sized, ribbed cylinders. Flowers yellow with a *dense, woolly outer covering.* Each spine cluster has 3–4 curved, red-gray central spines and 6–8 shorter ones below. 10–50 cm. Rocky slopes. Ariz.   APRIL–MAY

WHISKERED   *Ferocactus hamatacanthus*
BARREL CACTUS
Note the *very long, gray, whiskerlike spines* (5–20 cm). The longest spine is sharply *curved or fish-hooklike.* 4–10 nearly erect central spines and 6–18 smaller radial spines. Stem ribs close together. Flowers yellow to orange-yellow, may have red bases. *Fruit green.* Low, barrel-like stems. 10–60 cm. Rocky or gravelly places, often hidden under shrubs. Blooms in summer, in late afternoon. El Paso and southeasterly to Brownsville, Tex.   JUNE–AUG.

MESQUITE BARREL CACTUS   *Ferocactus setispinus*
Similar to Whiskered Barrel Cactus, but 1–3 central spines with curved or hooked tips. Lower *radial spines thin, threadlike,* usually in a *flat, starlike circle.* Flowers yellow with reddish bases. *Fruit red.* Stems round to cylindrical. 5–35 cm. Thickets. Cen. and coastal Tex.   APRIL–SEPT.

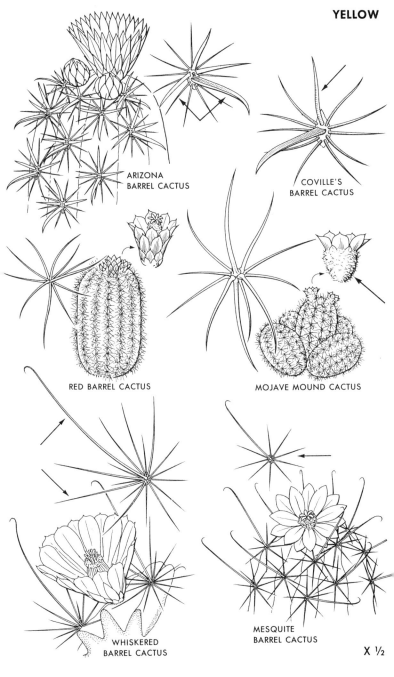

ARIZONA
BARREL CACTUS

COVILLE'S
BARREL CACTUS

RED BARREL CACTUS

MOJAVE MOUND CACTUS

WHISKERED
BARREL CACTUS

MESQUITE
BARREL CACTUS

X ½

LOW, COLUMNLIKE CACTI OR
LOW, ROUND CACTI

Cactus Family (Cactaceae)
See also pp. W 2–4; Y 126–142; R 252–270.

JOHNSON'S CACTUS *Echinomastus johnsonii*
Tangled, strawpilelike clusters of spines that are *pinkish red,* (becoming black with age). Spines all nearly the same length (3–5 cm). Central spine has a thick, bulblike base. Flowers yellow-green, pink, or red purple. Stem single, with a distinct *"squared" surface pattern* around each raised spine bump. 10–30 cm. Common. Deep soil on gentle hills. W. Ariz., Ut.   APRIL–MAY

GOLDEN-CASCADE CACTUS *Coryphantha recurvata*
Note the *flat-topped,* cylindrical stem with many *cascading, golden-brown, single* central spines. Many small, closely set stem nipples. Flowers yellow-green. S. Ariz.   JULY

NYLON HEDGEHOG CACTUS *Echinocereus viridiflorus*
Note the *long, teardrop-shaped* base of each spine cluster. The central portion has 0–3 main spines in a *vertical row.* Single main spine often twice as long as surrounding radial spines. Narrow, tubular flowers on the side of cylindrical or low, globelike stems. Flowers yellow-green, red, or red-brown. Stems single. 5–25 cm. In **Davis's Dwarf Cactus** (subspecies *davisii*), not shown, stems 1–3 cm tall. Rocky slopes, grasslands. W. Tex., e. N.M., Pl. Sts.
          MARCH–JUNE

CYLINDER BELLS *Echinocereus chloranthus*
Narrow, tubular, bell-like flowers, yellow-green to dark reddish brown. Columnlike stems, often single. Base of each spine cluster round or widely egg-shaped. 4–15 central spines *spreading.* 10–30 cm. Limestone hills. Southern N.M., Big Bend region of Tex.   MARCH–APRIL

LONG MAMA CACTUS *Mammillaria longimamma*
Soft, *nipplelike* stem bumps, highly visible due to the *few, thin, threadlike* radial spines and 1 straight central spine. Stems in large clumps. 5–10 cm. Grasslands, mesquite thickets. S. Tex.
          FEB.–MARCH

TEXAS HAIR CACTUS *Mammillaria prolifera*
Numerous white, hairlike lower radial spines and 4–8 spreading, *erect, red-brown,* straight central spines. Many spine clusters on small marble-sized stems, also in clusters. Flowers tubular, pale yellow to pale reddish yellow. 2–4 cm. Grasslands. Cen. and s. Tex.   FEB.–MAY

PANCAKE CACTUS *Mammillaria gummifera*
Stem a low tussock with a wide (5–12 cm), *flat, pancake-shaped top.* Numerous nipples, each with a cluster of brown spines of which only 1 is erect. Flowers white, cream, yellow, or pale pink. Petals lancelike. Milky sap. In some areas the stem is level with the ground. A highly variable species with many names. Rocky plains, very common. Tuscon, Ariz. to cen. Tex. and s. Tex.
          MARCH–MAY

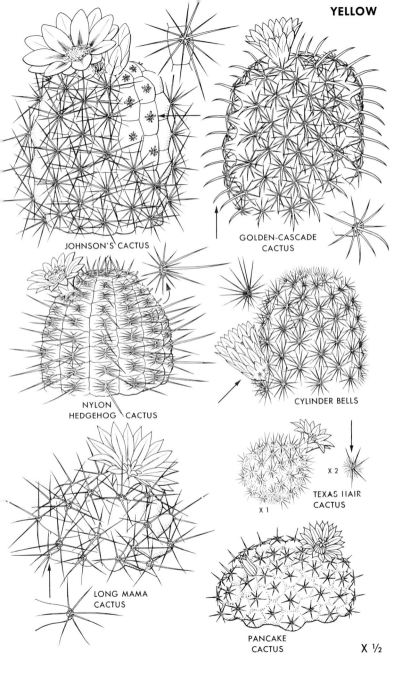

YELLOW

JOHNSON'S CACTUS

GOLDEN-CASCADE
CACTUS

NYLON
HEDGEHOG CACTUS

CYLINDER BELLS

LONG MAMA
CACTUS

X 1 X 2

TEXAS HAIR
CACTUS

PANCAKE
CACTUS

X ½

LOW, COLUMNLIKE CACTI OR
LOW, ROUND CACTI

Cactus Family (Cactaceae)
See also pp. W 2–4; Y 126–142; R 252–270.

BEADED STAR CACTUS   *Ancistrocactus asterias*
A flattened, *spineless pincushion.* Note the *small, beadlike tufts* in a row along each reverse-starlike stem segment. Large yellow flowers. 2–18 cm. Lower Rio Grande Valley, s. Tex.
JULY–DEC.

SCHEER'S CACTUS   *Ancistrocactus scheeri*
Large, cucumberlike stem with stem bumps in *slightly spiraling rows.* Spine clusters with a *short, flat,* lower row of radial spines and *long central spines,* of which *1 is fish-hooklike* and the others straight. Flowers yellow-green. Single stems. 10–20 cm. Common in mesquite brushlands. S. Tex.
FEB.–APRIL

TOBUSCH'S CACTUS   *Ancistrocactus tobuschii*
Similar to Scheer's Cactus, but low stem is conical. Each enlarged stem bump has *irregularly arranged* lower radial spines and 3 long, central spines of which *1 is curving* or fish-hooklike and *2 are straight.* Flowers pale yellow. 3–8 cm. Hill country, northwest of San Antonio, Tex.
MARCH–JULY

SIMPSON'S BALL CACTUS   *Pediocactus simpsonii*
Spines in *radiating clusters* on 8–14 spiral rows of *nipplelike bumps.* Each cluster has 3–13 *long,* straight, yellow to red-brown spines with thick bases, and 10–25 *smaller, thinner* ones below. Flowers yellow-green, white, or dark red, outer petals fringed with hairs. Small (5–20 cm), round, melonlike stems, single or clustered. Northern S.W., R. Mts.
MAY–JULY

SILER'S BALL CACTUS   *Pediocactus sileri*
Similar to Simpson's Ball Cactus, but *all* of the spines have *thick bases.* 3 central, erect spines are blackish while the 8–15 spines below are white or pale gray. Flowers yellow or with reddish veins. Petal edges fringed with tiny hairs. Single, ball-like stem with nipples. 5–15 cm. Ariz. strip region of nw. Ariz.
MAY

WHIPPLE'S CLAW CACTUS   *Sclerocactus whipplei*
Ribbed, cylindrical stem often looks *shaggy* due to the *long, semi-hooked* main spines. Each cluster usually has 4 main spines. Of the 2 longest main spines, *1 projects outward and downward* and is semi-hooked, while the other is long, *whitish, flat-based, straight, and daggerlike and points upward.* 8–12 shorter radial spines below 4 main spines. Flowers yellow-green, pink, or red-purple. 10–30 cm. Grasslands, juniper woodlands, high desert. Northern quarter of Ariz. and nw. N.M. and adjacent area in Four Corners area.
MAY–JUNE

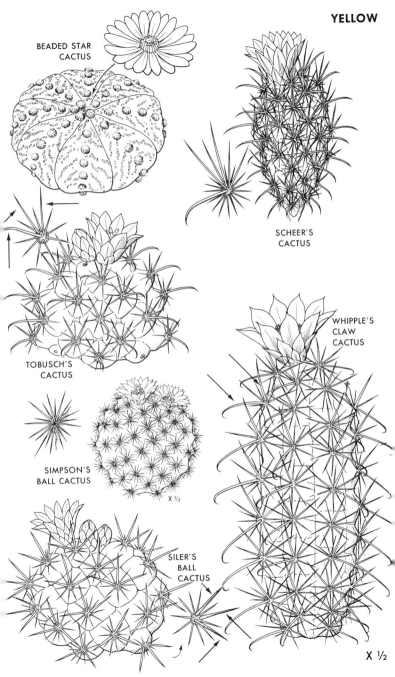

YELLOW

BEADED STAR
CACTUS

SCHEER'S
CACTUS

TOBUSCH'S
CACTUS

WHIPPLE'S
CLAW
CACTUS

SIMPSON'S
BALL CACTUS

X ⅓

SILER'S
BALL
CACTUS

X ½

4-PETALED MALTESE CROSS

Mustard Family (Cruciferae)
See also pp. W 26–32; Y 144–152; O 232; R 276.

ARIZONA BLADDERPOD　　　*Lesquerella arizonica*
Small, *silvery gray, erect, tufted stems* with short, *narrowly linear leaves. Short, headlike* flower clusters. 2–15 cm. Very common. Plateaus. Northern S.W., R. Mts.　　APRIL–AUG.

DANDELION BLADDERPOD　　　*Lesquerella rectipes*
Note the *flat* central circle of *silvery gray, strongly pinnate-lobed, dandelionlike* leaves. *Densely leaved,* spokelike flowering stems with narrow, spatula-like leaves. 10–40 cm. Common on high plateaus. Northern S.W., R. Mts.　　MAY–JUNE

FENDLER'S BLADDERPOD　　　*Lesquerella fendleri*
Note the *tall, erect,* silvery gray stems, *densely* covered with linear leaves. Elongated flower clusters. Smooth, pealike seed-pods on *long, straight pedicels.* 10–30 cm. *Gypsum flats.* Southern N.M., sw. Tex.　　FEB.–APRIL

GORDON'S BLADDERPOD　　　*Lesquerella gordonii*
Flat central circle of *dark green, shallowly lobed,* rounded leaves. Prostrate, spokelike flower stems with widely scattered, lancelike leaves. Hairless, pealike seedpods on *curved pedicels.* 5–40 cm. Common in masses. Desert flats, plains. S.W., Tex., Pl. Sts.　　FEB.–JUNE

MOUNTAIN BLADDERPOD　　　*Lesquerella montana*
Flat central circle of silvery gray, spoon-shaped leaves with *smooth margins* or a few *tiny teeth.* Spokelike flower stems. Seedpods with *gray hairs, on curved pedicels.* 10–20 cm. Plains, mountain slopes. N.M., R. Mts.　　MARCH–JUNE

ALPINE BLADDERPOD　　　*Lesquerella alpina*
Stem *tufted;* usually small (3–8 cm), but may reach 2–15 cm. Leaves on central tuft *long, narrow, lancelike, silvery gray.* Flower stem short, either included within or extended above the central tuft. *Seedpods silvery* (covered with gray hairs), on *curved pedicels.* Mountains, plains. Northern S.W., R. Mts.　　MARCH–JUNE

GASLIGHT BLADDERPOD　　　*Lesquerella recurvata*
Loosely arranged, long, *curved pedicels with gaslight-shaped* seedpods. Silvery gray leaves, *sharply toothed, on a long, slender petiole.* 10–50 cm. Cen. Tex.　　MARCH–MAY

GORGEOUS BLADDERPOD　　　*Lesquerella grandiflora*
Broad leaves with *many sharp teeth at margins,* and bases clasping the *long, erect stem. Large flowers* (3 cm wide) for a bladderpod. 10–60 cm. Cen. and s. Tex.　　MARCH–MAY

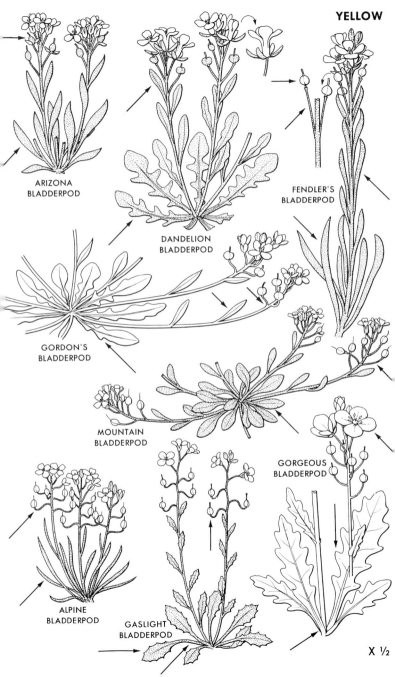

YELLOW

ARIZONA
BLADDERPOD

DANDELION
BLADDERPOD

FENDLER'S
BLADDERPOD

GORDON'S
BLADDERPOD

MOUNTAIN
BLADDERPOD

GORGEOUS
BLADDERPOD

ALPINE
BLADDERPOD

GASLIGHT
BLADDERPOD

X ½

4-PETALED MALTESE CROSS; OVAL SEEDPODS

Mustard Family (Cruciferae)
See also pp. W 26–32; Y 144–152; O 232; R 276.

GOLDEN DRABA *Draba aurea*
Egg-shaped leaves with *smooth edges* on the upper stem; long, *spoon-shaped* leaves at stem base. Golden petals. Seedpods (not shown) straight or corkscrewlike. Mid-mountain forests to alpine zone. N. Ariz., N.M., R. Mts. JUNE–JULY

HELLER'S DRABA *Draba helleriana*
Note the *toothed, oval* leaves, alternating *up the entire stem.* Seedpods *corkscrewlike.* Petals golden. 10–40 cm. Mountains. Ne. Ariz., northern N.M., R. Mts. JULY–AUG.

LANCELEAF DRABA *Draba streptocarpa*
Similar to Heller's Draba and Golden Draba. Leaves *narrow, lancelike;* margins *smooth.* 2–40 cm. Mountains. N.M., R. Mts. JUNE–SEPT.

COULTER'S LYREPOD *Lyrocarpa coulteri*
Long, twisted, dull yellow petals with red-brown backsides. Small, *lyre-shaped seedpods.* Leaves dandelionlike. 10–40 cm. Low deserts, under shrubs. Southwestern quarter of Ariz. JAN.–APRIL

SHIELD PEPPERGRASS Alien *Lepidium perfoliatum*
Heart-shaped leaves *surround* the stem; basal leaves divided, threadlike. Tiny flowers become *tiny, rounded seedpods.* 20–50 cm. Common in disturbed places. S.W., R. Mts. MARCH–JUNE

SPOONLEAF TWINPOD *Physaria australis*
Low, clustered plant. Simple, *rounded, spoonlike* leaf blades on short petioles. Flower and fruit stems twice as long as leaves. Extra-large twin seedpods, *notched at tip; pods equally round above and below.* 5–20 cm. Open slopes at lower elevations. Western N.M., R. Mts. APRIL–JUNE

MINER'S PEPPER *Lepidium densiflorum*
Linear leaves with *coarsely toothed* margins. Plants *hairy.* Petals often absent. Seedpods rounded, with a terminal notch. 30–60 cm. Middle elevations. S.W., n. Tex. FEB.–JUNE

NEWBERRY'S TWINPOD *Physaria newberryi*
Similar to Spoonleaf Twinpod, but leaf blades silvery gray and somewhat *squarish,* with a *few hints of a toothed margin.* Seedpod *deeply* V-*notched* on upper side. 2–8 cm. Lower elevations. Both n. Ariz. and N.M., R. Mts. MAY–JUNE

POINTTIP TWINPOD *Physaria floribunda*
Central cluster of leaves with *long flower stems.* Gray central leaf *tips* have *sharp points.* Long, spoonlike leaves with tapering "handles" and *very few side lobes.* Seedpod has a *broad, shallow notch* between the 2 rounded lobes. 10–20 cm. Lower elevations. Western two-thirds of N.M., R. Mts. APRIL–JUNE

ROUNDTIP TWINPOD *Physaria vitulifera*
Similar to Pointtip Twinpod, but grayish leaf *tip rounded. Many side lobes* on each leaf blade. Seedpod (not shown) *broad and deep* at top. 10–20 cm. Nw. N.M., sw. Colo. APRIL–JUNE

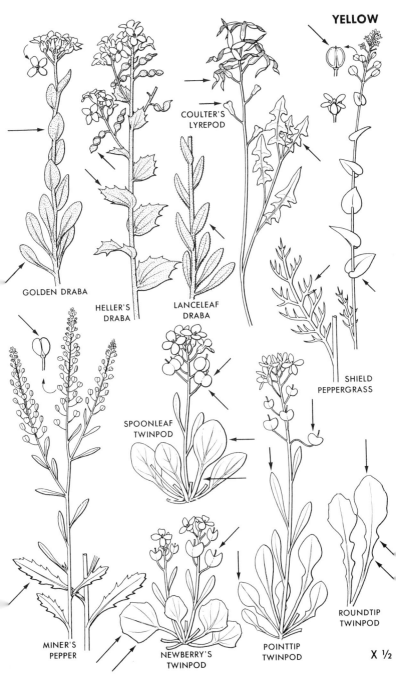

YELLOW

GOLDEN DRABA

HELLER'S DRABA

LANCELEAF DRABA

COULTER'S LYREPOD

SHIELD PEPPERGRASS

SPOONLEAF TWINPOD

MINER'S PEPPER

NEWBERRY'S TWINPOD

POINTTIP TWINPOD

ROUNDTIP TWINPOD

X ½

4-PETALED MALTESE CROSS; LINEAR SEEDPODS

Mustard Family (Cruciferae)
See also pp. W 26–32; Y 144–152; O 232; R 276.

LYRELEAF TWISTFLOWER *Streptanthus carinatus*
Similar to Arizona Jewelflower (below). *Purplish, urnlike calyx* (sepals) with tiny, twisted, purplish petals. Lower leaves *sharply reverse pinnate-lobed.* 20 cm–1 m. Sw. Tex.

JAN.–APRIL

ARIZONA JEWELFLOWER *Streptanthus arizonicus*
Calyx (sepals) large, *yellow to whitish, urnlike;* petals tiny, twisted, brownish purple with yellowish streaks (calyx and petals not shown). Large, pinnate-lobed, blue-green leaves with *bare petioles* and *2 basal lobes that resemble rooster combs.* Seedpods erect. 20 cm–1 m. Lower deserts. S.W., sw. Tex.

JAN.–APRIL

HEARTLEAF JEWELFLOWER *Streptanthus cordatus*
Pointed sepals with a *terminal tuft of hairs.* Urnlike flowers, yellow or red-purple with white tips. Seedpods erect. *Heart-shaped, yellow-green leaves* clasp the upper stem. 30 cm–1 m. Rocky slopes. N. Ariz. and N.M., R. Mts.

MARCH–MAY

LONGBEAK *Streptanthella longirostris*
Plant parts *all long and narrow,* including the hairy, urnlike calyx; *yellow petals;* and *hanging seedpods.* Leaves linear with *tiny, sharp lobes.* Stems and leaves waxy blue. 1–6 cm. Rocky slopes. S.W., R. Mts.

JAN.–JUNE

LONDON ROCKET Alien *Sisymbrium irio*
Pedicel *thinner* than the seedpod above it. Basal leaves, each with a broad, semi-triangular tip and broad side leaflets. 30 cm–1 m. Common. S.W., Tex.

DEC.–MAY

TUMBLING MUSTARD Alien *Sisymbrium altissimum*
Pedicels *as thick as* the long (5–10 cm), slender seedpods that *spread* from the stem. Pinnate leaves with narrow, opposite lobes. Flowers pale yellow. 50 cm–1 m. Common. Northern S.W., Tex., R. Mts.

APRIL–SEPT.

HEDGE MUSTARD Alien *Sisymbrium officinale*
Leaves and linear seedpods *closely pressed to the thin stems.* Lower stem leaves pinnate, with a *large terminal leaflet* and 1–4 pairs of linear leaflets. Small, pale yellow flowers. 50 cm–1 m. Occasional in S.W.; common in Tex., Pl. Sts.

MARCH–SEPT.

CALIFORNIA MUSTARD *Thelypodium lasiophyllum*
Broad leaves, sharply toothed. Whiskerlike seedpods, *bent strongly downward.* Pale yellow flowers in terminal spikes. 50 cm–1 m. Common at lower elevations, often under shrubs. Ariz.

FEB.–APRIL

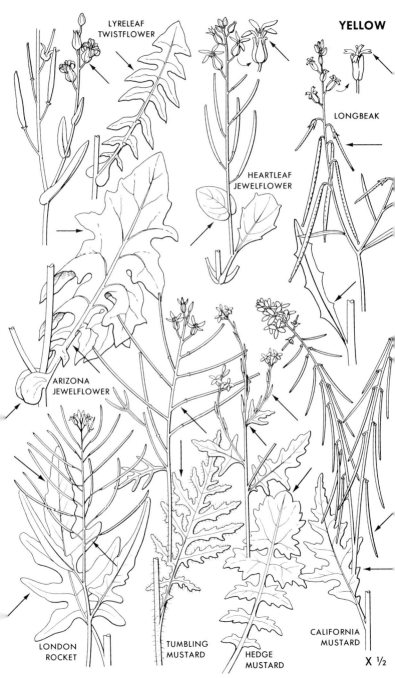

LYRELEAF
TWISTFLOWER

YELLOW

HEARTLEAF
JEWELFLOWER

LONGBEAK

ARIZONA
JEWELFLOWER

LONDON
ROCKET

TUMBLING
MUSTARD

HEDGE
MUSTARD

CALIFORNIA
MUSTARD

X ½

4-PETALED MALTESE CROSS;
LINEAR SEEDPODS

Mustard Family (Cruciferae)
See also pp. W 26–32; Y 144–152; O 232; R 276.

DOUGLAS' WALLFLOWER *Erysimum capitatum*
Gray basal leaves lancelike, with *toothed* margins. Seedpods
5–10 cm long, *somewhat 4-angled* in cross-section. Flowers yellow or orangish. 10 cm–1 m. Rocky slopes. S.W., n. Tex.

FEB.–SEPT.

SPREADING WALLFLOWER *Erysimum repandum*
Alien
Note the *sharply angled stem with 6 raised ribs* and many
sharply toothed, long, linear leaves. Flowers yellow-green, on
short pedicels. Seedpods nearly round. Stem becomes *strongly
branched* in age. 10–40 cm. Disturbed places. S.W., western and
n. Tex.

MARCH–JULY

ROUGH WALLFLOWER *Erysimum asperum*
Linear, gray-haired upper leaves have *smooth edges*. Seedpods
point upward; *square* in cross-section, not constricted between
seeds. Flowers yellow, tinted orange or reddish, 10 cm–1 m.
Plains. N.M., n. Tex., R. Mts., Pl. Sts.

APRIL–JUNE

SHY WALLFLOWER *Erysimum inconspicuum*
Petals *small* (1 cm or less across), pale yellow. Narrow, lancelike leaves, green, or with white hairs. Upward-pointing to erect
seedpods (2–5 cm) are 4-sided. 10–60 cm. N. Ariz. and northern
N.M., R. Mts.

JUNE–JULY

WESTERN TANSY MUSTARD *Descurainia pinnata*
Lacy leaves with numerous short segments. Upper stem leaves
simple-pinnate. Tiny, bright yellow flowers. Many short, *clublike seedpods* (each with *2 rows* of seeds) hang on threadlike
pedicels. *Seedpod short-tipped*. Stinging hairs. 10–30 cm. Common. S.W., Tex., R. Mts., Pl. Sts.

FEB.–JULY

MOUNTAIN *Descurainia richardsonii*
TANSY MUSTARD
Similar to Western Tansy Mustard, but *linear* seedpod has *1
row* of seeds and a *long, slender, seedless tip*. All stem leaves
simple-pinnate. 20 cm–1 m. Mountains. S.W., w. Tex., R. Mts.

MAY–SEPT.

FLIXWEED *Descurainia sophia*
Both upper and lower stem leaves pinnate. Linear seedpod has
1 row of seeds and *lacks* seedless tip. 10 cm–1 m. Disturbed
places. S.W., western and n. Tex., Pl. Sts., R. Mts.

FEB.–JUNE

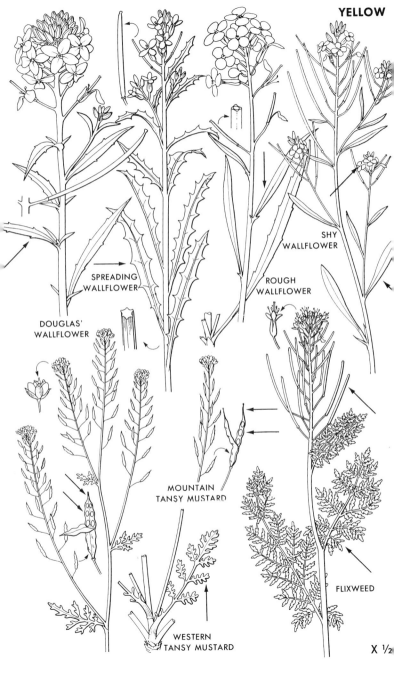

YELLOW

SHY
WALLFLOWER

SPREADING
WALLFLOWER

ROUGH
WALLFLOWER

DOUGLAS'
WALLFLOWER

MOUNTAIN
TANSY MUSTARD

FLIXWEED

WESTERN
TANSY MUSTARD

X ½

4-PETALED MALTESE CROSS;
LINEAR SEEDPODS

Mustard Family (Cruciferae)
See also pp. W 26–32; Y 144–152; O 232; R 276.

BLACK MUSTARD Alien *Brassica nigra*
Short seedpods (1 cm), *erect or spreading,* with several seeds.
Stems with coarse hairs. Lower leaves pinnate, with a large terminal lobe and small side lobes. Flowers bright yellow. 50 cm–2 m. Disturbed places. S.W., R. Mts. JAN.–JUNE

FIELD MUSTARD Alien *Brassica campestris*
Lower leaves *pinnate,* upper leaves arrowlike; all *clasping.*
Seedpods long, rounded. 20 cm–1 m. Disturbed places. S.W., Pl. Sts. JAN.–JUNE

TOWER MUSTARD *Arabis glabra*
Basal leaves hairy, *linear, with sawtoothed* (*reverse toothed*) *margins.* Smooth, narrow, arrowlike leaves clasp the *slender, towerlike stem.* Small, pale yellow flower. Slender, upright seedpods. 50 cm–1.5 m. Open slopes, foothills and mountains. Cen. and n. Ariz., northern N.M., R. Mts. MAY–JULY

GOLDEN PRINCE'S PLUME *Stanleya pinnata*
Long, linear petals with a *hairy surface on the lower inner portion* (see detail). Flowers in a *dense, terminal, brushlike spike.*
30 cm–2 m. Desert and foothill slopes, washes. S.W., w. Tex., R. Mts. APRIL–SEPT.

WESTERN YELLOW CRESS *Rorippa curvisiliqua*
The yellow flowers soon become *short, curved pods* (1 cm or less). Stem well-branched; 10–30 cm. Leaves divided into many irregularly toothed leaflets. Wet places, drying mud. Mountains. S.W. APRIL–SEPT.

AMERICAN WINTER CRESS *Barbarea orthoceras*
The pinnate basal leaves have a *large, rounded terminal lobe* and 1–2 pairs of *linear leaflets.* Pinnate upper leaves clasp the stout, succulent stem. Dense raceme of yellow flowers becomes a looser spike of numerous *long* seedpods. 20–40 cm. Streambanks. S.W., R. Mts. MARCH–SEPT.

Caper Family (Capparidaceae) See also pp. W 32; R 236.

YELLOW BEE PLANT *Cleome lutea*
Palmate leaves, usually with 5 leaflets. *Flat, banana-shaped seedpods* hang downward on long curving pedicels. 30 cm–1 m.
Sandy deserts. Ariz., nw. N.M. FEB.–JUNE

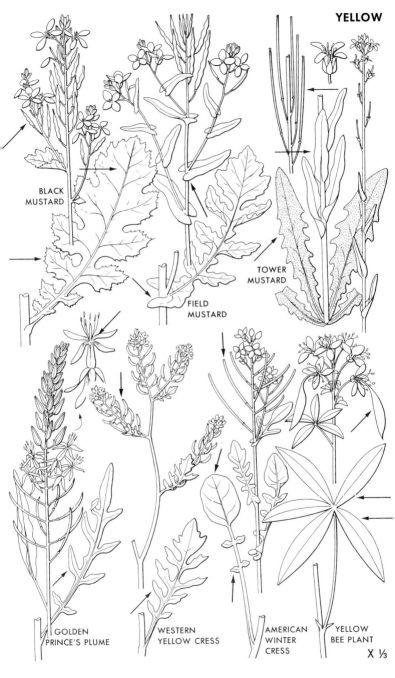

YELLOW

BLACK
MUSTARD

FIELD
MUSTARD

TOWER
MUSTARD

GOLDEN
PRINCE'S PLUME

WESTERN
YELLOW CRESS

AMERICAN
WINTER
CRESS

YELLOW
BEE PLANT

X ⅓

4 SHOWY PETALS ON TOP OF OVARY; STIGMA OF 4 LINEAR LOBES

Evening Primrose Family (Onagraceae)
See also pp. W 34–36; Y 154–158; R 278–280.

HOOKER'S EVENING PRIMROSE *Oenothera hookeri*
Stout, single, erect stem with many *long, lancelike* or narrow, elliptical leaves. Large yellow flowers, 5–10 cm wide. Thick, cylindrical ovary. 30 cm–1.5 m. Moist, springy places. S.W., w. Tex., R. Mts. JULY–OCT.

CUTLEAF EVENING PRIMROSE *Oenothera laciniata*
Note the *small* (1–2 cm wide), *pale yellow* flowers and *cut-lobed, broad leaves* on long, semi-erect stems. *4-sided, short, linear* ovary (and fruit). 10–60 cm. Semi-open places. Tex.; less common elsewhere in S.W. NOV.–JUNE

GRAND EVENING PRIMROSE *Oenothera grandis*
Similar to Cutleaf Evening Primrose, but with a *medium-sized* (2–3 cm wide) flower (not shown) above each leaf. Leaves strongly *cut-lobed.* 10–60 cm. Eastern half of Tex., Pl. Sts.
FEB.–JUNE, DEC.

BEACH EVENING PRIMROSE *Oenothera drummondii*
Large, showy, bright yellow flowers. *Short, oval, gray-haired* leaves. Long stems in clumps. 30 cm–1 m. Sandy beaches, dunes. Along Tex. Coast. MARCH–NOV.

FLUTTERMILLS *Oenothera missouriensis*
Note the *narrow, lancelike* leaves on *shiny, red,* semi-prostrate stems. *Very large flowers* with very long corolla tube and *basal (inferior) ovary.* Ovary and fruit short, with *thin, finlike wings.* 3–60 cm. Prairies, woodlands. Cen. Tex. and north; Pl. Sts.
APRIL–AUG.

BOTTLE EVENING PRIMROSE *Oenothera primiveris*
Stemless, flat tufts of gray, broadly lobed, *pinnate leaves.* Leaf-lobe tips *rounded.* Large flowers (5 cm across). Fruit *bottle-shaped,* with a *narrow "neck;"* surface rounded and angled, but *without wings.* Desert flats. S.W., w. Tex.
MARCH–MAY

SHORTFIN EVENING PRIMROSE *Oenothera flava*
Stemless tufts of leaves as in previous species, but each leaf blade has *many narrow, pointed lobes.* Ovary and fruit *short, squat, and 4-sided.* Ariz., northern N.M., R. Mts.
APRIL–SEPT.

LONGFIN EVENING PRIMROSE *Oenothera brachycarpa*
Stemless tufts of leaves as in previous species, but leaf blade *undivided, with smooth, wavy, or semilobed margins.* Ovary and seedpod *long,* 4-sided, with *4 winged fins along the entire length.* Rocky places. S.W., w. Tex., Pl. Sts. MARCH–JUNE

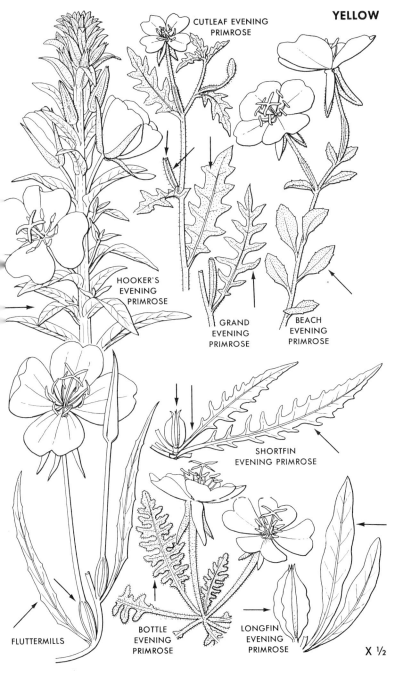

YELLOW

CUTLEAF EVENING PRIMROSE

HOOKER'S EVENING PRIMROSE

GRAND EVENING PRIMROSE

BEACH EVENING PRIMROSE

SHORTFIN EVENING PRIMROSE

FLUTTERMILLS

BOTTLE EVENING PRIMROSE

LONGFIN EVENING PRIMROSE

X ½

4 SHOWY PETALS ON TOP OF OVARY; ROUND, HEADLIKE STIGMAS

Evening Primrose Family (Onagraceae)
See also pp. W 34–36; Y 154–158; R 278–280.

BROWN EYES — *Camissonia clavaeformis*
Rounded petals, yellow or white, often with a *brown eyespot at base.* Flowers in a thick cluster, nodding when in bud. Basal rosette of strongly toothed, oval leaves. *Club-shaped* seedpod. 5–20 cm. Common on deserts. Ariz.   MARCH–MAY

YELLOW CUPS — *Camissonia brevipes*
Green, linear, pinnate leaves with *red veins.* Flower stem nodding until all flowers have opened. Flowers bright yellow. Seedpod has *constrictions* between seeds. 10–40 cm. Slopes, washes. Lower deserts. W. Ariz.   FEB.–MAY

MUSTARD EVENING PRIMROSE — *Camissonia californica*
Erect plant resembles members of the mustard family. Leaves narrow, lancelike with *irregularly toothed margins.* Flowers 1–3 cm wide. *Sepals swept backward;* petals sometimes have red dots. 30 cm–1 m. Lower deserts. W. Ariz.   FEB.–JUNE

MINIATURE EVENING PRIMROSE — *Camissonia micrantha*
Small, prostrate stem; 5–50 cm. *Tiny, gray, lancelike* leaves with *wavy margins.* Seedpods *curved, contorted.* Flowers tiny (5–10 mm). Common at lower elevations. Ariz.   MARCH–MAY

HEARTLEAF EVENING PRIMROSE — *Camissonia cardiophylla*
Heart-shaped leaves with short sharp teeth at margins. Stem erect, with *terminal flower buds* in a nodding curve. 10–60 cm. Flats, canyons of lowest deserts. Sw. Ariz.   FEB.–APRIL

FIELD EVENING PRIMROSE — *Camissonia dentata*
Note the *curved, snakelike* seedpods. Flowers tiny. *Long, narrowly linear* leaves with toothed margins. Petal bases with or without red dots. Stigma tip a rounded lobe. 10–20 cm. Deserts. Westernmost S.W., Nev.   MARCH–MAY

YELLOW WATERWEED — *Ludwigia peploides*
Note the *black, glandular bumps* on leaf bases. Ovary *bulges on one side,* below large yellow petals. An aquatic plant with numerous broad, shiny, green, lancelike leaves. Stem hairy, *floating;* 30 cm or more long. Slow streams, ponds. Common. Eastern half of Tex.   APRIL–OCT.

WINGED WATERWEED — *Ludwigia decurrens*
Tall, erect, well-branched stem with *raised, winglike margins* along the stem and *willowlike leaves.* Ovary and fruit 4-sided, with *winged margins.* 50 cm–1.5 m. Swamps, semi-wet places. E. Tex.   JUNE–OCT.

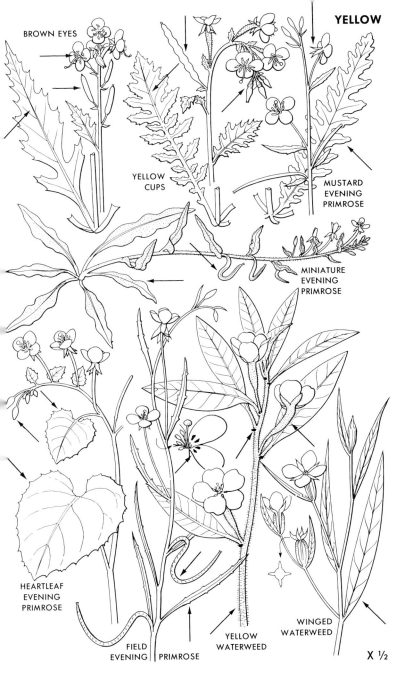

YELLOW

BROWN EYES

YELLOW CUPS

MUSTARD EVENING PRIMROSE

MINIATURE EVENING PRIMROSE

HEARTLEAF EVENING PRIMROSE

FIELD EVENING PRIMROSE

YELLOW WATERWEED

WINGED WATERWEED

X ½

4–6 PETALS; LARGE OR TINY FLOWERS

Evening Primrose Family (Onagraceae)
See also pp. W 34–36; Y 154–158; R 278–280.

HARTWEG'S SUNDROPS   *Calylophus hartwegii*
Note the *flat-sided, square* flowerbud tips and *broad, lancelike* leaves with smooth margins. Large, bright yellow petals with a *crinkly surface*. Long, trumpetlike corolla base. Stigma *doughnutlike*. Grows in large masses. 5–30 cm. S.W., western half of Tex., Pl. Sts.   MARCH–OCT.

DRUMMOND'S SUNDROPS   *Calyophus drummondianus*
Note the *raised, winglike* flowerbud tips and *long, narrow, stringlike* leaves with small, *sharp-toothed margins*. Stigma doughnutlike; *well above stamens* at pollen-shedding time. Large, bright yellow petals with crinkly surfaces. Long, trumpetlike corolla base. In large masses. 10–60 cm. Tex., adjacent N.M., Pl. Sts.
     MARCH–NOV.

HALFLEAF SUNDROPS   *Calylophus serrulatus*
Doughnutlike stigma *below stamens* at pollen-shedding time. Leaves *intermediate* between Hartweg's and Drummond's Sundrops — lancelike with toothed margins. Flowerbud *tips raised, winglike*. Crinkly petals small (1–2 cm long). 10–60 cm. S.W., western two-thirds of Tex., Pl. Sts.   MARCH–NOV.

LAVENDERLEAF SUNDROPS   *Calylophus lavandulifolius*
Flowers as above. *Leaves gray, linear, crowded up entire stem.* 5–20 cm. Dry slopes. S.W., Tex., Pl. Sts.   MAY–SEPT.

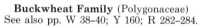

Buckwheat Family (Polygonaceae)
See also pp. W 38–40; Y 160; R 282–284.

DEVIL'S SPINYHERB   *Chorizanthe rigida*
Small, tufted plant with *broadly oval* leaves and a cluster of spiny flowers. Each flower surrounded by *3 long spines*. Plants persist as black spiny tufts. 2–10 cm. Stony places. Lowest deserts. Common. W. Ariz.   MARCH–MAY

HAVARD'S ERIOGONUM   *Eriogonum havardii*
Note the *small, erect* cluster of short, *grayish, oblong leaves*. The *single* long, bare flower stem divides into nearly equal forks, ending in few-flowered clusters. Yellow, starlike flowers. 30–60 cm. Rocky slopes. Southern N.M., Big Bend region, Tex.   JUNE–SEPT.

WINGED ERIOGONUM   *Eriogonum alatum*
Note the *flat, spokelike* basal cluster of *long, green spatula-like leaves*. Single *leafless,* erect flower stem divides into *graceful, nearly right-angled branches*. Tubular, yellow to tannish red flowers form *conelike umbel cups*. 50 cm–1.5 m. Open forests, grasslands. S.W., western and n. Tex., Pl. Sts.   MAY–NOV.

LONGLEAF ERIOGONUM   *Eriogonum longifolium*
Grayish, long, narrow leaf blades, scattered up the *main stem.* Yellow to whitish flowers within gray-haired clusters. 50 cm–1.5 m. Woods, plains. Tex., Pl. Sts.   JUNE–AUG.

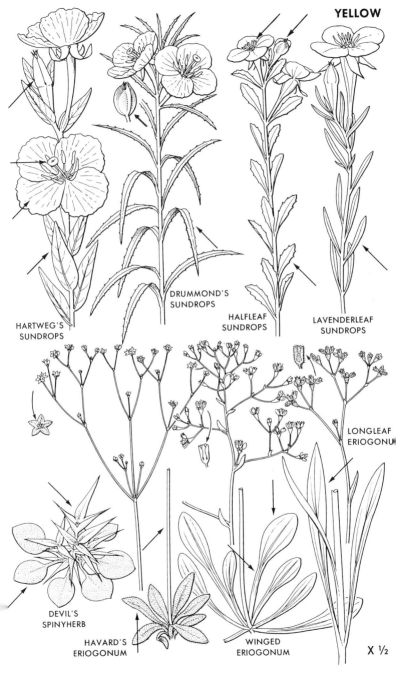

YELLOW

HARTWEG'S SUNDROPS

DRUMMOND'S SUNDROPS

HALFLEAF SUNDROPS

LAVENDERLEAF SUNDROPS

DEVIL'S SPINYHERB

HAVARD'S ERIOGONUM

WINGED ERIOGONUM

LONGLEAF ERIOGONU

X ½

4–6 PETALS; TINY TUBULAR FLOWERS IN CLUSTERS

Buckwheat Family (Polygonaceae)
See also pp. W 38–40; Y 158; R 282–284.

LITTLE TRUMPET *Eriogonum trichopes*
Numerous fine, threadlike stem and flower branches; umbels with few flowers. Crinkled, green, oval to oblong leaf blades with long petioles in a basal rosette. Lower central stem often inflates into 1 "trumpet." Annual. 30–60 cm. Very common on deserts. S.W., R. Mts. FEB.–OCT.

DESERT TRUMPET *Eriogonum inflatum*
Flowers yellow with hairy, red-brown midribs; on *thick pedicels*. Note the *inflated "trumpets"* produced by insect galls at the top of several to many branches of the leafless stem. Oval to rounded green leaves with stiff, curly margins in a basal cluster. Perennial. 30 cm–1 m. Common in lower deserts. W. Ariz., nw. N.M., Ut. MARCH–OCT.

PUNY ERIOGONUM *Eriogonum pusillum*
Gray *spoonlike* leaves in a basal rosette. Stem leafless, well-branched. Few-flowered umbels, pale yellow with red midribs. 10–30 cm. Common. W. Ariz. APRIL–MAY

KIDNEYLEAF ERIOGONUM *Eriogonum reniforme*
Felt-haired, kidney-shaped leaves in a flat basal rosette. Leafless stem branches in an orderly forking pattern. Single umbels of yellow flowers. 5–30 cm. Very common on lowest deserts. W. Ariz. MARCH–JUNE

SULPHUR ERIOGONUM *Eriogonum umbellatum*
Spatula-shaped gray leaves with *long petioles, both* in a basal rosette and as *whorls at each branching point.* Flowers sulphur yellow, tinted red, in compound umbels with a *whorl of linear leaves only* below the primary (first) umbel. 10–30 cm. Common in mountains. N. Ariz., R. Mts. APRIL–JUNE

EGGLEAF ERIOGONUM *Eriogonum ovalifolium*
A dense *basal mat of tiny white, woolly, egg-shaped leaves.* Flower stems with round heads of yellow, pink or white flowers. Umbel bracts not visible. 10–20 cm. Desert slopes to alpine. Northern S.W., R. Mts. APRIL–JUNE

YELLOW ERIOGONUM *Eriogonum flavum*
Linear, gray-haired leaves in a basal rosette. Leafless flower stem. 4–6 leaflike bracts immediately below many *headlike clusters* of pale to deep yellow flowers that are sometimes rose-tinted. Petal tips *rounded.* Grows in mats. Open ridges, pine forests. N. Ariz. AUG.

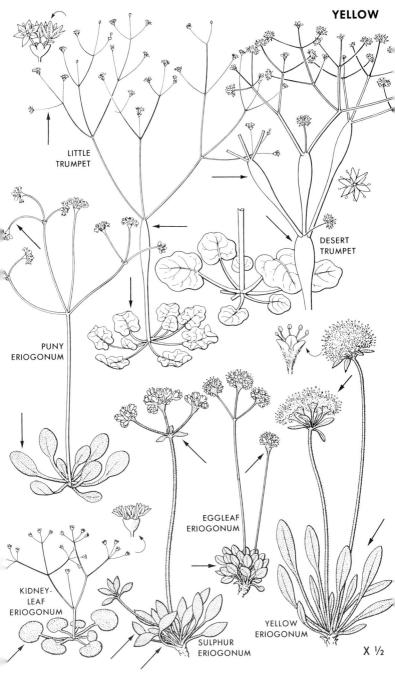

YELLOW

LITTLE
TRUMPET

DESERT
TRUMPET

PUNY
ERIOGONUM

EGGLEAF
ERIOGONUM

KIDNEY-
LEAF
ERIOGONUM

SULPHUR
ERIOGONUM

YELLOW
ERIOGONUM

X ½

5 TO MANY PETALS, MANY STAMENS

Buttercup Family (Ranunculaceae)
See also pp. W 42–44; Y 162–164;
R 236, 286; B 344, 356–358; G 396–406.

LONGSPUR COLUMBINE   *Aquilegia longissima*
Note the *very long spurs* (5–20 cm) on the flowers. Petals *dark yellow.* Tripinnate leaves, thin, *light yellow-green.* 50 cm–1 m. Near waterfalls. Chisos Mts., Tex.; Baboquivari and Huachuca Mts., s. Ariz.   MARCH–JULY

CANARY COLUMBINE   *Aquilegia chrysantha*
Flower spurs *medium-long,* 4–7 cm. Petals pale cream to *light canary yellow.* Flowers horizontal or pointing upward. Tripinnate leaves, thick, *waxy blue-green.* 30 cm–1 m. Common in shady forests. S.W., w. Tex., R. Mts.   APRIL–SEPT.

CHAPLINE'S COLUMBINE   *Aquilegia chaplinei*
(not shown)
Similar to Canary Columbine, but grows on dripping desert cliffs. Only in Guadalupe Mts. near Carlsbad, N.M.   APRIL–OCT.

HINCKLEY'S COLUMBINE   *Aquilegia hinckleyana*
(not shown)
Similar to Canary Columbine, but spurs *short,* 2–3 cm. Known only at Capote Falls, Presidio County, Tex.   MARCH–NOV.

GOLDEN COLUMBINE   *Aquilegia flavescens*
Flower *spurs short. Dark, nodding,* butter-yellow flowers. Leaves pinnate, blue-green. 30–90 cm. Moist mountain woods. Northern S.W., R. Mts.   APRIL–SEPT.

CLUSTERED BUTTERCUP   *Ranunculus inamoenus*
Note the *rounded to forklike* lobe tips of the lower leaves. *Middle stem bare,* with a terminal cluster of straplike leaves. Flowers small, *nestled among* the terminal leaves. Common in damp mountain meadows, woods. S.W., R. Mts.   APRIL–AUG.

BLACK BUTTERCUP   *Ranunculus macauleyi*
Note the *dense black hair on the sepals.* Large, bright yellow, *cuplike* flowers. Short stems with *toothed, spoonlike* lower leaves and *forklike upper leaves.* 5–20 cm. High mountains. Northern N.M., R. Mts.   JUNE–AUG.

SNOW BUTTERCUP   *Ranunculus adoneus*
Large flowers (2–3 cm). Leaves divided into *linear segments.* 10–20 cm. Edges of snowbanks in tundra zone of higher mountains. Northern N.M., R. Mts.   JUNE–AUG.

WOODLAND BUTTERCUP   *Ranunculus uncinatus*
Elongated, oval petals. Tripinnate leaves, often with pointed, partly linear lobes. Each seed has a *hooked beak.* Seedhead globular. 10 cm–1 m. Moist, shady places. Kaibab Plateau, Ariz.; R. Mts.   JULY–AUG.

MACOUN'S BUTTERCUP   *Ranunculus macounii*
Flowers small; petals *barely longer* than sepals. *Seedhead elongated.* Each seed (achene) is a fat oval with a short, curved beak. Stem sprawling, rooting at leaf bases. Leaves with *3–5 parts.* 30 cm–1 m. Marshy places in mountain woods. Northern half of Ariz., all of N.M., R. Mts.   JULY–AUG.

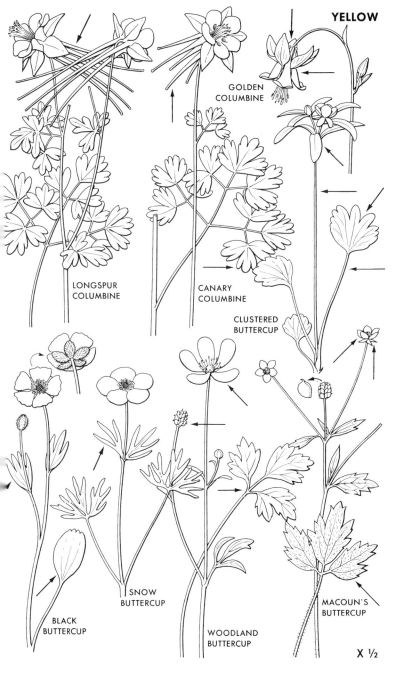

YELLOW

GOLDEN
COLUMBINE

LONGSPUR
COLUMBINE

CANARY
COLUMBINE

CLUSTERED
BUTTERCUP

BLACK
BUTTERCUP

SNOW
BUTTERCUP

WOODLAND
BUTTERCUP

MACOUN'S
BUTTERCUP

X ½

5–12 GLOSSY PETALS; MANY STAMENS

Buttercup Family (Ranunculaceae)
See also pp. W 42–44; Y 162–164;
R 236, 286; B 344, 356–358; G 396, 406.

CREEPING BUTTERCUP   *Ranunculus repens*
Pinnate *leaf blade* with 3 leaflets; each leaflet cut-lobed. Flower stems erect. Seedheads rounded; seeds smooth, oval, with a nearly straight beak. Leaves and stem hairy. 50 cm–1 m. Moist disturbed places. Northern S.W., Tex., R. Mts.   FEB.–SEPT.

PRICKLESEED   *Ranunculus muricatus*
BUTTERCUP Alien
Seeds flat, oval, with a *thick, birdlike beak;* seed walls covered with many *curved spines.* Shiny, *maplelike* leaves. 10–60 cm. Wet places. Eastern quarter of Tex.   MARCH–MAY

HEARTLEAF BUTTERCUP   *Ranunculus cardiophyllus*
Note the *heart-shaped leaves* on long pedicels and 5-petaled flowers. *Elongated seedheads* (not shown); seeds beaked. 10–40 cm. Mountain meadows, woods. S.W., R. Mts. JUNE–SEPT.

MALE BUTTERCUP Alien   *Ranunculus testiculatus*
Tiny gray plants with linear, *pinnate* leaves. *Urn-shaped,* pale yellow flowers. Seeds hairy, with a central shaft and 2 saclike bulges near the base. Seedhead cylindrical. 2–5 cm. Northern S.W., R. Mts.   APRIL–MAY

DESERT BUTTERCUP   *Ranunculus cymbalaria*
Leaves shiny green, *heart-shaped, with wavy margins.* Seeds oblong and *ribbed,* with a short, straight beak. Seedhead a *thumblike cylinder.* 5–12 petals. 5–30 cm. Marshy alkali meadows. S.W., Panhandle of Tex., R. Mts.   MAY–JULY

ESCHSCHOLTZ'S   *Ranunculus eschscholtzii*
BUTTERCUP
Low, tufted plants with *very large-petaled flowers.* Leaves shiny green, rounded in outline, but with 3 deeply-cut segments. Oval seeds with a long, straight beak. 2–15 cm. Alpine slopes. Northern S.W., R. Mts.   JULY–AUG.

SAGEBRUSH BUTTERCUP   *Ranunculus glaberrimus*
Shiny green leaves with *3-4 broad teeth* or lobes, somewhat similar to the tines of a broad butter fork. Upper stem leaves linear. Seeds slightly hairy. Stems erect to prostrate. 5–25 cm. On wet sagebrush flats. Northern N.M., R. Mts.

MARCH–JUNE

WATER PLANTAIN   *Ranunculus alismaefolius*
BUTTERCUP
Leaves shiny green, *lancelike,* on semi-sprawling stems. Seeds rounded with a nearly straight *beak pointed outward almost at a right angle.* First plant to flower in wet, high mountain meadows. 30 cm–1 m. Northern S.W., R. Mts.   MARCH–JULY

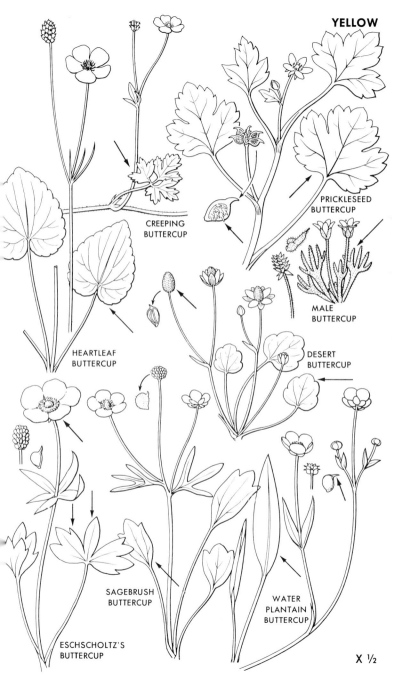

YELLOW

CREEPING
BUTTERCUP

PRICKLESEED
BUTTERCUP

MALE
BUTTERCUP

HEARTLEAF
BUTTERCUP

DESERT
BUTTERCUP

ESCHSCHOLTZ'S
BUTTERCUP

SAGEBRUSH
BUTTERCUP

WATER
PLANTAIN
BUTTERCUP

X ½

5 PETALS; COLUMN OF MANY STAMENS

Mallow Family (Malvaceae)
See also pp. W 44; O 238; R 288–290.

YELLOW FUGOSA   *Cienfuegosia drummondii*
Petals propellerlike. Plant smooth (hairless). 10–50 cm. Openings in brush. Coastal and s. Tex.   FEB.–OCT.

COULTER'S HIBISCUS   *Hibiscus coulteri*
Upper stem leaves *trilobed* with *scattered, shiny, starlike hairs.* Lemon or sulphur yellow flowers (2–5 cm). Small *linear bracts* immediately below the oval sepals. 30 cm–1 m. Rocky slopes, deserts. S.W., western third of Tex.   APRIL–AUG.

BALLOON SIDA   *Sida physocalyx*
Note the *inflated, sharply ridged "turk's cap" calyx* around the developing fruit or flower buds. Small (5–15 mm), pale yellow or buff petals, *not longer than* the heart-shaped sepals. Dark green, elongate, *ruffle-edged leaves.* Stems prostrate. 10–40 cm. Open places. Se. Ariz. to western two-thirds of Tex.   MARCH–OCT.

SPREADING SIDA   *Sida filicaulis*
Note the *spiny hairs on the stem and lancelike leaves. Open, spreading flowers* with yellow to salmon petals that are *longer than* the sepals. Erect or sprawling stems. 10 cm–1 m. Open waste places. S.W., western two-thirds of Tex.   MARCH–SEPT.

NEW MEXICO SIDA   *Sida neomexicana*
Dark red-brown margins on sepals and often on dark green leaves as well. Leaves *narrow, triangular.* Broad, pale yellow to salmon petals. Flowerbuds *ridged, pointed.* Hair on plant dense, velvety. 10–50 cm. Rocky slopes. S.W., w. Tex.
     MARCH–SEPT.

St. John's Wort Family (Hypericaceae)

SCOULER'S ST. JOHN'S WORT   *Hypericum formosum*
Note the *triangular to oval sepals without* a pointed tip. Petals sometimes black-dotted. Paired leaves *oblong* to oval, *flat.* 10–70 cm. Common in moist places in mountains. S.W., R. Mts.
     JULY–SEPT.

TINKER'S PENNY   *Hypericum anagalloides*
Tiny stem (2–7 cm); in creeping mats. Tiny, paired, oval to round leaves. Small yellow-orange flowers. Moist mountain meadows. Northern S.W., R. Mts.   JULY–SEPT.

KLAMATH WEED Alien   *Hypericum perforatum*
Leaves *linear to lancelike.* Petals yellow-orange, sometimes black-dotted. 20–70 cm. Occasional, in open fields. S.W., R. Mts.   JUNE–SEPT.

NITS-AND-LICE   *Hypericum drummondii*
Note the *smooth, wiry stems* with short, linear leaves that are *pressed against* the stem. Small, flattened flowers with funnel-like bases. Leaves and sepal tips *tiny, awl-like, pointed.* 10–50 cm. Open areas. Eastern half of Tex., Pl. Sts. APRIL–SEPT.

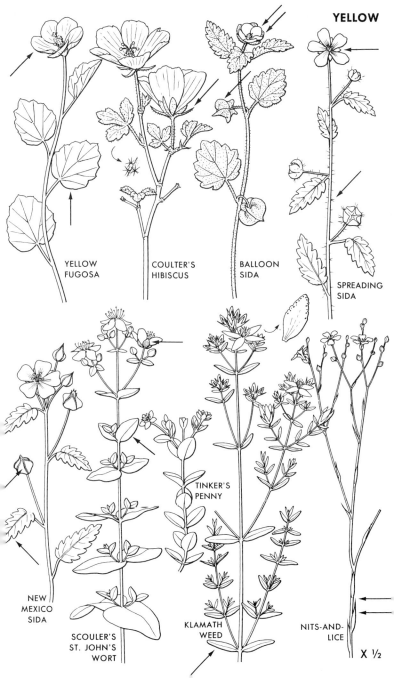

YELLOW

YELLOW
FUGOSA

COULTER'S
HIBISCUS

BALLOON
SIDA

SPREADING
SIDA

NEW
MEXICO
SIDA

SCOULER'S
ST. JOHN'S
WORT

TINKER'S
PENNY

KLAMATH
WEED

NITS-AND-
LICE

X ½

5 TO MANY PETALS; INFERIOR OVARY; NUMEROUS BUSHY STAMENS

Loasa Family (Loasaceae)

WHITESTEM STICKLEAF　　*Mentzelia albicaulis*
Small flowers (5–15 mm). *White, shiny stems* — erect, with *strongly sawtoothed,* linear to triangular leaves. 10–40 cm. Common. S.W., w. Tex.　　FEB.–AUG.

NEVADA STICKLEAF　　*Mentzelia dispersa*
Leaves narrow, linear, with *tiny teeth* along margins. Small flowers (1 cm). Petals on top of ovary. Slender white stems. 10–30 cm. Deserts. Western S.W.　　MAY–AUG.

WHITEBRACT STICKLEAF　　*Mentzelia involucrata*
Leaves somewhat triangular with *many coarse teeth. Large, cuplike,* satiny, cream to pale yellow flowers. Stems and leaves sticky-haired; surfaces *cling like Velcro.* 10–30 cm. Rocky places in lower deserts. Sw. Ariz.　　FEB.–APRIL

BULLET STICKLEAF　　*Mentzelia pumila*
Note the *blunt, bulletlike* inferior ovary below the medium-sized (3–5 cm wide), *many-petaled* dark yellow flowers. Long, *stringy leaves with tiny grayish lobes.* 20–80 cm. Dry streambeds, dunes. Ariz., R. Mts.　　FEB.–OCT.

WARNOCK'S ROCK NETTLE　　*Eucnide bartonioides*
Note the *large,* bright yellow, *funnel-like* flowers with *numerous projecting stamens.* Flat, low mounded plants with maple-like leaves that grow *horizontally or nearly upside down* in shade of overhanging ledges in limestone cliffs. 10–30 cm. W. Tex., particularly along Rio Grande and tributary canyons.
　　MARCH–AUG.

THREADPETAL STICKLEAF　　*Mentzelia strictissima*
Creamy yellow or nearly white *thistlelike* flowers with *numerous linear petals* and a few broad, similarly colored sepals below. Long, triangular leaves with *wavy, sawtoothed margins.* Long, cylindrical inferior ovary. Shiny, white stems; erect, well-branched. 20–90 cm. Gypsum soils. Se. N.M., w. Tex.
　　JUNE–OCT.

STINGING CEVALLIA　　*Cevallia sinuata*
Headlike clusters of dark yellow, *starlike flowers.* Triangular leaves, semi-pinnate-lobed; each lobe with *a few long, stinging hairs.* 10–60 cm. Open slopes. Se. Ariz. to w. Tex.
　　JUNE–OCT.

DESERT ROCK NETTLE　　*Eucnide urens*
Leaves *rounded* with coarse teeth, covered with velvety white hairs; they cling to clothing, like Velcro. Large, *cuplike, creamy yellow* flowers. Rounded, bushlike plants. 30–60 cm. Dry rocky places. W. Ariz., Ut.　　APRIL–SEPT.

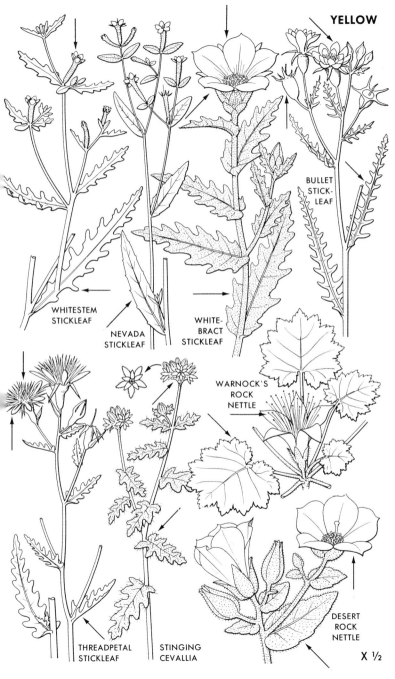

YELLOW

WHITESTEM STICKLEAF

NEVADA STICKLEAF

WHITE-BRACT STICKLEAF

BULLET STICK-LEAF

WARNOCK'S ROCK NETTLE

THREADPETAL STICKLEAF

STINGING CEVALLIA

DESERT ROCK NETTLE

X ½

5 FREE PETALS; STARS, VIOLETS, URNS

Saxifrage Family (Saxifragaceae)
See also pp. W 52–54; R 236; G 404.

WHIPLASH SAXIFRAGE *Saxifraga flagellaris*
Note the *reddish, whiplike runners* with clusters of tiny new plantlets at their tips. Bright yellow, cuplike flowers on erect stems. Lancelike leaves with *bristle-haired margins.* 5–10 cm. Rocky alpine slopes. Northern S.W., R. Mts. JULY–SEPT.

GOLDBLOOM *Saxifraga seryllifolia*
Note the *tiny basal clusters* of spatula-like leaves. Bright golden-yellow petals, *dotted with orange spots.* 2–10 cm. Rocky tundra slopes. Northern N.M., R. Mts. JULY–AUG.

Primrose Family (Primulaceae) See also pp. W 78; R 300.

FRINGED LOOSESTRIFE *Lysimachia ciliata*
Note the *shiny,* yellow, *flattened, cuplike* flowers (2–3 cm wide) on tall, well-branched, *squarish stems. Petal edges fringed.* Lancelike leaves in opposite pairs. 50 cm–1 m. Rich soil in mountain forests. Northern half of S.W., R. Mts.

JULY–SEPT.

Violet Family (Violaceae) See also pp. W 50; B 378.

MOUNTAIN VIOLET *Viola purpurea*
Nearly *triangular leaves* with toothed margins, tinted with purple. Petals deep lemon yellow, the lower 3 with purple veins. 5–20 cm. Mountains. Cen. Ariz. and north. APRIL–AUG.

NUTTALL'S VIOLET *Viola nuttallii*
Leaves *lancelike to oval,* hairy. Petals deep yellow, the lower 3 with brown-purple veins. 2–7 cm. A highly variable species. Dry mountain forests. S.W., R. Mts. APRIL–MAY

SMOOTH YELLOW VIOLET *Viola pubescens*
Bright green, *heart-shaped leaves on tall, erect stems.* Flowers yellow. 10–40 cm. Rich hardwood forests near streams. Ne. Tex. MARCH–MAY

SHELTON'S VIOLET *Viola sheltonii*
Fan-shaped, pinnate leaves. Flowers deep lemon yellow. Mountain forests. Northern S.W. APRIL–JULY

Wood Sorrel Family (Oxalidaceae). See also p. R 298.

CREEPING WOOD SORREL Alien *Oxalis corniculata*
Slender, creeping stems *rooting at leaf bases.* Small (5–10 mm), deep yellow-orange, funnel-like flowers. Cloverlike leaflets. 2–5 cm. Very common in lawns, etc. S.W., Tex., R. Mts., Pl. Sts. ALL YEAR

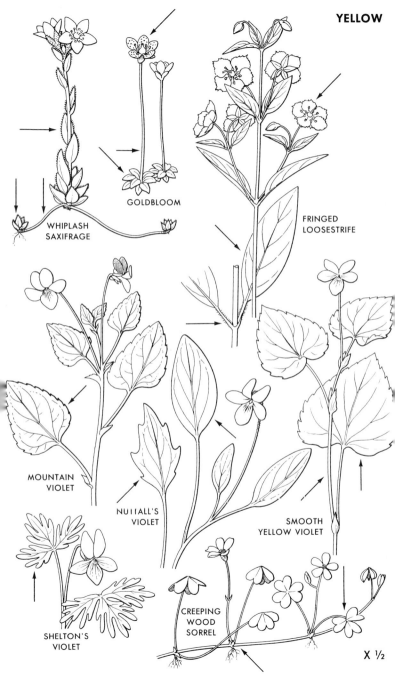

YELLOW

WHIPLASH
SAXIFRAGE

GOLDBLOOM

FRINGED
LOOSESTRIFE

MOUNTAIN
VIOLET

NUTTALL'S
VIOLET

SMOOTH
YELLOW VIOLET

SHELTON'S
VIOLET

CREEPING
WOOD
SORREL

X ½

5 PETALS; MANY STAMENS;
PINNATE LEAVES WITH STIPULES AT BASE

Rose Family (Rosaceae) See also W 50; R 298.

STICKY CINQUEFOIL *Potentilla glandulosa*
Leaves pinnate, with 5–9 strongly toothed, *oblong leaflets* in pairs, except for the terminal leaflet. Flowers lemon yellow to white. Sticky stems. 20–70 cm. Very common. Mountains. S.W., R. Mts. MAY–JUNE

FEATHER SILVERWEED *Potentilla anserina*
Long, silvery, featherlike leaves, each with 9–31 lancelike leaflets. Strawberry-like runners. 30–70 cm. Wet mountain meadows. S.W., R. Mts. MAY–AUG.

SHAGGY SILVERLEAF *Potentilla hippiana*
Tall, grayish semi-leafy stems. Leaves with 1–4 pairs of *shaggy, silver-gray leaflets* and a terminal leaflet. Lobes of leaflets do not penetrate to main veins. 30–60 cm. Mountain meadows and forests. S.W., R. Mts. JUNE–SEPT.

FIVEFINGER CINQUEFOIL *Potentilla gracilis*
Palmate, fanlike leaves, each with 5–7 *fingerlike leaflets.* Leaves bright green with silky hairs; leaflet margins may be slightly to deeply lobed. 10–50 cm. Mountains. N.M., R. Mts.

MAY–AUG.

CLUBLEAF CINQUEFOIL *Potentilla subviscosa*
Palmate leaves, each with 5–9 *clublike leaflets. Windmill-like* flowers with bilobed, square-tipped petals. 10–40 cm. Mountain meadows, forests. S.W. APRIL–JUNE

PENNSYLVANIA CINQUEFOIL *Potentilla pensylvanica*
5–9 *deeply lobed leaflets* per pinnate leaf. Bright yellow flowers. Closely related to Alpine Avens. 10–60 cm. S.W., R. Mts.

JULY–AUG.

ALPINE AVENS *Geum rossii*
Note the basal cluster of *dark green, elongate, featherlike* pinnate leaves. Erect, nearly naked stem with bright yellow flowers as in Pennsylvania Cinquefoil. 10–50 cm. Common in alpine meadows. N.M., R. Mts. JUNE–AUG.

LARGELEAF AVENS *Geum macrophyllum*
Each pinnate basal leaf has a *large, rounded terminal leaflet,* with smaller pairs of leaflets below. Leaves become smaller further up stem. 50 cm–1 m. Mountains. S.W., R. Mts.

JULY–SEPT.

PRAIRIE SMOKE *Geum ciliatum*
Flowerbuds are *nodding bells* of red sepals that become small, erect, yellow flowers. Basal leaves *pinnate,* with narrowly cleft leaflets. Stem leaves few. 10–60 cm. Rocky places, mountain forests. S.W., R. Mts. MAY–AUG.

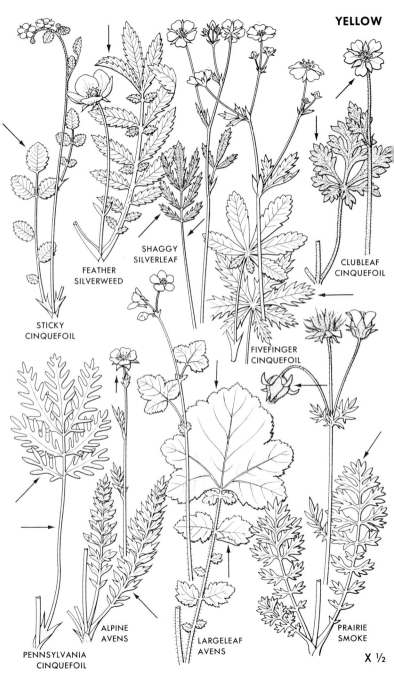

YELLOW

STICKY
CINQUEFOIL

FEATHER
SILVERWEED

SHAGGY
SILVERLEAF

CLUBLEAF
CINQUEFOIL

FIVEFINGER
CINQUEFOIL

PENNSYLVANIA
CINQUEFOIL

ALPINE
AVENS

LARGELEAF
AVENS

PRAIRIE
SMOKE

X ½

4 OR 5 PETALS; VARIOUSLY ARRANGED

Gentian Family (Gentianaceae)
See also pp. W 78; R 242; B 342; G 400.

SPUR GENTIAN *Halenia recurva*
Note the *4 short spurs* at the base of the dark yellow, pointed, short, cylindrical corolla. 4 tiny petal tips. Yellow-green, erect, well-branched stems that are flattened. *Short, linear leaves,* in opposite pairs. 10–50 cm. Mountain meadows, open conifer forests. Ariz., sw. N.M. JULY–SEPT.

EGGLEAF GENTIAN *Gentianella microcalyx*
Short, tapering, funnel-like, yellow-green flowers with *5 pointed petal lobes. Broad, heart- to egg-shaped leaves* without petioles, in opposite pairs on erect, well-branched stems. 20–60 cm. Shady mountain canyons. S. Ariz. AUG.–OCT.

UTAH SWERTIA *Swertia utahensis*
Flat, 4-petaled, *rich yellow-green flowers with purple dots and lines.* Each petal has an *elongated, keyhole-like basal gland* — lower portion has 2 lobes and is lined with yellow hair. Long, lancelike leaves in a basal cluster, with *brilliant white margins.* Flowering stem erect, *towerlike.* 50 cm–1 m. Grows on pink sand dunes in northern Ariz., northern N.M., and adjacent states to the north. JUNE–SEPT.

Bleeding Heart Family (Fumariaceae) See also p. R 298.

GOLDEN SMOKE *Corydalis aurea*
Arched, flattened, pale to dark golden yellow flowers, each with a *gaping mouth* and a *rounded, single spur.* Flat-sided, *bananalike seedpods.* Highly divided, waxy, blue-green (smoky) pinnate leaves. One of the first spring flowers. 5–60 cm. Sandy disturbed places. S.W., Tex., R. Mts., Pl. Sts.
FEB.–SEPT.

Pitcher Plant Family (Sarraceniaceae)

YELLOW TRUMPETS *Sarracenia alata*
Note the long, *yellow-green, trumpetlike leaf with a hooded lid.* Single, nodding, pale yellow flowers. Leaf partly filled with a liquid that digests trapped insects, converting protein to nitrogen that the plant can absorb. 30–60 cm. Acid boggy slopes, piney woods. Eastern fifth of Tex., S.E. MARCH–APRIL

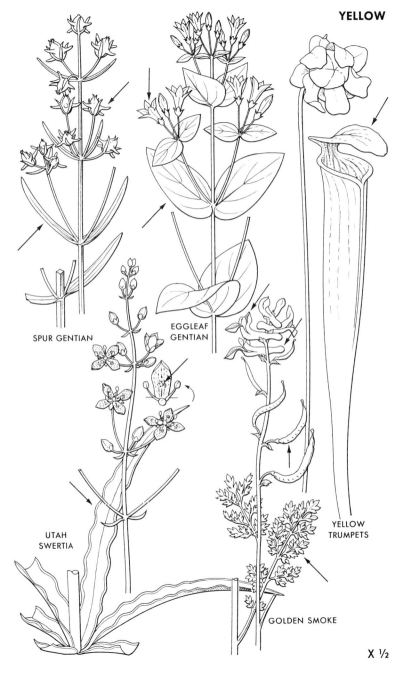

YELLOW

SPUR GENTIAN

EGGLEAF GENTIAN

UTAH SWERTIA

YELLOW TRUMPETS

GOLDEN SMOKE

X ½

5 TINY PETALS; FLOWERS IN UMBELS

 Carrot Family (Umbelliferae) See also pp. W 58–60; R 286.

SWEET FENNEL Alien *Foeniculum vulgare*
Tall, *waxy blue, canelike* stems. Leaves divided into *threadlike* lobes. Sweet licorice odor when handled. 1–2 m. Disturbed places. Edible. S.W., Tex., R. Mts. MARCH–MAY

MOUNTAIN PARSLEY *Pseudocympoterus montanus*
Note the *narrow, linear leaflets* on single or 3-branched petioles. *Leaves scattered up stem.* Stem base often purplish. Compound umbel. Flowers yellow, orangish, or purplish. A highly variable species. 20–70 cm. Common in grasslands, mountains. S.W., w. Tex., R. Mts. MAY–OCT.

STEMLESS ALETES *Aletes acaulis*
Note the *simple, broad-bladed leaflets* with sharp margins on the long central petiole. One compound flower umbel on a *leafless stem,* well above the basal leaves. 10–30 cm. Rocky cliffs, lower mountains. N.M., w. Tex., R. Mts. APRIL–AUG.

MACDOUGAL'S ALETES *Aletes macdougali*
Similar to Stemless Aletes, but *leaflets narrow and few,* on long, bare central petioles. 10–30 cm. Canyon rims, mesas. N. Ariz., nw. N.M., R. Mts. APRIL–JUNE

GOLDEN ALEXANDERS *Ziza aurea*
Leaves *pinnate;* lancelike to oval leaflets with *sawtoothed margins,* often in 3's. 30–60 cm. Sandy woods and floodplains. Eastern third of Tex., Pl. Sts., S.E. APRIL–AUG.

YELLOW PIMPERNEL *Taenidia integerrima*
Note the *undivided* oval leaflets with *smooth margins.* Leaves *sessile* (petioleless), but begin branching near base. *Leafy up entire stem.* Stem whitish. Compound flower umbels. 30 cm–1 m. Dry woods and bluffs. E. Tex., Pl. Sts., S.E.
MAY–JUNE

TEXAS PARSLEY *Polytaenia texana*
Note the tall (50 cm–1.5 m), coarse, yellow-green stem with a distinct *pyramid-shaped cluster* of basal leaves. *Reddish petiole bases.* Pinnate leaflets with *rounded* tips. Mature seeds have a *tapering lower end;* wing portion broader and thinner than seed body. 50 cm–1 m. Open prairies. Eastern half of Tex. APRIL–JULY

PRAIRIE PARSLEY *Polytaenia nuttallii*
Similar to Texas Parsley, but the pinnate leaflet tips are *sharply pointed.* Mature seeds *perfectly elliptical at both ends.* Wing portion narrow, thicker than seed body. 50 cm–1 m. Sandy soil, prairies, woods. Eastern half of Tex., S.E.
MAY–OCT.

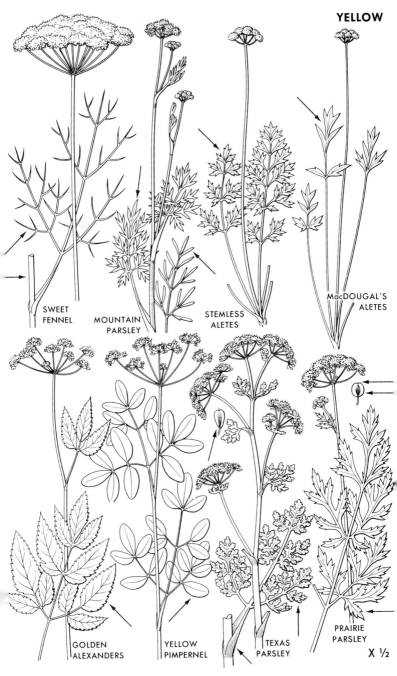

YELLOW

SWEET
FENNEL

MOUNTAIN
PARSLEY

STEMLESS
ALETES

MacDOUGAL'S
ALETES

GOLDEN
ALEXANDERS

YELLOW
PIMPERNEL

TEXAS
PARSLEY

PRAIRIE
PARSLEY

X ½

5 PETALS; FLOWERS IN UMBEL CLUSTERS; MILKY SAP: MILKWEEDS

Milkweed Family (Asclepiadaceae)
See also pp. W 66–72; O 234; R 302–304; G 404.

Note: See p. 67 for illustrations of special flower parts.

DESERT MILKWEED   *Asclepias erosa*
Tall, stout stems. Large, broadly oval, *bluish green* leaves with *feltlike gray hairs*. Flower has cream to dark yellow, *hollow-cheeked* hoods that resemble *corn kernels,* and *strongly down-swept* yellow-green petals below. Long horns usually protrude from hoods. 50 cm–1 m. Lower deserts along washes. W. Ariz.

APRIL–OCT.

LEMMON'S MILKWEED   *Asclepias lemmoni*
Tall, stout stems. *Broad, long, elliptical, bright green* leaves are *petioleless* and have 2 earlike basal lobes. Flowers pale pinkish with *earlike hoods* that have *short* projecting horns; on a *broad, triangular pedestal*. Downswept, yellow-green petals. 50 cm–1 m. Rocky slopes in mountains. S. Ariz.

JUNE–SEPT.

FOUR O'CLOCK MILKWEED   *Asclepias nyctaginifolia*
Low, *semi-prostrate stem.* Leaves oval to lancelike with *long petioles,* in opposite pairs. Hoods *elongated, erect cylinders,* with only the *horn tips protruding.* Flowers large, yellow-green, sometimes tinted with purple. Petals bent downward. 10–20 cm. Southern S.W.

MAY–AUG.

TUBA MILKWEED   *Asclepias tomentosa*
Stout, erect stems with broadly oblong to oval, dark green leaves in opposite pairs. Low, broad flowers. *Hoods short, tubalike,* with *protruding horns* ascending to the top of the column. Yellow-green petals bent downward, tinted with orange. 20–50 cm. Piney woods. E. Tex.

MAY–JULY

LONGHORN MILKWEED   *Asclepias macrotis*
Short, erect, *twiggy stem* with *narrow, grasslike leaves.* Pointed hoods *spread outward, like the horns of longhorn cattle.* Short, triangular horn tip protrudes near base of hood. Petals pale yellow-green to yellow with a reddish line on the back of each hood. Each umbel has few flowers. 10–30 cm. Dry limestone slopes. Se. Ariz. to w. Tex., se. Colo.

MAY–OCT.

SPERRY'S MILKWEED   *Asclepias sperryi*
Stem and leaves similar to Longhorn Milkweed. Few flowers yellow-green (may be purple-tinted), *flat, wheel-like.* Tubular hoods with *outer half bent at a right angle,* scooplike with a tiny pointed tip. 10–30 cm. Limestone ledges and open slopes. Se. N.M., w. Tex.

APRIL–AUG.

WHITERIM MILKWEED   *Asclepias involucrata*
Short, slender, *prostrate stems.* Leaves *troughlike,* narrowly triangular, and dark green with *white, wavy margins. Dark yellow,* urnlike hoods, taller than the *broad-based central column.* Short horns barely touch the column. Yellow-green petals. 5–20 cm. Gravelly dunes. S.W., R. Mts.

MARCH–MAY

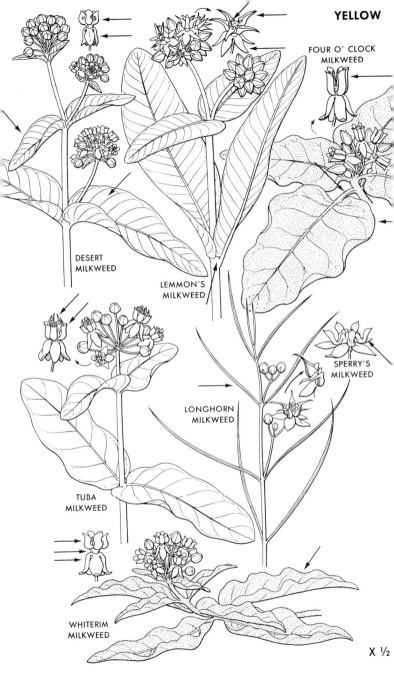

YELLOW

FOUR O' CLOCK MILKWEED

DESERT MILKWEED

LEMMON'S MILKWEED

SPERRY'S MILKWEED

LONGHORN MILKWEED

TUDA MILKWEED

WHITERIM MILKWEED

X ½

5 PETALS; STARS, URNS, TRUMPETS

Sedum Family (Crassulaceae) See also W 78; R 286.

PYGMY STONECROP *Tillaea erecta*
Tiny plant (2–5 cm) with short, fleshy, *oblong leaves* in oppo-site pairs. Stem well-branched. Many tiny flowers, becoming red with age. Grows in masses on rocks and mud. 2–10 cm. Lower elevations. Western half of Ariz. MARCH–APRIL

NUTTALL'S SEDUM *Sedum nuttallianum*
Starlike flowers on *prostrate, spreading stems*. Swollen, cylin-drical leaves in *alternate arrangement*. Shallow soil layers on open rocks. 5–15 cm. W.-cen. Tex. APRIL–JULY

LANCELEAF SEDUM *Sedum lanceolatum*
Both basal rosette and stem leaves *linear, round*. 5–20 cm. Rocky slopes. Northern S.W., R. Mts. JUNE–AUG.

COLLOM'S ECHEVERIA *Echeveria collomae*
Fleshy, lancelike leaves that are *broadest at basal end,* with *troughlike* upper sides. Bright yellow flowers, shaped like *long tubes*. 10–30 cm. Common on rocky slopes. Cen. Ariz.

MARCH–MAY

ARIZONA ECHEVERIA *Echeveria arizonica*
Basal cluster of *flat,* fleshy leaves that are *broadest at the upper end*. Tubular, urnlike flowers, apricot yellow to deep red. 5–30 cm. Shady cliffs. W. Ariz. FEB.–MARCH, OCT.–FEB.

Phlox Family (Polemoniaceae)
See also pp. W 88; O 234; R 308–312; B 360–362.

DESERT GOLD *Linanthus aureus*
Note the *golden, upright, funnel-like* flowers with orange to brown-purple throats. Branched, threadlike stems; 5–15 cm. Each leaf divided into 3–7 linear lobes. Common as massive carpets. Sandy places. S.W., w. Tex. MARCH–JUNE

YELLOW SKYPILOT *Polemonium viscosum*
This is subspecies *mellitum*. Dull yellow petals with short lobes on a long, trumpetlike tube. Flowers in terminal *headlike clus-ters on short stems*. Narrow, *long,* pinnate leaves with trilobed leaflets. 10–30 cm. Limestone cliffs. Scattered in mountains of S.W., R. Mts. JUNE–JULY

MARSH STARS *Polemonium flavum*
Broad, starlike yellow petal lobes on a very short tube hid-den within a sticky calyx tube. Flowers in headlike clusters on *tall stems* with alternate, *simple-pinnate leaves*. 50 cm–1 m. Marshy places in mountains. E. Ariz., sw. N.M. JULY–SEPT.

PINE TRUMPETS *Polemonium pauciflorum*
Note the *solitary, very long, pale yellow, trumpetlike flowers* scattered along the upper stem. Alternately arranged, simple-pinnate leaves. 50 cm–1 m. *Dry slopes* in higher mountains. Se. Ariz. JUNE–AUG.

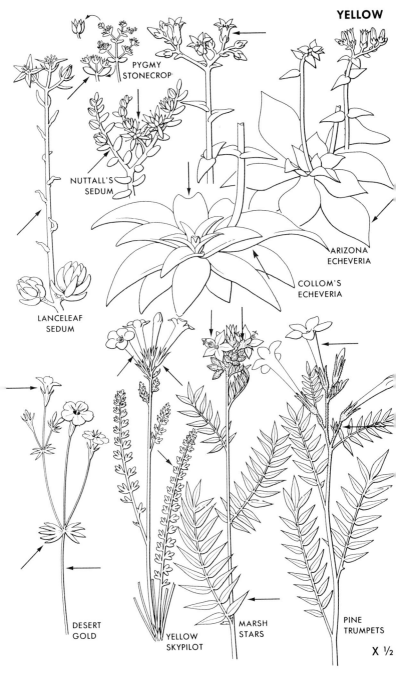

YELLOW

PYGMY STONECROP

NUTTALL'S SEDUM

LANCELEAF SEDUM

ARIZONA ECHEVERIA

COLLOM'S ECHEVERIA

DESERT GOLD

YELLOW SKYPILOT

MARSH STARS

PINE TRUMPETS

X ½

5 UNITED PETALS; SMALL PINWHEELS

Forget-me-not Family (Boraginaceae)
See also pp. W 84; O 234; R 314; B 344, 366.

PURPLE GROMWELL *Lithospermum multiflorum*
Note the *fat, semi-long, tapering, funnel-like,* deep yellow-orange flowers with *short petal lobes in nodding,* coiled clusters. Erect, tufted stems. Leaves *narrowly triangular and elongated.* Stems with *purple dye* at ground level. 30–60 cm. Open pine woods. S.W., R. Mts. MAY–JUNE

MOUNTAIN GROMWELL *Lithospermum cobrense*
Broad petal lobes on a short, semi-funnel-like corolla tube. Flowers pale yellow, on *erect coils* shaped like a *shepherd's crook.* Leaves *short,* lancelike, with *margins rolled under.* Stem and leaves gray with scattered short, stiff hairs. No purple dye on roots. 10–30 cm. Open conifer forests. S.W., w. Tex. JULY–AUG.

NARROWLEAF GROMWELL *Lithospermum incisum*
Note the dark yellow-orange, *ruffled* petal lobes above the *long, slender corolla tube.* Dark green, linear leaves, *slightly broader above the middle.* Erect stems. 10–30 cm. Common. S.W., Tex., R. Mts., Pl. Sts. NOV.–JUNE

TINYSTAR GROMWELL *Lithospermum tuberosum*
Tiny, pale yellow, starlike petal lobes on a short corolla tube *hidden within the calyx.* Coiled flower cluster, nearly hidden among the *broad, shiny, dark green,* lancelike leaves. Scattered coarse hairs on stem and under leaves. 30 cm–1 m. Hardwood forests. E. Tex., S.E. MARCH–APRIL

GIANT TRUMPETS *Macromeria viridiflora*
Note the *giant-sized cascading coils of hairy,* yellow-green, trumpetlike flowers. Stems tall, densely leaved. Dark green, broadly lancelike leaves. Erect stems in clusters. 50 cm–1 m. Midmountain meadows. N. Ariz., N.M. MAY–SEPT.

MOJAVE POPCORN FLOWER *Cryptantha confertiflora*
Note the *clublike cluster of both* pale and dark yellow flowers. Each petal has a conspicuous *small, toothlike inner lobe.* White, bristly-haired leaves. 10–60 cm. Often in juniper-pinyon pine plant community. Nw. Ariz., Ut. MAY–JUNE

Waterleaf Family (Hydrophyllaceae)
See also pp. W 82; R 312; B 364.

WHISPERING BELLS *Emmenanthe penduliflora*
Note the pale yellow, *nodding, bell-like* flowers on erect, glandular-haired stems. Leaves linear with *sawtoothed edges.* 10–50 cm. Lower elevations. W. Ariz., adjacent Ut.

MARCH–MAY

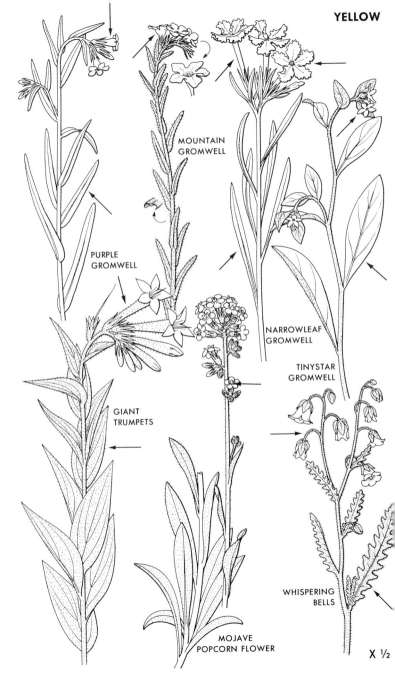

YELLOW

MOUNTAIN
GROMWELL

PURPLE
GROMWELL

NARROWLEAF
GROMWELL

TINYSTAR
GROMWELL

GIANT
TRUMPETS

WHISPERING
BELLS

MOJAVE
POPCORN FLOWER

X ½

5 PETALS; FLAT STARS, YELLOW BEAKS

Nightshade Family (Solanaceae)
See also pp. W 86; R 312; B 368.

BUFFALO BUR   *Solanum rostratum*
Note the *yellow-spined ovary and fruit. Watermelonlike,* pinnate leaves. Bright yellow, starlike flowers with projecting stamen beak. Spines cause intense pain if touched. 10–60 cm. Common in disturbed places. S.W., Tex., Pl. Sts.   APRIL–OCT.

VELVET FIVE-EYES   *Chamaesarcha sordida*
Sticky hairs variable, from short and feltlike to long and woolly. *All hairs unbranched.* Leaf blades with *wavy margins.* Flowers are flat stars, yellow, white, or bluish; note "eyes" at petal bases. 10–60 cm. Very common. S.W., western two-thirds of Tex., Pl. Sts.

           ALL YEAR

GREENLEAF FIVE-EYES   *Chamaesarcha coronopus*
Nonsticky green leaves with narrow blades; lobes have *narrow projecting tips.* Pale yellow flowers are flat, *rounded wheels* with sepals and petals fused (as in previous species); note the *white mounded spot* ("eye") at the base of each narrow, lancelike petal. 10–60 cm. Very common. S.W., western two-thirds of Tex., Pl. Sts.

           ALL YEAR

TOMATILLO Alien   *Physalis philadelphica*
Leaf blade *triangular.* Calyx becomes *lanternlike* around a purple berry. 30 cm–1 m. Disturbed places. S.W., Tex.   MOST OF YEAR

WRIGHT'S GROUND CHERRY   *Physalis acutifolia*
Flower *white,* disklike, with an *inner ring of yellow.* Leaves lancelike. 30 cm–1 m. S.W., w. Tex.   APRIL–SEPT.

HEARTLEAF GROUND CHERRY   *Physalis hederaefolia*
Leaves broad but short (less than 5 cm); *dark green* with some gray hairs. Leaf blades heart-shaped with *smooth, wavy margins.* The nodding, star-lobed petals are *bent downward* at margins; note the *solid black spots* on a lower base of pure white. Stems stickyhaired. 10–50 cm. S.W., Tex.   APRIL–SEPT.

CLAMMY GROUND CHERRY   *Physalis heterophylla*
Leaves *very broad and long* (5 cm or more). Leaf blades oval, yellow-green, with *rounded bases.* Nodding, star-lobed petals have *darker yellow basal areas* and a network of *dark brown lines.* Stems glandular, *clammy* to the touch. 30 cm–1 m. S.W., Tex., Pl. Sts.   APRIL–OCT.

VIRGINIA GROUND CHERRY   *Physalis virginiana*
Long, tapering leaf blades, *narrowly oval to lancelike.* Petals similar to Clammy Ground Cherry (above), but stem *not* clammy. 40 cm–1 m. Eastern half of Tex., Pl. Sts., S.E.   APRIL–OCT.

STARRYHAIR GROUND CHERRY   *Physalis viscosa*
Leaves lancelike with *long, tapering bases and no petiole.* Stem hairs *starlike* (use a hand lens to see) — the only ground cherry with starlike hairs. Flowers have black basal spots. 30–60 cm. N M., Tex., Pl. Sts.   MOST OF YEAR

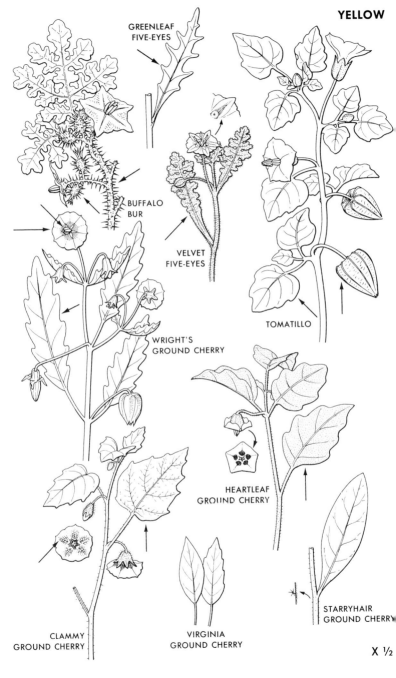

YELLOW

GREENLEAF
FIVE-EYES

BUFFALO
BUR

VELVET
FIVE-EYES

TOMATILLO

WRIGHT'S
GROUND CHERRY

HEARTLEAF
GROUND CHERRY

CLAMMY
GROUND CHERRY

VIRGINIA
GROUND CHERRY

STARRYHAIR
GROUND CHERRY

X ½

PASSION FLOWERS; WATER LILIES

Passion Flower Family (Passifloraceae)
See also pp. R 236; B 344.

YELLOW PASSION FLOWER   *Passiflora lutea*
Silver-dollar-sized flower has many *all-yellow, petal-like linear filaments* and a few broader, yellow-green petals below. *Broad, trilobed leaf blades.* Long, climbing vines with curling tendrils. Flowers open at dusk and last until the following midmorning. Shady woods. Cen. and e. Tex., Pl. Sts., S.E.   MAY–AUG.

BIRDWING PASSION FLOWER   *Passiflora tenuiloba*
Note the 2 *long, linear lobes* that resemble outspread *bird wings,* on either side of the short central lobe of each leaf blade. Each leaf has a central, *metallic-white area.* Yellow-green, linear filaments in a corona; *inner half* of filaments *purplish.* A few yellow-green, sepal-like petals below the corona. Vines with tendrils, climbing over shrubs. Southern N.M., sw. Tex.
APRIL–OCT.

Water Lily Family (Nymphaeaceae)
See also pp. W 6; B 344; G 406.

YELLOW COW LILY   *Nuphar luteum*
Round, dark yellow flowers (3–7 cm wide) with 6 petals. Large, shiny, heart-shaped leaves. Leaves floating, or well above the water level. Shallow ponds, sloughs, mudflats. Eastern half of Tex.   MARCH–OCT.

YELLOW LOTUS   *Nelumbo lutea*
Note the pale yellow flowers (10–20 cm across) with a *round, showerheadlike* central ovary. *Stamens radiate* around the edges of the ovary. Large, umbrella-like, floating or raised leaves. Shallow ponds, sluggish streams. Eastern third of Tex., Pl. Sts., S.E.   MAY–JULY

INDIAN POND LILY   *Nuphar polysepalum*
Flower yellow, with *9–12 petals.* Flowers wide, spreading. Large oval leaves, always floating. Shallow mountain ponds. Occasional in S.W., R. Mts.   APRIL–SEPT.

BANANA WATER LILY   *Nymphaea mexicana*
Large, bright yellow flowers with *about 25 petals and a center of many stamens.* Large, rounded to oval leaves with a narrow slit on one side. Banana-shaped roots in clusters. Ponds, lakes, sloughs. Eastern and s. Tex.   MAY–SEPT.

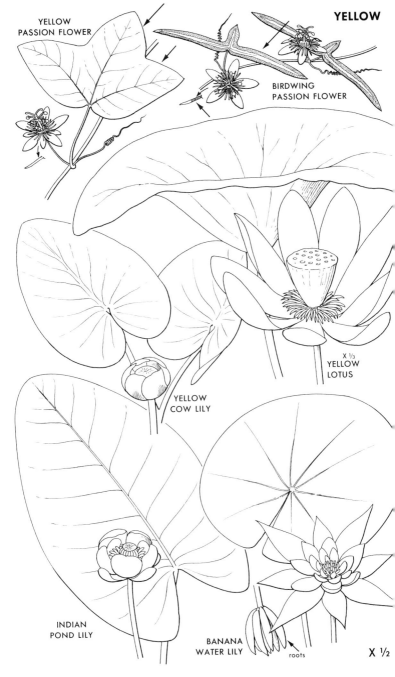

YELLOW
PASSION FLOWER

BIRDWING
PASSION FLOWER

X ⅓
YELLOW
LOTUS

YELLOW
COW LILY

INDIAN
POND LILY

BANANA
WATER LILY

roots

X ½

5 UNITED PETALS; 2-LIPPED FLOWERS

Bladderwort Family (Lentibulariaceae)
See also pp. W 92; R 298.

GREATER BLADDERWORT *Utricularia vulgaris*
Flowers protrude above the water. Spur petal *shorter than* lower lip. Threadlike leaves with scattered bladders that *float* horizontally below surface of water. 10–80 cm. Shallow or deep water. Scattered localities in S.W., Tex., Pl. Sts.

APRIL–AUG.

HORNED BLADDERWORT *Urticularia cornuta*
Note the *long, drooping spur petal* or "horn" (1 cm long). Bladders minute or absent. Simple, linear or grasslike leaves, embedded in mud. 10–40 cm. Muddy shores, bogs; near water but not in it. Eastern half of Tex., S.E. MAY–SEPT.

CONESPUR BLADDERWORT *Utricularia gibba*
Short stem (5–8 cm) with tiny flowers (5 mm across). *Tiny cone or hump-shaped spur* on back of each flower. Stems creep in mud and have few short filaments; bladders few. Mud, bogs, or on floating debris. Eastern half of Tex., Pl. Sts., S.E.

JUNE–AUG.

ZIGZAG BLADDERWORT *Utricularia subulata*
Note the *tiny, umbrella-shaped bracts* at base of each flower pedicel; *pedicel length equal* to corolla length. 10–20 cm. Grows in mud on seepage slopes, pond shores. E. Tex., S.E.

MARCH–JUNE

Broomrape Family (Orobanchaceae)
See also p. R 316.

MEXICAN SQUAWROOT *Conopholis mexicana*
Erect, *pale yellow, clublike stems.* Numerous curved flowers with *projecting, headlike stigmas.* Lower stem has scalelike, pale yellow leaves that lack chlorophyll. 10–30 cm. This plant is a saprophyte, living on decaying leaves and sticks in thick humus under pines, oaks, madrone. Mountains. S. Ariz. to Big Bend area of Tex. MARCH–JUNE

Mint Family (Labiatae)
See also pp. W 99; R 318; B 374–376.

YELLOW MINT *Agastache pallidiflora*
Note the *thick, long* terminal cluster of yellow-green bracts and pale yellow, 2-lipped, tubular flowers. *Stems square.* Leaves triangular with round-toothed margins, in opposite pairs. Strong mint odor. 10 cm–1 m. Coniferous forests. Mountains. Cen. Ariz., N.M., R. Mts. JULY–OCT.

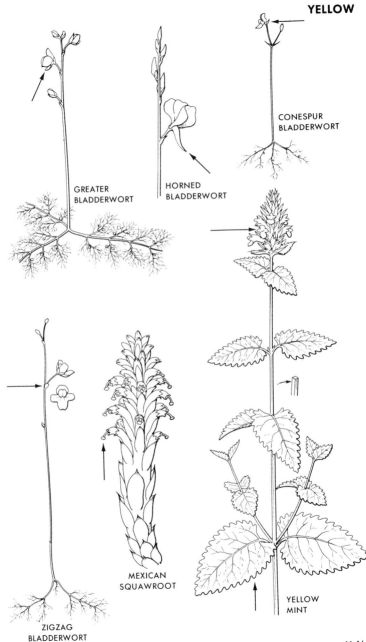

YELLOW

CONESPUR
BLADDERWORT

GREATER
BLADDERWORT

HORNED
BLADDERWORT

ZIGZAG
BLADDERWORT

MEXICAN
SQUAWROOT

YELLOW
MINT

X ½

MIMOSA & SENNA PEA SUBFAMILIES

Pea Family (Leguminosae)
See also pp. W 94–96; Y 190–196; R 320–328;
B 346–348, 380–382.

Pea Subfamily — Papilionoideae

Flowers *strongly asymmetrical (pealike),* with 1 upper banner
petal, 2 side wing petals, and 2 lower keel petals (see front
endpapers). 10 or fewer stamens with some or all of *basal filaments fused.* Leaves simple or once-pinnate. Members of the
pea family illustrated on all other pages belong to this subfamily.

Senna Subfamily — Caesalpinioideae

Differs from the main pea subfamily (Papilionoideae) in having
(1) *large flowers* that are (2) *barely asymmetrical* in shape and
irregular in arrangement, (3) 5–10 stamens, and (4) uppermost
petal the *most internal* in flowerbud.

PARTRIDGE PEA   *Cassia fasciculata*
Dark, red-purple stamens; red spots at base of each bright yellow petal. *Bright green, feathery* pinnate leaves that are *sensitive* (wilt when touched). Covers many areas in great masses.
50 cm–1 m. Eastern two-thirds of Tex., S.E.   JUNE–OCT.

TEXAS SENNA   *Cassia texana*
Flower parts *all bright yellow. Short, blue-green,* feathery
pinnate leaves. Many *short stems* arise from 1 central crown.
20–60 cm. S. Tex.   FEB.–MAY

TWOLEAF SENNA   *Cassia roemeriana*
Each leaf has *2 leaflets,* appearing *forked.* Large, deep yellow
flowers. 30–60 cm. Common in open fields, woods. Cen. and w.
Tex., N.M.   APRIL–MAY; SEPT.

Mimosa Subfamily — Mimosoideae

Differs from the main pea subfamily (Papilionoideae) in that
flowers are (1) *regularly* arranged, or nearly so; (2) leaves *doubly pinnate;* and (3) 4 to numerous stamens that are (4) *much
longer* than petals.

HOG POTATO   *Hoffmanseggia glauca*
Blue-green, twice-divided pinnate leaves in a basal cluster;
flower stem leafless. Open, irregular, pealike flower. Petals yellow or yellow-orange with *red-orange spots.* Underground,
potatolike tubers. 10–30 cm. Very common. S.W., w. Tex.

MARCH–SEPT.

YELLOW PUFF   *Neptunia lutea*
Note the *round or oval* flowerhead with *numerous stamens.*
Petals very small, not apparent. Compound pinnate leaves,
twice-divided; highly sensitive, folding (wilting) when touched.
Long, prostrate, running stems. Eastern half of Tex.

APRIL–OCT.

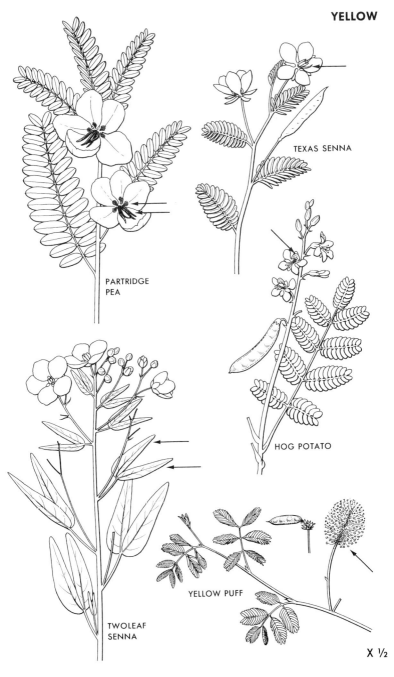

PARTRIDGE PEA

TEXAS SENNA

HOG POTATO

TWOLEAF SENNA

YELLOW PUFF

X ½

PEALIKE FLOWERS: LOTUS SPECIES

Pea Family (Leguminosae)
See also pp. W 94–96; Y 190–196; R 320–328;
B 346–348, 380–382.

GREENE'S LOTUS *Lotus greenei*
Stem and leaves covered with *dense gray hairs*. 1–2 large, banner-petaled, yellow flowers with reddish orange backsides. Each pinnate leaf has 4–5 *fanlike, clustered, short, spatula-like* leaflets. 30–60 cm. Rocky hillsides. Southern S.W.

MARCH–MAY

WIRY LOTUS *Lotus rigidus*
Very long, bare intervals between leaves. Stem and leaves *chalky gray*. 2–3 leaflets per pinnate leaf. 1–3 long, banner-petaled flowers on long peduncles. Ascending, wiry stems. 30 cm–1 m. Rocky slopes at lower elevations. Ariz.

NOV.–MAY

HILL LOTUS *Lotus humistratus*
A *single flower* above each *petioleless* leaf. Tiny yellow flower becomes red with age. Stem and leaves loosely gray-haired. 10–30 cm. Common at lower elevations. Ariz., sw. N.M.

MARCH–JUNE

UTAH LOTUS *Lotus utahensis*
Leaves dark green, pinnate, each with 4–5 *narrowly lancelike leaflets*. 2–3 large, yellow, banner-petaled flowers on long flower stalks and 2–3 leaflets directly below flowers. Petals bright yellow, either with or without a reddish tint. *Stems erect.* 10–30 cm. N. Ariz., Ut.

APRIL–SEPT.

WRIGHT'S LOTUS *Lotus wrightii*
Similar to Utah Lotus (above), but flowers *nestled next to leaflets; no flower stalk.* 20–40 cm. Very common in dry, open pine forests. S.W., R. Mts.

MAY–SEPT.

DESERT LOTUS *Lotus tomentellus*
Plants prostrate. Each succulent pinnate leaf has *5–6 blunt, grayish leaflets*. 1–2 flowers on each *long flower stem*. 5–25 cm. Very common on lowest deserts. Ariz., sw. Ut.

FEB.–MAY

BIRDSFOOT LOTUS Alien *Lotus corniculatus*
Note the *large pair* of almost *leaflike stipules* at the base of *each long leaf petiole*. 3 oblong leaflets per pinnate leaf. Flower yellow; the *extra long banner petal* may be tinted reddish. Dark green, prostrate stems; 10–60 cm. S.W., Tex., Pl. Sts.

JUNE–SEPT.

TORREY'S LOTUS *Lotus oblongifolius*
Each flower has a *yellow banner petal and white lower petals.* 1–3 leaflike bracts *immediately below* the flower umbel. 7–11 linear leaflets per pinnate leaf. Stem erect; 10–60 cm. Wet mountain meadows. S. Ariz.

JULY–SEPT.

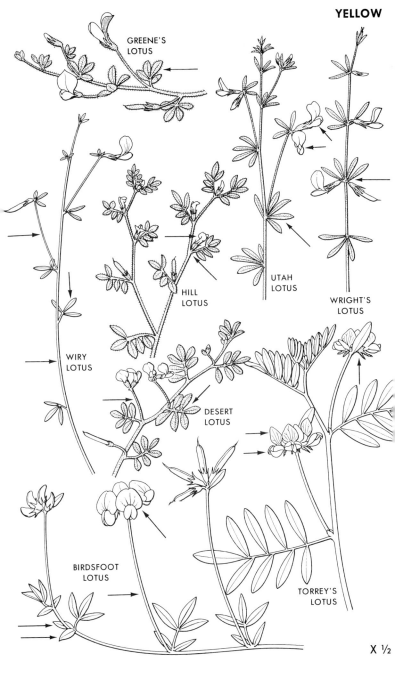

YELLOW

GREENE'S LOTUS

UTAH LOTUS

WRIGHT'S LOTUS

HILL LOTUS

WIRY LOTUS

DESERT LOTUS

BIRDSFOOT LOTUS

TORREY'S LOTUS

X ½

PEALIKE FLOWERS

Pea Family (Leguminosae)
See also pp. W 94–96; Y 190–196; R 320–328;
B 346–348, 380–382.

LANGUID WILD INDIGO   *Baptisia leucophaea*
Low, moundlike plant with *long, graceful sprays* of pale yellow
flowers that *curve downward* around the periphery. Mature
flower pedicels *3 or more cm* long. Each blue-green pinnate leaf
has 3 leaflets, and a *pair of leaflike stipules* at petiole base.
Yellow-green stems; 30 cm–1 m. Woods, dunes. Eastern third of
Tex., Pl. Sts., S.E.   FEB.–APRIL

UPRIGHT WILD INDIGO   *Baptisa sphaerocarpa*
Erect, oblong, mounded plant. Bright yellow flowers on *erect,
elongated* racemes. Flower *pedicels very short or absent.* Each
pinnate leaf has 3 leaflets. Yellow-green stem; 30 cm–1 m. Open
places in loamy soil. Eastern quarter of Tex., Pl. Sts., S.E.

MARCH–MAY

LITTLE-TREE WILD INDIGO   *Baptisia nuttalliana*
Erect, *treelike; lower stem bare.* Flowers pale yellow and *solitary.* Flowers seem to arise from the *central base* of the leaves;
each pinnate leaf has 3 leaflets. 50 cm–1 m. Common in woodlands. Eastern and n.-cen. Tex., Pl. Sts., S.E.   MARCH–MAY

LEAST SNOUTBEAN   *Rhynchosia minima*
Twining stringbeanlike vines. Each pinnate leaf has 3 *oval to
elliptical leaflets. Many* pale yellow to tan flowers with brownish markings on long flower stalks. Peapod broad, *limabeanlike.*
Common. S. Tex., east along Gulf Coast to Fla., also inland to
cen. Tex.   APRIL–DEC.

BROADLEAF SNOUTBEAN   *Rhynchosia latifolia*
Similar to Least Snoutbean, but *few flowers at tip* of each long
flower stalk. Peapod *long, slender.* Each pinnate leaf has 3 leaflets, which in turn have 3 *points each.* Long trailing vines.
Woodlands. Eastern third of Tex.   MAY–AUG.

PINE FALSE LUPINE   *Thermopsis pinetorum*
Large, bright yellow flowers in a terminal raceme much like
that of the lupines. However, each pinnate leaf has 3 *leaflets*
and a *large pair of oval, leaflike basal stipules.* 30–60 cm. Pine
forests, mountains. Ariz., northern N.M., R. Mts.

APRIL–JULY

LOW RATTLEBOX   *Crotalaria pumila*
Flowers yellow-orange with many *reddish streaks;* in a long
raceme. Each pinnate leaf has 3 leaflets. Stipules at base of
petiole *minute, threadlike.* Peapods *short, fat.* 10–30 cm. S.
Ariz. to sw. Tex.   JUNE–OCT.

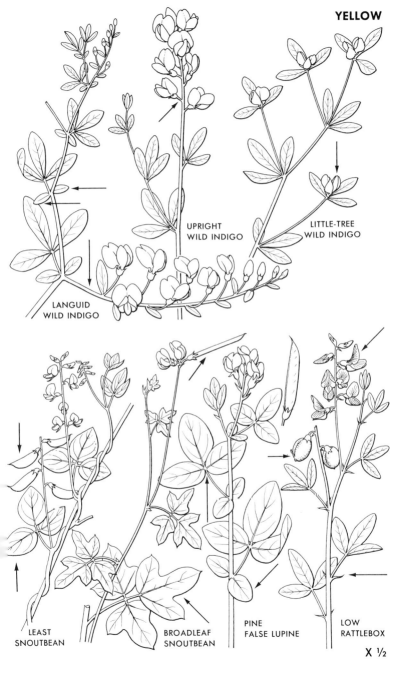

UPRIGHT
WILD INDIGO

LITTLE-TREE
WILD INDIGO

LANGUID
WILD INDIGO

LEAST
SNOUTBEAN

BROADLEAF
SNOUTBEAN

PINE
FALSE LUPINE

LOW
RATTLEBOX

X ½

PEALIKE FLOWERS

Pea Family (Leguminosae)
See also pp. W 94–96; Y 190–196; R 320–328;
B 346–348, 380–382.

GOLDEN SILKTHUMB *Dalea aurea*
Note the *silky, thumblike* terminal flowerhead with golden yellow flowers. Tall, erect, single stems with pinnate leaves, each having 5 (or 7) short, linear leaflets on a short petiole. 30–60 cm. E. Ariz.; more common in western two-thirds of Tex., occasional in rest of Tex. APRIL–JULY

SHAMROCK Alien *Trifolium dubium*
3 palmate leaflets with *blunt ends.* The leaf petiole base has *triangular, smooth-edged stipules. Tiny* pealike flowers in tiny *loose heads.* Stems prostrate, 10–50 cm. Many habitats. S.W., Tex. FEB.–JUNE

SPOTTED CLOVER Alien *Medicago arabica*
Each leaflet has a *reddish spot.* Seedpods are spiny spirals. 10–60 cm. Occasional. S.W., Tex., R. Mts. FEB.–JUNE

BUR CLOVER Alien *Medicago polymorpha*
Seedpods round, spiny spirals. Leaf stipules at base of leaf petiole *strongly fringed* with linear teeth. Each pinnate leaf has 3 leaflets with *strongly toothed margins.* Stem prostrate. 10–50 cm. Common in many habitats. S.W., Tex., Pl. Sts. MARCH–MAY

YELLOW SWEET CLOVER Alien *Melilotus indica*
Tiny pealike flowers in *long spikes.* Stem smooth. Each pinnate leaf has 3 leaflets on a long petiole. Large, triangular *stipules* at leaf petiole base. Emits a distinctive sweet odor on hot days. 30 cm–1 m. Disturbed places. S.W., Tex. APRIL–OCT.

COLORADO RIVER HEMP *Sesbania exaltata*
Long, feathery, pinnate leaves. Flowers with *purple-spotted banner* petals. Seedpod *pencil-like.* 30 cm–2.5 m. Floodplains, crop fields. Along Colorado R., w. Ariz., also eastern third of Tex. AUG.–OCT.

MOTTLED LOCOWEED *Astragalus lentiginosus*
Seedpod a strongly *inflated sausage* with a flattened, triangular tip that *curves upward.* Elongated, loose flower raceme. Pinnate blue-green leaves; each with 11–19 oval, nearly hairless leaflets that have *rounded tips.* Reddish stems. Flowers vary from yellow to white to red-purple. A highly variable species. 10–60 cm. S.W., R. Mts. FEB.–JUNE

CREAMY LOCOWEED *Astragalus racemosus*
Pale, creamy yellow flowers in *short terminal* (racemose) clusters on long, bare peduncles. 11–29 pinnate leaflets; *tips notched.* Stems pale yellow, erect, tufted. Seedpods flattened, peapodlike, with a *deep groove* on lower side. 30–60 cm. Plains region. Nw. Tex., e. N.M., Pl. Sts. MARCH–JUNE

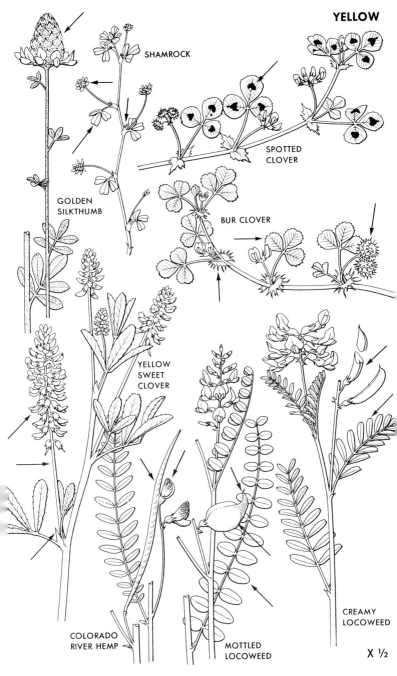

YELLOW

SHAMROCK

SPOTTED CLOVER

GOLDEN SILKTHUMB

BUR CLOVER

YELLOW SWEET CLOVER

COLORADO RIVER HEMP

MOTTLED LOCOWEED

CREAMY LOCOWEED

X ½

TRUE SUNFLOWERS

Sunflower Family (Compositae)

Sunflower Tribe: Heliantheae
See also pp. W 98–110; Y 198–222;
O 234; R 330–334; B 384–386; G 402.

KANSAS SUNFLOWER *Helianthus annuus*
The *petioled, broad, triangular leaf* blade has slightly toothed margins and is a dull green. Leaves *alternate.* Each flowerhead has numerous yellow ray flowers and a *reddish center* of disk flowers. State flower of Kansas. 20 cm–2.5 m. Very common. S.W., Tex., R. Mts. MARCH–OCT.

ASHY SUNFLOWER *Helianthus mollis*
Leaves *opposite,* with broad-based, ashy, gray-haired, oval to triangular leaf blades. Leaves *clasp* the stem and *lack petioles.* Large flowerheads with yellowish central disk flowers. 50 cm–1 m. Eastern half of Tex., Pl. Sts. JULY–OCT.

MAXIMILIAN'S SUNFLOWER *Helianthus maximiliani*
Note the *broad, long, linear leaves* that are folded upward in a V-*like trough.* Leaves alternate. Each stem has *many flowerheads in a towerlike column.* 30 cm–2.5 m. Tex., Pl. Sts.
SEPT.–NOV.

NUTTALL'S SUNFLOWER *Helianthus nuttallii*
Shiny, green, lancelike leaves, scattered in *pairs* along an elongated stem (30 cm–2 m). Leaves *with petioles.* Wet places. Northern S.W., R. Mts. AUG.–SEPT.

RIBBON SUNFLOWER *Helianthus angustifolius*
Narrow, ribbonlike leaves in *opposite pairs,* partly gray-haired. Each stem has a *few* flowerheads on *long, naked peduncles.* 50 cm–1.2 m. E. Tex. AUG.–OCT.

ARIZONA MULE'S EAR *Wyethia arizonica*
Note the *very large,* oblong to lancelike leaves that resemble *mule ears,* in a *low, mounded cluster.* Large, sunflowerlike flowerheads. 30 cm–1 m. S.W., R. Mts. JUNE–AUG.

SANDPAPER MULE'S EAR *Wyethia scabra*
Narrow, lancelike leaves in alternate arrangement, with a *stiff, rough, sandpaperlike surface.* Flowerhead bracts downturned. Low, mounded stem clusters. 30 cm–1 m. Open plains. N. Ariz., northern N.M., R. Mts. MAY–OCT.

PANAMINT SUNFLOWER *Enceliopsis argophylla*
Large, *silvery, spoonlike leaves* in a basal cluster. Huge sunflower heads on long naked stems. 30 cm–1 m. Rocky desert slopes. Nw. Ariz., adjacent Ut., Nev. APRIL–JUNE

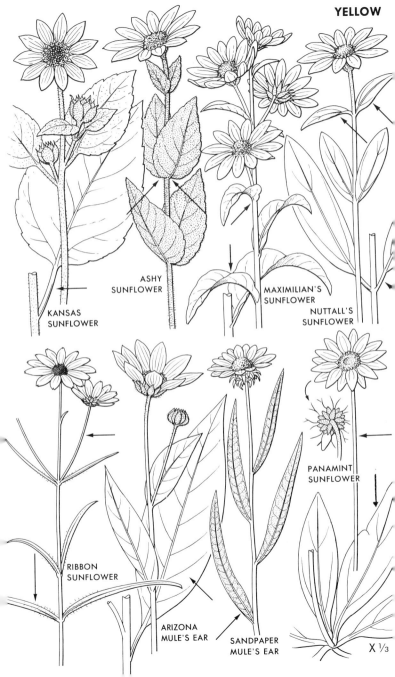

KANSAS
SUNFLOWER

ASHY
SUNFLOWER

MAXIMILIAN'S
SUNFLOWER

NUTTALL'S
SUNFLOWER

RIBBON
SUNFLOWER

ARIZONA
MULE'S EAR

SANDPAPER
MULE'S EAR

PANAMINT
SUNFLOWER

X ⅓

TRUE SUNFLOWERS

Sunflower Family (Compositae)

Sunflower Tribe: Heliantheae
See also pp. W 98–110; Y 198–222;
O 234; R 330–334; B 384–386; G 402.

PARRY'S SUNFLOWER *Helianthella parryi*
Note the *narrow, linear* basal leaves and a few similar ones further up the stem. Small flowerheads (5 cm wide). 20–50 cm. Near aspen groves in mountains. S.W., R. Mts.   JULY–SEPT.

FIVEVEINED SUNFLOWER *Helianthella quinquenervis*
Broad, lancelike leaf blades, mostly in a basal cluster. Leaves *petioleless;* leafblade veins divide into *5 major veins.* Sunflowerlike flowerhead. 50 cm–1 m. Often in meadows next to aspen groves. N.M., R. Mts.   JULY–OCT.

DESERT SUNFLOWER *Geraea canescens*
Leaf blades nearly *diamond-shaped* with a *sharp, triangular* upper half; occasional toothed margins. Covered by dense, velvety white hairs. Many golden flowerheads. 10 cm–1 m. Very common on desert flats. Western half of Ariz., Ut.

JAN.–JUNE

GOLDEN CROWNBEARD *Verbesina encelioides*
Note the *silver-gray, triangular* leaf blades with toothed margins. Stems develop many branches as plant ages. 10 cm–1 m. Very common. S.W., Tex.   APRIL–NOV.

CUTLEAF CONEFLOWER *Rudebeckia laciniata*
Leaves *large, deeply cut-lobed.* Large flowerhead *green, dome-shaped,* with all-yellow ray flowers. 50 cm–1 m. Mountain meadows and along streams. S.W., rarely in e. Tex., R. Mts., Pl. Sts.   JULY–SEPT.

BLACK-EYED SUSAN *Rudebeckia hirta*
Note the *red spots* at the bases of the yellow ray flowers (red spots absent in some areas). *Central cone of purplish* disk flowers. Leaves *short,* clasping the stem. 40–90 cm. Common. Eastern two-thirds of Tex., Pl. Sts., S.E.   MARCH–JULY

REDSPIKE MEXICAN HAT *Ratibida columnaris*
Note the *long, narrow, cylindrical* flowerhead with *dark red-purple* disk flowers. Ray flowers yellow or variously spotted with brown. Leaves *compound pinnate, with unequally cleft leaflets.* 10 cm–1 m. Common. S.W., Tex., R. Mts., Pl. Sts., S.E.   APRIL–SEPT.

GREEN MEXICAN HAT *Ratibida tagetes*
Note the *thick, short, drumlike* flowerhead with *yellow-green* disk flowers. Ray flowers all yellow or variously spotted with red-brown. Leaves pinnate with *simple linear leaflets.* 10–40 cm. N. Ariz. to cen. and n. Tex., Pl. Sts.   JUNE–SEPT.

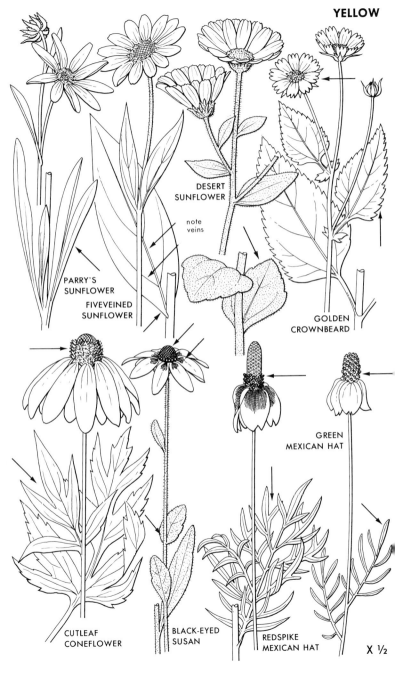

PARRY'S
SUNFLOWER

FIVEVEINED
SUNFLOWER

DESERT
SUNFLOWER

note
veins

GOLDEN
CROWNBEARD

GREEN
MEXICAN HAT

CUTLEAF
CONEFLOWER

BLACK-EYED
SUSAN

REDSPIKE
MEXICAN HAT

X ½

TRUE SUNFLOWERS

Sunflower Family (Compositae)

Sunflower Tribe: Heliantheae
See also pp. W 98–110; Y 198–222;
O 234; R 330–334; B 384–386; G 402.

TEXAS YELLOW STAR *Lindheimera texana*
Note the 5 *cupped,* bright yellow ray flowers. *Inner* flower-head bracts *large, rounded;* outer bracts *narrow, triangular.* Straplike leaves with a few toothed lobes. 10–40 cm. Common. Tex., Pl. Sts. FEB.–APRIL

TEXAS GREEN EYES *Berlandiera texana*
Note the *shallow, cuplike,* rounded flowerhead bracts below large yellow ray flowers. Central disk flower area *green, eyelike.* Petioled leaves, *broadly triangular* with coarsely toothed margins; *along the entire stem.* 30 cm–1 m. Woodland margins. Eastern half of Tex., Pl. Sts. MARCH–MAY

LYRELEAF GREEN EYES *Berlandiera lyrata*
Cuplike flowerhead bracts, as in Texas Green Eyes. Leaves *basal.* Leaf blades irregularly pinnate-lobed. Flowerheads on *long, leafless stems.* Red veins on undersides of ray flowers. 10 cm–1.2 m. Se. Ariz. to w. Tex., Pl. Sts. APRIL–OCT.

ENGELMANN'S SUNFLOWER *Engelmannia pinnatifida*
Pinnate leaves *lobed to base.* Lobes *short, linear;* tips vary from rounded right-angles to pointed. Many flowerheads on each stem. 10 cm–1 m. S.W., Tex., Pl. Sts. MARCH–SEPT.

PLAINS ZINNIA *Zinnia grandiflora*
Note the *few large* bright yellow, *nearly round* ray flowers and the tiny center with a few disk flowers in each flowerhead. Leaves linear, often somewhat *curled,* each with *3 ribs or veins.* 10–30 cm. Common in plains. S.W., w. Tex. MAY–OCT.

LAWNFLOWER *Calyptocarpus vialis*
Note *the tiny yellow flowerhead* with an elongated, dark green base. Flowerhead dwarfed by the surrounding dark green, *broadly oval leaves.* 2–10 cm. Frequent in lawns, disturbed places. Tex., S.E. ALL YEAR

ABERT'S DOME *Sanvitalia abertii*
Note the *sharp dome* of *elongated, greenish,* tubular disk flowers. Flowerhead *small,* with a *rim* of nearly round, bright yellow ray flowers. Long, lancelike leaves with 3 or more *lengthwise grooves;* in opposite pairs. 10–25 cm. Mountain slopes. S. Ariz., N.M., sw. Tex. JULY–SEPT.

ROUGH BLACKFOOT *Melampodium hispidum*
Small flowerheads; disk and ray flowers *both yellow.* Leaves opposite, narrowly lancelike, *broader toward tip.* 5–15 cm. Lower slopes of mountains in s. Ariz. and s. N.M. to Big Bend region of Tex. AUG.–OCT.

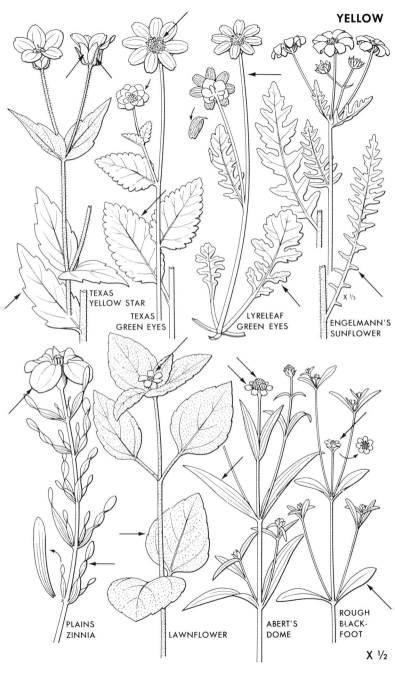

YELLOW

TEXAS
YELLOW STAR

TEXAS
GREEN EYES

LYRELEAF
GREEN EYES

ENGELMANN'S
SUNFLOWER

X ⅓

PLAINS
ZINNIA

LAWNFLOWER

ABERT'S
DOME

ROUGH
BLACK-
FOOT

X ½

COREOPSIS OR DAHLIALIKE FLOWERS

Sunflower Family (Compositae)

Sunflower Tribe: Heliantheae
See also pp. W 98–110; Y 198–222;
O 234; R 330–334; B 384–386; G 402.

GOLDENWAVES *Coreopsis tinctoria*
Outer flowerhead bracts *short, inconspicuous.* Ray flowers yellow with red-brown basal spots, or all yellow. Pinnate leaves with 2–3 pairs of *long, linear lobes.* 30 cm–1 m. Moist fields. S.W., Tex., Pl. Sts. FEB.–OCT.

DOUGLAS' COREOPSIS *Coreopsis douglasii*
Leaves basal, *nearly threadlike,* with 3 or more pinnate lobes. Outer row of flowerhead bracts *lancelike.* 5–25 cm. Rocky open places in lower deserts. Ariz. FEB.–MAY

NUECES COREOPSIS *Coreopsis nuecensis*
Leaves mostly basal, *pinnate* with *broad, oval lobes.* Outer flower-head bracts *linear, straplike.* Ray flowers often spotted with red-brown near bases. Upper flower stems naked. 10–60 cm. Common. S. Tex. MARCH–MAY

GOLDENMANE *Coreopsis basalis*
Stem leaves with 2 or more pairs of simple-pinnate leaves; leaflets vary from linear to elliptical. Some have an extra lobe shaped *like a rooster's spur* at the base. 20–50 cm. Common. Eastern third of Tex., occasionally west to N.M. FEB.–MAY

LANCELEAF COREOPSIS *Coreopsis lanceolata*
Note the *undivided, lancelike* leaf blades. Flowerhead has *triangular outer bracts.* 10–60 cm. E. Tex. MARCH–OCT.

BUR MARIGOLD *Bidens cernua*
Undivided, lancelike leaves with *toothed margins and no petioles.* Each flowerhead has a *few long, leaflike bracts* in the outer row. Older heads nodding. 50 cm–1.5 m. Marshes. Northern S.W., R. Mts., Pl. Sts. JULY–OCT.

NAVAJO GREENTHREAD *Thelesperma subnudum*
Blue-green inner flowerhead bracts form a cup; small outer row of bracts project *stiffly at right angles. Broadly diverging,* pinnate-lobed leaves. Single flowerheads on long, naked flower stalks. 30–60 cm. Northern S.W., R. Mts. MAY–SEPT.

SLENDER GREENTHREAD *Thelesprema simplicifolium*
Blue-green inner flowerhead bracts form a cup; *small outer row of bracts hugs* this inner cup. Yellow-green, *filamentlike,* pinnate leaves with 1 or a few pairs of side lobes. *Leafy up stem.* 30 cm–1 m. Western to n.-cen. Tex. APRIL–OCT.

HOPI-TEA GREENTHREAD *Thelesperma megapotamicum*
Note the *absence of ray flowers* in the flowerhead. Pinnate leaves *mostly basal,* with 2 or more *undivided, threadlike* side lobes. 30 cm–1 m. Eastern half of Ariz. to w. Tex. MAY–OCT.

DIVIDED GREENTHREAD *Thelesperma filifolium*
Ray flowers absent. Pinnate leaves divided 2–3 times. Stem and leaves gray, with cottony hairs. 30 cm–1 m. W. Tex. MAY–OCT.

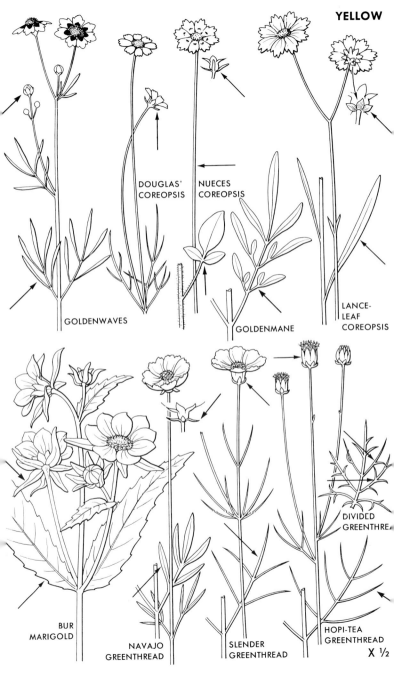

YELLOW

DOUGLAS'
COREOPSIS

NUECES
COREOPSIS

GOLDENWAVES

GOLDENMANE

LANCE-
LEAF
COREOPSIS

BUR
MARIGOLD

NAVAJO
GREENTHREAD

SLENDER
GREENTHREAD

HOPI-TEA
GREENTHREAD

DIVIDED
GREENTHRE

X ½

WOOLLY SUNFLOWERS

Sunflower Family (Compositae)

Woolly Sunflower Tribe: Helenieae
See also pp. W 98–110; Y 198–222;
O 234; R 330–334; B 384–386; G 402.

WOOLLY MARIGOLD *Baileya pleniradiata*
Many (20–40) *golden* to pale yellow ray flowers in each flowerhead. Plant parts with soft, white, woolly hairs. Leaves with *narrow, linear lobes,* withering rather early. Common on sandy plains. 10–60 cm. S.W., w. Tex., adjacent Ut.   FEB.–NOV.

DESERT MARIGOLD *Baileya multiradiata*
Similar to Woolly Marigold, but basal leaves *pinnate, broadly lobed, not withering early.* 10–60 cm. Sandy and rocky slopes. Deserts. S.W., w. Tex., Ut.   MARCH–NOV.

DROOPING MARIGOLD *Baileya pauciradiata*
5–7 drooping, pale lemon yellow ray flowers in each flowerhead. Stems well-branched, with soft, woolly hairs. Pinnate leaves with *linear teeth.* 10–60 cm. Common on sand dunes in lower deserts. Sw. Ariz.   MARCH–MAY

WOOLLY SUNFLOWER *Eriophyllum lanatum*
Numerous, solitary, large yellow flowerheads, each with 8–13 ray flowers on a *long, leafless* peduncle. Leaves and stem covered with *loosely clumping, gray, woolly hairs.* Upper leaves linear, lower leaves thin and pinnate. 10 cm–1 m. Very common in lower deserts. Western and s. Ariz., Ut.   FEB.–MAY

WALLACE'S WOOLLY DAISY *Antheropeas wallacei*
A miniature, tufted plant. Leaves spatula-like with dense, *white, woolly hairs; tips rounded.* Flowerheads on short, leafless peduncles. 2–10 cm. Sandy flats. Western half of Ariz., s. Ut.

MARCH–JUNE

PRINGLE'S WOOLLYLEAF *Eriophyllum pringlei*
Miniature, tufted plant. Leaves linear, with *3 lobes* at tips and *dense, white, woolly hairs.* Flowerheads all disk flowers (no rays). 2–5 cm. Sandy desert flats. Western and s. Ariz., s. Ut.

MARCH–MAY

COOPER'S PAPERFLOWER *Psilostrophe cooperi*
Note the large, *somewhat squat* ray flowers and *linear* leaves. Low, mounded plant. 10–60 cm. Rocky slopes, middle to low elevations. Ariz., w. N.M., s. Ut.   MOST OF YEAR

TAPERLEAF *Pericome caudata*
Note the triangular leaf blades with *long, tapering tips.* Flowerheads all disk flowers (no rays). 30 cm–1.5 m. S.W., w. Tex., R. Mts.   JULY–OCT.

YELLOWHEAD *Trichoptilium incisum*
Elongated leaves with *spiny teeth* and woolly hairs on a low, well-branched stem. *Pincushion-like* flowerheads with disk flowers only, well above the leaves. Grows in broad mats. 5–20 cm. Lower deserts. W. Ariz.   FEB.–MAY

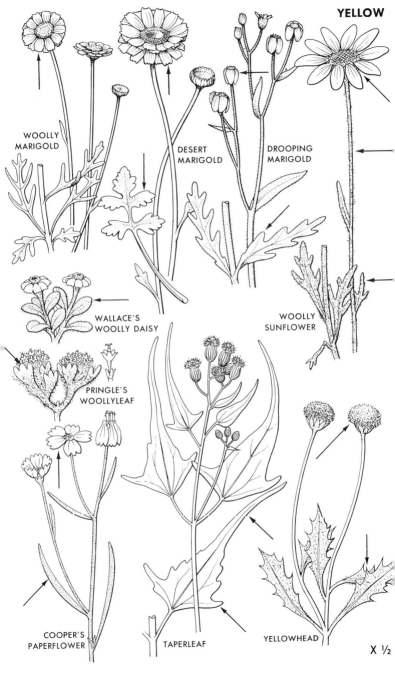

YELLOW

WOOLLY
MARIGOLD

DESERT
MARIGOLD

DROOPING
MARIGOLD

WOOLLY
SUNFLOWER

WALLACE'S
WOOLLY DAISY

PRINGLE'S
WOOLLYLEAF

COOPER'S
PAPERFLOWER

TAPERLEAF

YELLOWHEAD

X ½

WOOLLY SUNFLOWERS

Sunflower Family (Compositae)

Woolly Sunflower Tribe: Helenieae
See also pp. W 98–110; Y 198–222;
O 234; R 330–334; B 384–386; G 402.

ARIZONA BLANKETFLOWER *Gaillardia arizonica*
All parts of flowerhead bright yellow. Flowerheads on completely *leafless stems;* all leaves in basal clusters. Pinnate leaves with deeply cut, *round-lobed leaflets.* 10–30 cm. Lower mesas and desert plains. Ariz., s. Ut. FEB.–JULY

REDDOME BLANKETFLOWER *Gaillardia pinnatifida*
Ray flowers completely yellow; *rounded dome* of disk flowers *dark red.* Leaves *partly up stem.* Pinnate leaves with irregularly diverging, straplike lobes, each lobe edged with smaller, *spiny teeth.* 10–40 cm. Plains, forests. S.W., western and northern Tex., Pl. Sts. APRIL–NOV.

FINELEAF WOOLLYWHITE *Hymenopappus filifolius*
Grayish green, pinnate leaves, divided twice into *short, threadlike segments.* Stems with white to gray, feltlike hairs. Leaves may be basal *or* extend up most of stem. Flowerheads large, with all disk flowers that have enlarged, *doughnutlike corollas* and a *long, projecting* stamen and style column. A highly variable species. 10 cm–1 m. S.W., western and northern Tex., Pl. Sts. MAY–SEPT.

MEXICAN WOOLLYWHITE *Hymenopappus mexicanus*
Leaves mostly basal, with *single or partly lobed, lancelike* leaflets. Flowers similar to those of Fineleaf Woollywhite. 10 cm–1 m. Middle to high mountains. S.W., w. Tex. JUNE–SEPT.

RAGLEAF BAHIA *Bahia dissecta*
Short, compound pinnate leaves divided 2 or 3 times, dwarfed by the tall stem. Leaves widely spaced. 10 cm–1 m. Common in grasslands, forests. S.W., w. Tex., R. Mts. AUG.–OCT.

COMMON DOGWEED *Dyssodia pentachaeta*
Shiny, triangular flowerhead bracts, *fused, and dotted with orange glands.* Leaves with linear lobes, spine-tipped. Bad smelling if handled. Low mounds with wiry, naked flower stems. 10–30 cm. S.W., western two-thirds of Tex.
APRIL–NOV.

CHINCHWEED *Pectis papposa*
Shiny, linear, riblike flowerhead bracts are *free to base* and *dotted with orange glands.* Leaves linear-lobed, with spines near base. Bad odor if handled. 10–30 cm. Very common. Middle to lower elevations. S.W., w. Tex. JUNE–NOV.

LEMMON'S MARIGOLD *Tagetes lemmoni*
Note the *shiny, cylindrical* flowerhead bracts with *glandular orange streaks.* Few large, long-lobed pinnate leaves with sharply *sawtoothed* margins. Tall, leafy stems. 30 cm–1 m. Very common in mountain woods. S. Ariz. AUG.–OCT.

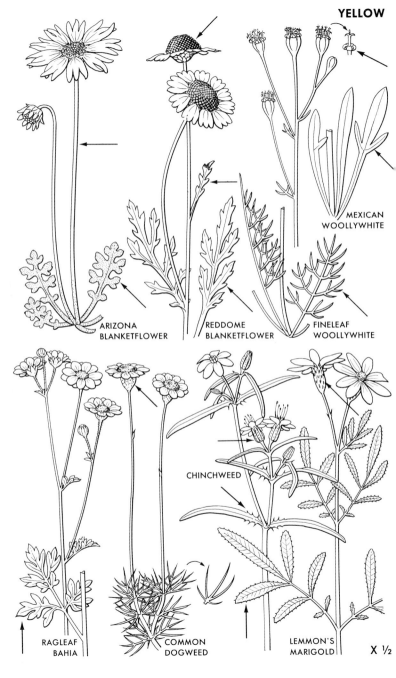

YELLOW

MEXICAN WOOLLYWHITE

ARIZONA BLANKETFLOWER

REDDOME BLANKETFLOWER

FINELEAF WOOLLYWHITE

RAGLEAF BAHIA

COMMON DOGWEED

CHINCHWEED

LEMMON'S MARIGOLD

X ½

GOLDFLOWERS

Sunflower Family (Compositae)

Woolly Sunflower Tribe: Helenieae
See also pp. W 98–110; Y 198–222;
O 234; R 330–334; B 384–386; G 402.

MOUNTAIN HELENIUM   *Helenium hoopesii*
Large, flat flowerheads with many *yellow-orange ray flowers.*
Leaves long and narrow; *base does not extend* down stem. 30 cm–
1 m. Common in mountain meadows. S.W., R. Mts. JUNE–SEPT.

WESTERN SNEEZEWEED   *Helenium autumnale*
Round, purple-brown flowerhead has 10–20 yellow ray flowers that
bend downward. Leaves with sawtoothed margins; *base extends
down stem.* 10–70 cm. Meadows. S.W., Tex., Pl. Sts. JULY–OCT.

LITTLEHEAD SNEEZEWEED   *Helenium microcephalum*
Small, red-brown flowerheads with many *short,* yellow *ray flowers*
that bend downward. Leaves *straplike with ragged, torn margins;
base extends down the main stem* in broad wings. 30 cm–1 m. Damp
places. Se. N.M., western two-thirds of Tex., Pl. Sts.

                                        MARCH–JUNE; FALL

DRUMMOND'S SNEEZEWEED   *Helenium drummondii*
Flowerhead of *narrow, yellow ray flowers* around a *bright yellow,
rounded dome* of disk flowers. *Narrow, sharp-pointed leaves;* leaf
bases extend winglike down the main stem. 30–60 cm. Standing
water. E. Tex.   MARCH–APRIL

DESERT GOLDFIELDS   *Lasthenia chrysotoma*
Bottom half of ray petals yellow-orange; *petal tips a lighter yellow.*
Flowerhead *bracts free* from each other. Stem slender, short, with
opposite pairs of linear leaves. Forms carpets of gold. 5–20 cm. Deserts. Ariz.   MARCH–MAY

STEMLESS GOLDFLOWER   *Hymenoxys acaulis*
Low, tufted, stemless clusters of linear, *undivided leaves.* Flowers
on leafless stems. A variable species. 10–30 cm. Lower plains to high
mountains. Northern S.W., R. Mts.   APRIL–OCT.

ALPINE GOLDFLOWER   *Hymenoxys grandiflora*
Low, basal clusters of linear leaves, *subdivided into a few lobes.*
Flower stems loosely woolly. *Large, broad* flowerheads. 10–30 cm.
Alpine tundra. N.M., R. Mts.   JUNE–SEPT.

CLUSTERED GOLDFLOWER   *Hymenoxys scaposa*
Similar to Stemless Goldflower (above). Leaves linear to lobed, all
in a basal tuft. Flowers on *very long, thin, wiry stems,* well above
leaves. Underside of yellow ray flowers may or may not have *red-
brown veins.* 10–40 cm. Very common. N.M., Tex., Pl. Sts.

                                 FEB.–JUNE, SEPT.–OCT.

STEMMED GOLDFLOWER   *Hymenoxys linearifolia*
Linear, spatula-like leaves, *scattered up stem. Outer half* of ray
flowers pale yellow. 10–50 cm. Eastern N.M., Tex. MARCH–NOV.

COOPER'S GOLDFLOWER   *Hymenoxys cooperi*
Note the *gray,* pinnate leaves with *linear lobes.* Leaves *thickly
cover the entire erect stem.* Many flowers on each stem. 30 cm–1 m.
Rocky slopes. N. Ariz., R. Mts.   MAY–SEPT.

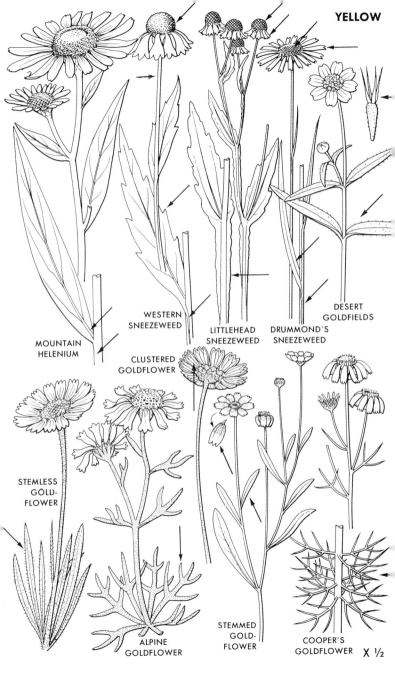

YELLOW

MOUNTAIN
HELENIUM

WESTERN
SNEEZEWEED

CLUSTERED
GOLDFLOWER

LITTLEHEAD
SNEEZEWEED

DRUMMOND'S
SNEEZEWEED

DESERT
GOLDFIELDS

STEMLESS
GOLD-
FLOWER

ALPINE
GOLDFLOWER

STEMMED
GOLD-
FLOWER

COOPER'S
GOLDFLOWER

X ½

ARNICAS, BUTTERWEEDS

Sunflower Family (Compositae)

Senecio Tribe: Senecioneae
See also pp. W 98–110; Y 198–222;
O 234; R 330–334; B 384–386; G 402.

HEARTLEAF ARNICA *Arnica cordifolia*
Note the *2–3 pairs of heart-shaped leaves.* Flowerhead of 9–14 ray flowers with *pointed tips.* 10–50 cm. Mountain forests. Northern S.W., R. Mts. JUNE–AUG.

MEADOW ARNICA *Arnica chamissonis*
Note the solitary, erect stem with *5–12 pairs of broad, lancelike leaves.* The flowerheads have somewhat round, pointed bracts, each with a *tuft of long hairs* just inside the tip. 30 cm–1 m. Moist mountain meadows. Northern S.W., R. Mts.

JUNE–AUG.

ALPINE BUTTERWEED *Senecio werneriaefolius*
Narrow, spatula-like leaves with *smooth margins* in basal clusters, well below the large, dark golden yellow flowerheads with *domelike centers.* 5–25 cm. Rocky, subalpine and alpine slopes. Northern S.W., R. Mts. JUNE–AUG.

THICKLEAF BUTTERWEED *Senecio crassulus*
Short, broad, variously oblong leaves with *torn margin lobes* that have *spiny tips.* Single, large, terminal flowerheads. 8–20 cm. Mountain meadows. Northern N.M., R. Mts.

JULY–AUG.

BITTERCRESS BUTTERWEED *Senecio cardamine*
Note the *large, rounded terminal leaflet* and 2 or more opposite pairs of similar, but smaller leaflets along the petiole. (Much like the leaves of Cardamine, on p. 32.) Single, erect stem. 30–60 cm. Mountains. E. Ariz., cen. N.M. JULY–AUG.

DANDELION BUTTERWEED *Senecio taraxacoides*
Narrow, spatulalike leaves with *sharply toothed margins,* similar to true dandelion leaves. The single large flowerhead has narrow, pointed ray flowers. 10–30 cm. Alpine meadows. Northern N.M., R. Mts. JULY–AUG.

COMMON BUTTERWEED Alien *Senecio vulgaris*
Pinnate leaves up entire stem. Clusters of pincushionlike flowerheads that are composed *entirely of disk flowers.* Flowerhead bracts *black-tipped.* Milky sap. 10–50 cm. Common. S.W., R. Mts. MUCH OF YEAR

FENDLER'S BUTTERWEED *Senecio fendleri*
Leaves *strongly pinnate-lobed,* in opposite pairs; the tips with a few rounded, notched edges. *Numerous small flowers* in terminal clusters. 5–20 cm. Mountains. N.M., R. Mts. JULY–AUG.

DESERT TURTLEBACK *Psathyrotes ramosissima*
White, velvety-haired leaves, round to kidney-shaped, in compact, *turtlelike mounds.* Yellow, pincushionlike heads (of disk flowers only) that turn purple with age. Strong turpentine odor. 2–12 cm. Common, lower desert flats. W. Ariz. FEB.–MAY

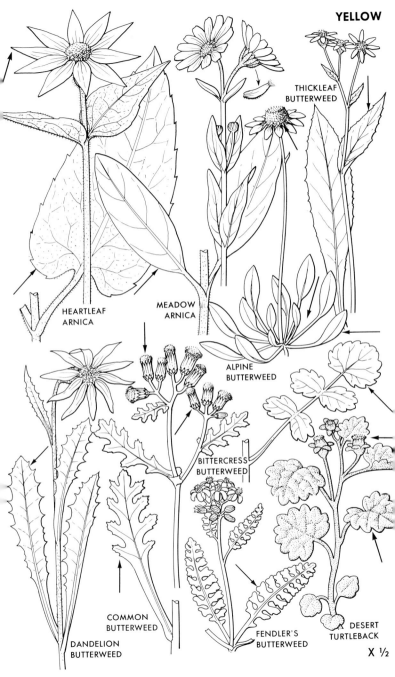

THICKLEAF BUTTERWEED

HEARTLEAF ARNICA

MEADOW ARNICA

ALPINE BUTTERWEED

BITTERCRESS BUTTERWEED

DANDELION BUTTERWEED

COMMON BUTTERWEED

FENDLER'S BUTTERWEED

DESERT TURTLEBACK

X ½

TALL-STEMMED BUTTERWEEDS

Sunflower Family (Compositae)

Senecio Tribe: Senecioneae
See also pp. W 98–110; Y 198–222;
O 234; R 330–334; B 384–386; G 402.

ARROWHEAD BUTTERWEED　　　　*Senecio triangularis*
Numerous *arrow-shaped leaves* alternating up entire stem. 30 cm–1 m. Wet mountain streamsides. Northern N.M., R. Mts.
JUNE–SEPT.

**ROCKY MOUNTAIN
BUTTERWEED**　　　　*Senecio cymbalarioides*
Blunt, toothed, somewhat butter-fork-like leaves in a basal rosette. Flower stem leafless. 10–40 cm. Mountain meadows. Northern N.M., R. Mts.
JULY–AUG.

LEMMON'S BUTTERWEED　　　　*Senecio lemmonii*
Leaves *elongated; narrowly spearlike,* with *earlike* bases that clasp the stem. Stems highly branched. 20 cm–1 m. Common on rocky slopes, low-elevation deserts. Western two-thirds of Ariz.
FEB.–MAY

TEXAS BUTTERWEED　　　　*Senecio ampullaceus*
Note the *clumpy, woolly gray hair* on the *spoonlike basal* leaves and the *narrow, triangular upper* stem leaves. 30 cm–1 m. Tex.
FEB.–APRIL

NEW MEXICO BUTTERWEED　　　　*Senecio neomexicanus*
Long, oval to lancelike leaf blades with *sharp, sawtoothed* (as if cut by pinking shears) *to wavy margins.* Plant parts with gray, woolly hairs. Single, erect stems with many basal leaves; leaves smaller toward top of stem. Many flowerheads in terminal clusters. 20–80 cm. Forests. *The most common butterweed* of S.W., R. Mts.
APRIL–AUG.

WOOTON'S BUTTERWEED　　　　*Senecio wootonii*
Bright green, smooth, spatula- to spoonlike leaves with a *narrow-leafed zone* between blade and petiole base. Leaves all basal. *Few* flowerheads at top of *single, leafless stem.* 20–60 cm. Higher mountains. S.W., w. Tex., R. Mts.
APRIL–SEPT.

SHOWY ALPINE BUTTERWEED　　　　*Senecio amplectens*
Large, broad, straplike leaves with base *clasping* the stem and small, coarse teeth at margins. Leafy up entire stem. Flower buds *nodding.* 10–50 cm. High mountains. N.M.
JUNE–OCT.

AXHEAD BUTTERWEED　　　　*Senecio multilobatus*
Pinnate leaves, divided into many *tiny, sharply-lobed* leaflets. Single, erect stem. Many flowerheads in a flat-topped cyme (not shown). 10 cm–1 m. Mesas. N. Ariz., R. Mts.
APRIL–AUG.

DOUGLAS' BUTTERWEED　　　　*Senecio douglasii*
Note the *gray,* woolly-haired, *stringy,* pinnate leaves with linear lobes. Leafy up entire stem. *Poisonous.* 30 cm–1.5 m. Common at lower elevations. S.W., western half of Tex.
MOST OF YEAR

COMB BUTTERWEED　　　　*Senecio monoensis*
Yellow-green, *comblike,* pinnate leaves with linear lobes, alternating up entire stem. Stem single, erect. 30 cm–1.5 m. Ariz., Ut.
MOST OF YEAR

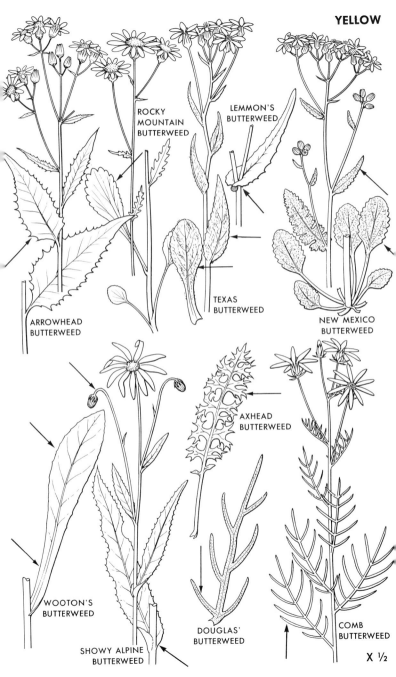

YELLOW

ROCKY MOUNTAIN BUTTERWEED

LEMMON'S BUTTERWEED

NEW MEXICO BUTTERWEED

ARROWHEAD BUTTERWEED

TEXAS BUTTERWEED

AXHEAD BUTTERWEED

WOOTON'S BUTTERWEED

SHOWY ALPINE BUTTERWEED

DOUGLAS' BUTTERWEED

COMB BUTTERWEED

X ½

ASTERS, GUMPLANTS, GOLDENRODS

Sunflower Family (Compositae)

Aster Tribe: Astereae
See also pp. W 98–110; Y 198–222;
O 234; R 330–334; B 384–386; G 402.

TEXAS SLEEPY ASTER   *Xanthisma texanum*
Note the *broad, sharply pointed, white-margined,* triangular flowerhead bracts. Alternate, straplike leaves up entire stem. Many *sharply pointed,* bright yellow ray flowers per head. 10–70 cm. Grows in great masses. Tex., Pl. Sts.   APRIL–NOV.

STRAPLEAF SPINE ASTER   *Machaeranthera spinulosa*
Note the *spine-tipped, narrow, linear* leaves with sharp, short lobes. Plant parts grayish, with cottony hairs. Wiry stems. 10–60 cm. S.W., Tex.   MARCH–OCT.

FEATHERLEAF SPINE ASTER   *Machaeranthera australis*
Pinnate, featherlike leaflets with *spiny tips.* Grayish cottony hairs. Narrow ray flowers. 10–40 cm. Common. Western third of Tex.
  APRIL–OCT.

MOUNTAIN GUMPLANT   *Grindelia aphanactis*
Ball-like flowerhead of many rounded, linear, *semi-hooked bracts;* flowerhead *all disk flowers.* Short, straplike leaves with sawtoothed margins. 10–40 cm. S.W., w. Tex., R. Mts.   JUNE–OCT.

CURLYCUP GUMPLANT   *Grindelia squarrosa*
Similar to Mountain Gumplant, but *ray flowers present.* 10–40 cm. S.W., western and northern Tex.   JUNE–OCT.

ALPINE GOLDENROD   *Solidago multiradiata*
Stem erect; leaves broadly *spatula-shaped.* Many small flowerheads in a *tight, clublike cluster.* 30 cm–1 m. Mountain meadows, tundra. S.W., R. Mts.   JULY–SEPT.

TELEGRAPH WEED   *Heterotheca grandiflora*
Note the many large, rounded flowerheads with linear yellow ray flowers. All flowerheads in a dense cluster near the top of the stem, which is usually *single, erect,* and *telegraph-pole-like.* Thick leaves, covered with dense, very short *white hairs.* Smells strongly like creosote. 30 cm–1 m. Open places. Ariz.   SEPT.–OCT.

HAIRY GOLDEN ASTER   *Heterotheca villosa*
Erect stems in bushy clumps. *Many oblong, gray-green leaves,* which are somewhat *glandular-haired.* Each flowerhead has 10–16 ray flowers. 5–50 cm. Common. S.W., w. Tex.   MAY–OCT.

GIANT GOLDENROD   *Solidago gigantea*
Note the widely branching flower stems with many small, cylindrical flowerheads. Tall stems, well covered by *lancelike* leaves with *3 main veins.* 50 cm–2 m. Moist hollows. Eastern N.M., Tex.
  AUG.–OCT.

CANADA GOLDENROD (not shown)   *Solidago canadensis*
Very similar to Giant Goldenrod, but found in mountains of Ariz., cen. N.M., and Pl. Sts.   AUG.–OCT.

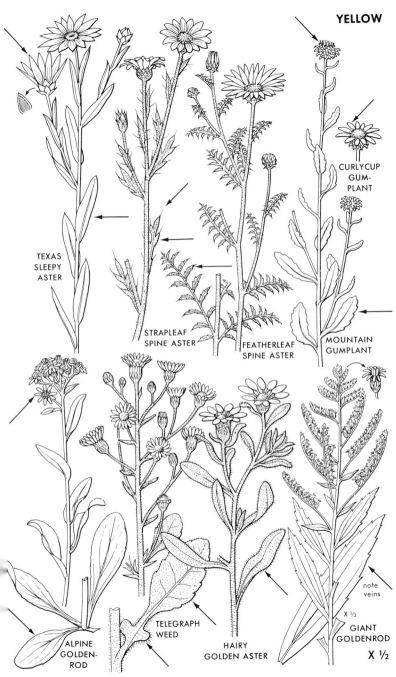

YELLOW

TEXAS
SLEEPY
ASTER

STRAPLEAF
SPINE ASTER

FEATHERLEAF
SPINE ASTER

CURLYCUP
GUM-
PLANT

MOUNTAIN
GUMPLANT

ALPINE
GOLDEN-
ROD

TELEGRAPH
WEED

HAIRY
GOLDEN ASTER

note
veins

X ⅓

GIANT
GOLDENROD

X ½

THISTLES, MAYWEEDS, CHICORIES

Sunflower Family (Compositae)
See also pp. W 98–110; Y 198–222;
O 234; R 330–334; B 384–386; G 402.

PARRY'S THISTLE *Cirsium parryi*
Note the *tall stem with thick clusters* of spiny, yellow-green
flowerheads. Leaf blades broadly triangular with *short,* spiny
margin lobes. 50 cm–1 m. Forest openings, mountain meadows.
S.W., R. Mts. JULY–SEPT.

YELLOW THISTLE *Cirsium horridulum*
Note the huge, *usually flat* (or nearly so) circle of *deeply
triangular-lobed* leaves with spiny tips. 1 or more huge, spiny,
central flowerheads. 10–60 cm. Eastern half of Tex.

MARCH–MAY

YELLOW STAR THISTLE Alien *Centaurea solstitialis*
Note the *long yellow spines* extending from the yellow flowerheads. Leaves linear, *extending like wings down the stem.* Stem
leaves with cottony hairs. Well-branched. 30 cm–1 m. Disturbed places. Occasional. S.W., Tex. APRIL–NOV.

Mayweed Tribe: Anthemidae

PINEAPPLE WEED Alien *Matricaria matricarioides*
Note the yellow-green, *pineapple-shaped flower cones* above
lacy, pinnate leaves. Strong odor. 5–30 cm. Disturbed places.
Occasional. S.W., R. Mts., Pl. Sts. ALL YEAR

Chicory Tribe: Cichorieae

YELLOW SALSIFY Alien *Tragopogon dubius*
Pointed, beaklike flower buds open into lemon yellow flowerheads during morning hours. Later they become *round balls* of
brown, parachuted seeds. Long, linear, grasslike leaves. 50 cm–
1 m. Occasional. N. Ariz., N.M., n. Tex., R. Mts. MAY–JULY

COMMON DANDELION *Taraxacum officinale*
Bright green leaves with sharply cut, *reversed lobes.* Bright yellow flowerheads. Soft, fluffy pappus (sepals) on long, beaked
seeds. 5–30 cm. Common. S.W., Tex., R. Mts., Pl. Sts.

ALL YEAR

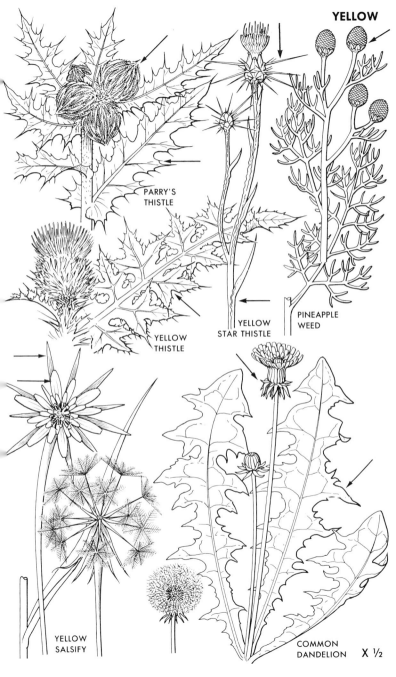

YELLOW

PARRY'S THISTLE

YELLOW THISTLE

YELLOW STAR THISTLE

PINEAPPLE WEED

YELLOW SALSIFY

COMMON DANDELION

X ½

DANDELION-LIKE FLOWERS; MILKY SAP

Sunflower Family (Compositae)

Chicory Tribe: Cichorieae
See also pp. W 98–110; Y 198–222;
O 234; R 330–334; B 384–386; G 402.

FENDLER'S DANDELION *Malacothrix fendleri*
Low, *flat, basal cluster* of *triangular-lobed* pinnate leaves.
Many leafless, *erect* flower stems with bright canary yellow
flowerheads. 10–30 cm. Common in plains, foothills. S.W.,
w. Tex. MARCH–MAY

STARPOINT *Microseris linearifolia*
Rosettes of erect, linear to partly linear, pinnate-lobed leaves.
Flowerhead bracts *extend beyond* the ray flowers as *starlike
points*. 10–30 cm. Common in plains, foothills below 5000 ft.
S.W., w. Tex. MARCH–MAY

FENDLER'S HAWKWEED *Hieracium fendleri*
Note the few broad, lancelike leaves. Many *long, soft hairs* on
leaves and stems. 20–30 cm. Midmountain pine forests. Ariz.,
northern N.M., R. Mts. MAY–AUG.

YELLOW TACKSTEM *Calycoseris parryi*
Stem covered with numerous tiny, *yellow, tack-shaped glands.*
Linear, pinnate-lobed leaves in basal rosettes. 10–30 cm. Lower
desert flats. W. Ariz., s. Ut. MARCH–APRIL

WESTERN HAWKSBEARD *Crepis occidentalis*
Broad, dandelion-like leaves. All plant parts covered with
short, *feltlike hair.* Erect stems have 10–30 flowerheads in
candelabra-like clusters. 10–30 cm. Rocky places. Northern
S.W., R. Mts. MAY–JUNE

TEXAS FALSE DANDELION *Pyrrhopappus multicaulis*
Bright yellow, half-dollar-sized flowerheads consisting entirely
of ray flowers. Upper stem leaves with 2–3 pairs of *pinnate
lobes.* Flowerhead buds with an outer row of *short, linear
bracts.* Milky sap. 20–80 cm. Forms giant *masses of yellow.*
Common. Eastern two-thirds of Tex., also N.M., Pl. Sts.
MARCH–MAY

DESERT DANDELION *Malacothrix glabrata*
Dandelion-like flowerheads; clear yellow, *centers red* until the
petals expand. *Hairless, linear, pinnate-lobed leaves* in basal
rosettes. 10–40 cm. Common in great showy masses. Sandy
flats of lower deserts. Ariz. MARCH–JUNE

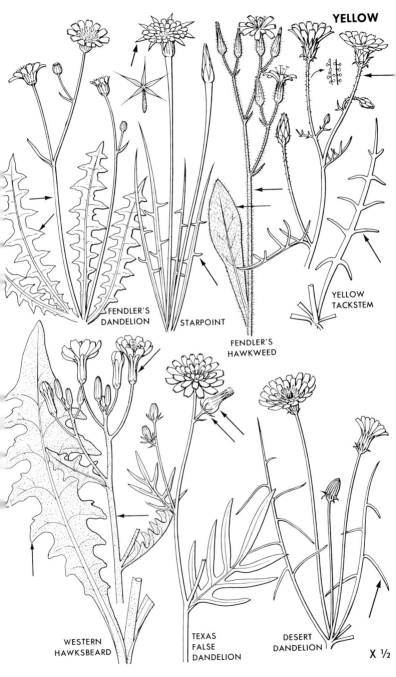

YELLOW

FENDLER'S DANDELION

STARPOINT

FENDLER'S HAWKWEED

YELLOW TACKSTEM

WESTERN HAWKSBEARD

TEXAS FALSE DANDELION

DESERT DANDELION

X ½

DANDELION-LIKE FLOWERS; MILKY SAP

Sunflower Family (Compositae)

Chicory Tribe: Cichorieae
See also pp. W 98–110; Y 198–222;
O 234; R 330–334; B 384–386; G 402.

COMMON SOW THISTLE Alien   *Sonchus oleraceus*
Stems smooth, well-branched. The lobed, spatula-shaped
leaves have *prickly margins* and *clasp* the stem. Flowerheads
small. Seeds sharp-beaked. 30 cm–1.5 m. Disturbed places.
S.W., Tex., R. Mts.   ANY TIME OF YEAR

WESTERN LETTUCE Alien   *Lactuca ludoviciana*
Note the broad, bright green, straplike leaves with *triangular
lobes* and earlike projections that *clasp* the stem. 50 cm–2 m.
S.W., Tex., Pl. Sts.   MARCH–AUG.

SCALEBUD   *Anisocoma acaulis*
Cylindrical, pale yellow flowerheads; covered with oblong
bracts that are both *dotted and edged with red*. Leaves basal.
5–20 cm. Sandy washes. W. Ariz.   MARCH–MAY

ROCKY MOUNTAIN   *Taraxacum eriophorum*
DANDELION
Straplike leaves and flower stem *thickened*. Gray flowerhead bracts that are *broadly rectangular*. 5–25 cm. Alpine
meadows. Northern S.W., R. Mts.   JUNE–AUG.

PRICKLY LETTUCE Alien   *Lactuca serriola*
Single tall, white, erect stem has *broad,* dark gray-green,
pinnate-lobed leaves. *Yellow prickles* cover *both sides* of each
leaf. Small flowerheads open during morning hours. Fluffy,
parachuted seedheads. 50 cm–1.5 m. Disturbed places. Common in S.W.; occasional in Tex.   MAY–SEPT.

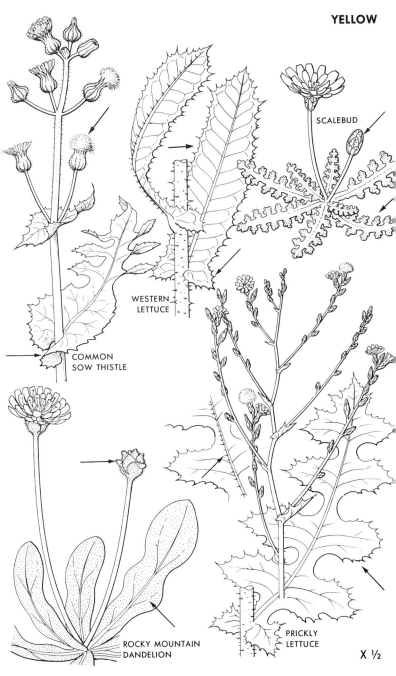

YELLOW

SCALEBUD

WESTERN LETTUCE

COMMON SOW THISTLE

ROCKY MOUNTAIN DANDELION

PRICKLY LETTUCE

X ½

Orange Flowers

Pink to Red or Red-Purple Flowers

Flowers that are truly orange or salmon are relatively few and are covered entirely by the next seven orange and red plates. The color spectrum shifts from the yellow band into the narrow orange band and then into the unmistakable pink and red colors. The pink and red section of this guide also includes the variable lavender, lilac, and purple shades that lean toward the red side. True purple is a 50–50 mixture of red and blue, and it is sometimes difficult to decide on which side of the line a color falls. Often a fresh red-purple flower will age to blue-purple. A majority of the purple flowers are in the red-purple category; if in doubt, check Violet to Blue or Blue-Purple Flowers on p. 337. The morning glories, peas, asters, and daisies are particularly tricky. When possible, the group characteristics given at the top of each text page are repeated in each color section, and in the same order. When the flowers on a page look nearly the same but your sample does not quite match, try using the cross reference given for other colors.

3 OR 6 PETALS; LILY-LIKE FLOWERS

Lily Family (Liliaceae)
See also pp. W 8–14; Y 114; R 272; B 338; G 390.

WOOD LILY   *Lilium philadelphicum*
Orange to bright red, *upturned flowers* in an umbel. Petal bases spotted with red-brown. Linear leaves in whorls. 30–90 cm. Semi-open aspen groves, wet places in mountains. N.M., Guadalupe Mts. of w. Tex., R. Mts.   MAY–AUG.

CAROLINA LILY   *Lilium michauxii*
Nodding flowers with red-pointed petal tips and orange-yellow bases with red-brown spots. Broad-tipped leaves in whorls. 30–90 cm. Oak, pine woods. E. Tex., S.E.   JULY–AUG.

KENNEDY'S MARIPOSA TULIP   *Calochortus kennedyi*
1–6 upright, cuplike flowers, orange to vermilion or bright yellow. *Brown-purple spots* may be present at petal bases. 10–20 cm. Lower elevations. Ariz.   MARCH–JUNE

GUNNISON'S MARIPOSA TULIP   *Calochortus gunnisonii*
Lower half of petal has a broad band of *many long, branching yellow hairs* above a *squarish outline* of short, thick hairs; note the *smooth, shiny, purplish* area below hairs at petal base. Petal color variable: pink, white, yellow or purplish. 10–60 cm. Mountain meadows. N.M., R. Mts.   JULY–AUG.

ARIZONA MARIPOSA TULIP   *Calochortus ambiguus*
Note the *narrow band of dark purple* (sometimes absent) above a broad band of *many long, branched* yellow hairs that are *enlarged* at their tips. Below the yellow hair band is a *feltlike semicircular mat* of pale purple, plus a *bare* darker purple, thumbnail-like *semicircle* below the mat. Petal color variable: white, pinkish, purplish. 10–60 cm. Rocky open slopes; woods. Ariz.   APRIL–AUG.

WINDING MARIPOSA TULIP   *Calochortus flexuous*
The lower part of each pink petal has (from top to bottom): a *white zone;* a *yellow band* with a central dark line at the top (this line may be absent); a *brownish mat* of short, feltlike hairs; and a *few short yellow hairs* on each side of this mat. Petal base is shiny, hairless, purple. Main portion of petal pink, purplish, or nearly white. Stems usually *bent, twisted, or wound* around nearby plants. 10–40 cm. Northern half of Ariz., southern R. Mts.   MARCH–JUNE

TORREY'S CRAG-LILY   *Anthericum torreyi*
Yellow-orange, *cometlike petals* partly swept backward. Flowers on leafless stems. Narrow, grasslike leaf blades have *no crossveins*. 10–30 cm. Frequent on grassy and rocky hillsides. Ariz., s. N.M., sw. Tex.   JUNE–NOV.

CHANDLER'S CRAG-LILY   *Anthericum chandleri*
Similar to Torrey's Crag-lily but leaves are wider, *with crossveins*. 10–40 cm. Thickets, prairies. Lower Rio Grande Valley, s. coastal Tex.   MAY–NOV.

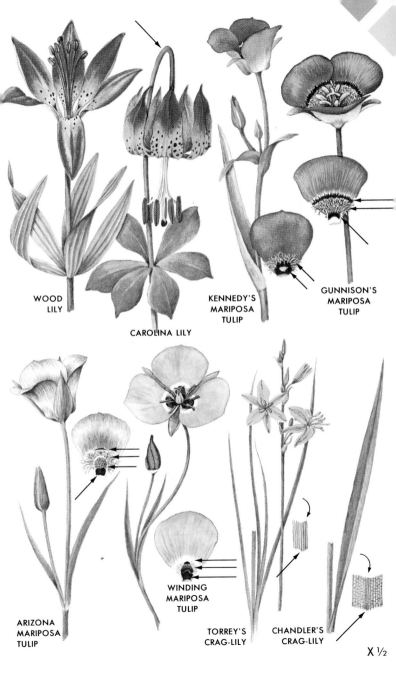

WOOD
LILY

CAROLINA LILY

KENNEDY'S
MARIPOSA
TULIP

GUNNISON'S
MARIPOSA
TULIP

ARIZONA
MARIPOSA
TULIP

WINDING
MARIPOSA
TULIP

TORREY'S
CRAG-LILY

CHANDLER'S
CRAG-LILY

X ½

3 IRREGULAR PETALS; ORCHIDS

Orchid Family (Orchidaceae)
See also pp. W 18–20; Y 114; R 230; G 390–394.

CINNABAR LADIES' TRESSES   *Spiranthes cinnabarina*
Note the thick flower spike of *long, tubular,* shiny orange to reddish flowers on a leafless stem above a few broad linear leaves. **Never pick** this rare, endangered orchid. 30–60 cm. Mountain hillsides. Big Bend region, Tex.   AUG.–OCT.

ORANGE EYELASH ORCHID   *Habenaria ciliaris*
Note the *orange* flowers (10–15 mm wide) that resemble an *animal's head;* petal lip *long, triangular, and fringed* like an eyelash. Slender *spur as long as ovary.* Many flowers in a spike. Scattered, long, lancelike leaves. 30–90 cm. Seepage slopes, bogs. Eastern quarter of Tex., S.E.   JULY–SEPT.

ORANGE CRESTED ORCHID   *Habenaria cristata*
Similar to Orange Eyelash Orchid, but flowers smaller, lip petal shorter. Spur *short, half as long* as ovary. 30–60 cm. Seepage spots, bogs. Eastern quarter of Tex., S.E.   JULY–SEPT.

TOOTHLIP ORCHID   *Habenaria integra*
Yellow-orange to saffron yellow, *tongue-shaped* petals; *margins with tiny teeth.* Flowers in a tight, cylindrical cluster. 20–60 cm. Wet pine savannahs. Se. Tex., S.E.   JULY–SEPT.

SPREADING CLEISTES   *Cleistes divaricata*
The single flower on each stem has 3 *upward-spreading,* red-brown to dark purplish sepals and a *downward tube* of pink to nearly white petals. Single leaf at mid-stem. 30–60 cm. **Rare; do not pick.** Pine savannahs, swamps. E. Tex.   APRIL–JULY

ROYAL GRASS PINK   *Calopogon pulchellus*
Note the *upward-pointing, triangular-lobed lip petal* with a central crest of long, yellow and rose hairs. Many *large* (3–8 cm), bright, rose-red flowers on a long leafless stem. Several *linear, grasslike* leaves. 30–90 cm. Wet grassy areas near bogs. Eastern quarter of Tex., S.E.   APRIL–JUNE

STREAM ORCHID   *Epipactis gigantea*
Flowers yellow-green to orangish. Orange, *heart-shaped lip petal* marked with *red lines.* Several leaves clasp the stem. 30–90 cm. Margins of seepage springs, streams, lakes. S.W., western two-thirds of Tex., R. Mts., Pl. Sts.   APRIL–JULY

ROSE POGONIA   *Pogonia ophioglossoides*
A *single* rose-pink flower (1–3 cm) and 1 leaf bract at the top of a long, leafless stem. A single, elliptical lower leaf. Lip petal with *many stringy points.* 10–50 cm. Pitcher-plant bogs, wet savannahs. Eastern quarter of Tex., S.E.   MARCH–JULY

CALYPSO ORCHID   *Calypso bulbosa*
Each plant has a single bright pink flower on a leafless stem above a *single oval leaf. Slipperlike lip petal tipped with 2 tiny horns,* mottled with orange, yellow, and white. 10–20 cm. Deep shade in mountain forests. S.W., R. Mts.   JUNE–AUG.

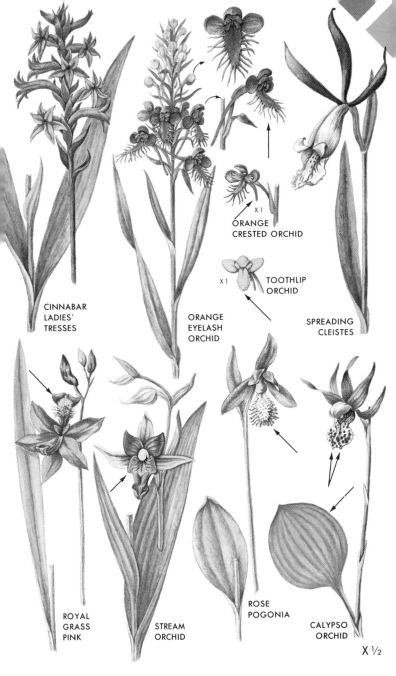

CINNABAR
LADIES'
TRESSES

ORANGE
EYELASH
ORCHID

ORANGE
CRESTED ORCHID

X 1

X 1 TOOTHLIP
ORCHID

SPREADING
CLEISTES

ROYAL
GRASS
PINK

STREAM
ORCHID

ROSE
POGONIA

CALYPSO
ORCHID

X ½

3 IRREGULAR PETALS; ORCHIDS

Orchid Family (Orchidaceae)
See also pp. W 18–20; Y 114; R 228; G 390–394.

SOUTHERN TWAYBLADE　　　　　　*Listera australis*
Lobes on lower lip petal resemble a *snake's forked tongue*. See p.
394 for full description. E. Tex.　　　　　　　　　FEB. MAY

THREE BIRDS ORCHID　　　　　*Triphora trianthophora*
Two alternate, oval leaves and 3 nodding flowers per stem. Lip petal
with *3 crests*. 10–20 cm. Forests. E. Tex.　　　　AUG.–OCT.

SPOTTED CORALROOT　　　　　　*Corallorhiza maculata*
Flowers orange, reddish, or yellow except for the *white, trilobed* lip
petal, which is *spotted with crimson*. Side sepals have *3 colored
veins*. 10–70 cm. Very common in mountain forests. S.W., w. Tex.,
R. Mts.　　　　　　　　　　　　　　　　　　JULY–AUG.

WISTER'S CORALROOT　　　　　　*Corallorhiza wisteriana*
Similar to Spotted Coralroot, but lip petal *entire (not lobed)*.
Flowers very early. 10–50 cm. Woods. S.W., Tex.　　FEB.–MAR.

STRIPED CORALROOT　　　　　　　*Corallorhiza striata*
Flowers *yellow* with *red stripes*. S.W., R. Mts.　　MAY–JULY

NORTHERN CORALROOT　　　　　　*Corallorhiza trifida*
Yellow-green to reddish sepals with *1 vein down midline*. Lip petal
white. 10–30 cm. Forests. Northern S.W., R. Mts.　　JUNE–JULY

EHRENBERG'S ADDER'S-MOUTH　　　*Malaxis ehrenbergii*
Flowers in a loose, *brushlike* raceme. See p. 394 for full description.
Southern S.W., sw. Tex.　　　　　　　　　　　　AUG.–SEPT.

CRESTED COCKSCOMB　　　　　　　*Hexalectris spicata*
Stem and most flower parts light yellow-brown. Trilobed lip petal
yellow-white with 5 *smooth, raised, parallel red-purple lines*. 20–
60 cm. Deep oak humus. S. Ariz., Tex.　　　　　　MAY–JULY

SHINING COCKSCOMB　　　　　　　*Hexalectris nitida*
Only lower lip petal is red-purple; other petals and sepals are *shiny*
reddish brown. Purple-red stems. 10–40 cm. Rocky streambeds.
Sw. Tex.　　　　　　　　　　　　　　　　　　JUNE–AUG.

CURLED COCKSCOMB　　　　　　　*Hexalectris revoluta*
Purplish, brownish yellow petals *rolled back in a curl*. Lip petal
deeply trilobed; lower half magenta with darker red lines. 10–40 cm.
Mountains. Big Bend area, Tex.　　　　　　　　　JUNE–AUG.

GREENMAN'S COCKSCOMB　　　　*Hexalectris grandiflora*
Flowers deep pink. Lip petal deep pink with a *central white bib* of
raised crests like cockscombs. Stems pink to red. 30–60 cm. Humus
along mountain streams. Big Bend area, Tex.　　　　　　JULY

WARNOCK'S COCKSCOMB　　　　　*Hexalectris warnockii*
Stem and flowers dark red-purple; lip petal white with 4 or 5 *yellow
"French ruffles"* and a broad, red-purple spot at tip. 10–30 cm. Oak
woods. S. Ariz. to sw. Tex.　　　　　　　　　　JUNE–AUG.

CRIPPLED CRANEFLY　　　　　　　　*Tipularia discolor*
Two seasonal phases: From fall to spring, leaves oval with *metallic
purple undersides*. Leaves disappear in late summer and are replaced by red-brown stems with numerous red-brown flowers that
have long spurs. White *lip petal trilobed*. 20–70 cm. Near moist
seeps in hardwood forests. E. Tex.　　　　　　　　JULY–AUG.

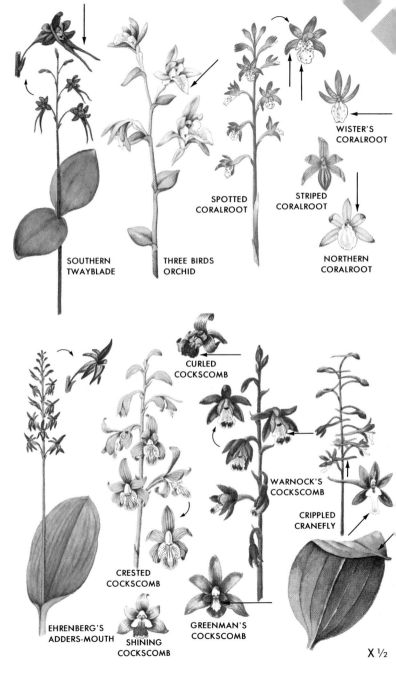

SOUTHERN
TWAYBLADE

THREE BIRDS
ORCHID

SPOTTED
CORALROOT

WISTER'S
CORALROOT

STRIPED
CORALROOT

NORTHERN
CORALROOT

CURLED
COCKSCOMB

WARNOCK'S
COCKSCOMB

CRIPPLED
CRANEFLY

CRESTED
COCKSCOMB

EHRENBERG'S
ADDERS-MOUTH

SHINING
COCKSCOMB

GREENMAN'S
COCKSCOMB

X ½

4 OR 5 PETALS; SHOWY FLOWERS

Poppy Family (Papaveraceae) See also pp. W 22; Y 128.

MEXICAN POPPY *Eschscholtzia californica*
Subspecies *mexicana*. The 4 *large petals* may be orange, yellow, cream, or white, with darker bases. *Distinct rim* below petals. Stems leafy. 10–30 cm. Often forms carpets of color. Ariz., s. N.M., sw. Tex., Ut. FEB.–MAY

PYGMY POPPY *Eschscholzia minutiflora*
4 *tiny* petals (5–10 mm), yellow-orange. Flower stem leafy. 10–40 cm. Lower deserts. W. Ariz., s. Ut. FEB.–MAY

MOJAVE POPPY *Eschscholtzia glyptosperma*
All leaves in a *flat basal cluster*. Flowers on *very long, naked stems, well above leaves*. 10–30 cm. Lower deserts. W. Ariz., sw. Ut., s. Nev., e. Calif. FEB.–MAY

RED PRICKLY POPPY *Argemone sanguinea*
Prickles *at right angles* on flower buds. Petals blood red, deep pink, or white. Stamen filaments lemon-yellow to dark red. Leaves deeply lobed. 30 cm–1 m. Southern Tex. FEB.–APRIL

CHISOS PRICKLY POPPY *Argemone chisoensis*
Very similar to Red Prickly Poppy. Petals deep pink to white. 30 cm–1 m. Big Bend region, Tex. MARCH–JUNE

Mustard Family (Cruciferae)
See also pp. W 26–32; Y 144–152; R 276.

WHEELER'S WALLFLOWER *Erysimum wheeleri*
4 petals form a Maltese cross; *both orange and orange-red* flowers in the same terminal cluster. Leaves nearly linear, with *spiny-toothed* margins. 30–90 cm. S.W., R. Mts. JUNE–JULY

Caltrop Family (Zygophyllaceae) See also p. Y 124.

SUMMER POPPY *Kallstroemia grandiflora*
Large (2–6 cm), *5-petaled poppylike* flowers with pale red veins on weak sprawling stems with *pinnate leaves*. Ovary base *slender*. Often forms massive orange carpets in midsummer. 10–70 cm. Lower deserts. S.W., w. Tex. JUNE–NOV.

WARTY CARPETWEED *Kallstroemia parviflora*
Similar to Summer Poppy, but petals *much smaller* (5–10 mm wide). Petals orangish, with *red basal markings*. Ovary base *wide*. 10–70 cm. Lower elevations. S.W., Tex. APRIL–NOV.

Cochlospermum Family (Cochlospermaceae)

ARIZONA YELLOW SHOW *Amoreuxia palmatifida*
Large, finger-lobed leaves *broad to base*. Large (5–8 cm wide), irregular flowers. Petals *orange or yellow;* upper 2 each have *2 red basal spots*. Side petals each have *1 red spot; no spots* on larger basal petal. Stamens in *3 distinct sets*. 10–50 cm. Open slopes. S. Ariz. JULY–SEPT.

WRIGHT'S YELLOW SHOW *Amoreuxia wrightii*
Similar to Arizona Yellow Show, but each fingerlike leaflet has a *narrow base*. 10–50 cm. Rocky flats. Southwest portion of cen. Tex. and along Rio Grande to south. MAY–JULY

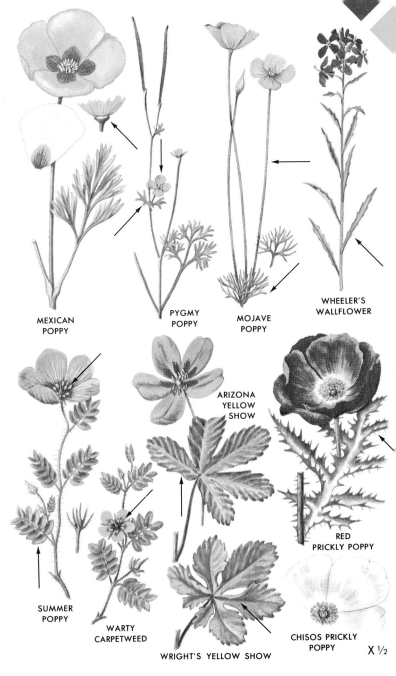

MEXICAN
POPPY

PYGMY
POPPY

MOJAVE
POPPY

WHEELER'S
WALLFLOWER

ARIZONA
YELLOW
SHOW

RED
PRICKLY POPPY

SUMMER
POPPY

WARTY
CARPETWEED

WRIGHT'S YELLOW SHOW

CHISOS PRICKLY
POPPY

X ½

MISCELLANEOUS FAMILIES

Dodder Family (Cuscutaceae)

DODDER *Cuscuta* species
Note the *mat of twining, orangish, leafless stems.* Tiny, white, tubular flowers. S.W., Tex., R. Mts., Pl. Sts. MOST OF YEAR

Forget-me-not Family (Boraginaceae)
See also pp. W 84; Y 182; R 314; B 344, 366.

ROUGH FIDDLENECK *Amsinckia intermedia*
Many small, trumpetlike flowers along the upper edge of a *coiled "shepherd's crook."* Calyx *5-lobed.* 4 brown, *irregular, rough-surfaced* nutlets per flower (use a hand lens to see). 10 cm–1 m. Ariz., w. N.M. FEB.–MAY

COBBLESTONE FIDDLENECK *Amsinckia tessellata*
Similar to Rough Fiddleneck, but calyx *3- or 4-lobed.* Seed surface smooth and rounded like a cobblestone. Ariz. FEB.–JUNE

Milkweed Family (Asclepiadaceae)
See also pp. W 66–72; Y 178; R 302; G 404.

CURAÇAO MILKWEED *Asclepias curassavica*
Dark yellow, upward-pointing hoods on a *long pointed pedestal; hoods the same size or shorter* than the central column. Petals bright red-orange to red. Flowers in umbels. *Large, broad,* lancelike leaves. 20 cm–1 m. S. Tex. APRIL–AUG.

ORANGE MILKWEED *Asclepias tuberosa*
Upward-pointing hoods on a *short pedestal; hoods much longer* than the central column. Flowers entirely yellow-orange to red-orange, in umbels. *Short* lancelike leaves. 20 cm–1 m. Common. S.W., Tex., Pl. Sts., S.E. APRIL–SEPT.

Sunflower Family (Compositae)
See also pp. W 98–110; Y 198–222; R 330–334; B 384–386; G 402.

CAPE MARIGOLD Alien *Dimorphotheca sinuata*
Shiny, pale orange to yellowish ray flowers with *inky black bases.* Central orangish disk flowers have *black anthers.* Straplike leaves with *toothed margins on sprawling stems.* 10–50 cm. Lower deserts. Sw. Ariz. JAN.–APRIL

ORANGE AGOSERIS *Agoseris aurantiaca*
Numerous burnt-orange *ray flowers* on a leafless stem; *no* disk flowers. Basal leaves lancelike. Milky sap. 10–60 cm. Mountain meadows. S.W., R. Mts. JUNE–AUG.

ORANGE SKYFLOWER *Haplopappus croceus*
Usually a single flowerhead on an erect stem. *Narrow, dark orange ray flowers* around central yellow disk flowers. Basal leaves long, linear. Stem leaves arrow-shaped. 10–60 cm. Mountain meadows. S.W., R. Mts. JULY–OCT.

Phlox Family (Polemoniaceae)
See also pp. W 88; Y 180; R 308–312; B 360–362.

GRAND COLLOMIA *Collomia grandiflora*
Single, erect stems topped by a *headlike cluster of long, trumpetlike* salmon flowers. 10 cm–1 m. Open and lightly wooded slopes. Ariz., w. N.M., R. Mts. MAY–JULY

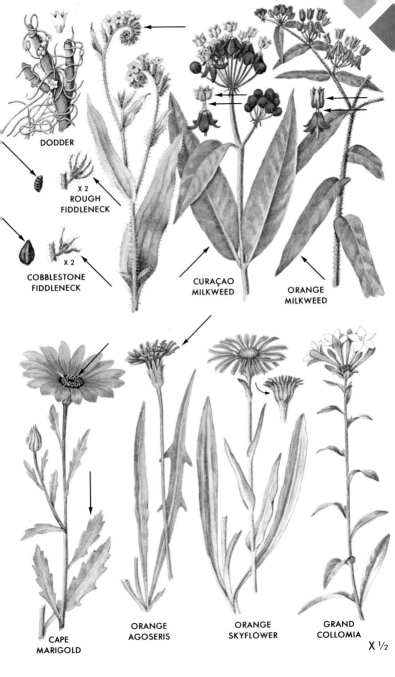

DODDER

X 2
ROUGH
FIDDLENECK

X 2

COBBLESTONE
FIDDLENECK

CURAÇAO
MILKWEED

ORANGE
MILKWEED

CAPE
MARIGOLD

ORANGE
AGOSERIS

ORANGE
SKYFLOWER

GRAND
COLLOMIA

X ½

MISCELLANEOUS FAMILIES

Saxifrage Family (Saxifragaceae)
See also pp. W 52–54; Y 170; G 404.

CORAL BELLS *Heuchera sanguinea*
Many small, *hairy, rosy pink, bell-like flowers* on leafless stems. Basal cluster of semi-rounded leaves with triangular pointed lobes. 30–60 cm. Mountains. Ariz. FEB.–OCT.

Caper Family (Capparidaceae) See also pp. W 32; Y 152.

ROCKY MOUNTAIN BEE PLANT *Cleome serrulata*
Pink, *4-petaled* flowers with *long, spiderlike stamens.* Seedpods *bananalike,* with a *thin base* above the pedicel. Upper leaves single, lower leaves trilobed. Skunky odor if handled. 20 cm–1 m. S.W., w. Tex., R. Mts., Pl. Sts. MAY–SEPT.

Bluebell Family (Campanulaceae)
See also pp. W 92; B 370, 376.

CARDINAL FLOWER *Lobelia cardinalis*
Note the bright red, 2-lipped, 5-petaled flowers. Leaves lancelike. 30 cm–1 m. Wet places. S.W., Tex., Pl. Sts. MAY–DEC.

Passion Flower Family (Passifloraceae)
See also pp. Y 186; B 344.

MEXICAN PASSION FLOWER *Passiflora mexicana*
Flowers with many *dark rust-red, linear, petal-like* lobes. Leaves U-*shaped.* Vines along streambanks. Southernmost Ariz.
JULY–AUG.

Logania Family (Loganiaceae)

INDIAN PINK *Spigelia marilandica*
Note the erect, *cockscomb-like row* of long, *vivid red,* tubular flowers. Petal lobes *yellow-green.* Stigma long, *black, projecting.* Vivid dark green, lancelike leaves. 20–60 cm. Shady hardwood forests. E. Tex., Pl. Sts., S.E. MAY–OCT.

Buttercup Family (Ranunculaceae)
See also pp. W 42–44; Y 162–164;
R 286; B 344, 356–358; G 396, 406.

COMET COLUMBINE *Aquilegia elegantula*
Yellow-petaled flower *narrow, cometlike,* with long spurs that are evenly tapered and often *spread apart.* Sepals red-orange, *shorter than or the same length as petals.* Stamens *barely* projecting. 10–50 cm. Mountains. Ne. Ariz., N.M., R. Mts. MAY–JUNE

TOP-HAT COLUMBINE *Aquilegia desortorum*
Yellow-petaled flower resembles a *top hat.* Sepals red-orange, *strongly spreading at right angles.* Leaves doubly tripinnate. 20–30 cm. N. Ariz. (Flagstaff area, Canyon de Chelly). JULY

CANADIAN COLUMBINE *Aquilegia canadensis*
Flowers pinkish red, triangular to cylindrical with *spur tips close to each other.* Sepals *not spreading.* 20–50 cm. Damp ledges, ravines. West-central Tex. and northward. MARCH–MAY

BARREL COLUMBINE *Aquilegia triternata*
Flowers squat, *barrel-like,* orange-red and yellow. Sepals *longer* than the yellow-tipped petals. Stamens *strongly projecting.* Leaves tripinnate. 20–60 cm. Very common in moist mountain forests. S.W., R. Mts. MAY–OCT.

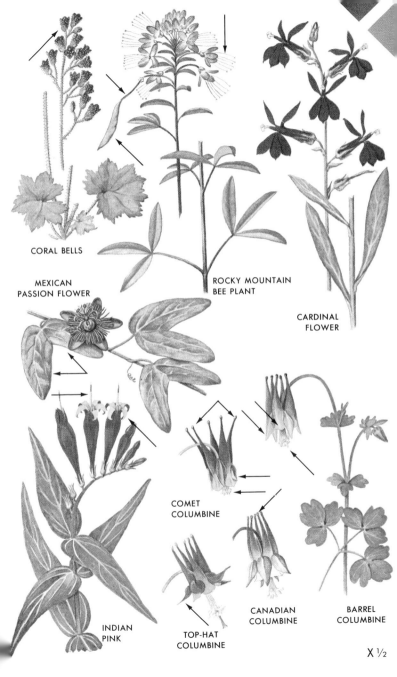

CORAL BELLS

MEXICAN
PASSION FLOWER

ROCKY MOUNTAIN
BEE PLANT

CARDINAL
FLOWER

INDIAN
PINK

TOP-HAT
COLUMBINE

COMET
COLUMBINE

CANADIAN
COLUMBINE

BARREL
COLUMBINE

X ½

5 PETALS; MISCELLANEOUS FAMILIES

Vervain Family (Verbenaceae) See also p. B 372.

CALICO BUSH *Lantana horrida*
Headlike clusters of asymmetrical, 2-lipped flowers, usually with *both* yellow orange and orange-red flowers. Stems armed with *spiny prickles.* Often 3 oval to heart-shaped leaves at each stem node; leaf margins with short teeth. 30 cm–1.2 m. S.W., Tex. MARCH–NOV.

DESERT LANTANA *Lantana macropoda*
Headlike flower clusters smallish, with pink, 2-lipped flowers; *bracts visible.* Stems *thornless.* Leaf blades *diamond-shaped with a tapering base,* margins with few teeth. 20 cm–1 m. Rocky hillsides. S. Ariz. to western two-thirds of Tex.
FEB.–NOV.

Mallow Family (Malvaceae)
See also pp. W 44; Y 166; R 288–290.
See other *Sphaeralcea* species on p. 290.

COULTER'S GLOBEMALLOW *Sphaeralcea coulteri*
Open, hollyhock-like flowers *bright orange.* Stem and leaves with *loose gray hairs.* 10–80 cm. Deserts. Sw. Ariz. JAN.–MAY

ORCUTT'S GLOBEMALLOW *Sphaeralcea orcuttii*
Similar to Coulter's Globemallow, but stem and leaves with *dense yellowish hairs.* 10–80 cm. Very common in lowest deserts. Sw. Ariz. JAN.–MAY

WINECUPS *Callirhoe involucrata*
Large, rose-purple, chalicelike flowers with *linear, leaflike bracts immediately* next to the calyx. Leaves palmate, each leaflet lobed. Long trailing or erect stems. 20 cm–1 m. Ne. N.M., Tex., Pl. Sts. FEB.–JUNE

TEXAS MALLOW *Malvaviscus arboreus*
Bright red petals always *twisted closed,* with a *long, projecting,* fused stamen column. Leaves heart-shaped. Low plant. 30 cm–1.5 m. Eastern half of Tex. MOST OF YEAR

Purslane Family (Portulacaceae) See also pp. R 294–296.

ORANGE FLAMEFLOWER *Talinum aurantiacum*
Large, round, *fluorescent* reddish orange and pink flowers. Shiny, succulent stems; *leaves succulent, rounded* in cross-section. 2 sepals. 10–40 cm. S. Ariz. to sw. Tex. JUNE–OCT.

SHOWY FLAMEFLOWER *Talinum pulchellum*
Petals *fluorescent,* light rose and orange, elliptical. A single flower above each succulent, *flattened,* linear leaf. 2 sepals. Stems many-branched. 5–30 cm. W. Tex. JUNE–OCT.

CLUBLEAF FLAMEFLOWER *Talinum brevifolium*
Semi-rounded, fleshy, *blue-green leaves.* Rose flowers with about 20 stamens. 2 sepals. Low, spreading stems. 2–10 cm. Juniper woodlands. Ne. Ariz., N.M., w. Tex., Ut. MAY–SEPT.

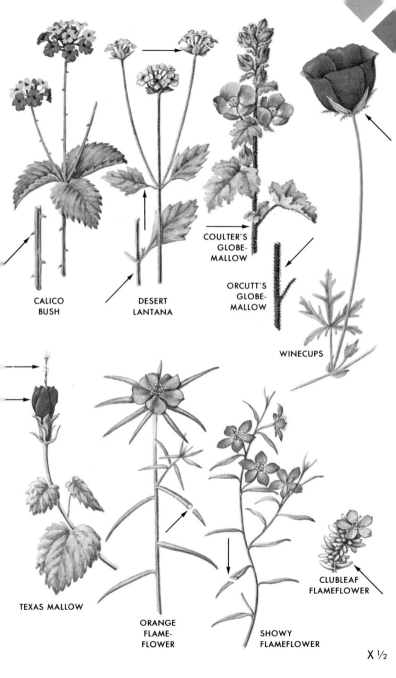

CALICO
BUSH

DESERT
LANTANA

COULTER'S
GLOBE-
MALLOW

ORCUTT'S
GLOBE-
MALLOW

WINECUPS

TEXAS MALLOW

ORANGE
FLAME-
FLOWER

SHOWY
FLAMEFLOWER

CLUBLEAF
FLAMEFLOWER

X ½

5 PETALS; MORNING GLORIES; VINES

Morning Glory Family (Convolvulaceae)
See also W 80; B 362.

Note: Blue-purple species may also have red-purple flowers;
many are represented only on this red page.

RAILROAD VINE   *Ipomoea pes-caprae*
Large, leathery, oblong to rounded leaves are shiny, yellow-green. Flowers rose-purple. 5–12 cm. Beaches and dunes. Tex. Coast.   JUNE–NOV.

SCARLET CREEPER   *Ipomoea hederifolia*
Note the red-orange flowers with *long tubes.* Leaves with 3 or 5 lobes. Vines. Common. S. Ariz. and N.M., also in thickets along Tex. coast.   JULY–NOV.

TIE VINE   *Ipomoea trichocarpa*
Leaves variable; may be arrow-shaped with 3 or 5 lobes, or unlobed and heart-shaped. Large, rose-lavender to purplish flowers with darker centers. E. $\frac{1}{3}$ Tex., Pl. Sts.   JUNE–OCT.

BUSH MORNING GLORY   *Ipomoea leptophylla*
Crowded, long, straplike leaves point upward on *prostrate stems.* Huge (8–10 cm), rosy to red-purple flowers. 50 cm–1 m. Frequent on open plains, dunes. Eastern N.M., nw. Tex., Pl. Sts.   MAY–JULY

LONGLEAF MORNING GLORY   *Ipomoea longifolia*
Similar to Bush Morning Glory, but large flowers *white with red-purple throats.* Open plains. S. Ariz.   JULY–SEPT.

PLUMMER'S MORNING GLORY   *Ipomoea plummerae*
Erect to prostrate vine has *long, threadlike, pinnate leaves* with 3–7 leaflets. Long, trumpetlike flowers rosy pink with *warty sepals.* Mountains. Ariz.   JULY–SEPT.

ALAMO VINE   *Ipomoea sinuata*
Note the *toothed, palmate-lobed leaves* and *large* white flowers with red-purple centers. Often cultivated. S. $\frac{1}{2}$ Tex.   MAY–NOV.

PAN'S FIDDLE   *Ipomoea pandurata*
Note the *heart-shaped* leaf blades and the *red-throated, white* flowers. *Sepals smooth (hairless).* Climbing, trailing vines. Cen. and e. Tex., Pl. Sts.   JUNE–SEPT.

IVYLEAF MORNING GLORY   *Ipomoea hederacea*
Alien (?)
Leaves variable; may be *heart-shaped to trilobed on the same vine. Short-tipped, oval sepals* with long hairs from enlarged, warty bases. Flowers variable, pink to deep blue-purple. Often cultivated. S.W., Tex., Pl. Sts.   JULY–NOV.

IMPERIAL MORNING GLORY Alien   *Ipomoea nil*
Very similar to Ivyleaf Morning Glory; leaves variable. *Long, tapering, oval sepals* with long hairs. Vines. Often cultivated. S.W., Tex.   JULY–NOV.

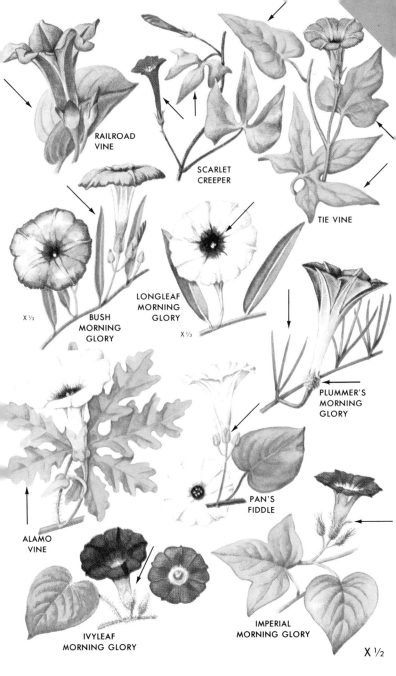

RAILROAD VINE

SCARLET CREEPER

TIE VINE

BUSH MORNING GLORY

X ⅓

LONGLEAF MORNING GLORY

X ⅓

PLUMMER'S MORNING GLORY

ALAMO VINE

PAN'S FIDDLE

IVYLEAF MORNING GLORY

IMPERIAL MORNING GLORY

X ½

5 PETALS; SHOWY BOWLS, PINWHEELS

Gentian Family (Gentianaceae)
See also pp. W 78; Y 174; B 342; G 400.

ROSITA *Centaurium calycosum*
Pink to dark rose petal lobes, each *broadly elliptical and as long as* the corolla tube. Corolla tube same length as calyx, and entirely *hidden within* the calyx. Leaves *lancelike.* Numerous flowers in colorful, long-lasting masses. 10–60 cm. S.W., western two-thirds of Tex., Ut. APRIL–JUNE

MOUNTAIN CENTAURY *Centaurium beyrichii*
Rosy pink petal lobes *narrowly oblong,* each lobe as long as the corolla tube. Part of corolla tube *protrudes above* calyx tips. Leaves linear, straplike or slightly lancelike. 10–30 cm. N.-cen. to w. Tex. MAY–AUG.

LADY BIRD'S CENTAURY *Centaurium texense*
Rosy pink petal lobes *narrow, much shorter* than the corolla tube. Corolla tube longer than calyx tube. Leaves linear, straplike or slightly wider at outer end. Named for the former First Lady, Lady Bird Johnson, who had seeds of this species gathered and planted along the presidential airstrip at her Texas ranch. 10–30 cm. Tex. MAY–AUG.

PRAIRIE ROSE GENTIAN *Sabatia campestris*
Calyx with *sharply raised ridges, lobes triangular.* Thin stem leaves *broadest at base.* Rosy pink flowers always 5-petaled. 10–50 cm. Dry open fields, wooded openings. Eastern half of Tex., Pl. Sts. APRIL–JULY

COAST ROSE GENTIAN *Sabatia arenicola*
Calyx tube with *sharply raised ridges,* lobes triangular. *Thick* stem leaves *broader above base.* Rosy pink flowers always 5-petaled. 10–30 cm. Beaches, dunes, flats along coast of Tex.
APRIL–JULY

SQUARESTEM ROSE GENTIAN *Sabatia angularis*
Short calyx tube *lacks ridges* or has *low ridges.* Calyx lobes *long, leafy.* Stem leaves broadly oval to heart-shaped. Stems strongly *4-angled* (squared). 5–6 rosy pink petals. 10–60 cm. Pine and hardwood forests. E. Tex., Pl. Sts. MAY–JULY

SPIDER ROSE GENTIAN *Sabatia gentianoides*
7–12 *rosy pink petals. Long, spiderlike calyx bracts* next to flower, longer than petals. Stem leaves long, *very narrow.* 20–50 cm. Wet pinelands. E. Tex. MAY–AUG.

GIANT ROSE GENTIAN *Sabatia dodecandra*
Similar to Spider Rose Gentian with 8–12 rosy pink petals, but no spiderlike calyx. *Calyx lobes short,* with 3 or 5 veins. 20–50 cm. Wet pinelands, coastal marshes. Sw. Tex. JUNE–AUG.

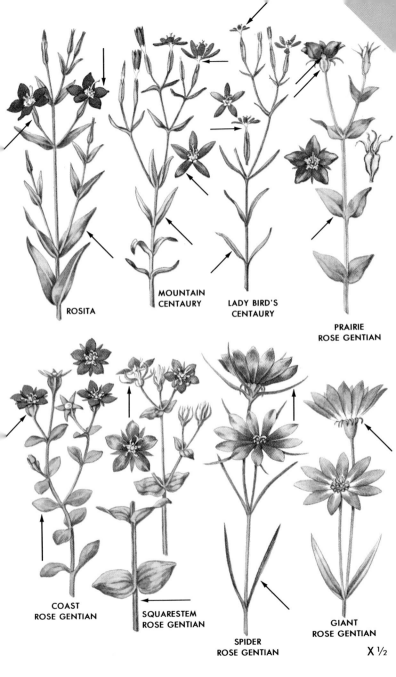

ROSITA

MOUNTAIN CENTAURY

LADY BIRD'S CENTAURY

PRAIRIE ROSE GENTIAN

COAST ROSE GENTIAN

SQUARESTEM ROSE GENTIAN

SPIDER ROSE GENTIAN

GIANT ROSE GENTIAN

X ½

5-PETALED; 2-LIPPED, TUBULAR COROLLAS

Snapdragon Family (Scrophulariaceae)
See also pp. W 88; Y 118–122; R 244–250; B 350–354.

BIGELOW'S MONKEY FLOWER   *Mimulus bigelovii*
Stigma hidden inside corolla throat. Nearly *equal lobed*, pink to
red-purple flowers. *Two round eyes* (may be pale) on opposite sides
of pale yellow throat with purple dots. 5–35 cm. Lower deserts.
W. Ariz.   FEB.–MAY

PYGMY MONKEY FLOWER   *Mimulus rubellus*
Tiny flowers (5 mm) somewhat *rectangular,* with a *long, lobed
lower petal.* Calyx lobes *broadly rounded and fringed.* 2–12 cm.
Common in masses. Sandy washes. Ariz., s. N.M., sw. Tex., R. Mts.
         MARCH–JULY

SCARLET MONKEY FLOWER   *Mimulus cardinalis*
Large, scarlet flower with upper petal lobes *projecting* farther than
the lower. All petal tips strongly *swept back.* Leaves oval, coarsely
toothed, with sticky hairs. 30 cm–1 m. Wet places. S.W., Ut.
         MARCH–OCT.

RED OWL'S-CLOVER   *Orthocarpus purpurascens*
Flowers and flower leaf bracts *both dark red-purple.* Corolla has a
prominent hooked beak and 3 yellow or white lower *sacs.* Leaves
threadlike. 10–40 cm. Very common at lower elevations. Western
and southern half of Ariz.   MARCH–MAY

PARROT'S BEAK   *Pedicularis racemosa*
The pale pink flowers consist of a curved, sickle-shaped upper petal
(parrot's beak) and 3 lower petals flattened behind it. Bright green
leaves *lancelike and entire.* 30–60 cm. Dry conifer woods, mid-
mountains. E. Ariz., northern N.M., R. Mts.   JULY–AUG.

BULL ELEPHANTS HEAD   *Pedicularis groenlandica*
Note the red-purple "elephant's head" formed by the *long, twisted*
upper petals (the long "trunk") and the *shorter* lower petals
("ears"). 30 cm–1 m. Wet mountain meadows. E. Ariz., N.M.,
R. Mts.   JULY–AUG.

TWOTONE OWL'S-CLOVER   *Orthocarpus purpureo-albus*
Lower side of corolla prominently *inflated into 3 sacs;* the hooked
beak above *dwarfed.* Flowers white and pink-purple on the *same
stem.* Leaves pinnate, linear. 10–40 cm. Mountain forests, meadows.
N. Ariz., w. N.M., R. Mts.   JULY–OCT.

JUNIPER LOUSEWORT   *Pedicularis centranthera*
Low, semi-flattened, pinnate leaves in a cluster. Flowers *broad, pur-
ple-white, with hooked corollas.* 2–12 cm. Juniper and pine woods,
mountains. S.W., R. Mts.   APRIL–JUNE

CALIFORNIA FIGWORT   *Scrophularia californica*
Short, red-brown, tubular flowers with *2 projecting upper petals.*
Coarse stems; *large, broadly triangular leaves.* 1–2 m. Moist thick-
ets. Cen. Ariz.   JUNE

RED FIGWORT   *Scrophularia coccinea*
Similar to California Figwort. Flowers *red. Narrow, arrow-
shaped leaves.* 1–2 m. Southern N.M.   JULY–AUG.

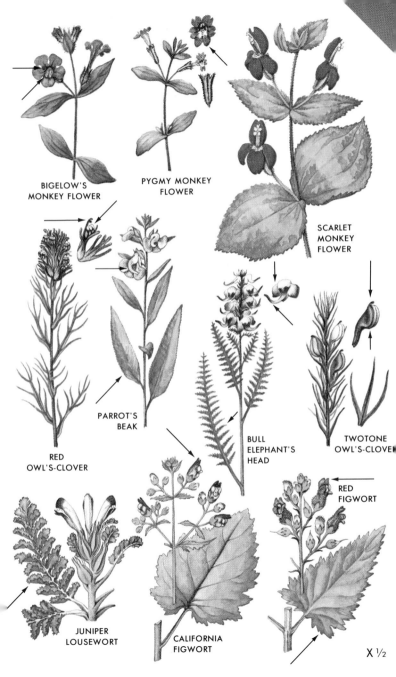

BIGELOW'S
MONKEY FLOWER

PYGMY MONKEY
FLOWER

SCARLET
MONKEY
FLOWER

RED
OWL'S-CLOVER

PARROT'S
BEAK

BULL
ELEPHANT'S
HEAD

TWOTONE
OWL'S-CLOVER

JUNIPER
LOUSEWORT

CALIFORNIA
FIGWORT

RED
FIGWORT

X ½

5-PETALED; 2-LIPPED, TUBULAR COROLLAS

Snapdragon Family (Scrophulariaceae)
See also pp. W 88; Y 118–122; R 244–250; B 350–354.

EATON'S FIRECRACKER *Penstemon eatonii*
Scarlet, tubular corolla with *petal lobes barely open, non-spreading.* Triangular leaves *green, without* a waxy blue coating. 30 cm–1 m. Common on rocky slopes at lower elevations. Ariz., northern N.M., sw. R. Mts. FEB.–JUNE

UTAH PENSTEMON *Penstemon utahensis*
Bright red-orange corolla tube shaped like a *pipe,* diameter nearly equal for most of its length. Petal lobes at *right angles* to corolla tube. Leaves *narrowly triangular,* waxy blue. 10–80 cm. Rocky mesas. N. Ariz., s. Ut. MARCH–MAY

BRIDGES' PENSTEMON *Penstemon bridgesii*
Scarlet, tubular corollas with 2 distinct lips; lower lip sharply bent backward, upper lip *protruding forward.* Upper petals with *round tips.* Gray-green, linear leaves. 30–90 cm. Among pinyons, ponderosa pine. Ariz., w. N.M., sw. R. Mts.
MAY–SEPT.

SOUTHWESTERN PENSTEMON *Penstemon barbatus*
Reddish orange corolla tube widens to form gaping, *mouthlike petal lobes.* Lower petal lobes with *white splotches;* the upper petals *sharp, pointed,* projecting forward with the *tips folded back* like ears. Leaves grasslike, dark green. 30 cm–1 m. Common in mountains. S.W., w. Tex., R. Mts. JUNE–OCT.

BIG BEND PENSTEMON *Penstemon havardii*
Note the *large, blue-green,* egg-shaped to wedge-shaped leaves without petioles. *Bright red* flower tubes narrow, with *distinct glandular hairs.* Petal lobes short, nearly equal; the upper 2 lobes project forward over the lower. 50 cm–1.5 m. Along streambeds. Big Bend area, Tex. APRIL–OCT.

PINE-NEEDLE PENSTEMON *Penstemon pinifolius*
Long, red-orange corolla with *sticky hairs* has a *slender base.* 3 *narrow* lower petal lobes widely spaced, upper lobes projecting straight out. Orangish yellow "mouth" of corolla has many *short yellow hairs.* Leaves *short, linear, like pine needles.* 30–60 cm. Higher mountains. Se. Ariz., sw. N.M. JULY–AUG.

CARDINAL PENSTEMON *Penstemon cardinalis*
Note the *thick mat of golden hair* at the corolla mouth. Cardinal red corolla tube looks *ready to burst;* petal lobes *miniature.* Large, *heart-shaped* leaves; fleshy, *bluish green.* 30–90 cm. Guadalupe Mts. of w. Tex., adjacent N.M., also White Mts., N.M. MAY–JULY

BACCHUS' PENSTEMON *Penstemon baccharifolius*
Dark scarlet red corolla tube *broad,* with a *short, tapered base* and *dense, sticky hairs.* Leaves yellow-green with *spiny, toothed* margins. Most of plant has many sticky hairs. 10–40 cm. Rocky bluffs. Western half of Tex. MAY–SEPT.

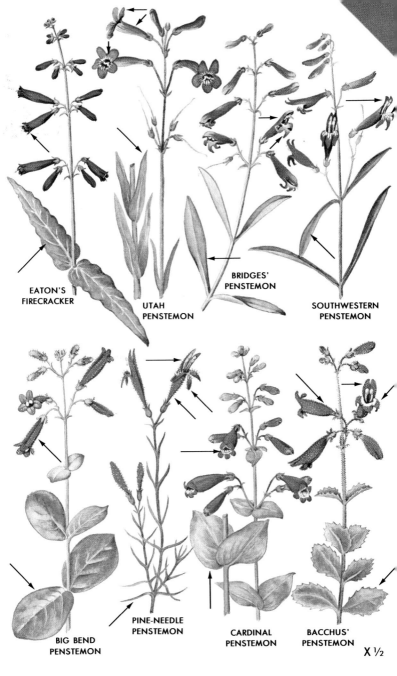

EATON'S
FIRECRACKER

UTAH
PENSTEMON

BRIDGES'
PENSTEMON

SOUTHWESTERN
PENSTEMON

BIG BEND
PENSTEMON

PINE-NEEDLE
PENSTEMON

CARDINAL
PENSTEMON

BACCHUS'
PENSTEMON

X ½

5-PETALED; 2-LIPPED TUBULAR COROLLAS

Snapdragon Family (Scrophulariaceae)
See also pp. W 88; Y 118–122; R 244–250; B 350–354.

MURRAY'S PENSTEMON *Penstemon murrayanus*
Corolla *bright red-orange,* gradually expanding outward. Short petal lobes. Leaves fleshy, *blue-green; paired bases fused together.* 30–90 cm. Common e. ¼ Tex., Ozarks, Pl. Sts., S.E.
APRIL–MAY

PALMER'S PENSTEMON *Penstemon palmeri*
Note the *short, bulging, light pink corolla tube.* Gray-green leaves with a waxy blue covering. The upper pairs of leaves are *joined together* and *surround* the stem. 30–90 cm. Rocky places, washes. Nw. Ariz., cen. N.M., s. R. Mts. MARCH–SEPT.

WANDBLOOM PENSTEMON *Penstemon virgatus*
Somewhat like Palmer's Penstemon. Corolla tube *short, broad, bulging, light pink* to dark blue-purple (sometimes white) with *dark purple lines* extending to the lower petal lobes. Leaves *linear, threadlike.* 10–60 cm. Pine woods, mountain meadows. S.W.
JUNE–AUG.

PARRY'S PENSTEMON *Penstemon parryi*
Lower petal lobes of the bright lavender-red corolla *project forward.* Corolla tube *evenly inflated* on both upper and lower sides. *Narrowly triangular* leaves fleshy, thick, blue-green. 20 cm–1 m. Lower deserts. S. Ariz. FEB.–APRIL

ARIZONA PENSTEMON *Penstemon pseudospectabilis*
Bright lavender-red corolla with a *lower, one-sided bulge.* Cheeklike petal lobes at right angles to corolla tube. *Broad,* triangular leaf pair *bases fused together* around the stem, leaf margins raggedly toothed. 20 cm–1 m. Common. Ariz., w. N.M.
FEB.–MAY

SNAPDRAGON VINE *Maurandya antirrhiniflora*
Note the *broad, arrow-shaped leaves on twining vines.* Flowers dark red or blue-purple with a yellowish throat. Calyx lobes nearly *as long as the corolla tube.* Vines, forming mats over shrubs. Common at lower elevations. S. Ariz. to sw. Tex., and se. to Brownsville. FEB.–OCT.

MOTH PENSTEMON *Penstemon ambiguus*
Large, *mothlike petal lobes slanted in line* with the long, curving, pinkish corolla tube. Petal lobes white or pale pink; corolla tube pale pink. A large, rounded, shrublike plant with *linear, grasslike leaves.* 30 cm–1 m. Common on plains, sand dunes. N. Ariz., N.M., w. ⅓ Tex. MAY–AUG.

PURPLE GERARDIA *Agalinis purpurea*
Dark red-purple corolla like an *upturned trumpet,* with equal petal lobes. Dense woolly hairs in throat. Tall, widely branching stems with *narrow, linear leaves.* 20 cm–1 m. Seepage areas, moist prairies. E. Tex., S.W. AUG.–NOV.

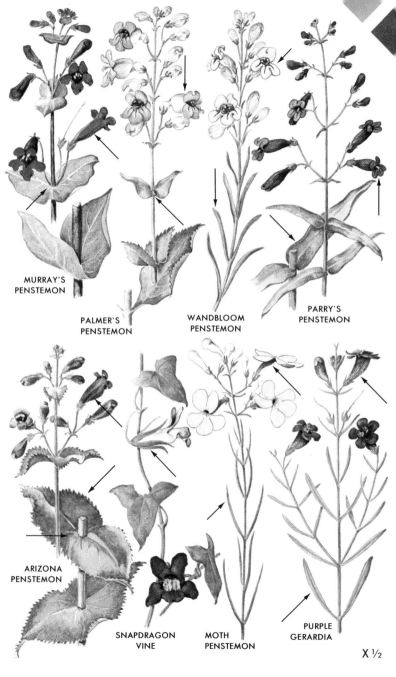

MURRAY'S
PENSTEMON

PALMER'S
PENSTEMON

WANDBLOOM
PENSTEMON

PARRY'S
PENSTEMON

ARIZONA
PENSTEMON

SNAPDRAGON
VINE

MOTH
PENSTEMON

PURPLE
GERARDIA

X ½

5-PETALED; 2-LIPPED, SPOUTLIKE FLOWERS

Snapdragon Family (Scrophulariaceae)
See also pp. W 88; Y 118–122; R 244–250; B 350–354.

WOOLLY PAINTBRUSH　　　　　*Castilleja lanata*
Feltlike leaves and stem with *dense, white, woolly hairs.* Each colored flower bract is evenly *trilobed, red on outer half.* Calyx tubular, *tricolored:* red, yellow, and green. Lower leaves linear, upper leaves lobed. 10–90 cm. Southern S.W., w. Tex.　　MARCH–AUG.

DESERT PAINTBRUSH　　　　　*Castilleja chromosa*
Each dark red-brown flower leaf bract is relatively narrow, with 5 *long, narrow lobes.* Stem leaves with 3 or 5 lobes. *Fluorescent* pink to red flowers. 10–60 cm. Northern two-thirds of Ariz., R. Mts.
　　　　　　　　　　　　　　　　　　　　　MARCH–AUG.

SOUTHWESTERN PAINTBRUSH　　*Castilleja integra*
Orange-red colored flower bracts. Lower bracts *broadly oblong;* upper bracts *trilobed;* center lobe *broadest, tips rounded.* Red-orange tubular calyx, with *sharp lobes.* Leaves linear, with dark gray hairs. 10–40 cm. Common. S.W., w. Tex.　MARCH–OCT.

TEXAS PAINTBRUSH　　　　　*Castilleja indivisa*
Broad, *oval, bright reddish pink flower leaf bracts. Cut-off, funnel-like* red-tipped calyx; corolla barely protruding. Leaves linear, with *folded, wavy margins.* 10–40 cm. Tex.　　MARCH–JUNE

WYOMING PAINTBRUSH　　　*Castilleja linariaefolia*
Long (5 cm), *widely spaced flowers* project at right angles from the stem, with 3-lobed leaf bracts at base. Leaves *linear,* yellow-green. Wyoming state flower. 50 cm–1 m. Common in forests, sagebrush flats. S.W., R. Mts.　　　　　　　　　　　APRIL–OCT.

PATRIARCH PAINTBRUSH　　　*Castilleja patriotica*
Similar to Wyoming Paintbrush, but corolla very long. Leaves *deeply divided.* 10–60 cm. Mountains. S. Ariz.　JULY–SEPT.

GIANT RED PAINTBRUSH　　　*Castilleja miniata*
Scarlet-colored leaf bracts and calyx have *3 or more narrow, sharp points.* Leaves *flat, lancelike.* 30–90 cm. Common in wet mountain meadows. Northern third of S.W., R. Mts.　　JUNE–OCT.

ARIZONA PAINTBRUSH　　*Castilleja austromontana*
Similar to Giant Red Paintbrush, but colored flower bracts either *shallowly trilobed or not lobed.* 30–60 cm. Moist high mountain slopes. S. Ariz. to northern rim of Grand Canyon.　MAY–AUG.

HAYDEN'S ALPINE PAINTBRUSH　　*Castilleja haydenii*
Fluorescent bright lavender-pink flower bracts *strongly lobed* with 2 or more lobe pairs. Pink calyx, narrowly pointed; yellow-green, spoutlike corolla *barely projecting.* Leaves linear. 10–30 cm. Alpine. Northern N.M., R. Mts.　　　　　　　　　　JULY–AUG.

LONGBILL PAINTBRUSH　　　*Castilleja sessiliflora*
See p. 120 for full description. S.W., Tex., Pl. Sts.　MARCH–MAY

THREADTORCH PAINTBRUSH　　　*Castilleja minor*
Long, threadlike, red to orange-tipped flower-bract leaves. Stem leaves also linear. 30–80 cm. Moist places. S.W., R. Mts.
　　　　　　　　　　　　　　　　　　　　　APRIL–AUG.

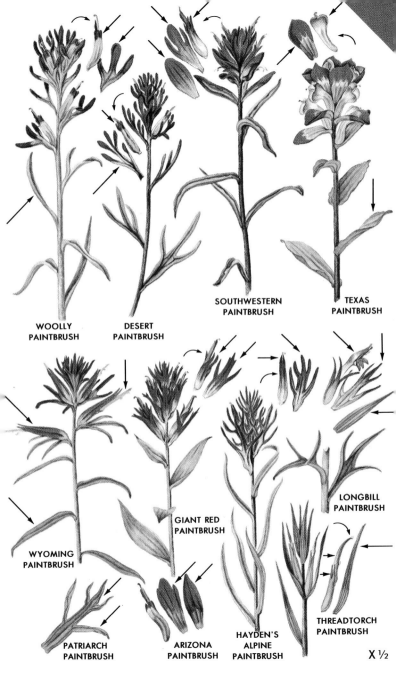

WOOLLY
PAINTBRUSH

DESERT
PAINTBRUSH

SOUTHWESTERN
PAINTBRUSH

TEXAS
PAINTBRUSH

WYOMING
PAINTBRUSH

GIANT RED
PAINTBRUSH

LONGBILL
PAINTBRUSH

THREADTORCH
PAINTBRUSH

PATRIARCH
PAINTBRUSH

ARIZONA
PAINTBRUSH

HAYDEN'S
ALPINE
PAINTBRUSH

X ½

HEDGEHOG CACTI IN LARGE CLUMPS

Cactus Family (Cactaceae)
See also pp. W 2–4; Y 126–142; R 252–270.

CLARET CUP *Echinocereus triglochidatus*
Flowers *scarlet-orange,* or bright red with yellow. *Long, curly spines* with *white, feltlike hairs* at base of larger spines (2–4). Short, yellow-green, oblong stems in low spreading mounds. 5–20 cm (to 50 cm). Widespread species. Rocky hills, juniper-oak woodlands, desert flats. S.W., w. Tex., R. Mts.   APRIL–JULY

FENDLER'S HEDGEHOG *Echinocereus fendleri*
One long, blackish central spine with 6–11 shorter, gray to white radial spines below in each spine cluster. Both main spine base and entire spine cluster *nearly round.* Flowers dark red-purple. Elongate, cylindrical stems in clusters. 10–30 cm. Common in mid-elevation grasslands, woodlands. S.W., w. Tex., sw. R. Mts.   APRIL–JUNE

COCKSCOMB HEDGEHOG *Echinocereus fasciculatus*
Similar to Fendler's Hedgehog. *Several* (2–4) pale blackish or brownish *central spines,* with 1 long spine and 1–3 shorter ones. Both main spine bases and entire spine cluster *nearly round.* 12–14 shorter radial spines below. Flowers dark red-purple. Cylindrical stems, 10–50 cm. Common in lower deserts. Southern two-thirds of Ariz., sw. N.M.   APRIL–JUNE

ENGELMANN'S HEDGEHOG *Echinocereus engelmannii*
Several central spines; main ones *flattened near base,* surrounded by 6–14 lower radial spines. Spines brownish black to golden yellow. Entire spine cluster base rounded. Flowers dark red-purple. Many hedgehoglike stems in clumps. 10–50 cm. Lower deserts. Western two-thirds of Ariz., Ut.   FEB.–MAY

GOLDEN HEDGEHOG *Echinocereus ledingii*
Downward-cascading, golden yellow main spines, 1 main spine per cluster. Tall, columnlike stems. 10–60 cm. Chaparral, oak woodlands of mid-mountains. Southeastern quarter of Ariz.
MAY–JUNE

STRAWBERRY HEDGEHOG *Echinocereus enneacanthus*
Large, sausagelike stems in *large mounds,* with sharply raised, even-margined ribs. Very long (2–10 cm), *downturned, straight,* swordlike central spines (some flat-sided) on ribs. 1–4 main spines and 6–18 similar radial spines. All spines *straight,* not curved. Flowers rose to red-purple. (The most thickly spined plants are sometimes called subspecies *stramineus* — **Strawpile Hedgehog.**) Fruit edible, tastes like strawberries. 30–60 cm. Flats, hills. Se. N.M., southern half of Tex.   FEB.–MAY

LLOYD'S HEDGEHOG *Echinocereus lloydii*
Similar to Claret Cup. All of the 2–5 reddish gray *central spines are similar and somewhat shorter* than the 8–10 lower radial spines. Flowers reddish orange to dark red. 10–20 cm. Uncommon. Carlsbad, N.M. to Ft. Stockton, Tex.   APRIL–MAY

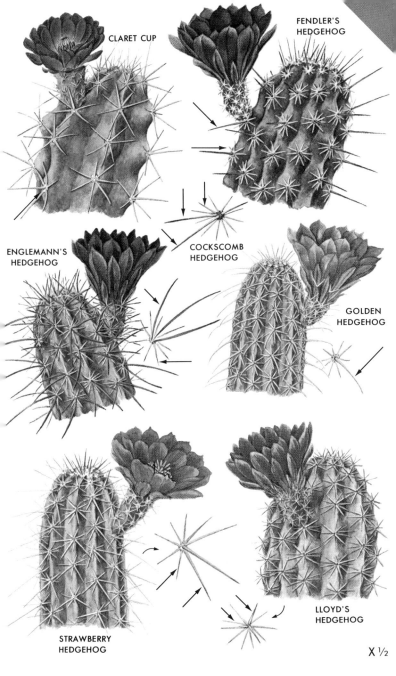

CLARET CUP

FENDLER'S HEDGEHOG

COCKSCOMB HEDGEHOG

ENGLEMANN'S HEDGEHOG

GOLDEN HEDGEHOG

STRAWBERRY HEDGEHOG

LLOYD'S HEDGEHOG

X ½

HEDGEHOG AND FLAT BARREL CACTI

Cactus Family (Cactaceae)
See also pp. W 2–4; Y 126–142; R 252–270.

RAINBOW CACTUS   *Echinocereus pectinatus*
Large, thick, cylindrical stems with *rainbowlike, alternating horizontal rows* of pinkish red and grayish, *comblike* spine clusters. Each spine cluster *vertically elongate* with a flattened circle of leglike spines and 0–9 vertical spines along the teardrop-shaped base. Immense, funnel-like flowers, yellow, orange, pink, or dark red. 10–30 cm. Grasslands, brushy scrub on limestone soil. Southeastern quarter of Ariz. in a southerly band to Del Rio, Tex.   MARCH–MAY

PICKLE CACTUS   *Echinocereus blanckii*
Note the strongly raised, *wartlike bumps* on the picklelike, globular (5–15 cm) stem joints. Large, funnel-like flowers, completely rose red or yellow with dark red basal stripes. Stems prostrate, in clumps under shrubs. 30–60 cm. Mesquite brushlands. Cen. and s. Tex.   FEB.–MARCH

LADYFINGER CACTUS   *Echinocereus pentalophus*
Note the *narrow, flat, 4- to 5-sided stem* with small, spreading clusters of 3–6 blackish spines. *No* central spines. Large magenta flowers. Stems prostrate, in fingerlike clumps. 10–30 cm. Under shrubs. S. Tex.   FEB.–APRIL

HORSE CRIPPLER   *Echinocactus texensis*
Low, broad, barrel cactus, often hidden in grass. *Sharply ridged, undulating ribs. Petal edges fringed.* Flowers pink with darker centers. 10–20 cm tall, 15–30 cm wide. Eastern N.M., western two-thirds of Tex.   FEB.–MAY

LACE HEDGEHOG   *Echinocereus reichenbachii*
Note the clearly *separated,* vertical rows of flat, silverfishlike spine clusters that give the stem a *uniform, delicate, lacy appearance.* Spines all white, reddish brown, or dark dirty brown. Usually no central spines, but sometimes 1–3 vertical ones present. Spine clusters on ovary with *dense, cobweblike hairs.* Large rose-purple flowers. Cylindrical stems in small clumps. 5–50 cm. Rocky plains. Eastern N.M., western two-thirds of Tex., Pl. Sts.   MARCH–MAY

CHISOS HEDGEHOG   *Echinocereus chisosensis*
Spines irregular in length. Central, erect spines *dark brown to black with conspicuous bulblike bases.* Lower radial spines mostly white or gray with tapering bases. Large red flowers with yellowish white centers. 10–20 cm. Creosote bush flats. Big Bend National Park, Tex.   MARCH–APRIL

EAGLESCLAW CACTUS   *Echinocactus horizonthalonius*
Note the *smooth, gently curving, blue-green ribs.* Petal edges *smooth.* Flowers fluorescent pink with dark red centers. Spines flattened or rounded, resembling the clawed foot of an eagle. Low, flattened stem. 5–30 cm. Rocky hills. S. Ariz. and s. N.M., Big Bend region, Tex.   JULY–AUG.

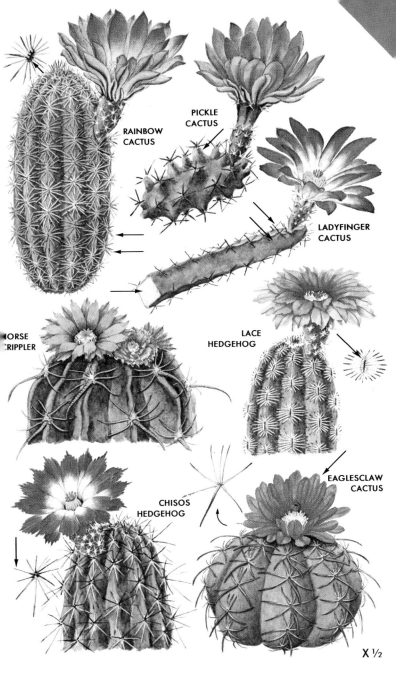

RAINBOW CACTUS

PICKLE CACTUS

LADYFINGER CACTUS

HORSE CRIPPLER

LACE HEDGEHOG

CHISOS HEDGEHOG

EAGLESCLAW CACTUS

X ½

PRICKLY PEAR, CHOLLA, BARREL CACTI

Cactus Family (Cactaceae)
See also pp. W 2–4; Y 126–142; R 252–270.

TREE CHOLLA   *Opuntia imbricata*
Cylindrical stem joints *very long, with sharply raised bumps.*
Many (15–40) spines in each cluster; spines usually short,
straw-colored. Flowers dark red, cuplike. *Fruits spineless, yellow.* An open branching shrub. 1–3 m. Se. Ariz., N.M., w. ⅓
Tex., Pl. Sts.   JUNE–AUG.

COMMON BEAVERTAIL   *Opuntia basilaris*
Blue-green or yellow-green *pads resemble beaver tails* and
have *small eyespots* ringed by tiny spines; otherwise spineless.
Pads leaden blue in winter. Flowers red-purple or yellow. 30–
60 cm. Deserts and mountains. W. ⅓ Ariz., S. Ut.
                                         MAY–JUNE

JUNIPER PRICKLY PEAR   *Opuntia polyacantha*
This is subspecies *juniperina.* Stem pads elongated and usually
spineless on lower portion; ovary also nearly spineless. Each
main spine *round* at base. A circle of gray, woolly spinelets
surround each spine cluster. *Flowers red.* All other subspecies
have yellow flowers. 10–30 cm. Juniper-pinyon woodlands.
Northern S.W., R. Mts.   APRIL–JULY

PORCUPINE PRICKLY PEAR   *Opuntia erinacea*
Long (10–30 cm), oblong or elliptical, green or blue-green pads
with *numerous long* (2–10 cm), *white or gray, whiskerlike*
spines. Longer spines slightly twisted, with *flattened bases.*
Flowers red, pink, or yellow at any one locality. Stems in low,
sprawling clumps. In Porcupine Prickly Pear (subspecies
erinacea) pads have moderately thick, *straight spines.* Grizzly
Bear Prickly Pear (subspecies *ursina*) has *very long, curving,
threadlike spines* that *densely cover* the pads in a tangled mass.
30–60 cm. Northern S.W., sw. R. Mts.   APRIL–JULY

ARIZONA BARREL CACTUS   *Ferocactus wislizenii*
Each cluster has *many slender, hairlike* radial spines *below* 4
large central spines, which are flattened and cross-ribbed; main
spine often hooked. Flowers red, yellow-orange, or yellow; all
colors often found in one place. Blooms in mid- to late *summer.*
Stem barrel-like. 30 cm–2 m. S. ½ Ariz., to El Paso, Tex.
                                         JULY–SEPT.

COVILLE'S BARREL CACTUS   *Ferocactus covillei*
Similar to Arizona Barrel Cactus, but note that the *lower radial spines* and all but 1 of the central spines look alike and are
round with thick bases. Main central spine flattened, the tip
curved to hooked. Columnlike barrel stem. Flowers red-purple
or yellow. Blooms in *summer.* 50 cm–2 m. Lower deserts.
Sw. Ariz. to Phoenix.   JULY–SEPT.

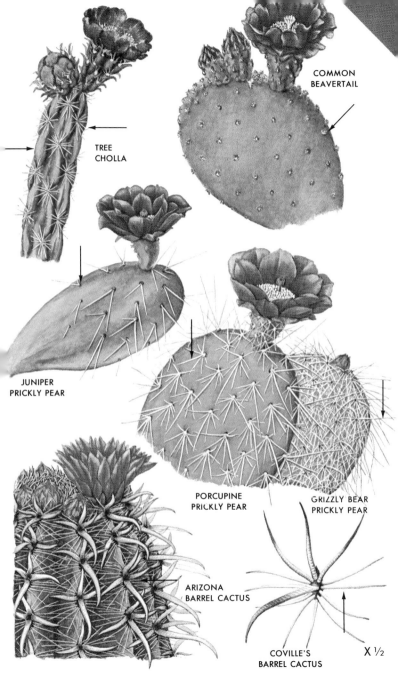

TREE
CHOLLA

COMMON
BEAVERTAIL

JUNIPER
PRICKLY PEAR

PORCUPINE
PRICKLY PEAR

GRIZZLY BEAR
PRICKLY PEAR

ARIZONA
BARREL CACTUS

COVILLE'S
BARREL CACTUS

X ½

CYLINDRICAL-STEMMED CHOLLA CACTI

Cactus Family (Cactaceae)
See also pp. W 2–4; Y 126–142; R 252–270.

CHAIN CHOLLA *Opuntia fulgida*
Hanging chains of smooth, *beadlike* fruits. Stem joints relatively short, thick; stem bumps short but nearly as broad (breastlike). Each spine cluster of 6 to many spreading spines. Pink to red-purple flowers arise from the tip of last year's fruit. Flowers open when night falls or when thunderclouds darken the afternoon sky. Stem joints detach easily and "jump." A treelike shrub. 1–4 m. Deep soils of plains at low elevations. Southern half of Ariz. JULY–AUG.

STAGHORN CHOLLA *Opuntia versicolor*
Each long (15–30 cm), narrow, *sticklike stem joint* has an *elongated* bump (2 cm long and 1 cm wide) with 6–9 short, spreading spines. Greenish *fruits spineless* with a shallow cup, in *short chains*. Some fruits remain for several years, with new flowers growing from the sides of the old fruit. Flowers yellow, bronze, red, or dark purple. Treelike shrub. 50 cm–3 m. S.-cen. Ariz.
APRIL–JUNE

HANDLEGRIP CHOLLA *Opuntia spinosior*
Note the *closely packed, short,* sharply raised stem bumps (2 cm or less long and 5 mm or less wide) that *resemble handlegrips*. Widely radiating clusters of 8–20 short (5 mm or less) spines; *5 rows* (from side to side) usually visible. Ovary and fruit spineless. Flowers yellow or red. Spreading, erect shrubs. 1–3 m. Common. Southeastern quarter of Ariz., s. N.M.
APRIL–JUNE

BUCKHORN CHOLLA *Opuntia acanthocarpa*
Stem joints *slender cylinders* (30 cm long) with *elongated,* raised bumps about 3 cm long and 1 cm wide. Each spine cluster has 10–12 stout (3–4 cm) straw-colored spines. Flowers yellow or red. Open, well-branched shrubs. 1–2 m. Dry slopes. Ariz.
APRIL–JUNE

KLEIN'S PENCIL CHOLLA *Opuntia kleiniae*
Note the *enlarged stem bumps with 1* or a few short (2 cm), *thin* spines on short, pencil-like stems. Flowers pale pink to red-purple. Vaselike fruit, bright red. Highly branched shrub. 20 cm–2.5 m. Rocky hillsides. Southern half of Ariz. to Big Bend area, Tex.
APRIL–MAY

SAGEBRUSH CHOLLA *Opuntia pulchella*
Note the *short, fingerlike* stem cylinders (2–8 cm) with a *diffuse, porcupinelike tangle* of long (2–5 cm), white to brownish black spines. Flowers red to red-purple. Small, low clumps of stems (5–12 cm wide) from a *larger, spine-covered underground tuber.* Dunes, low slopes. Nw. Ariz., Nev., w. Ut.
MAY–JUNE

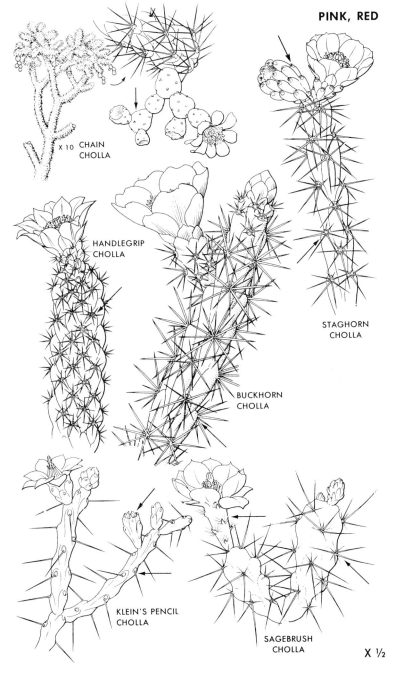

PINK, RED

X 10 CHAIN CHOLLA

HANDLEGRIP CHOLLA

STAGHORN CHOLLA

BUCKHORN CHOLLA

KLEIN'S PENCIL CHOLLA

SAGEBRUSH CHOLLA

X ½

FISHHOOK (MAMMILLARIA) CACTI

Cactus Family (Cactaceae)
See also pp. W 2–4; Y 126–142; R 252–270.

YAQUI FISHHOOK   *Mammillaria tetrancistra*
Similar to Tangled Fishhook, but with 1–4 reddish black central spines, *1 usually fish-hooked.* Lower radial spines numerous (30–50 or more). Stem *long, clublike,* with a *tapering base.* 10–30 cm. Western half of Ariz., s. Ut.   APRIL–MAY

TANGLED FISHHOOK   *Mammillaria microcarpa*
Broad-based, cylindrical stems with numerous close-set nipples, each with 1 fish-hooked central spine. Hooked spines point in *many disorganized (tangled) directions.* Long, dark red or black-purple main central spines consist of 1 "fish-hook" and *none, 1, or a few straight ones.* Note the flat circle of white to tannish red lower radial spines (15–40). Flower deep pink, with few petals (13 maximum). *Stigma green.* Fruit *club-shaped, bright red.* Juvenile form "olivae" has a *neat, golfball-like stem* with the central spine *straight* or missing. 2–5 cm. Grasslands, woodlands. Southern two-thirds of Ariz. to El Paso, Tex.
MAY–JULY

PALE FISHHOOK   *Mammillaria viridiflora*
Pale, *very narrow,* whitish or greenish petals striped with pink. 1 reddish brown central "fish-hook" and an *average of 18 radial spines* (13–42). Stigma green. 8–13 spirals of stem nipples. Fruit *small, clublike, green.* 5–10 cm. Granite soils of mid-mountains. Se. Ariz., sw. N.M.   APRIL–MAY

WRIGHT'S FISHHOOK   *Mammillaria wrightii*
Usually 2 (1–7 possible) *fish-hooked* central spines. 8–30 white to tan radial spines form a lower circle. *Huge, green, grapelike fruits.* Flowers bright red-purple. *Stigma yellowish. 5–8 spirals* of stem nipples. *Very low, round, turniplike stems* that shrink into the ground in dry times. 2–10 cm. Grasslands. Se. Ariz., southern half of N.M.   JULY–AUG.

COUNTERCLOCKWISE FISHHOOK
Mammillaria mainae
Spines *intensely yellow,* with brownish black, fish-hooked tips, *all twisted counterclockwise.* Usually 1 main central spine. 10–16 lower radial spines, also yellowish with red-brown tips. Flowers pink to red-striped, with white outer margins. *Stigma red.* Stems solitary or clumped. 5–15 cm. Slopes, washes. S. Ariz.   JULY

THORNBER'S FISHHOOK   *Mammillaria thornberi*
Short, bumpy, picklelike stems, usually in clumps. 1 main fish-hooked central spine surrounded by 15–25 yellow spines with red-brown tips. *Shallow, bowl-like flowers with very broad,* pale pink petals on *side of stem. Stigma bright red.* Fruit bright red, club-shaped. 2–25 cm. Floodplains, washes of low-elevation deserts. Cen. and sw. Ariz.   MAY–JUNE

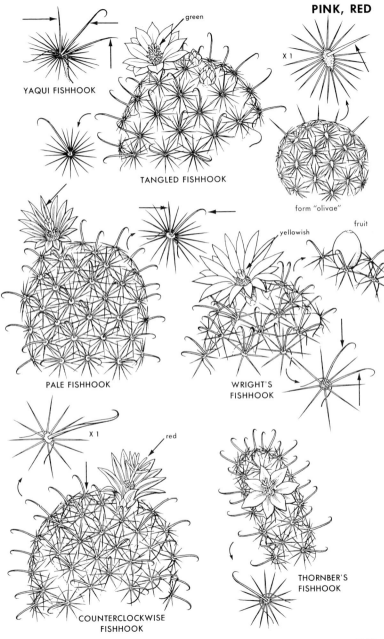

PINK, RED

YAQUI FISHHOOK

green

TANGLED FISHHOOK

X 1

form "olivae"

PALE FISHHOOK

yellowish

fruit

WRIGHT'S
FISHHOOK

X 1

red

COUNTERCLOCKWISE
FISHHOOK

THORNBER'S
FISHHOOK

X ½

MISCELLANEOUS CACTI

Cactus Family (Cactaceae)
See also pp. W 2–4; Y 126–142; R 252–270.

BUTTON CACTUS *Epithelantha micromeris*
Note the *open spaces* between tiny spine clusters, giving a *rough, latticelike* appearance to the golfball-sized stem. Spine cluster of 2–3 *relatively loose layers. Very tiny, tubular,* pale pink flowers *nearly hidden* inside the upward-pointing tuft of stem-top spines. 2–5 cm. Rocky slopes. Se. Ariz. to Del Rio, Tex.   FEB.–AUG.

BOKE'S CACTUS *Epithelantha bokei*
Note the *smooth, washed-out* appearance of the numerous tiny spine clusters with *4–5 layers* of spines. *Large, spreading,* pale pink flowers. Stems cylindrical. 2–10 cm. Rocky limestone ridges. Rio Grande, Big Bend area, Tex.   FEB.–AUG.

PANCAKE CACTUS *Mammillaria gummifera*
Flat, pancake-shaped top; see p. 140 for full description. S.W., Tex.   MARCH–MAY

LACYSPINE CACTUS *Mammillaria lasiacantha*
Stem top *not tufted.* Rounded spine clusters in *1 layer* of flattened, starlike spines. Spines *smooth or soft with feathery margins.* Large, saucerlike flowers with red-and-white-striped petals. Stems golfball-like. 2–10 cm. Limestone hills. Se. Ariz. to Big Bend region, Tex.   MARCH–AUG.

RATTAIL CACTUS *Mammillaria pottsii*
Long, *erect* stem shaped like *rat's tail,* with an outer fringe of *upward-pointing, red-brown, curved* spines. Tiny white *cottony hairs* at spine cluster bases. Radial spines *pure white.* Cylindrical, dark reddish brown flowers. 15–50 cm. Rocky hillsides. Big Bend region, Tex.   MARCH–APRIL

WHIPPLE'S CLAW CACTUS *Sclerocactus whipplei*
Main spines *more than 2 cm* long; see p. 142 for full description. In a closely related species, the **Dagger Claw Cactus,** *S. pubispinus,* upper main spine is *longer* than lower hooked spine; western Ut. **Wright's Claw Cactus,** *S. wrightae,* is very similar, but with brownish black main spines that are *less than 1.5 cm* long; southeastern Ut. **Blue Claw Cactus,** *S. glaucus,* has a waxy blue surface; main spines all straight. Eastern Ut., w. Colo. 10–30 cm. Desert plains, juniper woodlands. N. Ariz., nw. N.M., s. Ut., sw. Colo.   APRIL–JUNE

SIMPSON'S BALL CACTUS *Pediocactus simpsonii*
8–14 spiral rows of bumps. See p. 142. Northern S.W., R. Mts.
      MAY–JULY

KNOWLTON'S CACTUS *Pediocactus knowltonii*
Tiny (2–5 cm) rounded stem with many small, white or reddish-bodied, *spiderlike* spine clusters. Each spine cluster has a cottony, tear-shaped center and 16–24 leglike spines. Flowers dark pink to nearly white. 2–5 cm. Rare; on slopes in juniper-pinyon woodlands. Nw. N.M.   APRIL

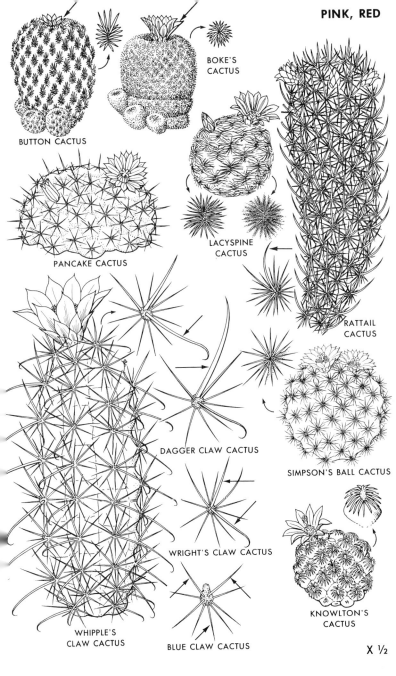

PINK, RED

BUTTON CACTUS

BOKE'S CACTUS

PANCAKE CACTUS

LACYSPINE CACTUS

RATTAIL CACTUS

DAGGER CLAW CACTUS

WRIGHT'S CLAW CACTUS

WHIPPLE'S CLAW CACTUS

BLUE CLAW CACTUS

SIMPSON'S BALL CACTUS

KNOWLTON'S CACTUS

X ½

SHORT, CYLINDRICAL-STEMMED CACTI

Cactus Family (Cactaceae)
See also pp. W 2–4; Y 126–142; R 252–270.

WOVEN PINEAPPLE CACTUS   *Echinomastus intertextus*
Note the *woven pattern* of the *flattened, chalky blue to brown* spine clusters in *spiraling rows* of low, nipplelike bumps. Spine cluster flattened, with *2 very long, central spines that point upward* and a whorl of stout radial spines below. Stem surface visible, green. Flowers pink to white; a central pink stripe on outside of petals. Usually solitary, football-like stems. 5–20 cm. Grasslands in limestone areas. Se. Ariz. to Big Bend region, Tex.   MARCH–APRIL

NEEDLED   *Echinomastus erectocentrus*
PINEAPPLE CACTUS
Note the *many, single, needlelike spines* projecting from the heavily spined, green, pineapple-shaped stem. One of the upper central spines pale straw-colored with a pinkish or red tip — *much longer* than other spines and *projecting upward and outward.* 1–4 central spines, lowermost spine shortest. Stem surface green. Flowers pinkish. Stems single, 5–30 cm. Deep soil of long slopes, plains. S.-cen. and se. Ariz.   APRIL–MAY

JOHNSON'S CACTUS   *Echinomastus johnsonii*
Note the *tangled, strawpilelike, pinkish red* (becoming black with age) *spines, all nearly the same length* (3–5 cm). Central spine thick with a bulblike base. Flowers red-purple, pink or yellow-green. Stem single with a distinctly *"squared"* surface pattern around each raised spine bump. 10–30 cm. Common. Deep soil of gentle hills. W. Ariz., Ut.   APRIL–MAY

WARNOCK'S CACTUS   *Echinomastus warnockii*
Central spines (3–4) dull gray or tan, with chalky blue or blue-green tips. Central spines *merge with 10–13 similar* but slightly smaller radial spines below. Stem surface waxy blue. Petals pale pink to white, with a dark central stripe. Flowers open in afternoon. 7–14 cm. Limestone slopes. Big Bend region, Tex.   MARCH–APRIL

SILVER COLUMN CACTUS   *Echinomastus mariposensis*
3–4 thick, central spines, dull gray or tan with chalky blue or blue-brown tips. *25–30 whitish radial spines.* Upper central spines longer than lower. Stem surface waxy blue. Flowers pale pink. Single, thickly spined, *silvery stem column.* 7–15 cm. Limestone slopes. Near Rio Grande in Big Bend region, Tex.   MARCH–APRIL

TEXAS CONE CACTUS   *Mammillaria conoidea*
Long, dark green, cylindrical stem with spiraling ribs. Large *black or brownish central* spine longer on the *lower side* of the cluster. 8–20 or more radial spines below each central spine. Flowers dark red or red-purple. Opens at mid-day. 5–20 cm. Limestone hills. El Paso to near Del Rio, Tex.   APRIL–MAY

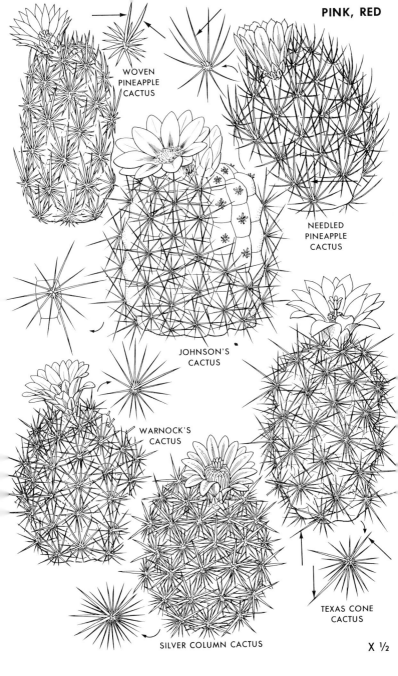

PINK, RED

WOVEN
PINEAPPLE
CACTUS

NEEDLED
PINEAPPLE
CACTUS

JOHNSON'S
CACTUS

WARNOCK'S
CACTUS

TEXAS CONE
CACTUS

SILVER COLUMN CACTUS

X ½

CORYPHANTHA NIPPLE CACTI; EACH NIPPLE WITH A GROOVE

Cactus Family (Cactaceae)
See also pp. W 2–4; Y 126–142; R 252–270.

BEEHIVE NIPPLE CACTUS *Coryphantha vivipara*
Grayish brown, baseball-sized or larger stems, usually in *beehivelike mounds.* Nipplelike stem bumps small (1 cm) and *completely obscured* by terminal clusters of 3–5 central, erect spines and 10–20 smaller ones in a flattened, circular pattern. Flowers red, pink, or yellow. 10–20 cm. Very common in woodlands, plains. S.W., western third of Tex., R. Mts., Pl. Sts.

MAY–JULY

FOXTAIL CACTUS *Coryphantha alversonii*
Stem an oblong cylinder. Each cluster includes 12–16 stout spines, surrounded by 25–35 slender spines that are *all the same length.* Spines *white with brown tips.* Flowers bright red-purple; each petal has a deep red central vein. 10–20 cm. Rocky slopes. Nw. Ariz., Calif.

MAY–JUNE

BIG NEEDLE CACTUS *Coryphantha macromeris*
Note the fist-sized, irregular *dark green stem with very long, nipplelike bumps,* each with a groove on the upper side. 4–6 *long (2–5 cm) needlelike, shiny coal black central spines* (can be grayish with age) and 5–15 smaller whitish radial spines below per cluster. Large rose-red to red-purple flowers. Stems usually in large clumps, sometimes solitary. 5–25 cm. Cen. N.M. southeasterly through Big Bend region to lower Rio Grande Valley of s. Tex.

JULY–SEPT.

WHISKERBRUSH *Coryphantha ramillosa*
Note the *upward-pointing, one-sided brush* of whitish radial spines below the 4–5 *long, black, needlelike,* erect central spines in each cluster. Flowers pale pink to rose. Stems in clustered mounds. 6–10 cm. Limestone ridges. Along Rio Grande, Big Bend Natl. Park to Del Rio, Tex.

APRIL–JUNE

HESTER'S DWARF CACTUS *Coryphantha hesteri*
Stem miniature, open-nippled. Short radial spines (5–10 mm) and 1–4 *central white spines* with brown tips. Flowers pale pink or lavender. Stems in mounded clusters. 5–10 cm. Grasslands. Rare in the wild, but commonly available from nurseries. Local species in Brewster Co., Tex.

APRIL

BIG BEND EGGS *Coryphantha dasyacantha*
Stems solitary, *egglike* (5–18 cm tall); rarely few-branched. 1 to 4 or 5 central spines are light pink, red and black (youngest). Central spines may fall off with age. 16–28 radial spines, white to straw-colored. Stigma lobes *dark green. Pink, bell-like flowers.* 5–18 cm. Rocky places. From El Paso southeastward through Big Bend region, Tex.

APRIL–MAY

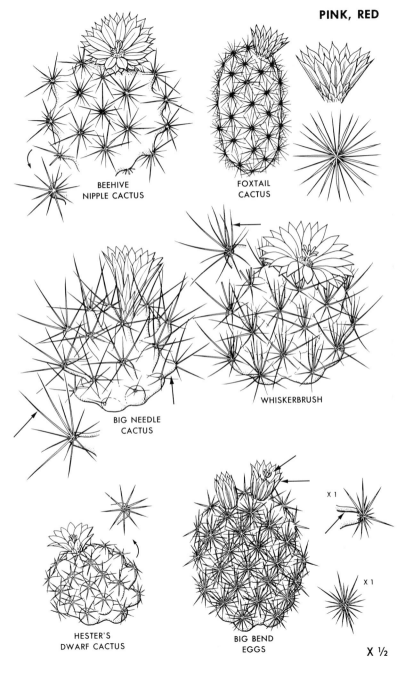

BEEHIVE
NIPPLE CACTUS

FOXTAIL
CACTUS

BIG NEEDLE
CACTUS

WHISKERBRUSH

HESTER'S
DWARF CACTUS

BIG BEND
EGGS

X 1

X 1

X ½

ESCOBARIA NIPPLE CACTI

Cactus Family (Cactaceae)
See also pp. W 2–4; Y 126–142; R 252–270.

CORNCOB ESCOBARIA *Coryphantha strobiliformis*
Tall, *erect, sausagelike stems in clumps*. Stem bumps and pale green surface easily seen through *flimsy* covering of spines. On old stems, *basal portion bare and corncoblike* where spine clusters have fallen away. 4 or 6 thick-based central spines, one longer than the others and *slanting downward,* pink-tipped. Lower radial spines *thin, numerous.* Flowers pink. Stigma lobes whitish. Fruit red. A highly variable species; many very similar segregate species have been proposed but are very difficult to separate. 10–30 cm. Common on rocky limestone ledges. Se. Ariz. (barely) to Big Bend region, Tex. APRIL–JULY

BIRDFOOT CACTUS *Coryphantha minima*
3 *large* central spines resemble a *bird's foot;* they point upward and are flattened against the *starlike clusters of radial spines* below. Flowers pink to rose-purple. Stems the size of sparrow eggs, in clusters. 2–8 cm. Big Bend region, Tex.

MARCH–APRIL

SNEED'S CARPET ESCOBARIA *Coryphantha sneedii*
Miniature (2–5 cm), round to thumblike stems in *carpetlike clusters.* Lower white radial spines on *top side* of stem. Central spines *erect,* white with pink-red tips, spreading in no particular direction. Stem surface not visible, but becoming bare and corncoblike with age. Petals pink-striped, red-purple, or brownish. *Fruit green.* 2–8 cm. Limestone ledges. Franklin Mts., w. Tex. JULY–AUG.

LEE'S CARPET ESCOBARIA *Coryphantha leei*
Miniature (2–5 cm), round to thumblike stems in carpetlike clusters. *Thick, stubby* central spines *flattened* against stem. Petals pink with lighter margins. Guadalupe Mts. of Guadalupe National Park in Tex. and adjacent N.M. JULY–AUG.

DUNCAN'S PINCUSHION *Coryphantha duncanii*
Small, 50-cent-sized, turnip-shaped stem with a *dense mat of long, white, dress-pin-sized spines* with brown tips. Each spine cluster has 2 *semi-visible layers* of similar-sized spines: outer layers with a few spines, inner layers with up to 80 spines on a large green nipple. Stigma tip *green.* Petals pale pink with a darker central stripe. 2–8 cm. Limestone ledges. Big Bend region, Tex.; also s.-cen. N.M. MARCH–APRIL

RUNYON'S ESCOBARIA *Coryphantha robertii*
Short (2–5 cm), *fat, brownish, dumpling-like stems* in large clusters. Central spines large, semi-erect, *tipped with dark brownish red.* Lower radial spines (20–30) smaller, thin, white. Narrow, tubular flowers pinkish with yellowish stripes. 2–5 cm. Grows in shade of shrubs. Along Rio Grande from Langtry to Brownsville, Tex. FEB.–MAY

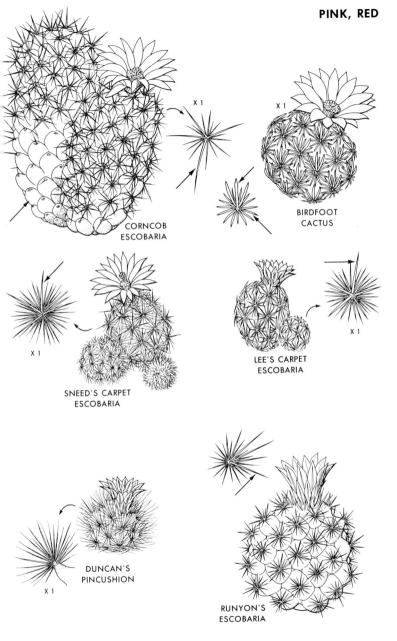

X 1

CORNCOB
ESCOBARIA

X 1

BIRDFOOT
CACTUS

X 1

SNEED'S CARPET
ESCOBARIA

LEE'S CARPET
ESCOBARIA

X 1

DUNCAN'S
PINCUSHION

X 1

RUNYON'S
ESCOBARIA

X ½

SPECIAL CACTI

Cactus Family (Cactaceae)
See also pp. W 2–4; Y 126–142; R 252–270.

SEÑITA or OLD MAN *Lophocereus schottii*
Note the *dense, manelike mantle* of spines on ends of upper stem.
Ribbed stems like a *giant, upturned bunch of bananas.* Pink flowers
within the spiny mane bloom at night. 1–5 m. Valleys. Organ Pipe
Cactus National Monument, Ariz. APRIL–JULY

CRACK STAR *Ariocarpus fissuratus*
Note the *warty, flat stem forming stars within stars;* stem *level* with
surrounding rocks. Beautiful deep pink flowers. Cracks of flat limestone slabs. Hard to find; you may have walked over hundreds of
these interesting plants without seeing one. 5–12 cm. Big Bend region to s. Tex. along the Rio Grande. LATE AUG.–DEC.

PEYOTE or DRY WHISKY *Lophophora williamsii*
Note the *spineless, blue-green, tomatolike stem* with a few *tufts of
silky hairs.* Flowers pink. Stem single or in clusters. Level with soil
surface to 7 cm. Formerly covered thousands of acres, but now rare
due to overcollecting. Southern N.M. and se. along the Rio Grande
to s. Tex. MARCH–APRIL

CATCLAW CACTUS *Ancistrocactus uncinatus*
Note the *extra long, hooked spines* that project upward from the
sharply ribbed, bluish green stem. Usually one of the main yellowish
brown central spines is hooked, the others straight. Lower, pale
reddish or gray radial spines often hooked. *Dark brownish, funnel-
like red flowers, nearly hidden* among spines. Stems solitary. 10–
30 cm. In a band from El Paso to Rio Grande City, s. Tex.
MARCH–APRIL

TEXAS PRIDE *Thelocactus bicolor*
Note the *egg-shaped stem* with most of the longer and larger
ribbonlike central spines sweeping upward. Spines straw-colored;
the uppermost spines have *pink tips.* Large, funnel-shaped, rose-red
flowers with dark red centers. Solitary stems. 7–12 cm. Gravelly
desert slopes. Big Bend region se. to s. Tex. MARCH–MAY

GEARSTEM CACTUS *Cereus striatus*
Gray-green, sticklike stems with 6–9 *barely distinguishable, broad,
flat ribs. Stem gearlike* in cross-section. Downward-projecting spine
clusters with 2 main spines. 1–2 m. Grows among other shrubs for
support. Sw. Ariz. near Organ Pipe Cactus National Monument.
JUNE

POSELGER'S CACTUS *Cereus poselgeri*
Long, snakelike stems taper to thin bases; 8–10 ribs on each stem.
Large pink to red-purple flowers. Upright stems, single or branched;
usually supported by nearby shrubs. 3–6 m. Brushlands. Laredo to
Brownsville, Tex. MARCH–APRIL

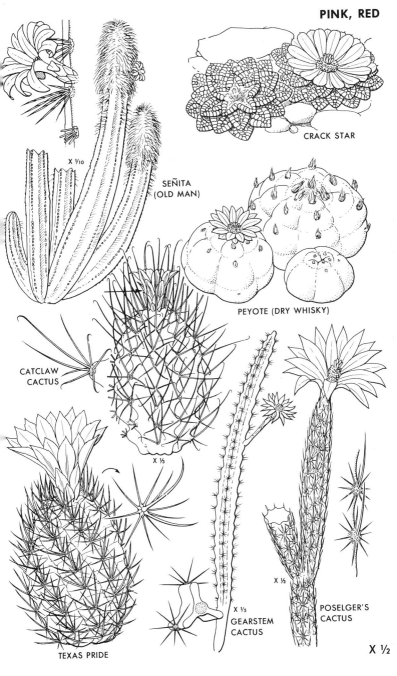

CRACK STAR

SEÑITA
(OLD MAN)

X 1/10

PEYOTE (DRY WHISKY)

CATCLAW
CACTUS

X 1/3

TEXAS PRIDE

X 1/5

GEARSTEM
CACTUS

POSELGER'S
CACTUS

X 1/3

X 1/2

3 PETALS; LEAVES PARALLEL-VEINED

Lily Family (Liliaceae)
See also pp. W 8–14; Y 114; O 226; B 338; G 390.

SLENDER TRILLIUM   *Trillium gracile*
*Slender, elliptical, green- and white-splotched leaves have
broad bases and no petioles.* 3 linear, erect dark red-purple
petals (sometimes yellow-green). *Round-tipped,* spreading
sepals. 10–30 cm. Very common. Pine, hardwood forests. Eastern quarter of Tex., S.E.   MARCH–MAY

HANDLED TRILLIUM   *Trillium recurvatum*
3 heart-shaped to elliptical, green- and white-splotched leaves,
each with a *narrow,* handlelike base (petiole). 3 erect, dark
red-purple petals. Sepals *sharp-tipped, triangular,* bent downward. 10–40 cm. Rich hardwood forests. E. Tex.

MARCH–MAY

WESTERN TRILLIUM   *Trillium ovatum*
Pink to whitish flower with *short, oval petals* on a *long pedicel*
above 3 oval, sharp-pointed green leaves. 10–60 cm. Moist,
shady woods. Northern S.W., R. Mts.   APRIL–JUNE

TAPERTIP TRILLIUM   *Trillium viridescens*
Leaf blades *petioleless,* broadly heart-shaped with *narrow, tapering tips.* Leaf surface *not mottled,* sometimes obscurely
marked. Petal color variable, purplish to yellow-green.
30–50 cm. Rocky slopes in hardwood forests. Ne. Tex. and north
through Ozark Mts.   APRIL–MAY

Iris Family (Iridaceae) See also pp. Y 116; B 340.

COPPER IRIS   *Iris fulva*
Iris-like flowers pink-red, red, or coppery red. *Ovary 6-sided.*
Petal tips *slightly notched* or bilobed. Tall, swordlike leaves in
flattened sheaths. 50 cm–1 m. Pond margins. Uncommon. E.
Tex.   MARCH–APRIL

Spiderwort Family (Commelinaceae)
Flower color variable in each species, pink to blue-purple. See
Blue section (p. 338) for most species in this family.

CLIFF SPIDERWORT   *Setcreasea brevifolia*
Note the pink, 3-petaled, *triangular* flowers *nestled among
channeled, leaflike bracts.* Alternate, parallel-veined, elliptical
leaves with clasping bases and *long, spidery hairs. No hairs* on
stamen filaments. 10–60 cm. Moist ledges, cliff cracks, mountains. W. Tex.   JULY–OCT.

PINE SPIDERWORT   *Tradescantia pinetorum*
Flower bud, pedicels, and sepals have *glandular hairs. Hairs*
on stamen filaments. All 3 pink to rose or purple petals equal-
sized. Two or more leaves or bracts enclose the flower cluster.
30–80 cm. Very common. Wooded slopes, particularly pine
woods. S.W., R. Mts.   JULY–SEPT.

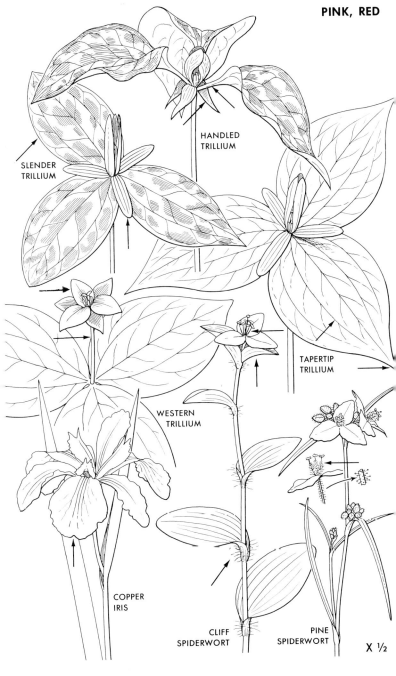

SLENDER
TRILLIUM

HANDLED
TRILLIUM

TAPERTIP
TRILLIUM

WESTERN
TRILLIUM

COPPER
IRIS

CLIFF
SPIDERWORT

PINE
SPIDERWORT

X ½

6 PETALS; UMBEL ON LEAFLESS STEM; WITH OR WITHOUT ONION ODOR

Amaryllis Family (Amaryllidaceae)
See also pp. W 14–16; Y 116; B 338.

PINK FUNNEL LILY *Androstephium breviflorum*
Note that the 6 stamen filaments are *fused into a long, protruding funnel*. Petals light pink to red-purple. *No onion odor.* 5–20 cm. Sandy ground. Northern S.W., R. Mts. MARCH–APRIL

HOOKER'S ONION *Allium acuminatum*
Three small, triangular, bright rose to dark red inner petals with *minutely sawtoothed, rolled margins*. Small urnlike flowers. 2–3 narrow leaves. Distinct onion odor. 10–30 cm. Semi-open to open slopes. Ariz., R. Mts. MAY–JULY

NODDING ONION *Allium cernuum*
Note the *nodding umbel* of pink to white *bell-like flowers*. Petals *nearly round*. Leaves linear. Distinct onion odor. 10–50 cm. Moist mountain soils. S.W., R. Mts. JULY–OCT.

GEYER'S ONION *Allium geyeri*
Flowers pink or white with a *distinct constriction* immediately below the *tiny, reflexed, sharply triangular petals*. Each petal has a thick rib on the back. In some areas the flowers are replaced by small bulblets. Distinct onion odor. 10 cm–1 m. Damp mountain meadows. S.W., R. Mts. MAY–JUNE

ARIZONA ONION *Allium macropetalum*
Flowers open, bowl-like; petals lancelike, palest pink with a dark red-brown stripe. *6 rounded, flattened crests* near ovary top. 2 leaves. Distinct onion odor. 5–25 cm. Open deserts. Extremely common. S.W., w. Tex., R. Mts. MARCH–JUNE

PLUMMER'S ONION *Allium plummerae*
Petal tips taper evenly to *sharp points*. Ovary walls with *6 jagged crests*. Papery umbel bracts with 3–5 veins. Flowers pink to white. 10–30 cm. Mountains. S. Ariz., sw. N.M. JULY–AUG.

BELLED ONION *Allium perdulce*
Deep rosy red flowers *open, bell-like*. Ovary walls *smooth, without crests*. 3 or more leaves. 10–30 cm. Open plains. North-cen. and Panhandle, Tex.; e. N.M., Pl. Sts. MARCH–APRIL

PALMER'S ONION *Allium palmeri*
Widely spreading, red-purple petals give the flower a *wheel-like appearance*. 6 prominent *linear crests in pairs* on the ovary wall. Distinct onion odor. 10–15 cm. Mid- to highest mountains. S.W., R. Mts. MAY–JULY

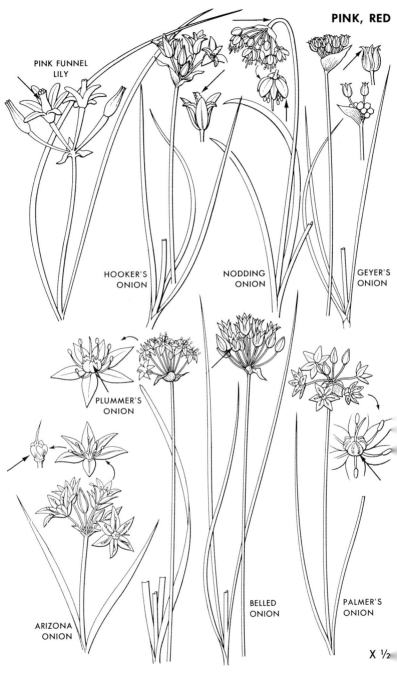

PINK FUNNEL LILY

HOOKER'S ONION

NODDING ONION

GEYER'S ONION

PLUMMER'S ONION

ARIZONA ONION

BELLED ONION

PALMER'S ONION

X ½

4-PETALED MALTESE CROSS

Mustard Family (Cruciferae)
See also pp. W 26–32; Y 144–152; O 232.

ARIZONA JEWELFLOWER   *Streptanthus arizonicus*
Large, *yellow, urnlike* calyx with tiny, twisted, brownish purple
petals. See p. 148 for details. Southern S.W.   JAN.–APRIL

HEARTLEAF JEWELFLOWER   *Streptanthus cordatus*
Pointed sepals with a *terminal tuft of hairs.* Urn-shaped flowers
have red-purple or yellow petals with white tips. Seedpods
erect. *Heart-shaped,* yellow-green leaves clasp the upper stem;
basal leaves are toothed, spatula-like. 30–90 cm. Rocky slopes.
Northern S.W., R. Mts.   MARCH–MAY

SQUAW CABBAGE   *Caulanthus crassicaulis*
Note the *long columns* of dark, red-purple flowers on *inflated,
coarse, cabbagelike stems.* Thick, succulent *waxy blue-green
arrow-shaped leaves* with clasping, *earlike* bases. 30 cm–1 m.
Lower mountain slopes. Nw. Ariz., R. Mts.   APRIL–JUNE

PINK WINDMILLS   *Sisymbrium linearifolium*
Note the *long, linear leaves* and the long, narrow, *upright seedpods.* Flowers rose-purple. 30–90 cm. Common in pine forests,
chaparral. S.W., sw. Tex., R. Mts.   APRIL–OCT.

PURPLE CROSS FLOWER Alien   *Chorispora tenella*
Seedpods *curve upward, with sharp points.* Long, narrow petals. Stem and calyx have *distinct, scattered, glandular hairs.*
10–50 cm. Disturbed places. S.W., R. Mts.   APRIL–JUNE

STIFFARM ROCK CRESS   *Arabis perennans*
Curving seedpods extend horizontally from the stem. Dense
basal cluster of gray-green, spatula-like leaves with a few teeth;
thick covering of straplike leaves on lower stem. Flowers pink
to red-purple. 20–60 cm. The most common *Arabis* species
throughout S.W. and R. Mts.   FEB.–OCT.

TAILED ROCK CRESS   *Arabis pulchra*
Narrow, linear leaves with smooth margins in both the basal
cluster and up the stem. Nearly straight seedpods on curving
pedicels form a *thick, downward-pointing "tail" or brush.*
Flowers pink to red-purple. 20–60 cm. Northern S.W., R. Mts.
MAY–JULY

HOLBOELL'S ROCK CRESS   *Arabis holboellii*
The nearly straight to curving seedpods are *strongly reflexed
downward.* Gray, spatula-shaped leaves with a few teeth in a
basal rosette. The stout stem has narrow, clasping, arrow-
shaped leaves. Flowers pink to white. 10 cm–1 m. Dry rocky
hills. Northern N.M., R. Mts.   MAY–AUG.

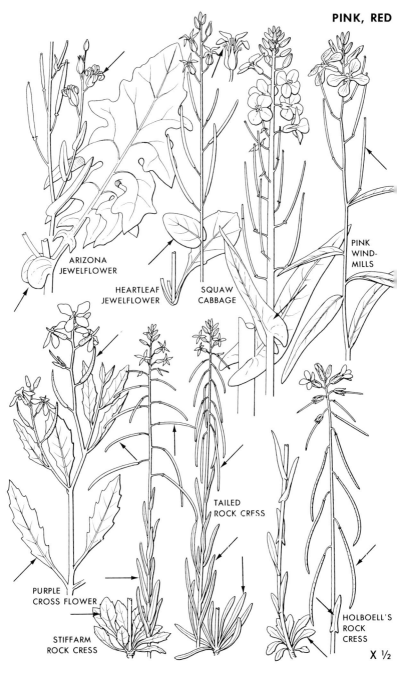

ARIZONA JEWELFLOWER

HEARTLEAF JEWELFLOWER

SQUAW CABBAGE

PINK WIND-MILLS

PURPLE CROSS FLOWER

STIFFARM ROCK CRESS

TAILED ROCK CRESS

HOLBOELL'S ROCK CRESS

X ½

4 SHOWY PETALS ON TOP OF OVARY

Evening Primrose Family (Onagraceae)
See also pp. W 34–36; Y 154–158; R 280.

PINK LADIES *Oenothera speciosa*
Four *large, rosy pink petals* with darker red veins and a *yellow basal spot*. Petals white when bud opens, but quickly turn pink. *Unopened buds nodding.* Inferior ovary club-shaped. Leaves somewhat lobed or entire. Occurs in great showy pink masses. 30–60 cm. Tex., occasionally to Ariz., Pl. Sts.

MARCH–JULY

BROWN EYES *Camissonia clavaeformis*
A *brown, eyelike spot* is often present at the base of each petal. Flowers pink, yellow, or white; petals rounded. Flower cluster of *nodding buds* above a basal rosette of oval, strongly-toothed leaves. Seed capsules (not shown) *club-shaped.* 10–20 cm. Common in lower deserts. Ariz.

JAN.–APRIL

WINECUP CLARKIA *Clarkia purpurea*
Small, cuplike flowers. Petals fan-shaped, solid purple, sometimes with a darker central spot. Flower buds erect. 10–60 cm. Open places in low mountains. S. Ariz.

APRIL–MAY

TONGUED CLARKIA *Clarkia rhomboidea*
Pink, *diamond-shaped* petals *with 2 rounded projections* opposite each other near the red petal base. 10 cm–1 m. Open to semi-shaded, dry slopes. Cen. and s. Ariz.

MAY–JUNE

STICKY FIREWEED *Epilobium glandulosum*
Stem has *tiny, sticky hairs.* Many small flowers (less than 10 mm) on long inferior ovaries. Petals vary from pink to white, with bilobed (notched) tips. *Opposite,* lancelike leaves with minutely sawtoothed margins. 30–90 cm. Moist places in mountains. Common. S.W., R. Mts.

JUNE–SEPT.

PARCHED FIREWEED *Epilobium paniculatum*
Leaves linear, *alternately arranged.* Petal lobes *deeply notched.* Stem surface has *peeling bark.* 10 cm–1.5 m. Common in dry places at mid-mountain elevations. S.W., R. Mts.

AUG.–OCT.

THREADSTEM FIREWEED *Epilobium minutum*
Similar to Parched Fireweed, but leaves *opposite.* A tiny (2–10 cm), well-branched plant found in *dry places* on open slopes, at mid to lower elevations. Ariz.

MAY

RED FIREWEED *Epilobium angustifolium*
Each *large,* bright red-purple petal has a single rounded tip. Numerous flowers in a long terminal spike. Leaves alternate. 50 cm–2 m. Common in mountains. S.W., R. Mts.

JULY–SEPT.

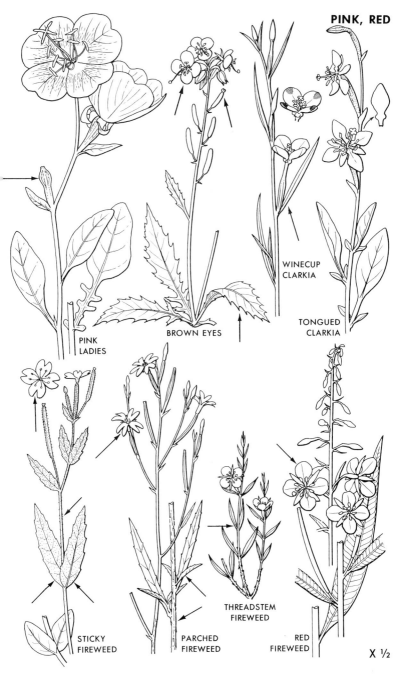

PINK
LADIES

BROWN EYES

WINECUP
CLARKIA

TONGUED
CLARKIA

STICKY
FIREWEED

PARCHED
FIREWEED

THREADSTEM
FIREWEED

RED
FIREWEED

X ½

4 OR 6 PETALS; CROSSES, WHEELS

Evening Primrose Family (Onagraceae)
See also pp. W 34–36; Y 154–158; R 278.

SCARLET BEEBLOSSOM *Gaura coccinea*
Four pink to deep scarlet petals arranged *irregularly* (asymmetrically). Leaves linear to elliptical with smooth or toothed margins. Seed capsule *club-shaped, with grooves.* Ovary inferior. Most *Gaura* species have white petals that turn pink (see p. 36). 10–40 cm. S.W., Tex., Pl. Sts.   MARCH–SEPT.

ARIZONA TRUMPET *Zauschneria latifolia*
Long, tubular, scarlet flowers look like *fushia flowers* (fuchsias also belong to this family). Leaves broadly lancelike with *toothed margins.* Ovary inferior, with glandular hairs. 10–50 cm. Rocky slopes, canyons. Southern half of Ariz., sw. N.M.
JUNE–DEC.

Meadow Beauty Family (Melastomataceae)

VIRGINIA MEADOW BEAUTY *Rhexia virginica*
Four *oval,* rose-purple petals with a *threadlike base.* Stigma *long, spoutlike.* Ovary *superior.* Leaves *broadly oval, without petioles.* 30 cm–1 m. Open seepage slopes, bogs. Eastern third of Tex., Pl. Sts., S.E.   JUNE–OCT.

LANCE-LEAF MEADOW BEAUTY *Rhexia mariana*
Similar to Virginia Meadow Beauty, but leaf *narrow, lancelike, with a petiole.* Flowers rose to pure white. 10–60 cm. Wet meadows, ditches, bogs. Common. Eastern quarter of Tex., Pl. Sts.
MAY–SEPT.

Bedstraw Family (Rubiaceae) See also p. W 24.

PRAIRIE BLUETS *Hedyotis nigricans*
Petal *tips sharply pointed* in a Maltese cross. Leaves thin, linear, in *opposite pairs.* Pedicel of seed capsule *erect* (not shown). Flowers pink, purplish, or white. 5–50 cm. S.W., Tex., Pl. Sts.
APRIL–NOV.

NEEDLELEAF BLUETS *Hedyotis acerosa*
Note the *spine-tipped, hairy* leaves and sepals. 5–35 cm. Se. N.M., western third of Tex.   APRIL–SEPT.

WRIGHT'S BLUETS *Hedyotis pygmaea*
Leaves *thick, succulent.* Pedicel of developing seed capsules *curves downward.* Stems spreading, prostrate. 5–50 cm. Mesas, dry rocky hills. S.W.   APRIL–AUG.

Loosestrife Family (Lythraceae)

CALIFORNIA LOOSESTRIFE *Lythrum californicum*
Small, red-purple flowers with pedicels; *4–7 petals, usually 6. Grooved, cylindrical calyx* looks like an inferior ovary, but is superior. Leaves alternate. 50 cm–1.5 m. Damp soil along streams, bogs. S.W., Tex.   MARCH–NOV.

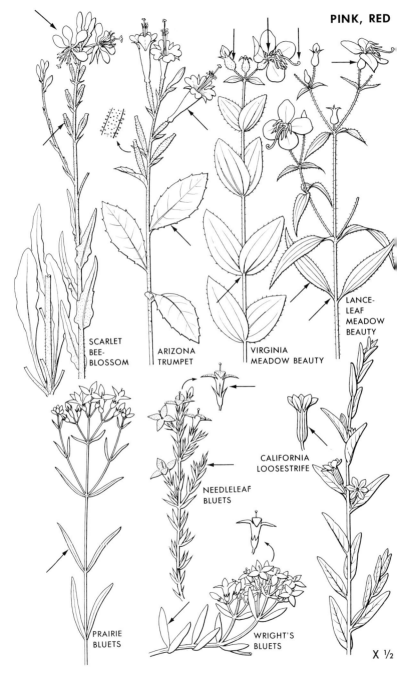

SCARLET
BEE-
BLOSSOM

ARIZONA
TRUMPET

VIRGINIA
MEADOW BEAUTY

LANCE-
LEAF
MEADOW
BEAUTY

CALIFORNIA
LOOSESTRIFE

PRAIRIE
BLUETS

NEEDLELEAF
BLUETS

WRIGHT'S
BLUETS

X ½

4 OR 5 PETALS; TINY TUBULAR FLOWERS IN CLUSTERS

Buckwheat Family (Polygonaceae)
See also pp. W 38–40; Y 158–160; R 284.

WATER SMARTWEED *Polygonum coccineum*
Large, oval leaves (5–15 cm long). *Smooth-edged,* papery sheaths at each stem joint. Stem erect to floating. A dense terminal cluster of pink flowers on a leafless stem. *P. amphibium* is now included in this species. 30–60 cm. Ponds, or nearly dry ground. S.W., Tex., R. Mts.   JUNE–OCT.

WHORLED DOCK Alien *Rumex conglomeratus*
Note the *whorls* of tiny red flowers, which soon become *conspicuous clusters* of red-brown seeds. Lower leaves oblong. 30–60 cm. Disturbed places. S.W., Tex.   FEB.–MAY

LADY'S THUMB Alien *Polygonum persicaria*
Papery stem *bracts fringed.* Erect stems with lancelike leaves and dense, pink, thumblike flower clusters. 30–120 cm. Common in moist places. S.W., Tex., R. Mts.   JUNE–DEC.

DAGGER SORREL *Rumex hastatulus*
Leaf blade *long, narrow, daggerlike,* with *thin, curled lobes.* Upper stem leaves daggerlike with only a suggestion of basal lobes. 10–90 cm. Very common. Eastern half of Tex., Pl. Sts.
FEB.–MAY

MOUNTAIN SORREL *Oxyria digyna*
Note the bright green, *kidney-shaped leaves,* mostly basal. Many small red to yellow-green flowers in a spike. 50 cm–2.5 m. Rocky alpine slopes. S.W., R. Mts.   JULY–SEPT.

SHEEP SORREL Alien *Rumex acetosella*
Note the *broad, arrow-shaped,* dark green, fleshy leaves with fairly *broad basal lobes.* Tiny red-yellow flowers in a loose terminal raceme. 10–40 cm. Disturbed places. S.W., Tex., Pl. Sts.
FEB.–NOV.

DESERT RHUBARB *Rumex hymenosepalus*
Note the *very large, oblong leaves* (10–30 cm). Stems in dense clumps. Tiny pink flowers in terminal racemes. Each of the heart-shaped, red-brown seeds has flat finlike membranes around it. 50 cm–1 m. Common in deserts. S.W., western half of Tex., R. Mts., Pl. Sts.   FEB.–MAY

CURLY DOCK Alien *Rumex crispus*
The lower leaves are lancelike with *curly margins.* Tiny red flowers in dense clusters. The tiny, red-brown seeds are heart-shaped. 50 cm–1 m. Disturbed places. S.W., Tex., R. Mts., Pl. Sts.   FEB.–MAY

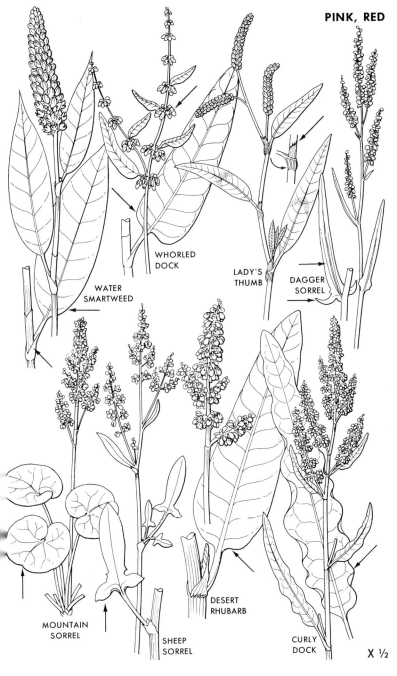

PINK, RED

WHORLED DOCK

LADY'S THUMB

DAGGER SORREL

WATER SMARTWEED

MOUNTAIN SORREL

SHEEP SORREL

DESERT RHUBARB

CURLY DOCK

X ½

4 OR 5 PETALS; TINY, TUBULAR FLOWERS IN CLUSTERS

Buckwheat Family (Polygonaceae)
See also pp. W 38–40; Y 158–160; R 282.

EGGLEAF ERIOGONUM   *Eriogonum ovalifolium*
A dense *basal mat of tiny, white, woolly, egg-shaped leaves.*
Flower stems protrude above mat in round heads of pink, white
or yellow flowers; Umbel bracts not visible. 10–20 cm. Desert
slopes to alpine. Northern S.W., R. Mts.   APRIL–JUNE

ABERT'S ERIOGONUM   *Eriogonum abertianum*
Heart-shaped to oval leaves with *sparse gray hairs* on long
petioles. Rosy red flowers in *round, flat-topped clusters* on long,
leafless stems. Stem erect, well-branched. 10–50 cm. Gravelly
slopes, flats at lower desert elevations. Frequent. S.W., w. Tex.
FEB.–NOV.

HAWKWEED ERIOGONUM   *Eriogonum hieracifolium*
Dark green, *spatulalike leaves* with long, tapering bases; most
are in a basal cluster. Dark red-brown to yellow flowers in
semi-loose clusters arise from *narrow, cuplike bases*. 10–60 cm.
Common in open places, low-elevation woodlands. S.W.
JUNE–NOV.

REDROOT ERIOGONUM   *Eriogonum racemosum*
Note the many *erect leaves* with *very long petioles* and leaf
blades, *all in a basal cluster*. Long, gray, leafless flower stems.
Pink or white flowers in a scraggly spike of loose clusters; note
dark pink ribs on petal backsides. 10–60 cm. Common in pine
forests. Northern S.W.   JUNE–OCT.

WICKERSTEM ERIOGONUM   *Eriogonum vimineum*
Clusters of pink, white or yellow flowers emerge from *elongated
cylinders* that *hug* the branches of the erect, red, wickerlike
stem. *Rounded* basal leaves. 10–60 cm. Upper desert slopes.
W. Ariz.   MAY–OCT.

THURBER'S ERIOGONUM   *Eriogonum thurberi*
Note the tiny wad of "cotton" at the base of each squared petal.
Oblong leaves in a basal cluster; upper surface green, *underside
white, feltlike.* 10–30 cm. Very common in sandy places on
lower desert slopes. Ariz.   MARCH–JUNE

FLATCROWN ERIOGONUM   *Eriogonum deflexum*
Flower clusters *hang upside-down*. The *felt-haired* basal leaves
are kidney-shaped to round. 10–80 cm. Common on rocky
slopes. Ariz., Ut.   MOST OF YEAR

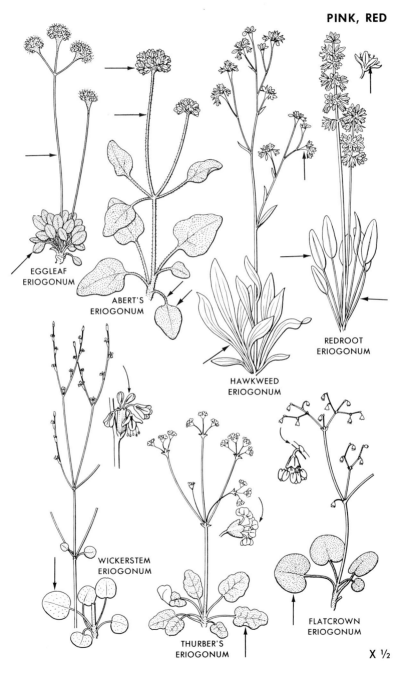

EGGLEAF
ERIOGONUM

ABERT'S
ERIOGONUM

HAWKWEED
ERIOGONUM

REDROOT
ERIOGONUM

WICKERSTEM
ERIOGONUM

THURBER'S
ERIOGONUM

FLATCROWN
ERIOGONUM

X ½

5 TO MANY PETALS

Carrot Family (Umbelliferae) See also pp. W 58–62; Y 176.

LEAVENWORTH'S ERYNGIUM — *Eryngium leavenworthii*
Note the *bright red-purple, headlike* flower cones and the rigid, *divided, spiny bracts.* Stems densely covered with similar but greenish bracts. Forms colorful carpets. 10–80 cm. Tex., Pl. Sts.

JULY–OCT.

Buttercup Family (Ranunculaceae)
See also pp. W 42–44; Y 162–164;
R 236; B 344, 356–358; G 396–406.

PITCHER'S CLEMATIS — *Clematis pitcheri*
Note the dark red-purple, *nodding, urnlike* (pitcherlike) flowers. The pinnate leaves have *raised, netlike* surfaces. Climbing vine. N.M., Tex., Pl. Sts.

APRIL–SEPT.

DESERT ANEMONE — *Anemone tuberosa*
Many light pink petals around a *cylindrical column.* Leaves *pinnate.* 10–30 cm. Frequent on lower deserts in rocky places. S.W., w. Tex., Ut.

FEB.–APRIL

Leadwort Family (Plumbaginaceae)

NASH'S SEA LAVENDER — *Limonium nashii*
Note the curving sprays of *tiny,* pink to violet, *trumpet-shaped* flowers. Each flower within a *long, papery bract.* Smooth, yellow-green, spatula-like leaves, all basal. 30–60 cm. Tex. Gulf Coast.

JUNE–NOV.

Sedum Family (Crassulaceae) See also pp. W 78; Y 180.

KING'S CROWN — *Sedum rosea*
Tiny (5 mm or less), dark red-purple flowers in *headlike clusters* on erect, fleshy stems. Leaves flattened. 10–30 cm. Rocky cliffs in higher mountains. N.M., R. Mts.

JULY–SEPT.

QUEEN'S CROWN — *Sedum rhodanthum*
Similar to King's Crown, but flowers in small clusters *above leaf base* of upper stem. Each flower longer (5–10 mm), red to nearly white. 10–50 cm. Wet streamsides of higher mountains. S.W., R. Mts.

JULY–SEPT.

CHALK DUDLEYA — *Dudleya pulverulenta*
Note the *huge, chalky white* basal cluster of pointed, oval leaves. Flower stem emerges from the side of the cluster. Upper leaves heart-shaped. Dark red, urnlike flowers. 30–60 cm. Rocky cliffs. W. Ariz.

APRIL, OCT.–DEC.

BIG BEND SUCCULENT — *Echeveria strictiflora*
Note the red to red-orange, *tapering, urnlike* flowers in long *nodding sprays* well above the basal cluster of leaves. Basal leaves fleshy, bright green, grooved, spatula-shaped; flower stem leaves *swollen, cylindrical.* 20–60 cm. Rocky ledges, crevices in higher mountains. Big Bend region of Tex.

JUNE–AUG.

RATTAIL SUCCULENT — *Villadia squamulosa*
Erect, *rat-tail-like* stem *crowded* with thick, fleshy cylindrical leaves. *Many tiny* pinkish flowers *clustered above* base of *each leaf.* 10–15 cm. Frequent on cliffs, crevices of higher mountains. Big Bend region of Tex.

JUNE–SEPT.

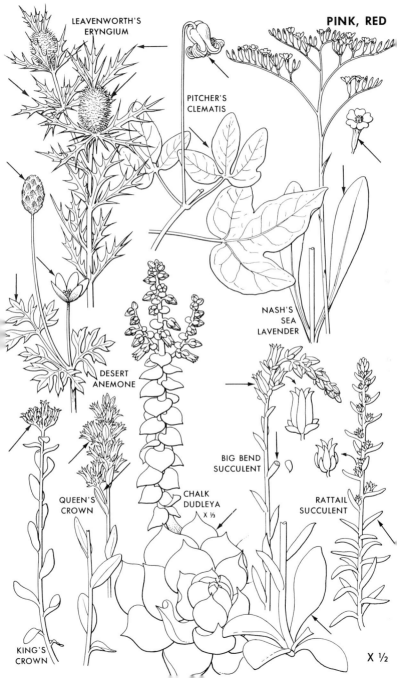

LEAVENWORTH'S ERYNGIUM

PINK, RED

PITCHER'S CLEMATIS

NASH'S SEA LAVENDER

DESERT ANEMONE

QUEEN'S CROWN

CHALK DUDLEYA
X ⅓

BIG BEND SUCCULENT

RATTAIL SUCCULENT

KING'S CROWN

X ½

5 PETALS; HOLLYHOCK FLOWERS; MANY STAMENS, IN A FUSED COLUMN

Mallow Family (Malvaceae)
See also pp. W 44; Y 166; O 238; R 290.

DESERT FIVESPOT *Malvastrum rotundifolium*
Large (3 cm), globe-shaped, rose pink flowers with *large, dark red spots* at the base of each petal. Leaves *rounded.* 10–50 cm. Common, lower deserts. W. Ariz. MARCH–MAY

TRAILING MALLOW *Malvastrum exile*
Small (5 mm), pale pink or white flowers along a *trailing stem.* Leaves *trilobed.* 10–50 cm. Sandy flats, lower elevations. S.W., Tex., R. Mts. APRIL–OCT.

UMBRELLA MALLOW Alien *Malva neglecta*
Small (10 mm), pale pink flowers with *petals longer than sepals.* Dark green, umbrellalike leaves. 10–60 cm. Common in disturbed places. S.W., Tex., R. Mts. APRIL–OCT.

CHEESEWEED Alien *Malva parviflora*
The tiny (5 mm), pink to white flowers have very short petals that are *the same length as the sepals.* Leaves have 5–7 broad, rounded lobes. 20 cm–1 m. Common in waste places. S.W., Tex., R. Mts., Pl. Sts. MARCH–SEPT.

HIGH MALLOW Alien *Malva sylvestris*
Large (3 cm), dark-veined rose-purple flowers. *Petal tips bilobed.* Leaves have 5–7 sharply pointed, triangular lobes. Stems erect. 20 cm–1 m. Disturbed places. Eastern third of Tex. MAY–AUG.

WHEEL MALLOW *Modiola caroliniana*
A *single* nearly flat, *wheellike,* dull red flower (5 mm) above each maplelike leaf. Prostrate stems. 20–60 cm. Waste places, lawns. S. Tex., occasionally elsewhere. MARCH–MAY

NEW MEXICO SIDALCEA *Sidalcea neomexicana*
Upper leaves with 5–9 *linear lobes;* basal leaves *rounded* with shallow lobes. The rose-colored flowers are on pedicels as long as or longer than the calyx. 10 cm–1 m. Moist mountain meadows, woods. S.W., R. Mts. JUNE–SEPT.

NAKED HIBISCUS *Hibiscus denudatus*
Cuplike, pale pink flowers with a series of *short red lines* on inner petal bases. Small, *yellow-green, velvety* oval leaves with toothed margins; *widely spaced on a semi-bare* stem. 20–60 cm. Lower deserts. S.W., sw. Tex. JAN.–OCT.

HEARTLEAF HIBISCUS *Hibiscus cardiophyllus*
Bright red petals, somewhat *propellerlike.* Leaves *heart-shaped.* 30–60 cm. Rocky slopes. Southern and sw. Tex. MOST OF YEAR

VIRGINIA HIBISCUS *Kosteletzkya virginica*
Petals pink. Leaves *sharply tripointed,* like an ancient military weapon. 20 cm–2.5 m. Eastern and n. Tex. MAY–NOV.

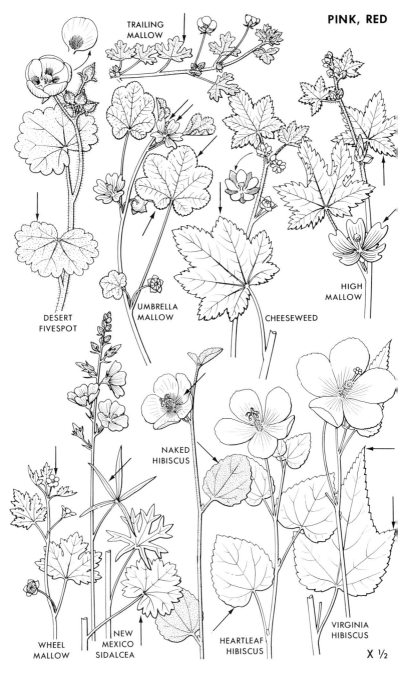

TRAILING MALLOW

DESERT FIVESPOT

UMBRELLA MALLOW

CHEESEWEED

HIGH MALLOW

NAKED HIBISCUS

WHEEL MALLOW

NEW MEXICO SIDALCEA

HEARTLEAF HIBISCUS

VIRGINIA HIBISCUS

X ½

5 PETALS; LARGE,
HOLLYHOCK-LIKE FLOWERS;
MANY STAMENS, IN A FUSED COLUMN

Mallow Family (Malvaceae)
See also pp. W 44; Y 166; O 238; R 288.
All globemallows have flowers similar to Desert Hollyhock.

EMORY'S GLOBEMALLOW   *Sphaeralcea emoryi*
Leaves somewhat *arrow-shaped, longer* than wide, 20–90 cm. Lowest deserts. Western and s. Ariz.   MARCH–JUNE

FENDLER'S GLOBEMALLOW   *Sphaeralcea fendleri*
Gray-green leaves with 5 lobes. Flowers grenadine (deep cherry red) or pink. 50 cm–1 m. Ponderosa pine forests. S.W., w. Tex.
JULY–SEPT.

DESERT HOLLYHOCK   *Sphaeralcea ambigua*
Note the gray, *maplelike leaves,* which are about *as wide as long.*
Globelike, red-orange to deep pink flowers. 50 cm–1.5 m. Common on lower deserts. Western two-thirds of Ariz., s. Ut.
MUCH OF YEAR

SILVERY GLOBEMALLOW   *Sphaeralcea leptophylla*
Silvery gray leaf blades, narrowly linear. Either 1 or 3 lobes. Flowers grenadine red. 30–60 cm. Ne. Ariz., nw. N.M., R. Mts.
MAY–SEPT.

RUSBY'S GLOBEMALLOW   *Sphaeralcea rusbyi*
Dark green leaf blades with scattered clumps of gray hairs. Leaves divided into 3 *unequal, narrow lobes;* each lobe has a few rounded lobes. Petals grenadine red to pinkish. 30 cm–1 m. Well-drained slopes at low to middle elevations (to 6000 ft.). Northern two-thirds of Ariz., s. Ut.   APRIL–SEPT.

WRINKLED GLOBEMALLOW   *Sphaeralcea subhastata*
Green leaf blades, somewhat *arrow-shaped* with *short* side lobes, margins *irregularly sharp, sawtoothed.* Petals grenadine to pink. 20–60 cm. Roadsides, open plains. S.W., w. Tex.   MARCH–OCT.

SCARLET GLOBEMALLOW   *Sphaeralcea coccinea*
Leaf blades deeply divided into 5 or more main, *relatively narrow lobes.* Leaf often *somewhat longer* overall than wide. Flowers scarlet to red-orange. 10–40 cm. *Open plains, mesas.* Ne. Ariz. to w. Tex., R. Mts.   MAY–OCT.

NARROWLEAF GLOBEMALLOW *Sphaeralcea angustifolia*
Thick, green leaf blades *narrowly elongate* with a *wider, non-lobed base;* margins smooth and/or gently wavy. Petals orange-red to pink. 2 cm–1.2 m. S.W., Tex., Pl. Sts.   MOST OF YEAR

JUNIPER GLOBEMALLOW   *Sphaeralcea digitata*
Leaf blade *deeply divided* into 3–5 main lobes of *equal length.* Lobes very narrow (5 mm). Flowers scarlet to red-orange. 30–60 cm. Usually among juniper trees. Northern S.W., w. Tex., s. Ut.
MAY–AUG.

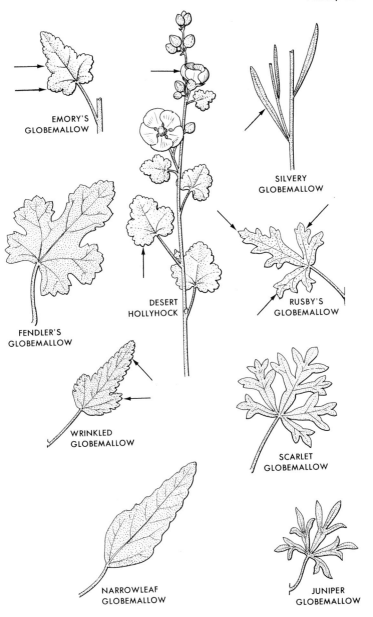

EMORY'S GLOBEMALLOW

SILVERY GLOBEMALLOW

FENDLER'S GLOBEMALLOW

DESERT HOLLYHOCK

RUSBY'S GLOBEMALLOW

WRINKLED GLOBEMALLOW

SCARLET GLOBEMALLOW

NARROWLEAF GLOBEMALLOW

JUNIPER GLOBEMALLOW

X ½

5 DELICATE PETALS;
LONG, BEAKLIKE OVARY

Geranium Family (Geraniaceae) See also p. W 50.

REDSTEM STORKSBILL Alien   *Erodium cicutarium*
Leaves *twice-pinnate;* divided into narrow, sharp-pointed lobes.
The long, beaklike seeds (1–5 cm) coil when dry. Red stems in
prostrate rosettes. Small, delicate, roselike petals. 1 cm–1 m.
Very common in pastures, lawns, disturbed places. S.W., west-
ern two-thirds of Tex., R. Mts., Pl. Sts.   FEB.–JULY

LONGBEAK STORKSBILL Alien   *Erodium botrys*
Elongated leaves with lobes *joined into a central leaf blade
area.* Seed beak to 10 cm. Stem 1 cm–1 m. Cen. Tex.
    MARCH–MAY

TEXAS STORKSBILL   *Erodium texanum*
Leaves *trilobed* with a *larger middle lobe. Very large flowers*
(1–3 cm). Dry sandy places. 10–60 cm. Lower plains, mesas.
S.W., western half of Tex., s. Ut.   FEB.–APRIL

CAROLINA GERANIUM   *Geranium carolinianum*
Beaklike, *yellow-green style tips,* ending in a *short* tapering
neck. Tiny flowers on short pedicels in compact clusters. Sepals
awn-tipped (spinelike). Petals pale pink, notched. Leaves
deeply divided 5 times, *round-tipped.* 20–40 cm. S.W., Tex.,
Pl. Sts., S.E.   MARCH–MAY

CUT-LEAVED GERANIUM Alien   *Geranium dissectum*
Similar to Carolina Geranium, but beaklike *style tips purple,*
ending in a slender, *elongated, constricted beak.* Densely
haired. Leaves narrowly lobed, *sharp-pointed.* Pale pink flowers in loose clusters. 30–60 cm. Disturbed places. Ne. Tex.,
Pl. Sts., S.E.   APRIL–MAY

RICHARDSON'S GERANIUM   *Geranium richardsonii*
Stem hairs tipped with *red glands.* Large rounded petals, pale
pink or all white, always with purple veins. 30–90 cm. Common
in moist mountain meadows, forests. S.W., R. Mts.
    APRIL–OCT.

PURPLE GERANIUM   *Geranium caespitosum*
Petals *dark red-purple* with white streaks; *many hairs on
lower half only.* Stems well-branched, slightly gray-haired.
Leaves straplike, deeply lobed. 10–60 cm. Very common in
shady pine forests. S.W., w. Tex., R. Mts.   MAY–SEPT.

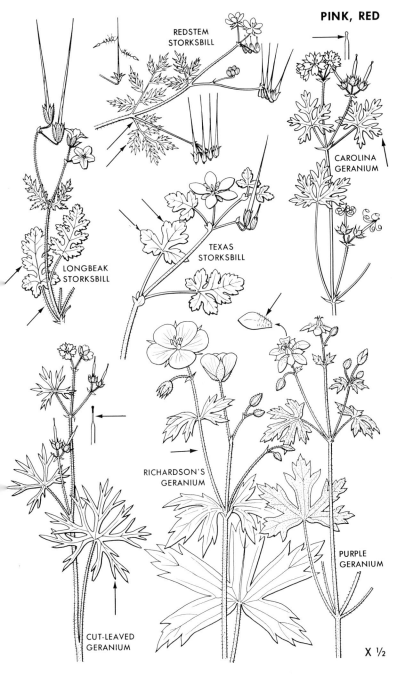

PINK, RED

REDSTEM
STORKSBILL

CAROLINA
GERANIUM

LONGBEAK
STORKSBILL

TEXAS
STORKSBILL

RICHARDSON'S
GERANIUM

PURPLE
GERANIUM

CUT-LEAVED
GERANIUM

X ½

5 TO MANY PETALS; 2 SEPALS; LEAVES OFTEN FLESHY AND SMOOTH

Purslane Family (Portulacaceae) See also pp. O 238; R 296.

SOUTHWESTERN LEWISIA *Lewisia brachycalyx*
Large, pale pink (may seem white) flowers with red lines, *nestled in a flat rosette of smooth, broadly linear leaves.* 20–80 cm. Rocky meadows, flats in mountains. Northern two-thirds of Ariz., southern Ut. MARCH–MAY

BITTERROOT *Lewisia rediviva*
Note the *very large* (5–8 cm), pink or white flowers with numerous petals that nearly hide the tufted, *fleshy, linear leaves.* State flower of Montana. 2–10 cm. Open rocky flats. N. Ariz., R. Mts. APRIL–JUNE

DWARF LEWISIA *Lewisia pygmaea*
Many rounded, fleshy, *linear leaves* in a tuft. Pink to white flowers in among the leaves. 2–8 cm. High mountain meadows. Northern S.W., R. Mts. JUNE–AUG.

ALPINE SPRING BEAUTY *Claytonia megarhiza*
A low cluster of *fleshy, broad, spatulalike leaves* with pink to white flowers and pink veins. 2–5 cm. Rocky places, alpine tundra. N.M., R. Mts. JULY–AUG.

WESTERN SPRING BEAUTY *Claytonia lanceolata*
A single pair of dark green, *lancelike leaves without petioles.* Flowers light pink or rosy. Petal tips *notched.* 5–12 cm. Moist mountain meadows. S.W., R. Mts. FEB.–JUNE

VIRGINIA SPRING BEAUTY *Claytonia virginica*
Similar to Western Spring Beauty, but leaves *very narrow, linear,* 10–30 cm. Woods. Eastern third of Tex., Pl. Sts. FEB.–MARCH

CHAMISSO'S MONTIA *Montia chamissoi*
Stems have *several opposite pairs* of fleshy, lancelike leaves, and runner branches that bear bulblets. Flowers pink to white. 5–12 cm. Wet places, mountain forests. S.W., R. Mts. JUNE–AUG.

MINER'S LETTUCE *Montia perfoliata*
Fleshy, green, *umbrella-like leaves* with clusters of pale pink flowers that seem to rise from the top. 10–30 cm. Common in moist places. Ariz., R. Mts. FEB.–MAY

RED MAIDS *Calandrinia ciliata*
Petals *bright red* with *round tips.* Sepals with *hairy margins.* 5–7 cm. One of the first spring flowers. Common at lower elevations. Ariz. FEB.–APRIL

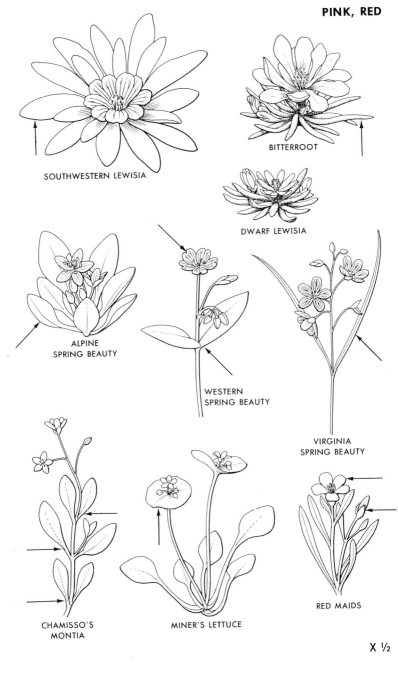

SOUTHWESTERN LEWISIA

BITTERROOT

DWARF LEWISIA

ALPINE
SPRING BEAUTY

WESTERN
SPRING BEAUTY

VIRGINIA
SPRING BEAUTY

CHAMISSO'S
MONTIA

MINER'S LETTUCE

RED MAIDS

X ½

5 TO MANY PETALS; 2 OR 5 FREE SEPALS

Purslane Family (Portulacaceae)
See also pp. O 238; R 294.

CHINESE HAT *Portulaca umbraticola*
Seed capsule resembles a *chinese hat* with a pointed, removable lid and surrounded by a *raised rim*. 2 sepals. Roselike flowers with yellow orange bases nestled at the bases of thick, fleshy, spatula-like yellow-green leaves. 5–25 cm. Southern S.W., Tex.

MARCH–NOV.

Pink Family (Caryophyllaceae)
See also pp. W 46–48; Y 158–160.

STICKY SAND SPURRY *Spergularia macrotheca*
Leaves, stems, and sepals covered with *numerous long, gray, glandular hairs*. Stems sprawling. 10–50 cm. Salt marshes, alkali sinks. S.W., Tex.

MARCH–JUNE

MARSH SAND SPURRY Alien *Spergularia media*
All plant parts *smooth,* or rarely with very tiny, non-sticky, thornlike hairs. Seed capsules *hang downward.* The bright yellow-green, fleshy, linear leaves are usually in pairs. 10–30 cm. S.W.

MARCH–JUNE

RUBY SAND SPURRY Alien *Spergularia rubra*
Tiny linear leaves (1 cm) in *dense whorls* with *large papery bracts. Only the sepals* are glandular. 10–30 cm. Very common in gardens, etc. S.W.

MARCH–JULY

MEXICAN PINK *Silene laciniata*
Each *scarlet* petal is divided into 4 *narrow, linear lobes* with *sharp points.* 30–60 cm. Wooded slopes, pine forests. S.W., w. Tex.

JULY–OCT.

SCOULER'S CATCHFLY *Silene scouleri*
Note the *strongly forked, narrow-lobed,* pink to rosy petals with tiny skirtlike basal lobes. Calyx strongly *balloonlike.* 10–20 cm. Common in midmountains. S.W., R. Mts.

JULY–SEPT.

SLEEPY CATCHFLY *Silene antirrhina*
Pale pink petals with *slightly notched tips. Tall, smooth stems* with bright green, lancelike leaves. Numerous flower branches. 30–60 cm. Very common on lower deserts; an early spring flower. S.W., Tex., Pl. Sts.

FEB.–SEPT.

MOSS CATCHFLY *Silene acaulis*
Petals *pink to lavender;* tips *nearly rectangular* with 2 short, round lobes. Note the 2 small lobes at petal base. 2–5 cm. Forms mats on alpine slopes. San Francisco Peaks, Ariz., northern N.M., R. Mts.

JULY–SEPT.

Carpetweed Family (Aizoaceae)

SHORE PURSLANE *Sesuvium portulacastrum*
Grayish, *fleshy, linear leaves* on very long, sprawling stems. Deep red-purple to lavender flowers. Ocean salt flats, alkaline streamsides, lake shores. S.W., Tex.

ALL YEAR

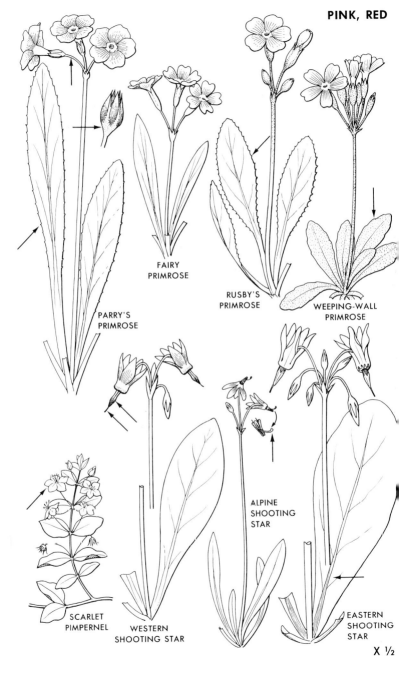

PINK, RED

PARRY'S PRIMROSE

FAIRY PRIMROSE

RUSBY'S PRIMROSE

WEEPING-WALL PRIMROSE

SCARLET PIMPERNEL

WESTERN SHOOTING STAR

ALPINE SHOOTING STAR

EASTERN SHOOTING STAR

X ½

5 PETALS; FLOWERS IN UMBEL CLUSTERS; MILKY SAP: MILKWEEDS

Milkweed Family (Asclepiadaceae)
See also pp. W 66–72; Y 178; O 234; R 304; G 404.

Note: See p. 67 for special flower part names.

SHOWY MILKWEED *Asclepias speciosa*
Long, *outward-curving, toothlike, pale pink* hoods with inward-curving horns. White, velvety oval leaves in opposite pairs. 30 cm–1 m. Very common. S.W., Tex., R. Mts.

MAY–SEPT.

HALL'S MILKWEED *Asclepias hallii*
Note the dark bluish green, *broad, lancelike leaves.* Bright white, *closed, scooplike hoods* have only the *inner center sides pinched together,* on a short broad pedestal above pale to dark pink-red petals. 10–50 cm. Rocky slopes with juniper, pinyon, or ponderosa pine. Northern S.W., R. Mts. JUNE–AUG.

MAHOGANY MILKWEED *Asclepias hypoleuca*
Note the dark green, *heart-shaped leaf blades* with petioles. *Rich, deep red-brown flowers.* The broad, pointed hoods each have *2 pinched points* on the inner side. Horns usually absent. Pedestal below horns *spindlelike* with a central constriction. Downswept petals, red-brown with yellowish bases. 10–60 cm. Ponderosa pine forests in mountains. Se. Ariz., sw. N.M.

JUNE–AUG.

HUMBOLDT MILKWEED *Asclepias cryptoceras*
Brilliant, dark red-purple hoods; each rounded, with the 2 inner edges *raised into slender points.* 10–30 cm. Rocky high desert slopes. Nw. Ariz., w. R. Mts. APRIL–JUNE

FOURLEAF MILKWEED *Asclepias quadrifolia*
Note the bright green, broadly lancelike leaf blades with petioles, in *whorls of 4* on the lower stem. Upper stem leaves often paired. Flowers on *long, threadlike pedicels.* Downswept petals delicate pink, lavender, or white. Bright white *hoods boatlike,* each with a *pinched* portion on inner column side. Prominent, inward-curving horns. 30 cm–1 m. Rocky slopes in shady woods. Ne. Tex., Pl. Sts. APRIL–JULY

SWAMP MILKWEED *Asclepias incarnata*
Short, erect, scooplike hoods, white tinted with pale pink. Erect, *pointed horns protrude* above pedestal-like column. Petals *downswept, bright rose pink.* Broad, bright green, lancelike leaves. 30 cm–1 m. Marshy ground. Se. N.M., northern half of Tex., Pl. Sts. JUNE–OCT.

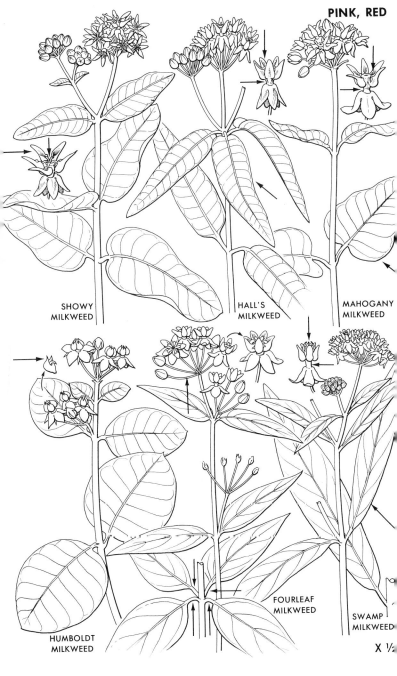

SHOWY
MILKWEED

HALL'S
MILKWEED

MAHOGANY
MILKWEED

HUMBOLDT
MILKWEED

FOURLEAF
MILKWEED

SWAMP
MILKWEED

X ½

5 PETALS; FLOWERS IN UMBEL CLUSTERS MILKY SAP, MILKWEEDS

Milkweed Family (Asclepiadaceae)
See also pp. W 66–72; Y 178; O 234; R 302; G 404.

Note: See p. 67 for special flower part names.

PINK BALLOONS *Asclepias amplexicaulis*
Note the *tight clusters* of *rosy pink*, balloonlike *hoods* and large, *downswept*, yellow-green petals (sometimes rose-tinted) below a short pedestal. Large, oblong, dark green leaves with *wavy margins*, on *reddish stems*. 30 cm–1 m. Open woods. Eastern half of Tex.
MARCH–SEPT.

SPIDER ANTELOPE HORNS *Asclepias asperula*
Hoods *low, curved, dark red-purple* (pale green in some areas), *nestled among upward-cupped* to wheel-like, pale green petals. Hoods *almost as long* as petals. Leaves *narrow*. 10–60 cm. Very common. S.W., western two-thirds of Tex.
MARCH–AUG.

GREEN ANTELOPE HORNS *Asclepias viridis*
Similar to Spider Antelope Horns, but leaves *broadly* oval to semi-lancelike. Pink to red-purple *hoods, half as long or shorter* than the *upward-cupped*, yellow-green petals. 10–60 cm. Prairies, pine woods. Eastern half of Tex., Pl. Sts., S.E.
APRIL–AUG.

SHORTCROWN MILKWEED *Asclepias brachystephana*
Note the *long, narrow, lancelike leaves*. *Small* flowers with *rosy, short, saclike hoods*; horns *tonguelike*, compressed and projecting upward. Dark red-purple to violet, downswept petals. 10–40 cm. Rocky plains, gullies. Very common. S. Ariz. east to southern half of Tex.
APRIL–SEPT.

CUTLER'S MILKWEED *Asclepias cutleri*
Note the *downswept, dark red-purple* petals in a *"wheel"* below the *low, boatlike white hoods*. Basal lobes of hoods earlike; horns compressed, tonguelike. Leaves *linear*, troughlike, with gray hairs. Low, tufted stem. 2–14 cm. Red sandy soil. Ne. Ariz., se. Ut. in Four Corners region.
MAY–JUNE

RUTH'S MILKWEED *Asclepias ruthiae*
Similar to Cutler's Milkweed, but leaves small, broadly heart-shaped. Low stems. 10–20 cm. Nw. S.W.
MAY–JUNE

WHEEL MILKWEED *Asclepias uncinalis*
Similar to Cutler's Milkweed (above), but leaves *narrow, lance-like*. 10–20 cm. Plains. N.M., e. Colo.
APRIL–JUNE

TUFTED MILKWEED *Asclepias nummularia*
Low tuft of very broad, oval, blue-green leaves with gray feltlike hairs along the veins. *Urnlike flower hoods* rosy, inner horns *curved downward*. Downswept, rose-purple petals. 5–10 cm. Open rocky foothills. S. Ariz. to w. Tex.
MARCH–AUG.

TORREY'S MILKVINE *Sarcostemma torreyi*
Whitish *wheel-like* flowers with *red-purple* bases. *Shiny green*, lancelike leaves on long *twining vines*. Mountain hillsides. Big Bend region, Tex.
MAY–AUG.

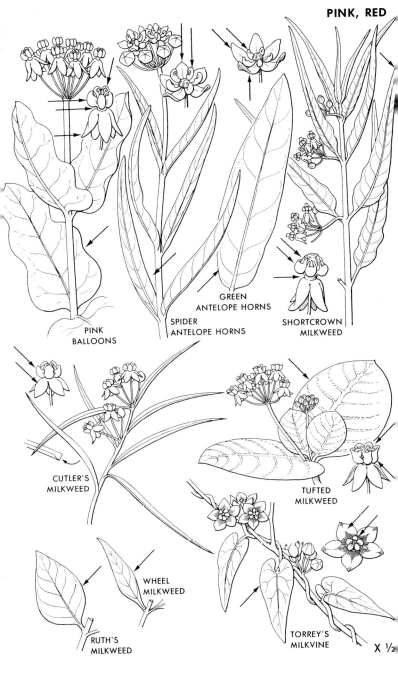

PINK
BALLOONS

SPIDER
ANTELOPE HORNS

GREEN
ANTELOPE HORNS

SHORTCROWN
MILKWEED

CUTLER'S
MILKWEED

TUFTED
MILKWEED

RUTH'S
MILKWEED

WHEEL
MILKWEED

TORREY'S
MILKVINE

X ½

3- TO 5-LOBED, TUBULAR FLOWERS IN UMBELS WITH LARGE BRACTS

Four O'Clock Family (Nyctaginaceae) See also p. W 64.

RIBBON FOUR O'CLOCK *Mirabilis linearis*
Very tall, long-stemmed plants with *very long, linear leaves* and a few broad, trumpet-shaped, red-purple flowers nestled or dangling near leaf bases. 30 cm–1 m. Middle elevations, often in pine forests. S.W., western two-thirds of Tex. MAY–SEPT.

TUFTED FOUR O'CLOCK *Mirabilis comata*
Broad, heart-shaped or *spearhead-like* leaf blades with *smooth surfaces* (no sticky hairs) on *short* petioles. Dark red-purple, funnel-shaped flowers. 30 cm–1 m. Meadows, foothill thickets. S.W., w. Tex. MAY–OCT.

SAND PUFFS *Abronia carnea*
Note the orangish, *puffy balls of thin, net-veined fins* on the clusters of papery seeds. Leaf blades *lancelike* on *very long* petioles. Umbel-like clusters of slender, tubular, bright pink flowers. 10–30 cm. Dry sandy places, open plains. Eastern N.M., w. Tex., Pl. Sts. FEB.–NOV.

DESERT SAND VERBENA *Abronia villosa*
Tubular, rose red flowers with white centers, in *umbels*. Flowers, bracts, and stems all have *long, sticky whiskery hairs*. Leaves *broadly oval* on long trailing stems. Flower umbels have lancelike bracts. 10–50 cm. Sandy places, lower deserts. W. Ariz. FEB.–MAY

NARROWLEAF SAND VERBENA *Abronia angustifolia*
Similar to Desert Sand Verbena (above), but leaves *elongate, spearhead-like*. Eastern two-thirds of Ariz. to w. Tex. MARCH–JULY

TRAILING WINDMILLS *Allionia incarnata*
Rose to cream, windmill-like flowers, *usually in threes* (often looks like one flower). Trailing stem has gray, oval leaves with wavy margins. Stem and leaves with sticky hairs. Flowers open in morning hours. Dry rocky slopes. S.W., western two-thirds of Tex. APRIL–OCT.

DESERT FOUR O'CLOCK *Mirabilis multiflora*
Huge (5–12 cm) *leaves* broadly triangular to oval. Several rose red, tubular flowers within a *large cup of calyx-like bracts*. 30–60 cm. Dry rocky places. Very common. Juniper woodlands, mesas. S.W., w. Tex., R. Mts. APRIL–SEPT.

DEVIL'S BOUQUET *Nyctaginia capitata*
Note the *triangular leaf blades* and *intensely brilliant scarlet-orange flowers* in terminal umbels. 10–60 cm. Sandy open places. Se. N.M., Tex. MARCH–OCT.

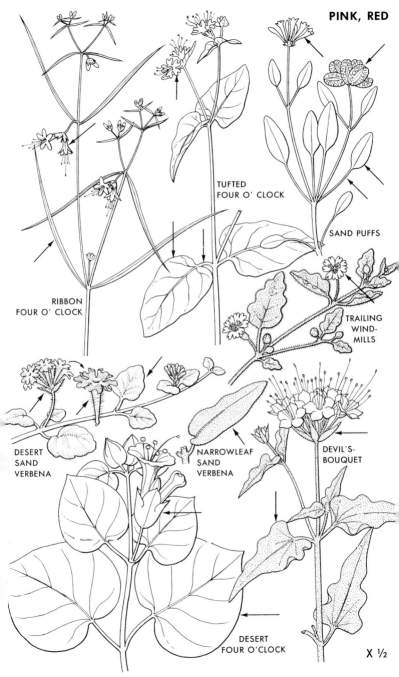

PINK, RED

TUFTED
FOUR O' CLOCK

SAND PUFFS

RIBBON
FOUR O' CLOCK

TRAILING
WIND-
MILLS

DESERT
SAND
VERBENA

NARROWLEAF
SAND
VERBENA

DEVIL'S-
BOUQUET

DESERT
FOUR O'CLOCK

X ½

5 PETALS; SMALL UPRIGHT TRUMPETS

Phlox Family (Polemoniaceae)
See also pp. W 88; Y 180; O 234; R 310–312; B 360–362.
Species of the Southwest and westernmost Texas.

THREADLEAF PHLOX *Phlox mesoleuca*
Somewhat similar to Longleaf Phlox (below). *Very long* (5–12 cm), *threadlike leaves*. Broad, oval, pink (also purple, white or yellow) petal lobes and a ring of white or pale yellow around the dark tube throat. Corolla tube *equal to or slightly longer* than sepals. 10–60 cm. Se. Ariz., s. N.M., w. Tex.

MARCH–MAY

SPREADING PHLOX *Phlox diffusa*
Pink or white flowers with *broad petals*. Often in *showy mats*. Low stems with *sharp, needlelike yellow-green leaves. Hairy clusters* between sepals and at leaf bases. 10–30 cm. Very common on higher plateaus. North Rim of Grand Canyon, Ariz., and northward. R. Mts. APRIL–JUNE

DESERT MOUNTAIN PHLOX *Phlox austromontana*
Similar to Spreading Phlox, but *petal lobes narrow*. Calyx and leaf bases *hairless*. The *gray-green, sharp, needlelike* leaves have a pungent odor. 2–12 cm. Dry rocky slopes in mountains. Ariz., nw. N.M., R. Mts. APRIL–JUNE

CARPET PHLOX *Phlox caespitosa*
Very dense, *thin, cushiony carpets* (2–5 cm thick) made of tiny linear leaves. Small, solitary, pale pink flowers seem to *dot the carpet*. Tiny linear leaves with a *flat upper surface*. Sticky-haired. High mountain meadows. Northern S.W., R. Mts.

MAY–JULY

STANSBURY'S PHLOX *Phlox stansburyi*
Flower tube *very long, 2–4 times longer than* the sepals. Pink, salmon, or white petal lobes, *narrow with small, notched tips*. Leaves linear, flat. 10–20 cm. Sagebrush, juniper woodlands. Ariz., w. N.M., R. Mts. APRIL–JUNE

WOODHOUSE'S PHLOX *Phlox woodhousei*
Note the pink, *wedge-shaped* petal lobes with *notched tips*. Corolla tube *barely longer than* the sepals. *White "eye"* at tube mouth. Leaves shiny dark green. 10–25 cm. Open woods or rocky slopes. N. Ariz., w. N.M. APRIL–JUNE; SEPT.

LOVELY PHLOX *Phlox amabilis*
Note the pink, *wedge-shaped* petal lobes with *rounded tips* (or slightly notched). Corolla tube protrudes and is *2–3 times longer* than the sepals. Corolla entirely pink, or with a *white zone* on lower half of petal lobe. Leaves dull green. 10–30 cm. Cen. Ariz. MARCH–MAY

LONGLEAF PHLOX *Phlox longifolia*
Long (1–3 cm) flower tube and sepals of *equal length*. Flowers *broad-petaled*. Long (10–50 cm), linear leaves. 10–40 cm. Open flats. Northern half of S.W. MARCH–MAY

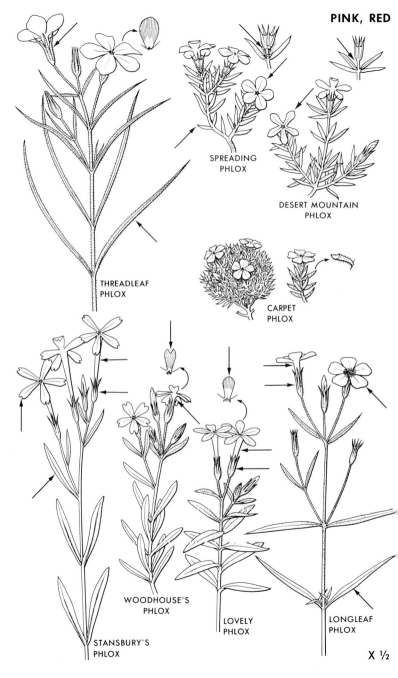

PINK, RED

THREADLEAF PHLOX

SPREADING PHLOX

DESERT MOUNTAIN PHLOX

CARPET PHLOX

STANSBURY'S PHLOX

WOODHOUSE'S PHLOX

LOVELY PHLOX

LONGLEAF PHLOX

X ½

5 PETALS; SMALL UPRIGHT TRUMPETS

Phlox Family (Polemoniaceae)
See also pp. W 88; Y 180; O 234; R 308–312; B 360–362.
Phlox species of Texas; also to the north and east.

DRUMMOND'S PHLOX *Phlox drummondii*
Petals brilliant pink, red-purple, violet, or white. Often a *dark star or ring* on inner portion of petal lobes. Corolla tube 1 or 2 times longer than calyx. Short, shiny, yellow-green, lancelike leaves. 10–50 cm. Eastern half of Tex. MARCH–MAY

GOLDEYE PHLOX *Phlox roemeriana*
Note the *conspicuous yellow "eye"* surrounded by white zone on the pink flowers. Corolla tube the same length as sepal. Leaves mostly alternate. 10–40 cm. Cen. Tex. MARCH–APRIL

DOWNY PHLOX *Phlox pilosa*
Note the *spine-tipped sepals.* Each pink to purple petal lobe often has a *dark purple bilobed mark within a bilobed white zone* (marking may be indistinct). Corolla tube slightly longer than sepals. Leaves alternate above, opposite below. A variable species. 10–60 cm. Common. Eastern two-thirds of Tex., Pl. Sts. MARCH–MAY

RIO GRANDE PHLOX *Phlox glabriflora*
Leaves *broadly ribbonlike.* Most plant parts *heavily long-haired.* Pink petal lobes with a bilobed white inner zone. Corolla tube *shorter* than the sepals. Leaves alternate above, opposite below. 10–25 cm. Lower Rio Grande Valley and Tex. Gulf Coast. FEB.–APRIL

BROADLEAF GILIA *Gilia latifolia*
The basal cluster of *broad leaves* has coarse, ragged margins with *spiny teeth* and sticky hairs. Short, funnel-shaped flowers red-pink. Bad odor if handled. 10–30 cm. Common on low-elevation desert flats. W. Ariz. MARCH–APRIL

ROCK GILIA *Gilia scopulorum*
Rose-lavender, funnel-shaped flowers with a *long tube* that is paler lavender or yellow. Stem erect, *well-branched.* Most of the *broad, keylike* pinnate leaves have sticky hairs and are in a basal rosette. 10–30 cm. Lower deserts. W. Ariz., s. Ut. MARCH–APRIL

SLENDER PHLOX *Microsteris gracilis*
Petal tips *notched.* Tiny (10 mm or less) rose to lavender, phloxlike flowers with long, slender, yellow-throated tubes; in *terminal clusters.* Calyx tips narrow, short. *Sticky-haired,* lancelike leaves. 5–20 cm. Open grassy places. Ariz. FEB.–MAY

TINY TRUMPET *Collomia linearis*
The *long, narrow,* trumpetlike, pink to purple flowers (1–2 cm) in dense, headlike clusters. Single erect stems with many long, broad, lancelike leaves. 10–60 cm. Open places. Common in mountains. Northern half of Ariz., N.M., R. Mts. JULY–AUG.

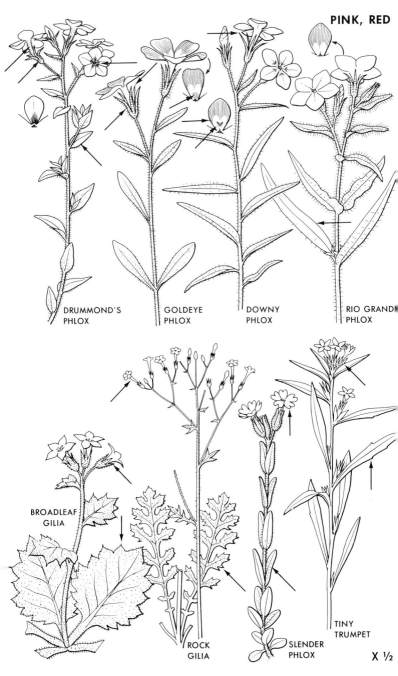

PINK, RED

DRUMMOND'S
PHLOX

GOLDEYE
PHLOX

DOWNY
PHLOX

RIO GRANDE
PHLOX

BROADLEAF
GILIA

ROCK
GILIA

SLENDER
PHLOX

TINY
TRUMPET

X ½

5 UNITED PETALS; FUNNEL-LIKE OR TRUMPET-LIKE FLOWERS

Phlox Family (Polemoniaceae)
See also pp. W 88; Y 180; O 234; R 308–312; B 360–362.

CORAL GILIA *Gilia subnuda*
Note the *brilliant coral pink,* funnel-like flowers and the *toothed,* spatula-like basal cluster of leaves. 15–40 cm. Sandy, rocky hills. Northern S.W., s. R. Mts. MAY–AUG.

TEXAS PLUME *Ipomopsis rubra*
A *long, spikelike* series of brilliant scarlet, trumpetlike flowers on *tall stems.* Petal lobes *spotted with yellow-orange.* Feathery pinnate leaves. 50 cm–1.5 m. Eastern half of Tex., Pl. Sts.
MAY–SEPT.

DESERT TRUMPET *Ipomopsis aggregata*
Fluorescent red to pink, narrow, trumpetlike flowers with long, *narrow petal lobes.* Sticky stems. Pinnate leaves. 20–90 cm. Forests, sagebrush flats. S.W., R. Mts. MAY–SEPT.

Waterleaf Family (Hydrophyllaceae)
See also pp. W 82; Y 182; B 364.

ROTHROCK'S NAMA *Nama rothrockii*
Note the *terminal headlike cluster* of lavender to red-purple, tubular flowers. *Erect stems.* Short, lancelike leaves with *toothlike* margins. Strongly sticky-haired. 12–30 cm. Open sandy slopes. Nw. Ariz. SEPT.

PURPLE MAT *Nama demissum*
Short, linear calyx lobes. Flat mats of *solitary,* dark red-purple, trumpetlike flowers on short stems. Sticky linear leaves. 2–12 cm. Sandy desert flats. W. Ariz. FEB.–MAY

FREMONT'S PHACELIA *Phacelia fremontii*
Coils of large, long, pale pink to bluish flowers with yellow throats and tubes. Bright green, pinnate leaves with *rounded* lobes. 10–40 cm. Nw. Ariz. MARCH–JUNE

CURLED NAMA *Nama hispidum*
Erect stems. Leaves usually taper to base; *not* clasping. Leaf margin *inrolled.* Flowers solitary or in small terminal clusters. 10–50 cm. Common. S.W., Tex. FEB.–JULY

WHITEWHISKER NAMA *Nama undulatum*
Leaves *straplike,* edges *flat* (not curled). All plant parts with *bristly white hairs.* 10–30 cm. Southern half of Tex. JUNE–AUG.

EGGLEAF NAMA *Nama pusillum*
Leaves broadly *egg-shaped, thick, succulent.* 2–10 cm. Nw. Ariz.
MAY–JUNE

Nightshade Family (Solanaceae)
See also pp. W 86; Y 184; B 368.

MIDGET PETUNIA *Petunia parviflora*
Note the *broad, spatula-like calyx lobes;* compare with the Namas (above). Sprawling, much-branched stems with *thick,* dark green, lancelike leaves and *tiny, petunialike,* pink to lavender flowers with yellow tubes. Mats 5–30 cm wide, 1–2 cm tall. Moist streambeds, flats, beaches. S.W., Tex. APRIL–SEPT.

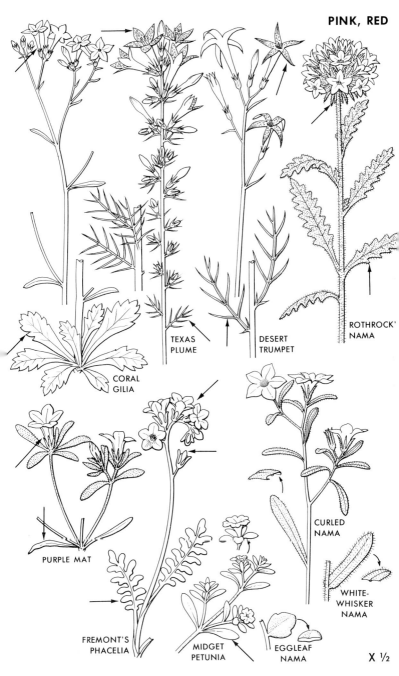

PINK, RED

ROTHROCK' NAMA

TEXAS PLUME

DESERT TRUMPET

CORAL GILIA

PURPLE MAT

FREMONT'S PHACELIA

MIDGET PETUNIA

EGGLEAF NAMA

CURLED NAMA

WHITE-WHISKER NAMA

X ½

5 UNITED PETALS; REGULAR FLOWERS

Wintergreen Family (Pyrolaceae) See also p. W 76.

PINEDROPS *Pterospora andromedea*
Red to white, urnlike flowers, *pendulous* and loosely scattered on single, spikelike, red-brown stems. 20–90 cm. Dry shady conifer forests. A saprophyte, feeding on decaying material. S.W., w. Tex., R. Mts.   JULY–AUG.

WESTERN PRINCE'S PINE *Chimaphila unbellata*
Lancelike, dark green, leathery leaves with *spiny* toothed margins, in *whorls. Nodding, crownlike,* pink to red flowers. 10 stamens. 10–30 cm. Frequent in dry conifer forests. S.W., R. Mts.
JULY–AUG.

AMERICAN PINESAP *Monotropa hypopithys*
Note the *"shepherd's crook"* of several nodding, bell-like flowers and the fleshy stem, *both bright red* (or occasionally whitish yellow). 5–30 cm. A saprophyte without chlorophyll, living on decaying humus in dark conifer forests of higher mountains. S.W., ne. Tex., R. Mts.   APRIL–AUG.

INDIAN PIPE *Monotropa uniflora*
Note the translucent waxy-white stems and the *single, nodding,* bell-like flower. The pink to white flowers turn black with age. Leaves are small, colorless scales. A saprophyte. 10–30 cm. Dark moist woods. E. Tex., possibly northern S.W.
APRIL–JULY

Dogbane Family (Apocynaceae) See also pp. W 72; B 356.

SPREADING DOGBANE *Apocynum androsaemifolium*
Note the *drooping pairs of oval leaves* and terminal cymes of small, pink to white, *bell-shaped flowers.* Thick milky sap. 10–60 cm. Frequent on mountain slopes. S.W., w. Tex., R. Mts.
APRIL–SEPT.

Spurge Family (Euphorbiaceae) See also pp. W 74; G 398.

RAGGED JATROPA *Jatropa macrorhiza*
Note the very large (5–20 cm) wide leaves with *fingerlike lobes and ragged margins.* Many *short,* trumpetlike, deep to pale pink flowers. 10–50 cm. Open foothills, plains. Southern S.W., sw. Tex.   MAY–OCT.

Forget-me-not Family (Boraginaceae)
See also pp. W 84; Y 182; O 234; B 344, 366.

BURGUNDY HOUND'S TONGUE Alien *Cynoglossum officinale*
Thick-flowered, coiled sprays of small, nodding, *red-purple, wheel-like* flowers with an *inner row* of similar-colored teeth. 4 nutlets (seeds) per flower. Numerous linear leaves. 20 cm–1 m. Disturbed places. N.M., R. Mts.   JUNE–AUG.

OREJA DE PERRO *Coldenia canescens*
Note the numerous, *tiny, gray,* felt-haired, oval leaves. Pink flowers with tubular bases. 4 nutlike seeds per flower. Forms extensive mats. 1–20 cm tall. S.W., sw. Tex.   MARCH–SEPT.

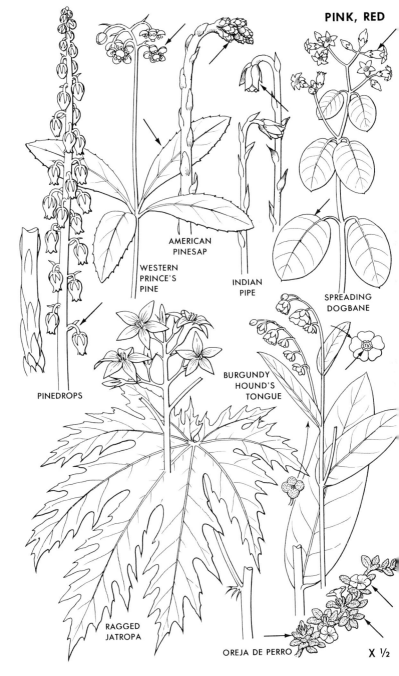

PINK, RED

AMERICAN
PINESAP

WESTERN
PRINCE'S
PINE

INDIAN
PIPE

SPREADING
DOGBANE

PINEDROPS

BURGUNDY
HOUND'S
TONGUE

RAGGED
JATROPA

OREJA DE PERRO

X ½

5 PETALS; 2-LIPPED, TUBULAR FLOWERS

Devil's-claw Family (Martyniaceae) See also p. Y 122.

RED DEVIL'S-CLAW *Proboscidea parviflora*
Large, tubular, semi-hanging, 2-lipped flowers, often hidden by
large, dark green, *heart-shaped leaves.* Plant with sticky hairs.
Large, *clawlike seedpods* (see p. 123). 30–90 cm. Lower elevations.
S W , w. Tex. APRIL–OCT.

Acanthus Family (Acanthaceae) See also p. B 372.

SHAGGY NARROWMAN *Stenandrium barbatum*
Large, 2-lipped, *mouthlike,* rose to lavender flowers *streaked with
white, nestled* in a ground-hugging mound of *shaggy,* white-haired,
linear leaves. 5–10 cm. Rocky ridges, slopes. Se. N.M., w. Tex.
MARCH–JUNE

Valerian Family (Valerianaceae) See also p. W 92.

ROTUND PLECTRITIS *Plectritis macrocera*
Upper portion of the corolla tube *broad,* with a *fat rounded spur.*
Lower corolla tube longer than the spur. *Leaves broad.* 10–60 cm.
Moist shaded slopes. Cen. Ariz. MARCH–APRIL

LONGSPUR PLECTRITIS *Plectritis ciliosa*
Note the *long, slender spur* that extends well beyond the inferior
ovary. Flower with 2 red dots, one on each side of the middle
petal lobe. *Leaves narrow.* 10–40 cm. Open, moist grassy places.
Southern two-thirds of Ariz. APRIL–MAY

Honeysuckle Family (Caprifoliaceae)

TWINFLOWER *Linnaea borealis*
Note the *twin pair of nodding,* pink, tubular flowers on a leafless
stem. Stem trailing with *shiny, oval leaves.* 5–15 cm. Semi-shaded
spruce-fir woods in mountains. Northern S.W., R. Mts.
MAY–AUG.

Broomrape Family (Orobanchaceae) See also p. Y 188.

COOPER'S BROOMRAPE *Orobanche cooperi*
Erect, *conelike stems* with many long, tubular, purple flowers on
very short pedicels. A root parasite. 10–30 cm. Sandy deserts. S.W.,
w. Tex., R. Mts. FEB.–SEPT.

NAKED BROOMRAPE *Orobanche uniflora*
Calyx lobes *longer than the calyx tube.* A *single* purple flower on
each stem; often in clumps. A root parasite. 2–6 cm. Woods. Tex.,
R. Mts. APRIL–MAY

CLUSTERED BROOMRAPE *Orobanche fasciculata*
Much like Naked Broomrape, but calyx lobes *shorter than calyx
tube.* Numerous flowers are in a *cluster of stems.* A root parasite.
2–12 cm. Midmountains. S.W., Tex., R. Mts., Pl. Sts.
MARCH–AUG.

BEECHDROPS *Epifagus virginiana*
Note the *open, well-branched,* purplish yellow stems are leafless,
with many scattered, *slender purple flowers.* A parasite on beech
tree roots. 10–50 cm. Beech woods. E. Tex., S.E. FEB.–JUNE

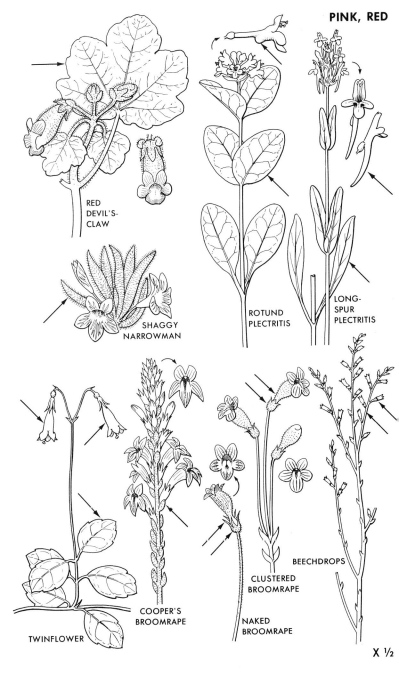

RED DEVIL'S-CLAW

SHAGGY NARROWMAN

ROTUND PLECTRITIS

LONG-SPUR PLECTRITIS

TWINFLOWER

COOPER'S BROOMRAPE

NAKED BROOMRAPE

CLUSTERED BROOMRAPE

BEECHDROPS

X ½

5 PETALS; 2-LIPPED, TUBULAR FLOWERS
SQUARE STEMS; MINT ODOR

Mint Family (Labiatae) See also pp. W 90;
Y 188; B 374–376.

SCARLET SAGE   *Stachys coccinea*
Scarlet flowers in whorls. 4 stamens. Leaf blades triangular with
netlike surfaces. Stems *square* in cross-section. 30–90 cm. Rocky
places. Southern half of S.W., w. Tex.   MARCH–OCT.

CEDAR SAGE (not shown)   *Salvia roemeriana*
Similar to Scarlet Sage, but with *2 stamens.* Cen. and w. Tex.
MARCH–SEPT.

MINTLEAF BEEBALM   *Monarda menthifolia*
Lavender to rose purple flowers in a *single terminal headlike cluster*
with purplish leaves. Bright yellow-green, lancelike leaves. Other
Beebalms have either white or pink flowers and are shown on p. 90.
30–90 cm. Mountains. S.W., R. Mts.   MAY–JULY

TRIANGLE LION'S-HEART   *Physostegia angustifolia*
Note the *thick, long spike* of large (2–5 cm) pink to lavender flowers,
spotted within. Narrow, *triangular* leaves. Stem *square.* 50 cm–
1.5 m. Marshy places. Eastern half of Tex., S.E.   APRIL–JULY

FALSE FOXGLOVE   *Physostegia digitalis*
Similar to Triangle Lion's-heart, but leaves *oblong* to elliptical.
Swampy areas, pinelands. 1–2 m. E. Tex., S.E.   JUNE–AUG.

COYOTE MINT   *Monardella odoratissima*
Note the *flat head* of numerous slender, pale red-purple to dirty
white flowers. Note *fringe of hairs* at top of the calyx tube. Stem
leaves *lancelike.* 10–60 cm. A variable species found at many elevations, but mostly in mountains. Ariz., w. N.M., R. Mts.
JUNE–SEPT.

FIELD MINT Alien   *Mentha arvensis*
Note the *dense whorls* of pale pink flowers nearly *hidden* by *long
leaves.* Leaves bright green with sharp, *sawtoothed* margins. 10–
90 cm. Moist places. S.W., Tex., Pl. Sts.   MAY–OCT.

SPEARMINT Alien   *Mentha spicata*
Note the whorls of pale lavender flowers that *form a spike well
above the crinkly, lancelike leaves.* 2 flower lips not widely separated. Plant nearly hairless. 10 cm–1 m. Moist disturbed places.
S.W., Tex., Pl. Sts.   JUNE–OCT.

RED HENBIT Alien   *Lamium purpureum*
Note the *distinct petiole* below the small, heart-shaped leaf blade.
Upper stem a *4-sided pagoda* of numerous flowers *hidden* under
the leaves. 5–30 cm. Disturbed places. E. Tex., Pl. Sts.
MARCH–SEPT.

CLASPING HENBIT Alien   *Lamium amplexicaule*
Long, slender, bright red-purple tubular flowers in whorls. *Rounded*
upper leaves *clasp the stem.* 5–50 cm. Disturbed places. S.W., Tex.,
Pl. Sts.   ALL YEAR

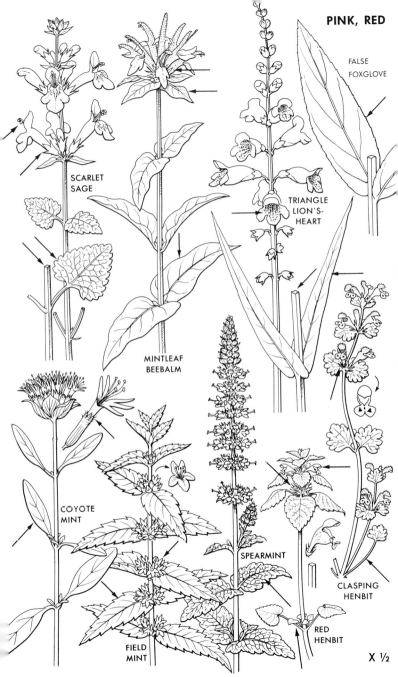

PINK, RED

SCARLET
SAGE

MINTLEAF
BEEBALM

TRIANGLE
LION'S-
HEART

FALSE
FOXGLOVE

COYOTE
MINT

FIELD
MINT

SPEARMINT

RED
HENBIT

CLASPING
HENBIT

X ½

PEALIKE FLOWERS; INFLATED SEEDPODS; LOCOWEEDS; LONG PINNATE LEAVES

Pea Family (Leguminosae)
See also pp. W 94–96; Y 190–196; R 320–328;
B 346–348, 380–382.

MOTTLED LOCOWEED   *Astragalus lentiginosus*
Seedpod a strongly *inflated sausage with a flattened triangular* tip that curves upward. 11–19 oval leaflets, *hairless*. Reddish stems. Flowers vary from purple to creamy white. A highly variable species. 10–30 cm. S.W., R. Mts.   FEB.–JUNE

WOOLLY LOCOWEED   *Astragalus mollissimus*
Numerous stems in clusters with pink-purple to dull pink flowers, well above *long, feathery* pinnate leaves. *Rounded* leaflets; stems *woolly-haired*. Short, curved seedpods. 10–30 cm. S.W., w. Tex., Pl. Sts.   JAN.–JUNE

LAMBERT'S CRAZYWEED   *Oxytropis lambertii*
Brilliant red-purple, pealike flowers in a long, loose raceme well above the *pointed, silvery, silky-haired leaves*. 30–60 cm. Extremely common in early spring. S.W., w. Tex., R. Mts., Pl. Sts.   APRIL–SEPT.

WESTERN SWEET VETCH   *Hedysarum occidentale*
A *long spike* of 20–75 red-purple flowers *cascading downward*. Each pinnate leaf has 9–21 oval leaflets. *Seedpods beadlike*. 20 cm–1 m. Mountains. Northern S.W., R. Mts.   JUNE–AUG.

BIGELOW'S LOCOWEED   *Astragalus bigelovii*
Note the *gray, felt-haired, elliptical leaflets*. Wing petals *white-tipped;* rest of petals dark red-purple. Seedpods short, white-woolly, triangular, with *pointed tips*. 10–40 cm. Open slopes, mesas. E. Ariz., to w. Tex.   APRIL–MAY

THURBER'S LOCOWEED   *Astragalus thurberi*
Short, gray, felt-haired, *troughlike leaflets* on very long pinnate leaves. Short, small, dark red-purple flowers with a *white patch* on banner petal, in dense racemes. *Numerous round, inflated seedpods* with slightly inflated triangular tips. 10–30 cm. Open flats. Southern third of N.M., w. Tex.   MARCH–APRIL

ALADDIN'S-SLIPPERS   *Astragalus amphioxys*
Low, *silvery mounds* of egg-shaped, silvery-haired pinnate leaflets. Long bright pink-purple flowers. *Curved, aladdin's-slipperlike seedpods*. 1–7 cm. S.W., w. Tex.   APRIL–JUNE

LAYNE'S LOCOWEED   *Astragalus layneae*
Purple-mottled, *sickle-shaped seedpod* with a distinct *groove* on the underside. 13–21 leaflets per leaf. Yellow flowers, *wing petals purple-tipped*. 5–45 cm. Nw. Ariz.   APRIL

KING'S LOCOWEED   *Astragalus calycosus*
Wing petals narrow; *tips bilobed*. 2–6 pink to dark red-purple flowers. Low, silvery, tufted stems. Short seedpods. 5–15 cm. Juniper woods. Northern S.W., R. Mts.   APRIL–MAY

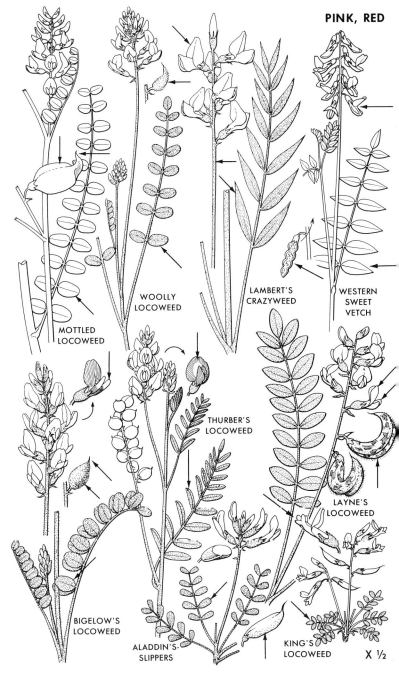

PINK, RED

MOTTLED
LOCOWEED

WOOLLY
LOCOWEED

LAMBERT'S
CRAZYWEED

WESTERN
SWEET
VETCH

THURBER'S
LOCOWEED

LAYNE'S
LOCOWEED

BIGELOW'S
LOCOWEED

ALADDIN'S-
SLIPPERS

KING'S
LOCOWEED

X ½

PEALIKE FLOWERS; 3-LEAFED CLOVERS

Pea Family (Leguminosae)
See also pp. W 94–96; Y 190–196; R 320–328;
B 346–348, 380–382.

RED CLOVER Alien   *Trifolium pratense*
Each oblong leaflet has a *central white chevron. Large* (3 cm), oval, red flowerhead with *no bract* below it. Leaf stipules *pointed.* 10–60 cm. S.W., eastern half of Tex., R. Mts., Pl. Sts.
                APRIL–JULY

CRIMSON CLOVER Alien   *Trifolium incarnatum*
Elongated cylindrical flowerhead of *bright red* flowers, with *no bract* below it. Leaflets *wedge-shaped.* 10–60 cm. Roadsides. Eastern half of Tex.; occasionally elsewhere. MARCH–MAY

MAIDEN CLOVER   *Trifolium microcephalum*
Note the *tiny, pale pink flowerheads* (5 mm) surrounded by a *shallow, bowl-like bract* with broad, *spine-tipped lobes.* Leaflets have *bilobed tips* and serrated margins. Stipules triangular. 10–50 cm. Lower mountains. Ariz.   MARCH–MAY

WHITETOP CLOVER   *Trifolium variegatum*
Leaflets narrowly oblong, margins sawtoothed. Leaf stipules with *ragged edges.* Each red-purple flower with white or pink tips. Calyx lobes broadly triangular, each with a *single long spine.* 10–40 cm. Ariz., occasionally elsewhere. FEB.–MAY

PINE CLOVER   *Trifolium pinetorum*
Flowerhead *bracts deeply divided* to near base into narrow, lancelike lobes. Elongated pink to whitish flowers. Stipules at leaf petiole base *broadly triangular* with a *tailed tip.* Leaflets semi-wedge-shaped, hairless. 5–50 cm. Forested mountain slopes. S.W.   JUNE–OCT.

TUNDRA CLOVER   *Trifolium dasyphyllum*
Large flowerhead of rose, pealike flowers *without* a bract. Leaflets *long, lancelike,* loosely covered with short hairs. Stipules at leaf petiole base *linear.* 0.5–4 cm. Alpine tundra. N.M., R. Mts.   JUNE–SEPT.

CUSHION CLOVER   *Trifolium nanum*
One to a few very long, pinkish, pealike flowers per head; no basal bract below head. Sepal tips *short, triangular.* Leaflets *long,* lancelike, yellow-green with smooth surfaces. Forms large cushiony tussocks. 5–25 cm. Alpine slopes. Northern N.M., R. Mts.   JUNE–AUG.

UTAH CLOVER   *Trifolium macilentum*
Note the *downward-cascading,* bright rose red, pealike flowers in a *long, shaggy head,* ending in a *tendril.* Leaflets short, oval, bluish green with smooth surfaces. 10–50 cm. Subalpine and alpine slopes. N.M., R. Mts.   JUNE–AUG.

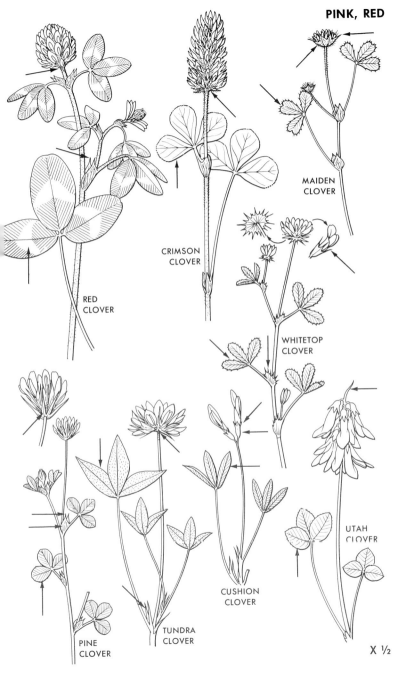

PINK, RED

RED
CLOVER

CRIMSON
CLOVER

MAIDEN
CLOVER

WHITETOP
CLOVER

PINE
CLOVER

TUNDRA
CLOVER

CUSHION
CLOVER

UTAH
CLOVER

X ½

PEALIKE FLOWERS; TENDRIL-TIPPED LEAVES, OR TRIFOLIATE WITH NO TENDRIL

Pea Family (Leguminosae)
See also pp. W 94–96; Y 190–196; R 320–328;
B 346–348, 380–382.

AMERICAN VETCH — *Vicia americana*
4–9 *long* (1–2 cm), dark red to blue-purple flowers in each raceme. 4–8 pairs of *oval* leaflets, *spine-tipped.* Slightly haired vines. 50 cm–1 m. Open fields. Common in pine forests. S.W., nw. Tex., R. Mts., Pl. Sts. APRIL–SEPT.

SPRING VETCH Alien — *Vicia sativa*
1–2 red-purple flowers *near the base* of each leaf. 4–8 pairs of *narrow* leaflets, blunt-tipped, with *tiny bristles.* 3–90 cm. S.W., ne. Tex. MAY–JUNE

SHOWY VETCH — *Vicia pulchella*
5–8 leaflet pairs. Leaflets *narrow, lancelike.* Many lavender and white (or all white), pealike flowers per raceme. Narrow, *sharp, winglike stipules* at side of leaf petiole base. Erect to matted vines. Common in mountain forests. S.W. JUNE–SEPT.

WINTER VETCH Alien — *Vicia villosa*
10 to many rose to violet flowers per raceme. 8–12 pairs of linear leaflets per leaf. Stems slightly *haired.* Vines. 10 cm–1.5 m. Disturbed places. Eastern and n.-cen. Tex., Pl. Sts., S.W. APRIL–AUG.

SPANISH LOTUS — *Lotus purshianus*
Solitary *pale rose flowers,* each with *1 leaflike bract* and on a long peduncle above trifoliate, lancelike leaflets. Numerous long, pale gray hairs. 10 cm–1 m. Open pine forests. S.W., R. Mts. JULY–OCT.

PINE SWEET PEA — *Laythrus eucosmus*
Note the *narrow, lancelike stipules* at the base of each leaf petiole. 6–8 lancelike leaflets per leaf; *tendril poorly developed.* 3–5 large, red-purple to bluish flowers. 15–50 cm. Common in pine forests. Ariz., northern N.M., R. Mts. MAY–AUG.

EVERLASTING PEA Alien — *Lathyrus latifolius*
Flower peduncle *very long,* placing the 5–15 bright red-purple flowers *well above* the stem and leaves. Some plants have white flowers. Each leaf with *2 lancelike leaflets. Tendrils well developed.* Main stem flattened. Vines, 1–2 m long. Common in old towns, etc. S.W., Tex., R. Mts. APRIL–JULY

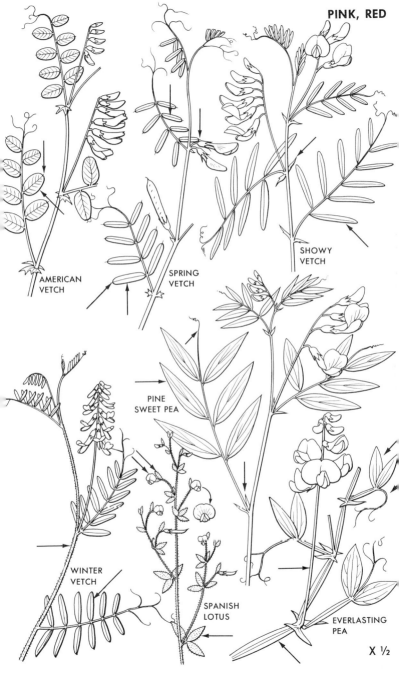

AMERICAN VETCH

SPRING VETCH

SHOWY VETCH

PINE SWEET PEA

WINTER VETCH

SPANISH LOTUS

EVERLASTING PEA

X 1/2

PEALIKE FLOWERS; COMPOUND LEAVES

Pea Family (Leguminosae)
See also pp. W 94–96; Y 190–196; R 320–328;
B 346–348, 380–382.

ROEMER'S SENSITIVE BRIAR *Schrankia roemeriana*
Note the pinkish red, *fluffy flower balls* on sprawling, *thorn-covered stems*. Lower mature stem portions more or less *rounded* in cross-section. Feathery compound leaves sensitive, collapsing when touched. Long, running stems. Northern two-thirds of Tex., Pl. Sts. APRIL–JULY

KARNE'S SENSITIVE BRIAR *Schrankia latidens*
Similar to Roemer's Sensitive Briar, but lower mature stems 4- or 5-sided, Plains. S. Tex. APRIL–SEPT.

EGGLEAF STRINGBEAN *Phaseolus ritensis*
Note the 3 *simple, oval leaflets* per leaf. Beanpods more or less equally wide for entire length. Many flowers per peduncle. Keel petal *coiled;* wing petals rose pink; banner petal dull red-brown. Vines. Southern half of Ariz., sw. N.M. JULY–SEPT.

PURPLE STRINGBEAN *Phaseolus atropurpureus*
Note the two lower leaflets *with basal lobes;* central leaflet lancelike, without lobes. Stringbeanlike peapods more or less *equally wide* for entire length. Flowers *few, deep, brick red.* Vines. S. Tex. MARCH–OCT.

SILVERSPOT LIMABEAN *Phaseolus pedicellatus*
All 3 leaflets with *3 pointed lobes* and *silvery central splotches.* Seedpod *limabean-shaped.* Flower has coiled keel petal and 2 wing petals; banner petal pale pink. Vines. Mountains. S. Ariz. east to sw. Tex. JULY–SEPT.

SLIMLEAF LIMABEAN *Phaseolus angustissimus*
Each leaflet *simple, narrow, lancelike. Limabean-like* peapod with outer end wider. Flowers rose pink. Vines. Common on mesas. S.W., sw. Tex. MAY–OCT.

WRIGHT'S LIMABEAN *Phaseolus wrightii*
Similar to Slimleaf Limabean, but each leaflet has 3 *long rounded lobes, spearlike.* Vines. S.W., sw. Tex. ALL YEAR

DOLLARLEAF *Rhynchosia americana*
Note the large, *crinkly,* kidney-shaped to round leaf blades the size of *silver dollars.* Pale pinkish to yellowish flowers. Corolla equal to or shorter than sepal length. Vines. Southern half of Tex. MARCH–OCT.

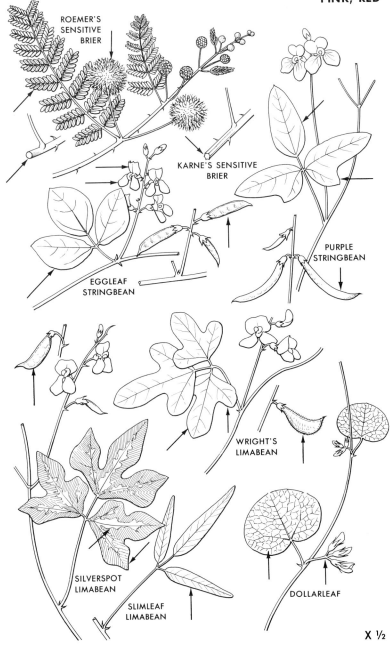

ROEMER'S SENSITIVE BRIER

KARNE'S SENSITIVE BRIER

EGGLEAF STRINGBEAN

PURPLE STRINGBEAN

WRIGHT'S LIMABEAN

SILVERSPOT LIMABEAN

SLIMLEAF LIMABEAN

DOLLARLEAF

X ½

PEALIKE FLOWERS

Pea Family (Leguminosae)
See also pp. W 94–96; Y 190–196;
R 320–328; B 346–348, 380–382.

SEARLS' PRAIRIE CLOVER   *Dalea searlsiae*
Leaf of 3–9 *narrow, troughlike leaflets.* Sausagelike spike of tiny, rose-purple, pealike flowers on *long, naked, wiry stems.* 30–60 cm. Middle elevations. N. Ariz., Ut.   APRIL–JUNE

TRICOLOR DALEA   *Dalea mollis*
Note the broad-based, *silky cone of tiny, 3-colored,* pealike flowers. Banner petal *large, rosy pink,* with a lower *yellow crescent* within an area of white. *Stem prostrate.* 5–9 squarish, white-haired leaflets per leaf. 10–30 cm. Lower deserts. Ariz.   JAN.–APRIL

BEARDED DALEA   *Dalea pogonathera*
Note the rose purple, *paddlelike keel petal.* Banner petal tricolored: rose purple, white, and yellow. Silky-haired flowerhead. Stems erect. 10–30 cm. Tex.   MARCH–SEPT.

GOAT'S-RUE   *Tephrosia virginiana*
Note the large, *bicolored, pealike flowers* with large lemon yellow to cream banner and keel petals and 2 rosy pink wing petals. Compound pinnate leaves. Leaflets narrow, *lancelike,* with *spiny tips.* 30–60 cm. Woods. Northern and e. Tex., Pl. Sts.   APRIL–JUNE

LINDHEIMER'S HOARY PEA   *Tephrosa lindheimeri*
Note the *white-rimmed,* oval to round leaflets. Stems semi-declining. Large, rose purple flowers with a *tiny white spot* or banner petal. 50 cm–1 m. S. Tex.   APRIL–SEPT.

GRAHAM'S TICK CLOVER   *Desmodium grahamii*
Note the broadly oval, slightly-haired trifoliate leaflets. *Spoutlike column of stamens projects* from the pink flowers. Banner petal large, rounded, with a *yellowish, bilobed* basal spot *outlined in dark red-purple.* Lower petals all fold downward. *Beadlike* seedpods. 30–60 cm. Pine woods. Ariz., s. N.M., sw. Tex.   AUG–SEPT.

BUSHY TICK CLOVER   *Desmodium batocaulon*
Much like Graham's Tick Clover, but leaflets *narrowly lancelike* with a *white central splotch.* Banner petal *diamond-shaped;* the bilobed yellow basal spot *not outlined.* 20 cm–1 m. Mountains. S. Ariz., sw. N.M.   JUNE–SEPT.

NARROWLEAF TICK CLOVER   *Cologania angustifolia*
Note the 1 or 2 large, rose pink flowers *nestled* next to the petiole base. Palmate compound leaves with 3 or 5 *long, narrow (very variable) leaflets.* Vines. 10 cm–1 m. Ariz., s. N.M., sw. Tex.
     JULY–OCT.

Ratany Family (Krameriaceae)

THREE FANS   *Krameria lanceolata*
Note the 5 irregularly arranged, dark wine red petals, 4 above and 1 below. *3 fanlike stigma lobes.* Prostrate stems with *lancelike* leaves. 10 cm–1.5 m. Southern S.W., Tex., Pl. Sts.   MARCH–SEPT.

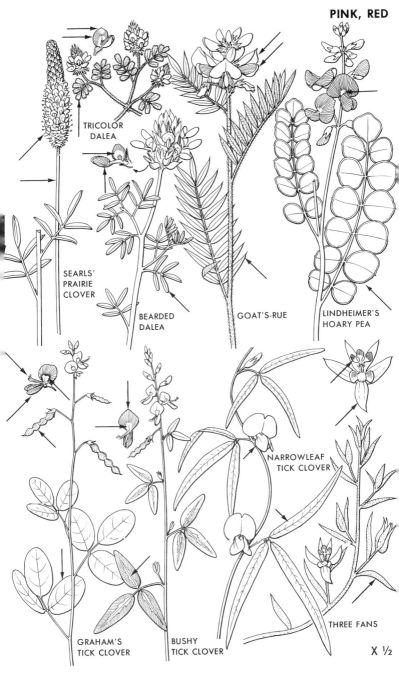

TRICOLOR DALEA

SEARLS' PRAIRIE CLOVER

BEARDED DALEA

GOAT'S-RUE

LINDHEIMER'S HOARY PEA

NARROWLEAF TICK CLOVER

GRAHAM'S TICK CLOVER

BUSHY TICK CLOVER

THREE FANS

X ½

VARIOUS SUNFLOWER TRIBES

Sunflower Family (Compositae)
See also pp. W 98–110; Y 198–222;
O 234; R 330–334; B 384–386; G 402.

Woolly Sunflower Tribe: Helenieae

FIREWHEEL *Gaillardia pulchella*
Note the *"comet's tail" of yellow-tipped, red-brown* ray flowers
below a large *reddish dome* of disk flowers. Leaves arrow-shaped.
20–50 cm. S.W., Tex., Pl. Sts. MARCH–SEPT.

Sunflower Tribe: (Heliantheae)

REDSTAR ZINNIA *Zinnia multiflora*
Dark reddish brown ray flowers around a shaggy dome of dark disk
flowers. Flowerhead *bracts resemble fish scales*. Oval leaves. 10–
40 cm. Wooded canyons. S. Ariz. AUG.–SEPT.

HANDLELESS CONEFLOWER *Echinacea sanguinea*
Note the *drooping,* straplike, dark-red, pink, or whitish ray flowers
below the brownish, *pointed, hemispherical cone* of disk flowers.
Leaves lancelike, *without a petiole* or nearly so. 30–90 cm. Pine
woods. E. Tex. MAY–SEPT.

HANDLELEAF CONEFLOWER *Echinacea angustifolia*
Similar to Handleless Coneflower, but disk flowers in a *rounded
cone.* Leaves linear with a *distinct petiole.* 10–50 cm. Prairies.
Nw. N.M. to cen. Tex., Pl. Sts. MAY–JULY

BLACK SAMPSON *Echinacea purpurea*
Similar to Handleleaf Coneflower, but leaves *broadly lancelike
with coarsely toothed margins.* 30 cm–1 m. Rocky open woods.
Nc. Tex., Pl. Sts. MAY–SEPT.

Everlasting Tribe: Inuleae

ROSY EVERLASTING *Antennaria rosea*
Small, rosy, cylindrical or round flowerheads with *tiny white centers and papery bracts.* Stem and leaves covered with a layer of
soft, feltlike hair. 5–50 cm. Northern N.M., R. Mts. JUNE–SEPT.

Chicory Tribe: Cichoriaeae

TEXAS SKELETON PLANT *Lygodesmia texana*
Showy flowerhead of broad, pink to rosy bluish ray flowers; no disk
flowers. Smooth, skeletonlike stems. Straplike leaves with a *few
lobes.* Milky sap. 10–60 cm. N.M., Tex. APRIL–OCT.

GRAND SKELETON PLANT *Lygodesmia grandiflora*
Showy flowerhead of a *few* (5–10) pink to lavender ray flowers; no
disk flowers. Leaves *grasslike, without* side lobes. Milky sap. 5–
40 cm. Common on sandy plains. Northern S.W., R. Mts.
MAY–JUNE

Mutisia Tribe: Mutisiaeae

PEONIA *Perezia runcinata*
Flowerhead of pinkish straplike ray flowers only. Sap *not milky.*
Highly divided, spiny, thistle-like leaves in a basal rosette.
10–40 cm. Cen. and e. Tex. MARCH–NOV.

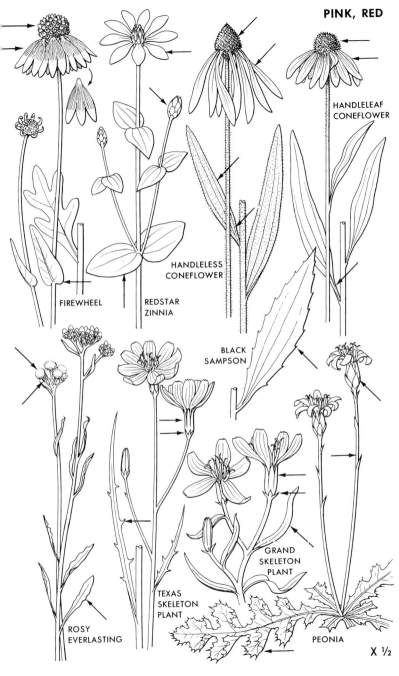

PINK, RED

HANDLELEAF
CONEFLOWER

HANDLELESS
CONEFLOWER

FIREWHEEL

REDSTAR
ZINNIA

BLACK
SAMPSON

ROSY
EVERLASTING

TEXAS
SKELETON
PLANT

GRAND
SKELETON
PLANT

PEONIA

X ½

SPINY THISTLES

Sunflower Family (Compositae)

Thistle Tribe: Cynareae
See also pp. W 98–110; Y 198–222;
O 234; R 330–334; B 384–386; G 402.

Note: Other thistles shown under White or Yellow can also have pink to red flowers, but are not shown under Red.

BULL THISTLE Alien   *Cirsium vulgare*
Note the spiny, dark green leaf blade, *clasping and extending down the stem.* Flowerheads red-purple. 50 cm–1 m. Disturbed places. Northern S.W., R. Mts.   AUG.–OCT.

CANADA THISTLE Alien   *Cirsium arvense*
Pink to red-purple, *marblelike* flowerheads, numerous and small (1 cm). Flowerheads, stems and leaves *shiny and smooth, as if varnished.* Slender, lancelike leaves with *shallowly lobed,* spiny margins; *green on both sides.* 20 cm–1 m. Disturbed places. Northern S.W., R. Mts.   MAY–SEPT.

MOUNTAIN THISTLE   *Cirsium pulchellum*
Leaf blades *narrow,* straplike with *widely spaced spiny lobes;* upper surfaces *bright green,* undersides with *gray hairs.* Narrow red-purple flowerheads, bracts broad. 10 cm–1 m. Mountains. S.W.   JUNE–OCT.

AMERICAN BASKETFLOWER   *Centaurea americana*
Very large (2–8 cm wide) flowerheads of *pink, threadlike* petals as an outer fringe and a *yellowish center.* Flowerhead bracts straw-colored with *long side spines.* Leaves lancelike, *spineless.* 30 cm–1.5 m. S.W., Tex.   APRIL–JULY

TEXAS THISTLE   *Cirsium texanum*
Flowerheads *broader than tall,* lavender-rose or pink-purple, on *long, naked upper stems. Shiny* flowerhead bracts, *long, narrow,* lancelike. Upper leaf surface dark green. 1–2 m. Tex., Pl. Sts.   MARCH–SEPT.

SANTE FE THISTLE   *Cirsium ochrocentrum*
Flowerheads *broader than tall,* of purple, rosy, or creamcolored flowers with shiny, semi-broad flowerhead bracts. Broad *green* leaf blades *with thin woolly hairs* on *upper* surface; *densely white-haired* below. Stem with dense, white, woolly hairs. 30 cm–1 m. Open places. S.W., western two-thirds of Tex., Pl. Sts.   MAY–OCT.

WAVYLEAF THISTLE   *Cirsium undulatum*
Much like Sante Fe Thistle, but the broad leaves nearly *equally gray-haired on both sides.* 30 cm–1.5 m. Eastern half of Ariz. to western third of Tex., Pl. Sts.   MAY–OCT.

MILK THISTLE Alien   *Silybum marianum*
Note the *spiny, shiny green* leaves with *white veins and spots.* Stout, erect stem with many red-purple flowerheads. 1–2 m. Disturbed places. S.W., Tex.   MAY–SEPT.

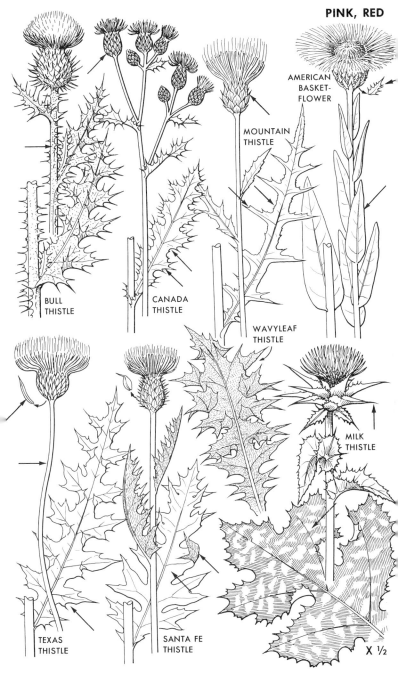

PINK, RED

AMERICAN BASKET-FLOWER

MOUNTAIN THISTLE

BULL THISTLE

CANADA THISTLE

WAVYLEAF THISTLE

TEXAS THISTLE

SANTA FE THISTLE

MILK THISTLE

X ½

VARIOUS SUNFLOWERS

Sunflower Family (Compositae)
See also pp. W 98–110; Y 198–222;
O 234; R 330–334; B 384–386; G 402.

Eupatory Tribe: (Eupatorieae)

SHARP GAYFEATHER   *Liatris acidota*
Note the slender stem of *hugging, linear, grasslike* leaves and the
spike of pink, *5-pointed disk flowers* in elongated flowerheads. Usually 5 flowers per head. 20 cm–1 m. Standing water. E. Tex.
                                                        JULY–DEC.

PINKSCALE GAYFEATHER   *Liatris elegans*
Similar to Sharp Gayfeather, but the long, linear, grasslike leaves
loosely at right angles to stem. Long spike of flowerheads, usually 5
flowers per head. 20 cm–1.5 m. Dry sandy fields. Eastern third
of Tex.   AUG.–OCT.

BALDWIN'S IRONWEED   *Vernonia baldwinii*
Strongly *5-lobed,* red-purple disk flowers above a *rounded* flowerhead of *broad, overlapping, shinglelike bracts.* Widely branched
flowering stems; a single stem below. Numerous broad, lancelike leaves with *sawtoothed* margins. 50 cm–1.5 m. Common.
Northern half of Tex., Pl. Sts.   JUNE–SEPT.

Everlasting Tribe: Inuleae

CANELA   *Pluchea purpurascens*
Note the numerous *rosy pink, urnlike* flowerheads with *2 layers* of
disk flowers: the lower layer numerous and *very thin,* the upper
layer with a *few larger* central flowers. Leaves *broadly lancelike.*
20 cm–1 m. Muddy places. Tex., Pl. Sts.   JUNE–OCT.

Woolly Sunflower Tribe: Helenieae

SMALL PALAFOXIA   *Palafoxia callosa*
Long, narrow, linear leaves with a slight central bulge. Loose flowerheads. 10–60 cm. Rocky limestone slopes. Cen. Tex.
                                                        APRIL–OCT.

SPANISH NEEDLES   *Palafoxia arida*
Leaves *linear.* On top of each seed are *needlelike bristles* with a
central midrib. *Pincushion-like* flowerheads of disk flowers only.
10–90 cm. Sandy washes, dunes. W. Ariz.   JAN.–SEPT.

Aster Tribe: Astereae

WANDERING DAISY   *Erigeron peregrinus*
Lower stem leaves *lancelike, clasping,* with only a few scattered
hairs. Pale pink to rose-purple ray flowers (30–80 per head), *broad
and flat.* 10–70 cm. Moist, high mountain meadows. Northern S.W.,
R. Mts.   JULY–AUG.

COLORADO SPINE ASTER   *Machaeranthera coloradensis*
Low basal cluster of straplike leaves with short, sharp-pointed
lobes. Several *broad* flowerheads with broad, rosy to violet ray
flowers. 5–10 cm. Mountains. Northern S.W., R. Mts.
                                                        JUNE–AUG.

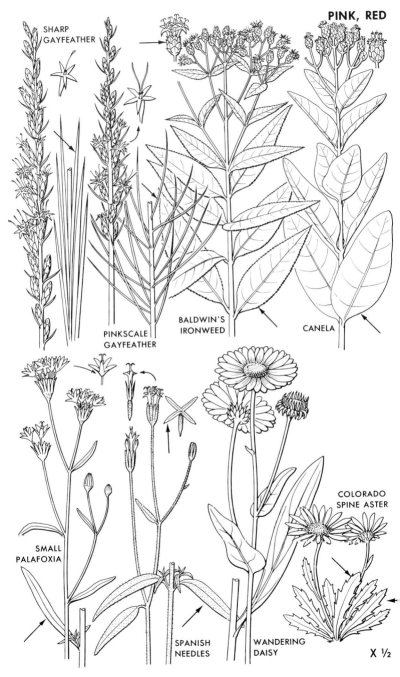

SHARP
GAYFEATHER

PINKSCALE
GAYFEATHER

BALDWIN'S
IRONWEED

CANELA

SMALL
PALAFOXIA

SPANISH
NEEDLES

WANDERING
DAISY

COLORADO
SPINE ASTER

X ½

Violet to Blue or Blue-Purple Flowers

The truly violet and blue flowers are in this category. Blue-purple flowers are also presented here, but are difficult to separate from the red-purples. True purple is a 50–50 mixture of red and blue; thus it is sometimes difficult to decide on which side of the line a color falls. Often a fresh red-purple flower will age to blue-purple. A majority of the purple flowers are in the red-purple category—if in doubt, check Pink to Red or Red-Purple Flowers, p. 225. When possible, the group characteristics given in the text page titles are repeated in each color section, and in the same order. Where the flowers on a page look nearly the same but your sample does not quite match, use the cross references given for other colors.

3 OR 6 PETALS; LILIES, DAYFLOWERS

Lily Family (Liliaceae)
See also pp. W 8–14; Y 114; O 226; R 272; B 338; G 394.

EASTERN CAMAS *Camassia scilloides*
Note the *broad column* (raceme) of pale blue to lavender, 6-petaled flowers well above the grasslike basal leaves. 10–60 cm. Prairies. Cen. and n. Tex., Pl. Sts., S.E. MARCH–MAY

Amaryllis Family (Amaryllidaceae)
See also pp. W 14–16; Y 116; R 274.

BLUE FUNNEL LILY *Androstephium coeruleum*
Note the 6 stamen filaments *fused into a long projecting funnel.* Petals pale blue to violet. Flowers in an umbel on top of a bare stem. 5–25 cm. N. Tex., Pl. Sts. FEB.–MAY

PALMER'S BAJA LILY *Triteliopsis palmeri*
Note the *clamlike structures* between the petal lobe bases. Many *short, funnel-shaped,* blue-purple flowers in an umbel on naked stems. 10–70 cm. Packed sand, dunes. Sw. Ariz. FEB.–MAY

BLUE DICKS *Dichelostemma pulchellum*
Blue to pink flower tube resembles a *short, round, inflated ball.* 6 *hidden anthers* within a series of white projections. Flowers in an umbel. 10–50 cm. Common at lower elevations. Ariz., sw. N.M.
FEB.–MAY

Spiderwort Family (Commelinaceae) See also p. R 272.

BIRDBILL DAYFLOWER *Commelina dianthifolia*
Long, boatlike flower spathe *open (free) to base* on upper side. Three dark blue petals: 2 large upper ones and 1 *slightly smaller lower one.* Stamens *hairless.* 5–25 cm. Pine woods. S.W., w. Tex.
JULY–SEPT.

WHITEMOUTH DAYFLOWER *Commelina erecta*
Short, boatlike spathe *fused at base* into a *right angle* on upper side. 2 large blue side petals and *1 tiny, white, bilobed lower one.* Stamens *hairless.* 30 cm–1.5 m. Common. Southern S.W., Tex., Pl. Sts. MAY–OCT.

BOULDER DAYFLOWER *Commelinantia anomala*
Yellow-green leaves *broad,* grasslike, with conspicuous *collarlike* clasping bases. 2 showy lavender-blue side petals and a diminutive, whitish lower one. Some *stamens with terminal hair clusters,* others hairless. 30–80 cm. Among boulders. W.-cen. Tex.

APRIL–JULY

OHIO SPIDERWORT *Tradescantia ohioensis*
Three *equal-sized* blue-purple to rose petals. 2 or more leaves at each flower cluster. Flower *sepals hairless.* Stamen *filaments hairy.* 10–80 cm. Very common. Eastern two-thirds of Tex., Pl. Sts., S.E. FEB.–MAY

WESTERN SPIDERWORT *Tradescantia occidentalis*
Similar to Ohio Spiderwort. Sepals *nearly hairless,* with just a few *glandular hairs.* Stamen filaments hairy. 10–80 cm. Woods. S.W., Tex., Pl. Sts. MARCH–SEPT.

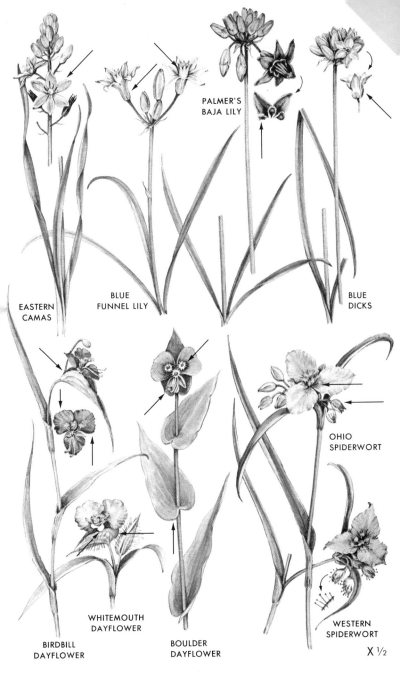

PALMER'S
BAJA LILY

EASTERN
CAMAS

BLUE
FUNNEL LILY

BLUE
DICKS

OHIO
SPIDERWORT

WHITEMOUTH
DAYFLOWER

BIRDBILL
DAYFLOWER

BOULDER
DAYFLOWER

WESTERN
SPIDERWORT

X ½

3 OR 6 PETALS; IRIS-LIKE FLOWERS

Iris Family (Iridaceae) See also pp. Y 116; R 272.

PURPLE PLEATLEAF *Alophia drummondii*
3 large, rounded, dark royal purple outer petal segments and 3 *boatlike inner* petals with a *yellow spot* at central *pinched-in area.* Inner petals spotted. Iris-like leaves. 10–70 cm. Woods. Eastern and s. Tex. MAY–OCT.

PRAIRIE NYMPH *Trifurcia lahue*
Note the 3 long, *wedgelike,* dark to light blue-purple outer petal segments and 3 *tiny, triangular inner* ones. Outer petal bases with a *blue chevron* and white-spotted base. Flat, iris-like leaves. 10–30 cm. Prairies. S. Tex. MARCH–MAY

CELESTIAL GHOST IRIS *Nemastylis geminiflora*
Pale blue, *short, broadly lancelike* petals with *narrow yellow bases.* Blooms at night; fades by mid-morning. Filament *bases of stamens free,* not fused. 10–50 cm. Limestone areas. Cen. Tex., Pl. Sts. FEB.–MAY

CIÉNAGA GHOST IRIS *Nemastylis tenuis*
Pale blue petals long, *wedgelike,* with a *similarly colored or whitish base.* Filament *bases of stamens fused.* Night blooming; fades by mid-morning. 10–30 cm. Soggy foothills, ciénagas. S. Ariz. to sw. Tex. JULY–AUG.

ROCKY MOUNTAIN IRIS *Iris missouriensis*
Flower tube above ovary a *short, bowl-like* enlargement; pedicel below very long (to 20 cm). Flowers dark blue or paler. Petals elongated with a *central, dark yellow-orange stripe and diverging dark blue lines on a white background.* 20–90 cm. Damp to marshy places in mountains. S.W., R. Mts. MAY–SEPT.

SHORTSTEM IRIS *Iris brevicaulis*
Large, *dark blue-purple, rounded* petal lobes held in a *distinct flat plane;* note the yellow-orange, *triangular patch* in a field of white on each petal. Ovary and seedpod 3-sided in cross-section. *Broad, erect,* blue sepals with *round tips.* 30–90 cm. Wet ditches. E. Tex., S.E. MARCH–JUNE

SOUTHERN BLUE FLAG *Iris virginica*
Broad, *arching, pale powdery blue* petals with a *spadelike central yellow patch* in a field of white. Ovary and seedpod 3-*sided* in cross-section. Broad, *pale blue,* semi-erect, *pointed* inner petals. 30–90 cm. Marshes. E. Tex., S.E. APRIL–JUNE

DIXIE IRIS *Iris hexagona*
Large, *dark blue-purple,* oval petals *arching downward.* Note the linear, dark yellow-orange, raised patch surrounded by a paler yellow area. Ovary and seedpod 6-*sided* in cross-section. *Narrow,* semi-erect, blue outer sepals *notch-tipped.* 60–90 cm. Wet places. E. Tex., S.E. MARCH–MAY

BLUE-EYED GRASS *Sisyrinchium* species
Dark blue-purple, *6-petaled stars.* Wiry stem with narrow, swordlike leaves. Many similar species. 5–50 cm. Common. S.W., Tex., R. Mts., Pl. Sts., S.E. MOST OF YEAR

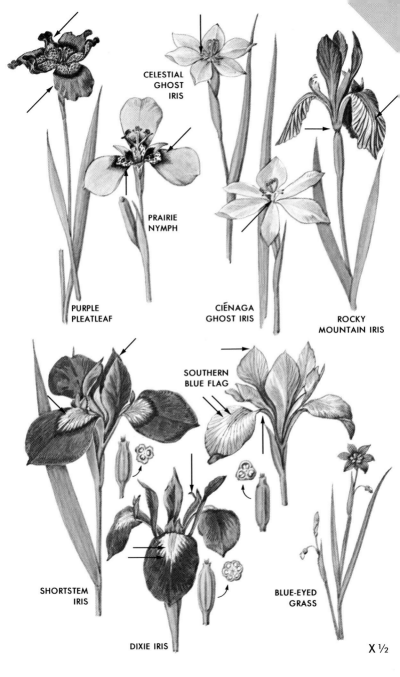

CELESTIAL
GHOST
IRIS

PRAIRIE
NYMPH

PURPLE
PLEATLEAF

CIÉNAGA
GHOST IRIS

ROCKY
MOUNTAIN IRIS

SOUTHERN
BLUE FLAG

SHORTSTEM
IRIS

DIXIE IRIS

BLUE-EYED
GRASS

X ½

4- OR 5-PETALED VASES, CHALICES

Gentian Family (Gentianaceae)
See also pp. W 78; Y 174; R 242; G 400.

ALKALI CHALICE *Eustoma exaltatum*
Small (2–5 cm), *punchbowl-like,* blue-pink flowers with a white central ring and *bilobed purple basal spots.* Petal lobe up to 2 *times as long* as basal tube. 30–60 cm. Alkali-encrusted streams, ocean flats. S.W., Tex. JUNE–OCT.

BLUEBELL GENTIAN *Eustoma grandiflorum*
Very similar to Alkali Chalice, but flowers *much larger* (5–10 cm). Petal lobe *3 or more times longer* than basal tube. Many common names. Prairies, open fields. 30–60 cm. Eastern third of N.M., Tex., Pl. Sts. JUNE–SEPT.

EXPLORER'S GENTIAN *Gentiana calycosa*
Note the broadly *forked filaments* between the rounded, reflexed petal lobes. Corolla deep blue, broadly vaselike, often with tiny yellow dots. Calyx lobes highly variable in size and shape. Thick oval leaves. 10–60 cm. Moist mountain meadows. S.W., R. Mts. AUG.–OCT.

MARSH GENTIAN *Gentiana affinis*
Elongated flower tube *narrowly vaselike.* Inner area between petal lobes has a *single short tooth.* Flower blue-purple, somewhat green-bronze on petal backs. Leaves nearly linear. 10–50 cm. Marshy places in mountains. Northern S.W., R. Mts.
AUG.–OCT.

NORTHERN GENTIAN *Gentiana amarella*
Note the *fringe of hairs* (actually 2 sets of hairs per petal) across the inside of the 5 petal lobe bases. Tubular, light purple to pink flowers. Leaves lancelike. 5–50 cm. Mountains. S.W., R. Mts. JULY–SEPT.

FRINGED GENTIAN *Gentianopsis detonsa*
4 *short, broadly rounded* petal lobes arranged like a Dutch windmill. Petal margins *raggedly fringed or smooth.* Leaves *broadly oval.* 10–60 cm. Streamsides, mountain meadows. S.W., R. Mts. JULY–OCT.

WINDMILL GENTIAN *Gentianopsis barbellata*
4 *long, narrow* petal lobes arranged like a Dutch windmill. Petal margins *raggedly fringed.* Leaves narrow on short stems. 5–15 cm. Subalpine slopes. Northern S.W., R. Mts.
AUG.–OCT.

STAR SWERTIA *Swertia perennis*
Dull blue-purple to greenish, *flat, starlike* flowers with 2 *round patches* of fringed hairs at the base of each petal. 10–30 cm. Mountain marshes. Northern S.W., R. Mts. AUG.–SEPT.

BOTTLE GENTIAN *Gentianopsis saponaria*
Deep blue, *bottlelike* flower, barely open. Lancelike leaves. 20–80 cm. Ditches, swamps. E. Tex. SEPT.–NOV.

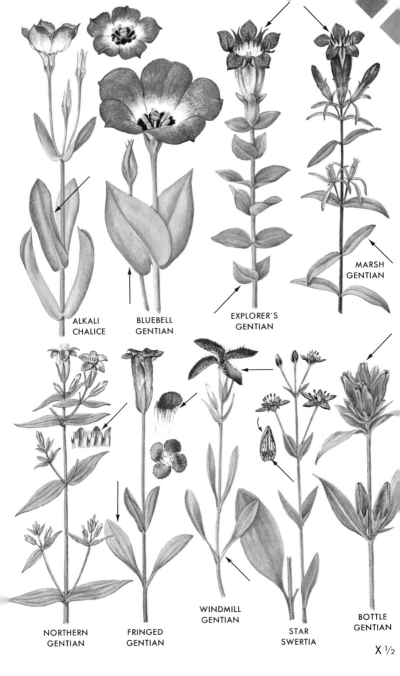

ALKALI
CHALICE

BLUEBELL
GENTIAN

EXPLORER'S
GENTIAN

MARSH
GENTIAN

NORTHERN
GENTIAN

FRINGED
GENTIAN

WINDMILL
GENTIAN

STAR
SWERTIA

BOTTLE
GENTIAN

X ½

4 TO MANY PETALS; VARIOUS FAMILIES

Buttercup Family (Ranunculaceae)
See also pp. W 42–44; Y 162–164;
R 236, 286; B 356–358; G 396, 406.

COLORADO COLUMBINE *Aquilegia caerulea*
Note the *5 blue spurs and outer sepals.* Inner petals *white.* Twice-pinnate, blue-green leaves. Colorado state flower. 30–90 cm. Damp woods in mountains. Northern S.W., R. Mts. JUNE–AUG.

ROCKY MOUNTAIN CLEMATIS *Clematis pseudo-alpina*
Single, pale to dark blue, *4-petaled, nodding* flowers on leafless peduncles. *Trilobed* leaflets on *trilobed* leaves. Vine. Damp woods. Northern S.W., R. Mts. JUNE–JULY

Water Lily Family (Nymphaeaceae)
See also pp. W 6; Y 186; G 406.

BLUE WATER LILY *Nymphaea elegans*
Flowers raised *above* water surface. Many blue to pale lavender petals, appearing white from a distance. Large, oval, floating leaves. Ponds. S. Tex. APRIL–AUG.

Passion Flower Family
(Passifloraceae) See also pp. Y 186; R 236.

MAYPOP *Passiflora incarnata*
Numerous flower filaments, pale blue with *bands* of darker violet or purple. Leaves deeply trilobed; *leaflet tips pointed.* Vine. Woods. Eastern third of Tex., Pl. Sts., S.E. APRIL–AUG.

CORONA DE CRISTO *Passiflora foetida*
Pale yellowish flower filaments *evenly purple to violet-streaked* above, bases forming a *tight circle* around the stigma column. Yellow-green, trilobed leaves with *rounded lobe tips.* Climbing vines. S. Tex., s. Ariz. APRIL–OCT.

CUPPED PASSION FLOWER *Passiflora bryonioides*
Pale yellow flower filaments with *one inner ring* of lavender to purple on the rim of the *wide inner cup* around the stigma column. *Dark green,* trilobed leaves, *margins toothed.* Climbing vines. Wooded canyons. S. Ariz. AUG.–SEPT.

Forget-me-not Family (Boraginaceae)
See also pp. W 84; Y 182; O 234; R 314; B 366.

BARE STICKSEED *Hackelia floribunda*
Tiny, *light powdery blue, pinwheel-like* flowers with *tiny inner teeth.* Each nutlet has *no prickles on the middle,* but has a row of stalked, hook-tipped spines at margins. Leaves linear, *petioleless.* 30 cm–1.5 m. Mountains. S.W., R. Mts. JULY–AUG.

PINE STICKSEED *Hackelia pinetorum*
Leaves *broad,* lancelike, with a *short, distinct petiole.* Each nutlet has *short prickles on the middle and longer,* stalked, hook-tipped *spines* at margins. Flowers *deep blue.* 20–50 cm. Mountain slopes. S.W., w. Tex. JUNE–AUG.

CRINKLE MATS *Coldenia plicata*
Small, oval leaves with a *crinkly appearance from gray, feltlike hairs* in ridges and dark green "canyons." Tiny violet to red-purple, funnel-like flowers. Low spreading mats. 10–20 cm. Very common. Low rocky ridges, desert plains. S.W. APRIL–OCT.

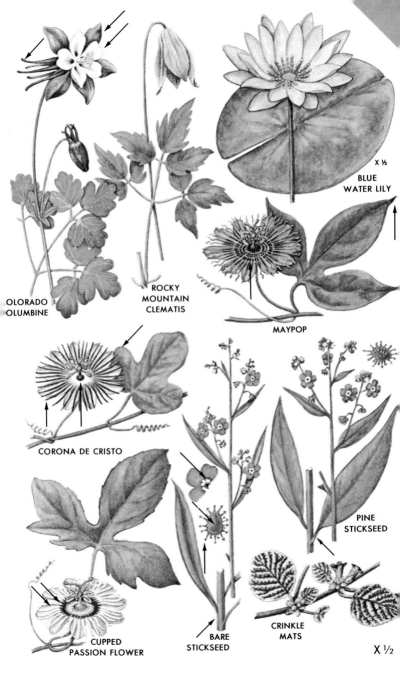

COLORADO
COLUMBINE

ROCKY
MOUNTAIN
CLEMATIS

X ⅓
BLUE
WATER LILY

MAYPOP

CORONA DE CRISTO

PINE
STICKSEED

CUPPED
PASSION FLOWER

BARE
STICKSEED

CRINKLE
MATS

X ½

PEALIKE FLOWERS, PALMATE LEAVES; LUPINES

Pea Family (Leguminosae)
See also pp. W 94–96; Y 190–196; R 320–328; B 348, 380–382.

ARIZONA LUPINE · · · · · · · · · *Lupinus arizonicus*
Leaflets *broad, bright green,* with *long hairs* on undersides. Flowers purple-pink with yellow centers. Often found with Coulter's Lupine (compare below). 30–60 cm. Very common in lower deserts. Western half of Ariz. · · · · · · · · · JAN.–MAY

COULTER'S LUPINE · · · · · · · · · *Lupinus sparsiflorus*
Tall plants. Leaflets *linear* with *scattered flattened hairs on upper surfaces.* Flowers light blue to violet, in a loosely arranged raceme; banner petal has a *yellow spot.* Keel petals short and broad, curved upward; hairy fringe on lower margins near base and often above as well. 1–30 cm. Below 4500 ft. Ariz., sw. N.M. · · · · · · · · · JAN.–MAY

BAJADA LUPINE · · · · · · · · · *Lupinus concinnus*
Low, *prostrate stems.* Short flower clusters *nearly hidden* among leaves. Plants *densely-haired.* Petals lilac, *edged with red-purple.* Banner petal with a *yellow center.* 5–20 cm. Desert pavements, bajadas. S.W. · · · · · · · · · MARCH–MAY

SPURRED LUPINE · · · · · · · · · *Lupinus caudatus*
Leaflets *somewhat* silvery-haired. *Long, dense cylinders* of numerous flowers. Flowers deep blue with a *white central area* which may have pale yellow at the bottom. 30–60 cm. Plains and open hills, aspen groves; often found with sagebrush. Northern N.M., R. Mts. · · · · · · · · · APRIL–SEPT.

SHORTSTEM LUPINE · · · · · · · · · *Lupinus brevicaulis*
Long (more than 3 cm) *flower cluster, stem,* and leaves have *long bristly hairs except* on the cupped, dull green upper leaflet surfaces, which are *bare.* Leaflets *narrow, lancelike.* Royal purple flowers with a squared white or yellowish "eye" with dark flecks in the banner petal. Banner petal *broader at base.* Short, reddish stems. 5–20 cm. Frequent on open sandy slopes. S.W., R. Mts. · · · · · · · · · APRIL–JULY

DWARF LUPINE · · · · · · · · · *Lupinus pusillus*
Somewhat similar to Shortstem Lupine, but flowers in a *short terminal cluster, often nestled* among the flat cluster of bristly-haired leaves and stems. Cupped leaflets *much broader at outer end,* with *no hairs* on upper surface. Royal blue flowers with a squared *white "eye"* on the banner petal. Banner petal *broadest in middle.* 2–15 cm. Sandy plains. S.W., R. Mts., Pl. Sts. · · · · · · · · · APRIL–JUNE

MINIATURE LUPINE · · · · · · · · · *Lupinus bicolor*
Tiny (5 mm), *deep blue* flowers. Banner petal *oblong,* with a *squared top* and a white spot with dark dots. Pedicel *shorter* than the flowers. 1–3 *distinct whorls* of flowers. Linear leaflets, hairy above. 10–40 cm. Cen. Ariz. · · · · · · · · · MARCH–MAY

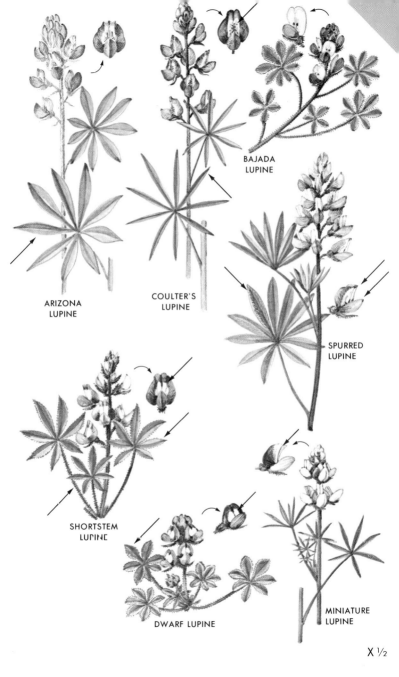

ARIZONA
LUPINE

COULTER'S
LUPINE

BAJADA
LUPINE

SPURRED
LUPINE

SHORTSTEM
LUPINE

DWARF LUPINE

MINIATURE
LUPINE

X ½

PEALIKE FLOWERS; LUPINES, BLUEBONNETS

Pea Family (Leguminosae)
See also pp. W 94–96; Y 190–196; R 320–328; B 346, 380–382.

BIG BEND LUPINE *Lupinus havardii*
Long, spirelike flower stems. Note the *square zone* of creamy white with many *dark yellow spots* on the banner petal, becoming red with age. Usually 7 leaflets, *tips pointed.* 30–90 cm. Common in Big Bend region of Tex. FEB.–APRIL

SHY BLUEBONNET *Lupinus subcarnosus*
Leaflet tips *broadly rounded to squared-off.* Wing petals *strongly inflated, cheeklike.* Flowers bright blue, banner petal with a white center that turns purplish with age. Tips of undeveloped terminal flowers *not conspicuous* (shy) from a distance. 10–40 cm. S.-cen. Tex. MARCH–APRIL

TEXAS BLUEBONNET *Lupinus texensis*
Leaflet tips with *sharp points.* Wing petals *shallowly cupped,* like *hands in prayer.* Flowers dark blue. Banner petal has a *pale yellow "eye" in the center* that ages reddish. Tips of undeveloped terminal flowers have *conspicuous white tips,* visible from a distance. 10–40 cm. Eastern ⅔ of Tex. MARCH–MAY

BLUMER'S LUPINE *Lupinus blumeri*
Banner petal *tricolored* (*changes* with age). In young flowers, inner banner petal *bright yellow* surrounded by white, outer edges blue; wing and keel petals blue. In older flowers, yellow area of banner petal becomes *rusty red* and the white area red-purple. Flowers in *whorls.* Broad, dark green, lancelike leaflets *without hairs* on upper surfaces. Tall stems. 30–90 cm. Mountains. Se. Ariz., sw. N.M. JUNE–AUG.

KING'S LUPINE *Lupinus kingii*
Flat, very short flower clusters on a relatively *tall, long-haired, leafless stem.* Entire plant has *long, bristly hairs. Tiny, dark blue* flowers with a *clean white central "eye"* on the *long, teardrop-shaped* banner petal. *Dull, blue-green,* troughlike leaflets, short-stemmed overall; 5–30 cm. Dry pine forests. S.W., R. Mts. JUNE–SEPT.

HILL'S LUPINE *Lupinus hillii*
Short, dense, cylindrical flower racemes. Flowers in *whorls.* Squat, dark blue-purple flowers with *wide, earlike* wing petals; wing petals become *semi-reflexed and edges enroll* with age. Center of banner petal *dark burgundy red.* Dark green, troughlike leaflets with flattened, silvery hairs. Short-stemmed; 10–30 cm. Mountain meadows. N. Ariz. MAY–SEPT.

SILVERSTEM LUPINE *Lupinus argenteus*
Stems with *silver hairs.* Leaflets somewhat narrow, *troughlike;* usually hairless, but sometimes with scattered hairs. Small flowers blue or lilac; *back* of banner petal *hairy.* Lower leaves dry up before flowering time. Extremely common and *highly variable.* 20–60 cm. Dry slopes, open plains, or moist pine forests. Northern S.W., R. Mts. JUNE–OCT.

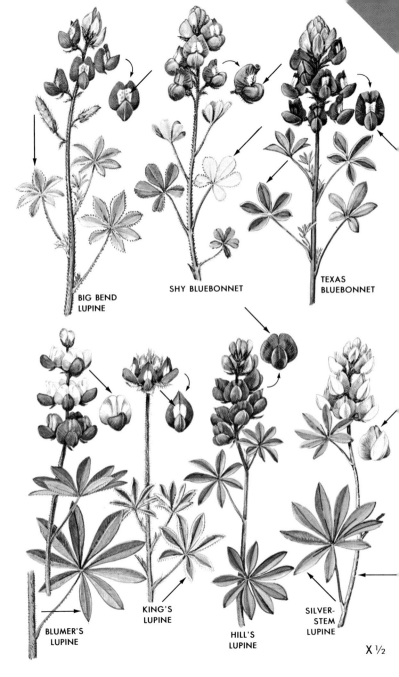

BIG BEND
LUPINE

SHY BLUEBONNET

TEXAS
BLUEBONNET

BLUMER'S
LUPINE

KING'S
LUPINE

HILL'S
LUPINE

SILVER-
STEM
LUPINE

X ½

5 PETALS; 2-LIPPED, TUBULAR FLOWERS

Snapdragon Family (Scrophulariaceae)
See also pp. W 88; Y 118–122; R 244–250; B 350–354.

SNAPDRAGON VINE *Maurandya antirrhiniflora*
Broad, arrow-shaped leaves on a *twining vine.* Flowers dark blue-purple or dark red with a pale yellowish throat. Common on lower deserts. S.W., sw. Tex. to Brownsville. FEB.–OCT.

MEADOW PENSTEMON *Penstemon rydbergii*
Dense clusters of tiny (1 cm long) blue-purple flowers with distinct white throats, in an *ascending position.* 10–60 cm. Higher mountain meadows. Northern N.M., R. Mts. JULY–AUG.

WHIPPLE'S PENSTEMON *Penstemon whippleanus*
Rich dark purple, sticky-haired corolla with *both* upper and lower petal lobes projecting forward. Note the *tuft of white hair* on the longer, *platformlike lower* petal lobes. Flowers *droop downward, in several thick clusters.* Lancelike leaves. 10–60 cm. Mountain meadows. Northern S.W., R. Mts. JUNE–AUG.

NEW MEXICO PENSTEMON *Penstemon neomexicanus*
Short, squat corolla tube, *equally inflated* above and below. Note the *dark guide line* on each lower petal lobe (to guide insects into flower) and the white-margined throat. *Naked staminode* (sterile stamen) *notched.* Flowers in *loose arrangement.* 30–60 cm. Mountains. N.M. JULY–AUG.

WANDBLOOM PENSTEMON *Penstemon virgatus*
Similar to New Mexico Penstemon. See p. 248 for details.

TUBTOP PENSTEMON *Penstemon oliganthus*
Light blue corolla tube, partly *inflated on upper side,* the lower lip petal slightly longer. Lower half of corolla white with hairs; note the dark yellow hairs on the *protruding staminode* (sterile stamen). Lancelike leaves on *long petioles. Loose* flower arrangement. Stem and flowers with sticky hairs. 10–60 cm. Mountain forests. E. Ariz., N.M., R. Mts. JUNE–AUG.

JAMES' PENSTEMON *Penstemon jamesii*
Blue-purple, glandular-haired corolla tube expands slightly outward, *appearing somewhat swaybacked.* Petal lobes cupped, projecting forward; upper lobes broad, earlike. Flowers in a *tight, spikelike panicle.* Lancelike, fleshy leaves. 10–60 cm. Pine forests. Northern S.W., R. Mts. MAY–JULY

THICKLEAF PENSTEMON *Penstemon pachyphyllus*
Dark royal blue to blue-purple corolla tube, *equally inflated* on all sides. Note the prominent *golden hair cluster* in outer corolla throat. Flowers in *dense clusters* along a *tall, spirelike stem.* Thick, fleshy, blue-green, lancelike leaves. 20–70 cm. Dry pine woods. N. Ariz., Ut. MAY–JUNE

PORCH PENSTEMON *Penstemon strictus*
Broad, royal purple to violet corolla tube, with the 2 *upper petals projecting straight forward, like a porch roof.* Spirelike flower stem. Straplike leaves, smooth, dark green. 30–90 cm. Mountains. Ne. Ariz., northern N.M., R. Mts. JUNE–JULY

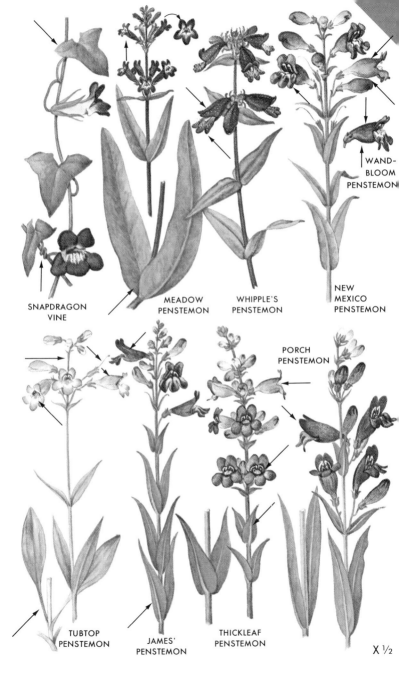

SNAPDRAGON
VINE

MEADOW
PENSTEMON

WHIPPLE'S
PENSTEMON

WAND-
BLOOM
PENSTEMON

NEW
MEXICO
PENSTEMON

TUBTOP
PENSTEMON

JAMES'
PENSTEMON

THICKLEAF
PENSTEMON

PORCH
PENSTEMON

X ½

5 PETALS; 2-LIPPED, TUBULAR FLOWERS

Snapdragon Family (Scrophulariaceae)
See also pp. W 88; Y 118–122; R 244–250; B 350–354.

FOXGLOVE PENSTEMON *Penstemon cobaea*
Note the *giant* (3–6 cm), pale lavender to all white, *bell-like* corolla tube with *dark purple lines inside.* Broad, bright green, lancelike to elliptical leaves. 30–60 cm. Common on prairies. Eastern two-thirds of Tex., Pl. Sts., S.E. APRIL–JUNE

PINEY WOODS PENSTEMON *Penstemon laxiflorus*
Note the *purple lines on the flat, projecting* lower lip of the *very pale* pink-blue corolla that *appears white.* A *golden hair cluster* on the projecting staminode (sterile stamen). Leaves narrow, *toothed.* 30–90 cm. Piney woods. E. Tex. MARCH–JUNE

FENDLER'S PENSTEMON *Penstemon fendleri*
Lavender to violet flowers *declined, with a slender, swaybacked* corolla tube and a white throat with *dark red-purple lines.* A cluster of *golden hairs* visible in the corolla throat. Thick, fleshy, blue-green, triangular, folded leaves. 30–60 cm. Open plains. E. Ariz to w. Tex., Pl. Sts. APRIL–AUG.

WHITERIM PENSTEMON *Penstemon lanceolatus*
Many *long, straplike, yellow-green* leaves with *spiny toothed margins.* Flowers pale violet to pinkish; note the *white rim* on lower throat with *many white hairs and a colored line* to each lower petal lobe. 10–60 cm. Guadalupe Mts., N.M.

MAY–JUNE

BROADBEARD PENSTEMON *Penstemon angustifolius*
Many dark lavender to violet, *trumpet-shaped* flowers with a *broad, curled, bearded, notch-tipped staminode* (sterile stamen) projecting out of the throat. Waxy blue-green leaves, straplike. 10–60 cm. Mesas, grasslands. Northern S.W., Pl. Sts.

MAY–JUNE

THOMPSON'S PENSTEMON *Penstemon thompsoniae*
Tiny, spatula-like gray leaves. Purple and lavender corolla elongated and hairy, the upper side inflated. A cluster of golden hairs in throat. Low, clustered stems. 5–30 cm. Pinyon woods, openings. N. Ariz., Ut. MAY–JUNE

LINARIALEAF PENSTEMON *Penstemon linarioides*
Many *short, upward-pointing,* linear leaves, which resemble those of the garden plant, *Linaria.* Flowers dark blue-purple. 10–60 cm. Plains. S.W., R. Mts. JUNE–AUG.

PARK PENSTEMON *Penstemon leiophyllus*
Large purple flowers with a nearly hairless throat; several large white spots on the lower side. Upper stem leaves linear, with a pale waxy blue coating; the lowermost may be broader. 10–40 cm. Subalpine meadows (parks). N. Ariz., s. Ut.

JUNE–AUG.

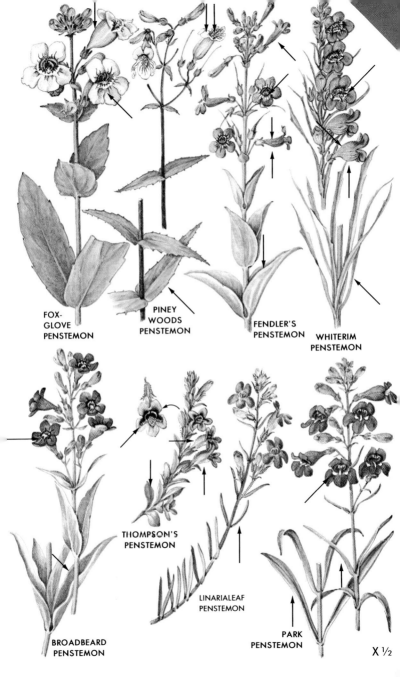

FOX-
GLOVE
PENSTEMON

PINEY
WOODS
PENSTEMON

FENDLER'S
PENSTEMON

WHITERIM
PENSTEMON

THOMPSON'S
PENSTEMON

LINARIALEAF
PENSTEMON

BROADBEARD
PENSTEMON

PARK
PENSTEMON

X ½

5 PETALS; 2-LIPPED, TUBULAR FLOWERS

Snapdragon Family (Scrophulariaceae)
See also pp. W 88; Y 118–122; R 244–250; B 350–354.

NUTTALL'S SNAPDRAGON *Antirrhinum nuttallianum*
Small, snapdragonlike, violet flowers with the 2 upper petal lobes erect and *sharply earlike. All* lower petals like a matron's skirt. *Pedicel as long as or longer than* the calyx. Leaves *lancelike.* Plant parts with sticky hairs. Long flower spikes. 10–80 cm. Lower elevation canyons. Cen. and sw. Ariz.   MARCH–MAY

FROG SNAPDRAGON *Antirrhinum cyathiferum*
Flowers small, rose-violet, *squat;* they look *froglike* from the front. Upper 2 petal lobes *reflexed backward,* the 2 outer and lower petals toed-in. The middle lower petal sticks straight out like a tongue. Leaves *oval to elliptical.* All plant parts with *long white hairs.* 10–80 cm. Lowest deserts. Sw. Ariz.

JAN.–MARCH

TEXAS TOADFLAX *Linaria texana*
Note the *long slender spur* on the back side of the sky blue, 2-lipped flowers. Leaves *linear.* 10–60 cm. Very common. S.W., Tex., Pl. Sts.   MOST OF YEAR

SHARPWING MONKEY FLOWER *Mimulus alatus*
One 2-lipped blue flower above each *lancelike* leaf; leaves with *coarse, sawtoothed margins.* 10–60 cm. Wet wooded areas. N.-cen. and e. Tex., Pl. Sts.   JUNE–NOV.

MAIDEN BLUE-EYED MARY *Collinsia parviflora*
Tiny (5 mm) flowers attached to the calyx at a *45-degree angle;* flowers *nearly hidden* among long, *lancelike* leaves. Corolla tube strongly inflated at top of bend. Upper petal lobes *rounded.* Stems smooth. 5–30 cm. Moist shady places. Ariz., northern N.M., R. Mts.   FEB.–JUNE

ALPINE BROOKLIME *Veronica alpina*
Stems erect; leaves *oval,* thin and hairy. Loose terminal clusters of tiny 2-lipped flowers (5 mm). 2 stamens. 10–90 cm. Wet places in mountains. N.M., R. Mts.   JUNE–AUG.

AMERICAN BROOKLIME *Veronica americana*
Large, lancelike leaves. Flowers in *long sprays.* 10–60 cm. Marshy streamsides. S.W., Tex., R. Mts.   MAY–AUG.

ALPINE KITTENTAILS *Besseya alpina*
Many dark blue-purple, *snoutlike* flowers in a *dense woolly spike.* 2 stamens. Leaf blades *oval to nearly heart-shaped.* 5–10 cm. Alpine tundra, mountain meadows. N. Ariz., R. Mts.

MAY–AUG.

FOOTHILL KITTENTAILS *Besseya plantaginea*
Similar to Alpine Kittentails, but *leaf blade oblong.* 10–50 cm. Foothills to midmountains. E. Ariz., N.M., R. Mts.

MAY–AUG.

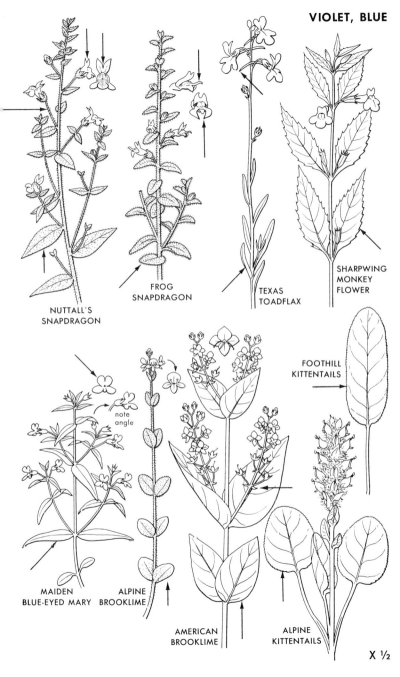

VIOLET, BLUE

NUTTALL'S
SNAPDRAGON

FROG
SNAPDRAGON

TEXAS
TOADFLAX

SHARPWING
MONKEY
FLOWER

note
angle

MAIDEN
BLUE-EYED MARY

ALPINE
BROOKLIME

FOOTHILL
KITTENTAILS

AMERICAN
BROOKLIME

ALPINE
KITTENTAILS

X ½

5 TO MANY PETALS

Buttercup Family (Ranunculaceae)
See also pp. W 42–44; Y 162–164; R 236,
238; B 344, 356–358; G 396, 406.

SILKY PASQUEFLOWER   *Anemone patens*
Large, upright, bell-like, blue-purple or all-white flowers with 5–8
petals. *Silky-haired,* deeply divided, linear-lobed leaves. Flowers
appear before leaves fully expand. 1–40 cm. Prairies to higher
mountain woods. Nw. Tex., Pl. Sts., R. Mts.   APRIL–JUNE

BASKET ANEMONE   *Anemone heterophylla*
Each leaf divided into *short, diverging lobes.* Open, *basketlike
flower* with linear, deep blue or all-white petals around an elongated
dome of seeds. 10–40 cm. Woods. Tex.   FEB.–APRIL

Flax Family (Linaceae) See also p. Y 122.

WESTERN BLUE FLAX   *Linum perenne*
Large, blue-petaled flowers on a tall, slender stem. *Short, linear,
lancelike* leaves. 10–60 cm. Common in open places. S.W., Tex.,
R. Mts., Pl. Sts.   MARCH–OCT.

Dogbane Family (Apocynaceae) See also pp. W 72; R 314.

PERIWINKLE Alien   *Vinca major*
Note the dark blue, *pinwheel-like* flowers on semi-vinelike stems
with short, *oval,* dark green leaves. Grows in masses. Milky sap.
30–60 cm. S.W., Tex.   MOST OF YEAR

FELTLEAF BLUE STAR   *Amsonia tomentosa*
Note the *pale lead-blue, pinwheel-like* flowers in *terminal clusters*
on long stems. Green or *felt gray,* lancelike leaves. *Milky sap.* 30–
60 cm. S.W.   MARCH–JUNE

FRINGED BLUE STAR (not shown)   *Amsonia ciliata*
Similar to Feltleaf Blue Star, but grows in cen. Tex.

    MARCH–MAY

Lennoa Family (Lennoaceae)

SAND FOOD   *Ammobroma sonorae*
The *tan* cluster of hairs and purple flowers looks like *one-half of a
tennis ball.* 1–3 cm. Sand dunes. Sw. Ariz.   APRIL

DESERT CHRISTMAS TREE   *Pholisma arenarium*
The dense *cluster* of tubular purple flowers with white borders resembles a *Christmas tree.* 10–20 cm. Sandy places. W. Ariz.

    APRIL

Pickerel Weed Family (Pontederiaceae)

WATER HYACINTH Alien   *Eichhornia crassipes*
Note the *globelike petiole base* that acts as a buoy for this floating
plant. Large flowers, pale purple; the uppermost petal has a large
yellow spot (6 petals in all). 30–60 cm. Waterways, ponds. E. Tex.,
S.E.   APRIL–JULY

PICKEREL WEED   *Pontederia cordata*
Large *triangular leaf blades.* Dark blue-purple, 6-petaled flowers
in a cylindrical cluster. Note the spindlelike, bilobed yellow spot
on the middle upper petal. 30–90 cm. Marshy ground. Eastern quarter of Tex., Pl. Sts., S.E.   APRIL–SEPT.

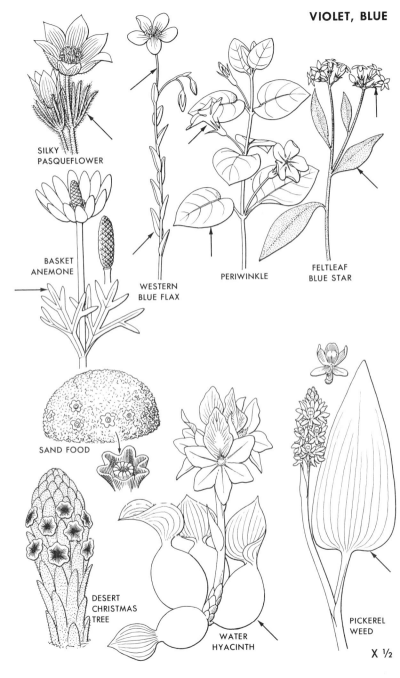

VIOLET, BLUE

SILKY
PASQUEFLOWER

BASKET
ANEMONE

WESTERN
BLUE FLAX

PERIWINKLE

FELTLEAF
BLUE STAR

SAND FOOD

DESERT
CHRISTMAS
TREE

WATER
HYACINTH

PICKEREL
WEED

X ½

5 PETALS; SPURRED DELPHINIUMS

Buttercup Family (Ranunculaceae)
See also pp. W 42–44; Y 162–164;
R 236; 286; B 344; 356–358; G 396, 406.

MONKSHOOD *Aconitum columbianum*
Upper sepal forms a *hood much like a monk's* (not spurred) over a *round head* of purple petals. Leaves deeply cleft 3–5 times. 30 cm–2 m. Mountain meadows. S.W., R. Mts.
JUNE–SEPT.

NAKED DELPHINIUM *Delphinium scaposum*
Stems leafless. Leaves strictly basal, often withered. Leaf segment *tips rounded.* Flowers *deep dark sky or royal blue.* 10–80 cm. Common on lower deserts. S.W. MARCH–JUNE

PALEFACE DELPHINIUM *Delphinium amabile*
Leaves *scattered up lower stem,* main segments linear to wedge-shaped with *tips sharply pointed. Flowers pale* blue, violet, or blue-purple. 20–90 cm. Rocky lower deserts. Ariz., sw. Ut. FEB.–MAY

BILOBE (NELSON'S) *Delphinium nuttallianum*
DELPHINIUM
Short stem. Leaves few, divided into 3–5 segments, or undivided and linear, *tips sharply pointed.* Flowers dark blue or whitish. Lower 2 petals *strongly bilobed.* 10–60 cm. Previously known by many different names. Northern S.W., R. Mts.
JUNE–JULY

DUNCECAP DELPHINIUM *Delphinium occidentale*
Middle and lower stem leaves divided into nearly parallel, *straplike leaflets* of nearly equal width for entire length; leaflets with short, sharply pointed tips. Leaves *dark green with hairs* on upper surface. Flowers blue-purple. 50 cm–1.5 m. Common in moist mountain meadows. Northern S.W., R. Mts.
JUNE–AUG.

BARBEY'S DELPHINIUM *Delphinium barbeyi*
Broad, linear leaf segments spreading wider on outer ends with *shorter lobes* near uppermost end. Leaves *shiny green and hairless* on upper surface. Stem with *sticky hairs* in flowering portion. 50 cm–2 m. Damp subalpine meadows (parks). E. Ariz., northern N.M., R. Mts. JULY–SEPT.

TOWERING DELPHINIUM *Delphinium tenuisectum*
Tall towerlike stem (50 cm–2 m) *leafy up to* flowering portion. Semi-broad, linear leaf segments *divided up middle* by long lobes. *No sticky hairs* in flowering portion of stem. *Small* blue-purple to greenish flowers. Mountain meadows, openings in woods. Se. Ariz., N.M. JULY–SEPT.

CAROLINA DELPHINIUM *Delphinium carolinianum*
Rich dark blue to bluish-white flowers. Lowermost leaves *broad, fanlike.* Upper leaves forked and *narrow,* daggerlike. A *dense tuft* of short, thick, *sideburnlike hairs* on the short lower and inner petals. 50 cm–1 m. Open woods. Eastern third of Tex., Pl. Sts. APRIL–JULY

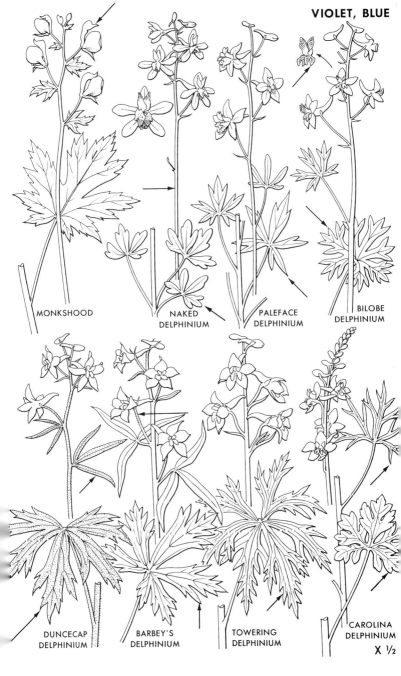

VIOLET, BLUE

MONKSHOOD

NAKED
DELPHINIUM

PALEFACE
DELPHINIUM

BILOBE
DELPHINIUM

DUNCECAP
DELPHINIUM

BARBEY'S
DELPHINIUM

TOWERING
DELPHINIUM

CAROLINA
DELPHINIUM

X ½

5 PETALS; SMALL, UPRIGHT TRUMPETS

Phlox Family (Polemoniaceae)
See also pp. W 88; Y 180; O 234; R 308–312; B 362.

BLUE BOWLS *Gilia rigidula*
Bright blue, bowl-shaped flowers; calyx with *brownish ridged lines.* Leaves *short,* pinnate-lobed. 10–40 cm. Eastern half of Ariz. to western half of Tex., Pl. Sts. APRIL–SEPT.

MINIATURE WOOL STAR *Eriastrum diffusum*
Tiny (5 mm), pale blue to white, short tubular flowers in terminal clusters, each above a 3–7-lobed bract that *arches slightly.* Pinnate leaves, *shiny green.* 5–15 cm. Sandy places. Deserts, plains. S.W., w. Tex. MARCH–JUNE

THURBER'S TRUMPET *Ipomopsis thurberi*
Note the *long,* dark blue to claret-colored, trumpetlike flowers with *protruding stamens.* Petals regularly arranged. *Narrow,* linear-lobed, pinnate leaves. 20–40 cm. Open mountain slopes. S. Ariz., s. N.M. AUG.–SEPT.

MACOMB'S TRUMPET *Ipomopsis macombii*
Purple-violet petals *irregularly arranged;* the uppermost ones tend to fold backward. *Corolla tube arched.* Stamens protrude strongly. Grayish pinnate leaves *stiffly spreading, spine-tipped.* 10–50 cm. Common on dry mountain slopes, often under pines. Ariz., western half of N.M. JULY–OCT.

BLUE TRUMPETS *Ipomopsis longiflora*
Note the *very long, straight* corolla tube below *pale blue to white* petals. Few-lobed, *threadlike,* pinnate leaves. 10–40 cm. Common on dry plains. S.W., w. Tex. MARCH–OCT.

TWO EYES *Ipomopsis polyantha*
Purple-violet petal lobes irregularly arranged, with *eye spots* at base of upper 2 lobes. Note the 2 lines on each side petal, and no marks on the lower 2 petals. Flower semi-short. *Stamens protrude. Shiny, yellow-green,* pinnate leaf lobes; contorted, spine-tipped. 10–50 cm. Mountains. Eastern half of Ariz., northern N.M., R. Mts. AUG.–SEPT.

CALIFORNIA GILIA *Gilia achilleaefolia*
Note the *dense, fan-shaped* flowerheads on a naked peduncle. Flowers blue-violet throughout. Pinnate leaves linear-lobed with terminal leaflet tips *scythe-shaped.* 10–60 cm. Open places. S.-cen. Ariz. MARCH–MAY

DESERT GILIA *Gilia sinuata*
Simple, round-lobed, yellow-green pinnate leaves mostly basal, but ascending up most of stem in a reduced form. Corolla tube *slightly to 2 times longer* than calyx. 5–27 cm. Very common below 700 ft. S.W., w. Tex., R. Mts. FEB.–JUNE

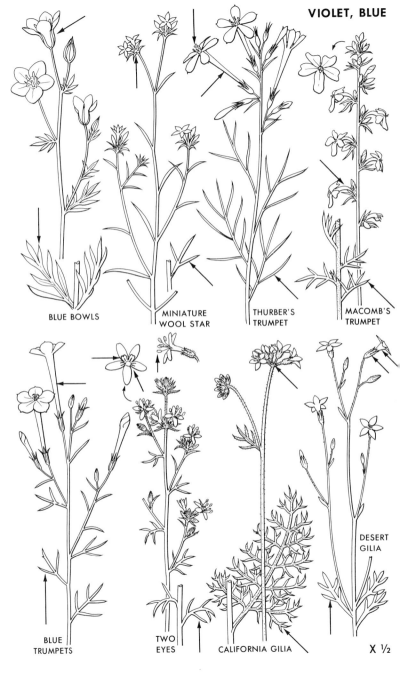

VIOLET, BLUE

BLUE BOWLS

MINIATURE
WOOL STAR

THURBER'S
TRUMPET

MACOMB'S
TRUMPET

BLUE
TRUMPETS

TWO
EYES

CALIFORNIA GILIA

DESERT
GILIA

X ½

5 UNITED PETALS; TRUMPETS, OPEN BELLS

Phlox Family (Polemoniaceae)
See also pp. W 88; Y 180; O 234; R 308–312; B 360–362.

SHOWY POLEMONIUM   *Polemonium pulcherrimum*
Short-stemmed. Small, *pale blue flowers* form a *shallow bowl* with a yellow tube. 11–25 pale yellow-green leaflets with *sticky hairs.* Bad odor if handled. 5–30 cm. Shady conifer forests in mountains. S.W., R. Mts.   JUNE–AUG.

TOWERING POLEMONIUM   *Polemonium foliosissimum*
Tall-stemmed. Large, pale to medium blue flowers form a *shallow bowl,* the *inner bowl with dark branching lines* in a field of palest yellow. Pinnate leaves with *simple, lancelike* leaflets to *near base* of the central petiole. 20 cm–1.5 m. Moist shady woods, along streams in mountains. S.W., R. Mts.
JUNE–AUG.

STICKY SKYPILOT   *Polemonium viscosum*
Short-stemmed. Note the *semi-nodding, headlike cluster* of dark blue-purple flowers. Trumpetlike corolla tube. Pinnate leaves with *numerous tiny, 3- to 5-parted leaflets.* 10–30 cm. Alpine meadows. San Francisco Peaks, Ariz.; N.M.; R. Mts.
JUNE–SEPT.

Morning Glory Family (Convolvulaceae)
See also pp. W 80; R 240.

Note: Blue-purple species may often also be reddish purple. See p. 240 in red-purple section for other species that may be blue-purple at times.

LANCEHAIR MORNING GLORY   *Ipomoea pubescens*
Note the 3–7 *broad leaf lobes* per leaf. Large, blue-purple to red-purple flowers with conspicuous long hairs on *broad to very narrow, lancelike sepals.* Vines. S. Ariz., N.M., w. Tex.
AUG.–SEPT.

HAIRY BIRD'S-FOOT   *Ipomoea leptotoma*
Very narrow, linear-lobed leaves resemble *bird feet.* Sepals *linear,* backs *long-haired. Large* blue-purple to reddish flowers on *semi-short* stalks. Vines. Common on grassy plains in oak and pine woods. Eastern two-thirds of Ariz. to w. Tex.
JULY–OCT.

SILVER MORNING GLORY   *Evolvulus sericeus*
Short, prostrate stems crowded with *silvery, linear leaves* that are strongly *folded together.* Flowers all blue or all white. 5–30 cm. Lower elevations, open areas. S.W., western and s. Tex.
APRIL–OCT.

CRESTRIB MORNING GLORY   *Ipomoea costellata*
Note the *small* leaves that look like *bird feet,* and the *small* flowers on *very long stalks.* Backs of *broad* sepals *crested or warty.* Vines. Common on grassy plains in southern S.W.
JUNE–OCT.

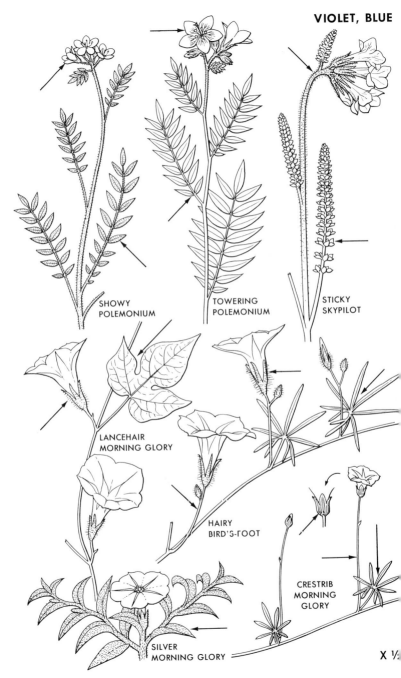

VIOLET, BLUE

SHOWY
POLEMONIUM

TOWERING
POLEMONIUM

STICKY
SKYPILOT

LANCEHAIR
MORNING GLORY

HAIRY
BIRD'S-FOOT

CRESTRIB
MORNING
GLORY

SILVER
MORNING GLORY

X ⅓

5 UNITED PETALS, AS BELLS OR BOWLS; FLOWERS IN COILED CLUSTERS

Waterleaf Family (Hydrophyllaceae)
See also pp. W 82; Y 182; R 312.

WATER OLIVE *Hydrolea ovata*
Stout, semi-woody stems with a *spine above each leaf* petiole base. Bright blue flowers. Shrubby. 20 cm–1 m. Edges of streams, ponds. E. Tex. JULY–OCT.

BRANCHING PHACELIA *Phacelia ramosissima*
Stems coarse, sprawling or weakly erect. Pinnate leaflets *alternately arranged,* with *coarse* teeth. Flowers blue to dirty white, in dense, tightly coiled cymes. 50 cm–1 m. Among shrubs. Western two-thirds of Ariz. MARCH–MAY

ALPINE PHACELIA *Phacelia sericea*
Note the tall, *pokerlike* clusters of deep purple flowers well above the *silvery-haired leaves.* Leaves pinnate with deeply cut, linear lobes. 10–40 cm. Rocky places, alpine tundra. Northern S.W., R. Mts. JUNE–AUG.

TIGHT PHACELIA *Phacelia congesta*
Small, dark blue-purple flowers with a *white interior.* Yellow-green leaves with *large, irregular pinnate lobes* that are often partly fused. 10–50 cm. Frequent on rocky soil. Se. Ariz., N.M., Tex. MARCH–JUNE

PRAIRIE PHACELIA *Phacelia strictiflora*
Note the *large, oval sepals.* Large flowers, *semi-bell-shaped,* with dark purple petal lobes and a *pure white interior.* Oblong leaf blades, margins entire with *simple lobes.* Leaves in low rosettes. 10–30 cm. Eastern half of Tex., Pl. Sts. MARCH–MAY

SPOTTED PHACELIA *Phacelia hirsuta*
Large lavender flowers form shallow bowls; each petal lobe has *2 dark purple spots.* Leaves *partly* pinnate-lobed with smooth margins. 10–50 cm. Openings in woods. E. Tex., Pl. Sts. MARCH–MAY

TEXAS BLUE EYES *Nemophila phacelioides*
Broad, shallow, bowl-like violet to bluish flower with a *white inner bowl.* Oval petal lobes *bilobed.* Long, straggling stems with *keylike, pinnate-lobed* leaves. 30–90 cm. Open woodlands. E. Tex., Pl. Sts. MARCH–MAY

SCALLOPED PHACELIA *Phacelia crenulata*
Note the many curving sprays of *dark blue-purple flowers* above *shiny red stems.* Broad, *elongated leaves,* dark shiny green, varying from a few lobes to many. 10–60 cm. *Very common.* Sandy desert flats. Ariz., nw. N.M., s. Ut. FEB.–JUNE

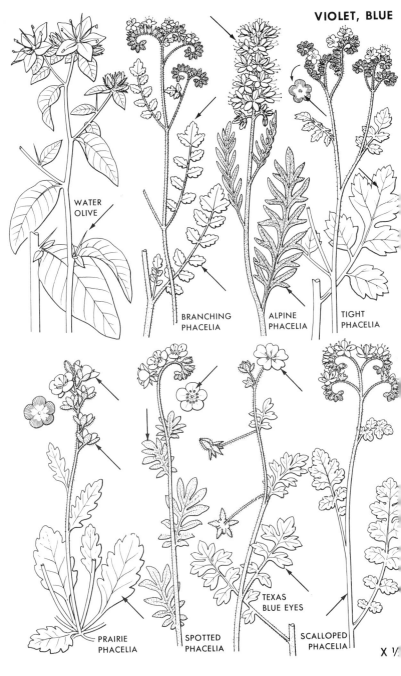

VIOLET, BLUE

WATER OLIVE

BRANCHING PHACELIA

ALPINE PHACELIA

TIGHT PHACELIA

PRAIRIE PHACELIA

SPOTTED PHACELIA

TEXAS BLUE EYES

SCALLOPED PHACELIA

X ½

5-PETALED TRUMPETS; 4 NUTLIKE SEEDS

Forget-me-not Family (Boraginaceae)
See also pp. W 84; Y 182; O 234; R 314; B 344.

SKYMAT *Eritrichium nanum*
A *tiny, tufted plant. Tiny, powder blue*, pinwheel-like flowers with an *inner row of tiny teeth* and an inner ring of yellow. Tiny, spatula-like leaves with *woolly hairs*. 2–15 cm. Very common. Alpine tundra. Northern N.M., R. Mts.   JUNE–AUG.

FRANCISCAN LUNGWORT *Mertensia franciscana*
Dark to pale blue flowers with a *long lower tube that extends well beyond* the calyx. *Sepal margins fringed* with hairs. Upper stem leaves lancelike, *without petioles.* Tall stems. 50 cm–1 m. Mountain forests. S.W., R. Mts.   JUNE–SEPT.

MacDOUGALL'S LUNGWORT *Mertensia macdougalii*
Dark to pale blue flowers with a *long lower tube that extends well beyond* the calyx. Sepal lobes and flower pedicels *hairless*. Upper leaves *waxy-blue, lancelike, without petioles.* Basal leaves broadly spatula-like. Low stem. 10–20 cm. South Rim of Grand Canyon to Mogollon Rim, Ariz.   MARCH–JUNE

LANCELEAF LUNGWORT *Mertensia lanceolata*
Leaves *narrowly lancelike* with *margins rolled inward.* Long corolla tube *bulges slightly*, and is *somewhat longer* than the calyx and about *equal to* the outer, skirted "bell" portion. Low-stemmed. 30–60 cm. Mountains. Northern N.M., R. Mts.   JUNE–JULY

ALPINE LUNGWORT *Mertensia alpina*
Deep blue-purple corolla with a *sharply flaring, funnel-like outer portion. Thick, fleshy, bright green,* lancelike leaves. Short stem. 10–30 cm. Alpine tundra. N.M., R. Mts.   JUNE–JULY

BELLED LUNGWORT *Mertensia viridis*
Sky blue corolla with a *rounded, bell-like* outer portion. *Thick leaves, broadly egg-shaped.* Short-stemmed, 10–30 cm. Open subalpine slopes. Northern N.M., R. Mts.   JUNE–JULY

FRINGED LUNGWORT *Mertensia ciliata*
Sepal margins *fringed with hairs, tips rounded.* Leaves *broadly lancelike, without petioles.* Dark blue flowers with a short, rounded tube below a wider, funnel-like portion; "funnel" *same length or shorter than* lower tube. Along subalpine streams, meadows. Tall-stemmed. 50 cm–1 m. Northern S.W., R. Mts.   JUNE–AUG.

ARIZONA LUNGWORT *Mertensia arizonica*
Similar to Fringed Lungwort, except *sepals triangular* with *sharp tips;* margins fringed with hairs, but *sepal backs nearly smooth.* Wide, funnel-like portion of corolla *longer than* lower tube. Tall-stemmed. 50 cm–1 m. Mountain meadows, woods. Nw. Ariz., R. Mts.   JUNE–SEPT.

WILD COMFREY *Cynoglossum virginianum*
Usually 3 spreading flower sprays on a naked upper stem. Basal leaves *tonguelike, with petioles.* 4 squat nutlets evenly covered with tiny stalks with hooked spine tips. Tiny, flat, blue to white flowers with an *inner row of tiny teeth.* 50 cm–1 m. Woods. E. Tex., Pl. Sts.   MARCH–APRIL

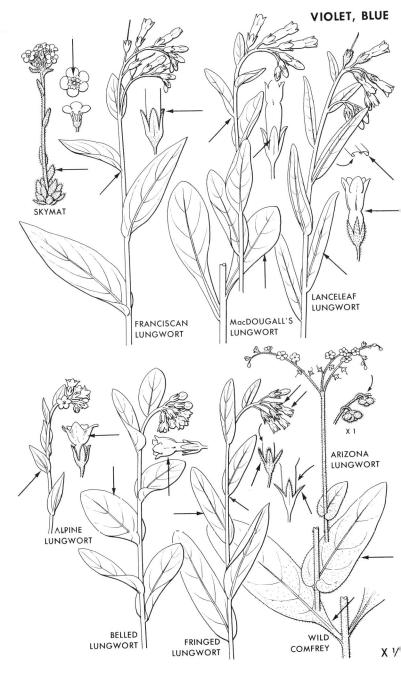

VIOLET, BLUE

SKYMAT

FRANCISCAN LUNGWORT

MacDOUGALL'S LUNGWORT

LANCELEAF LUNGWORT

ALPINE LUNGWORT

BELLED LUNGWORT

FRINGED LUNGWORT

ARIZONA LUNGWORT

WILD COMFREY

X ½

X 1

5 UNITED PETALS IN FLAT STAR
WITH BEAK, OR LARGE AND TRUMPETLIKE

Nightshade Family (Solanaceae)
See also pp. W 86; Y 184; R 312.

PURPLE NIGHTSHADE   *Solanum xanchi*
Note the flat, deep violet to lavender, *starlike flowers* on somewhat bushy stems. *Leaves oval.* Greenish berry. 30–90 cm. Rocky slopes. Ariz.   APRIL–NOV.

SILVERLEAF NIGHTSHADE   *Solanum elaeagnifolium*
Note the *scruffy, silvery-green, oblong to lancelike leaves with wavy margins.* Stem and undersides of leaves with *dark spines.* Flowers violet. 10 cm–1 m. Very common in disturbed places. S.W., Tex., Pl. Sts.   MARCH–OCT.

FENDLER'S POTATO   *Solanum fendleri*
Note the *crinkly-surfaced, dark green,* pinnate-lobed leaves. Several lavender to purple, *starlike flowers* per cluster. Tiny (5 mm wide) underground potato tubers; the commercial potato is a near relative. 10–50 cm. Deep loamy soils on steep mountain slopes. Se. Ariz. to sw. Tex.   JULY–SEPT.

PURPLE GROUND CHERRY   *Physalis lobata*
Note the dark purple, shiny, *narrow-lobed star* within the *round* purple corolla. 5 *hairy spots* at base of star lobes. Leaf blades elongated with *rounded, triangular margin lobes* or pinnate lobes. 10–50 cm. Ariz. to western two-thirds of Tex., Pl. Sts.   MARCH–OCT.

WATERMELON NIGHTSHADE   *Solanum citrullifolium*
Note the *lacy, watermelon-like leaves.* Leaves, stems, and seed capsules with *yellow spines.* Purple-petaled, starlike flower with a "beak" of yellow stamens. 10–60 cm. Open disturbed fields, roadsides. Ariz. to cen. Tex., Pl. Sts.   APRIL–OCT.

JIMSONWEED   *Datura meteloides*
Note the *very large, trumpetlike flowers* (10–20 cm) which may be white or various shades of pale purple. Calyx *tubular.* Leaves grayish, unequally oval. *Poisonous.* 50 cm–1 m. Dry open places. S.W., Tex., Pl. Sts.   MAY–OCT.

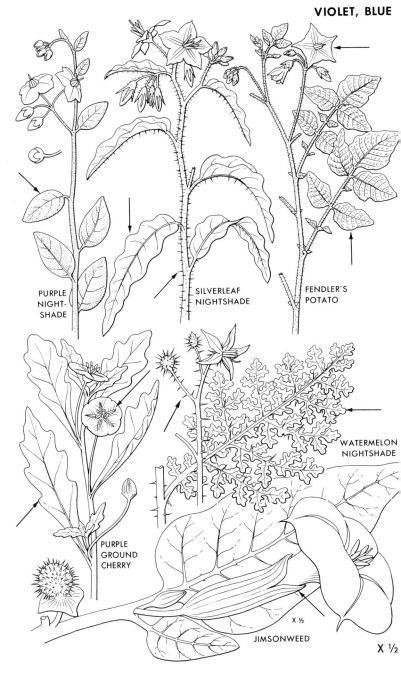

PURPLE
NIGHT-
SHADE

SILVERLEAF
NIGHTSHADE

FENDLER'S
POTATO

PURPLE
GROUND
CHERRY

WATERMELON
NIGHTSHADE

X ⅓

JIMSONWEED

X ½

5-PETALED BLUEBELLS, OR 2-LIPPED FLOWERS WITH AN INFERIOR OVARY BELOW

Bluebell Family (Campanulaceae)
See also pp. W 92; R 236; B 374.

SCOTCH BLUEBELL   *Campanula rotundifolia*
Petal lobes *not reflexed,* on broad, bell-like, blue flowers. Sepal lobes *linear, short.* Most leaves *linear.* 10–50 cm. Very common in *dry* mountain meadows. S.W., R. Mts.   MAY–AUG.

PARRY'S BLUEBELL   *Campanula parryi*
Petal lobes reflexed (bent), on broad, shallow, bowl-like purple flowers. Sepal lobes *triangular, longer than* the flower bowl. Leaves narrow to broadly lancelike. 5–30 cm. *Damper* meadow edges, *streamsides.* Often found with Scotch Bluebell, which would grow in the *drier* portion of the same meadow. Mountains. S.W., R. Mts.   JUNE–SEPT.

TUNDRA BLUEBELL   *Campanula uniflora*
Sepals *not reflexed. Tiny, narrow, funnel-like* dark purple flower. Sepals short, lancelike. Leaves *spatula-like.* 5–15 cm. Alpine tundra, mountains. N.M., R. Mts.   JULY–AUG.

BASIN BLUEBELL   *Campanula reverchonii*
Light blue flower with a *round tube below* large, reflexed petal lobes. Stem nodes between leaves *elongated.* Leaf blades *spatula-like* with a *few toothed* margin lobes. 10–40 cm. Grows in tiny basins of soil on *granite rocks.* Enchanted Rocks. W.-cen. Tex.   MAY–JULY

VENUS' LOOKING GLASS   *Triodanis perfoliata*
Blue to lavender flowers *nestled* above round to heart-shaped, *clasping* leaves. Calyx lobes equally broad and long. 10–30 cm. S.W., eastern two-thirds of Tex., S.E.   APRIL–JULY

THREAD PLANT   *Nemacladus glanduliferus*
2-lipped flowers with 2 *long lower lobes.* The 3 shorter upper lobes are tipped with purple or red-brown. Flowers on *long wiry pedicels.* A bushy cluster on *semi-zigzag* stems, with a few *linear* leaves near ground level. 10–30 cm. Frequent on open sandy deserts. Western half of Ariz., s. Ut.   FEB.–MAY

Teasel Family (Dipsacaceae)

FULLER'S TEASEL Alien   *Dipsacus fullonum*
Note the elongated terminal *cone of spiny bracts* above several linear, spiny leaves. Irregularly shaped rose to blue-purple flowers nearly hidden below each bract. Stem and midribs spiny. 30 cm–2 m. Disturbed places. Northern S.W., R. Mts.

       MAY–SEPT.

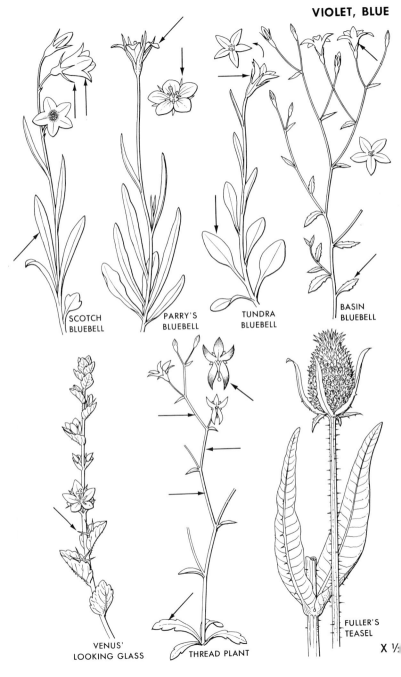

VIOLET, BLUE

SCOTCH BLUEBELL

PARRY'S BLUEBELL

TUNDRA BLUEBELL

BASIN BLUEBELL

VENUS' LOOKING GLASS

THREAD PLANT

FULLER'S TEASEL

X ½

5 UNITED PETALS; 2-LIPPED FLOWERS

Acanthus Family (Acanthaceae) See also p. R 316.

LONGNECK RUEL   *Ruellia nudiflora*
Note the *twin pairs* of large, lavender to purplish, 2-lipped, tubular flowers, *well above* the leafy stem. Leaves oval to lancelike, *with petioles.* 10–70 cm. Southern two-thirds of Tex.
                             ALL YEAR

ZIGZAG RUEL   *Ruellia humilis*
Often *single, long-tubed,* large, lavender to light blue, 2-lipped flowers *alternating up stem.* Dark green, lancelike leaves loosely arranged, with many *stiff hairs.* Leaves *petioleless.* 10–80 cm. Eastern half of Tex.   APRIL–OCT.

HAIRY TUBETONGUE   *Siphonoglossa pilosella*
Note the *strongly 2-lipped* flowers with *long, slender* corolla tubes emerging from *cupped leaf bases.* Flowers blue-purple to pinkish. 10–30 cm. Rocky hillsides. Southern two-thirds of Tex.
                           APRIL–OCT.

SPREADING SILVERLEAF   *Dyschoriste decumbens*
Broad, 2-lipped lavender to purplish flowers *without pedicels.* *Prostrate stems* with narrow, somewhat shiny, lancelike to spatula-like leaves with *silvery hairs.* 30–90 cm. Plains, oak and juniper woodlands. S. Ariz. to w. Tex.   APRIL–OCT.

Vervain Family (Verbenaceae) See also p. O 238.
Note: *Verbena* species are numerous and difficult to separate. This genus has 2 distinct subsections: 1) broad flowerheads with large flowers, and 2) narrow, stringy spikes with tiny flowers. Only a few species can be presented here. Flower color varies from blue-purple to pinkish in each species.

WRIGHT'S VERVAIN   *Verbena wrightii*
Flowerhead a *broad cluster* of slightly 2-lipped, purple, lavender, or pinkish flowers. Leaves *trilobed* with smaller terminal lobes. 10–30 cm. S.W., w. Tex., R. Mts.   MARCH–JUNE

SOUTHWESTERN VERVAIN   *Verbena gooddingii*
Similar to Wright's Vervain, but leaf blades *triangular.* S.W., Ut.   FEB.–OCT.

BLUE VERVAIN   *Verbena hastata*
Long, stringy flower spikes with tiny, slightly 2-lipped flowers. Leaf blade pinnate with long, *forward-thrusting* lobes. 10 cm–2.3 m. S.W., R. Mts., Pl. Sts.   JULY–OCT.

NEW MEXICO VERVAIN   *Verbena macdougalii*
Long, cylindrical *spike* of tiny flowers. Numerous *lancelike* leaves with ragged, *sawtoothed margins.* 50 cm–1 m. S.W., w. Tex.   JUNE–OCT.

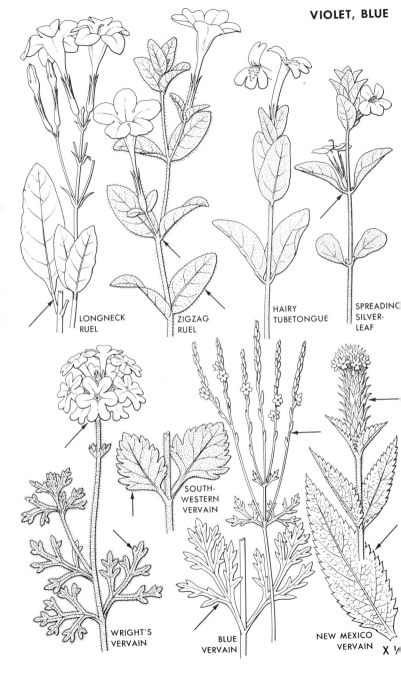

VIOLET, BLUE

LONGNECK RUEL

ZIGZAG RUEL

HAIRY TUBETONGUE

SPREADING SILVER-LEAF

WRIGHT'S VERVAIN

SOUTH-WESTERN VERVAIN

BLUE VERVAIN

NEW MEXICO VERVAIN

X ½

5-PETALED, 2-LIPPED, TUBULAR FLOWERS
SQUARE STEM, 4 NUTLIKE SEEDS

Mint Family (Labiatae) See also pp. W 90; Y 188; R 318; B 376.

CHIA
Salvia columbariae

Headlike clusters of tiny, 2-lipped purple flowers. 2 stamens. Bracts spine-tipped. Dark green, *pinnate* leaves. 10–50 cm. Lower deserts. Ariz.   MARCH–MAY

ARIZONA SAGE
Salvia arizonica

Purple to violet corolla with a *short, rounded upper "snout."* Leaves *broadly triangular,* in opposite pairs up entire stem. 30–60 cm. Rocky places. Mountains in oak and pine zone. Southeastern third of Ariz. to sw. Tex.   JULY–OCT.

MEALY SAGE
Salvia farinacea

Upper stem and calyx *mealy white.* Flowers *dark blue-purple;* upper corolla lip projects *straight out* with *many blue-purple hairs,* lower lip projects out *shovel-like* with a white zone on it. Leaves drooping, *straplike,* with wavy, toothed margins. 30–90 cm. N.M., Tex.   APRIL–NOV.

BLUE SAGE
Salvia azurea

Light sky blue corolla tube short, *curving upward. Upper petal lip scooplike,* with short, pale blue hairs. Yellow-green, *lance-like* leaves with slightly *sawtoothed* margins. 20 cm–1.3 m. Open places. Tex., Pl. Sts.   MAY–NOV.

LYRELEAF SAGE
Salvia lyrata

Leaves all in a *flat basal rosette.* Dark green leaves *partly* pinnate-lobed with *blackish veins;* main petiole *pinkish. Long, tapering* blue to blue-purple flowers in a *semi-cascading pattern.* Upper corolla lip *tiny.* 20–90 cm. Open woods, meadows. Eastern quarter of Tex., Pl. Sts.   DEC.–MAY

HOARY MINT
Poliomintha incana

Pale purple-pink outer corolla tube *much inflated.* Calyx covered with *long soft hairs.* Narrow, yellow-green, *smooth* leaves. 10–50 cm. Sandy places. S.W., w. Tex.   APRIL–JUNE

SWEET SCENT
Hedeoma hyssopifolium

Long, slender-tubed corollas with a *straight, projecting* upper lip above the *wide, gaping throat.* Flowers purple to rose-purple, in pairs. Stem leaves slender. 10–50 cm. Rocky hillsides of lower mountains. Se. Ariz., s. N.M.   MAY–OCT.

SELFHEAL
Prunella vulgaris

Note the *thick, oblong spike* of purple-brown bracts with blue flowers. Calyx consists of 2 long and 3 shorter spur-tipped lobes. Leaves *oval.* Often in matted clusters. 10–50 cm. Very common in moist, semishaded places. S.W., eastern quarter of Tex., R. Mts., Pl. Sts.   APRIL–SEPT.

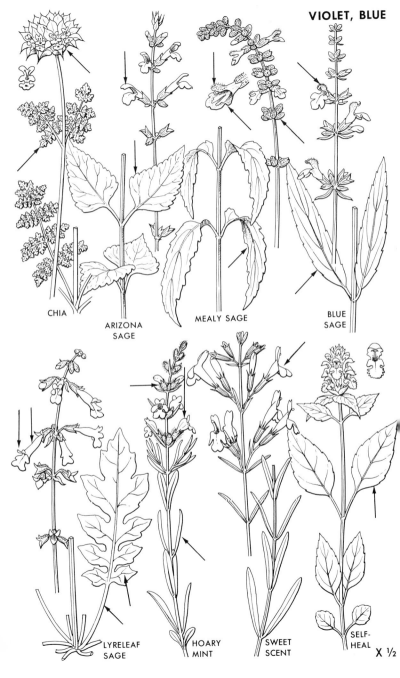

VIOLET, BLUE

CHIA

ARIZONA
SAGE

MEALY SAGE

BLUE
SAGE

LYRELEAF
SAGE

HOARY
MINT

SWEET
SCENT

SELF-
HEAL

X ½

5 PETALS; 2-LIPPED, TUBULAR FLOWERS

Mint Family (Labiatae) See also pp. W 90;
Y 188; R 318; B 374.

DRUMMOND'S SKULLCAP
Scutellaria drummondii

Numerous short purple flowers, each with a low, moundlike upper "beak." Note the *open, flat lower lip* with a *square, purple-dotted, white area.* Seeds (not shown) resemble skullcaps. Leaves green, oval, *hairy.* 10–40 cm. Very common. Se. N.M., Tex., Pl. Sts.

FEB.–JULY

ROUGH SKULLCAP
Scutellaria integrifolia

Very long purple flowers, each with a *long, curving "beak"* above a *closed "mouth."* Lower sides of petal lip folded. Seeds resemble skullcaps. Leaves *long, lancelike.* 30–90 cm. Edges of woods. E. Tex., S.E.

APRIL–JUNE

EGGLEAF SKULLCAP
Scutellaria ovata

Shiny, dark green leaves, broadly lancelike to *egg-shaped,* with *rounded, scalloped margins.* Corolla tube *sharply bent* near base. Lavender and white flowers nearly erect. Seeds resemble skullcaps. 10–60 cm. Woodlands. Southern and e. Tex.

APRIL–JUNE

MAD-DOG SKULLCAP
Scutellaria lateriflora

Note the *1-sided (asymmetrical) flower racemes* above each leaf base. Blue corolla tube *short, nearly straight.* Seeds resemble skullcaps. 30–90 cm. Woods, marshes. S.W., Tex., Pl. Sts.

JULY–SEPT.

Bluebell Family (Campanulaceae)
See also pp. W 92; R 236; B 370.

PURPLE DEWDROP
Lobelia puberula

Blue to red-purple flowers, each with *2 short, earlike upper petals and 3 broad, wedge-shaped lower petals* that are *fused* for most of their length. Note the *white U-shaped marking* formed by 2 white side spikes. Main stem covered with *stiff downy hairs.* Leaves lancelike, with similar hairs. 10–20 cm. Woods. E. Tex., Pl. Sts.

AUG.–DEC.

BERLANDIER'S LOBELIA
Lobelia berlandieri

Light blue lower lip petals with a *large white "eye"* that contains a smaller, *2-humped, yellow-green* zone. Upper petals dark purple, narrow, often *curled and offset backward* (see lateral view). Stamen tube also *curls backward* inside corolla. *Broad, oval leaves.* 10–60 cm. Moist places. Western and s. Tex.

APRIL–SEPT.

MOUNTAIN LOBELIA
Lobelia anatina

Dark purple flowers with *long, narrow petal lobes* both above and below. Lowermost lip petals *free almost to base,* with a *short white line* on each side of base. *Short stems* erect, with *shiny, yellow-green,* linear to spatula-like leaves. 10–50 cm. Moist mountain meadows. Ariz., N.M.

JULY–OCT.

STEEPLE LOBELIA
Lobelia fenestralis

Tall, *steeplelike stem; densely flowered, leafy.* Leaves and sepals *coarsely toothed.* Completely dark purple flowers *angle downward* from the inferior ovary. 50 cm–1.3 m. Damp summer swales (ciénagas). S. Ariz. to Big Bend region, Tex.

JULY–OCT.

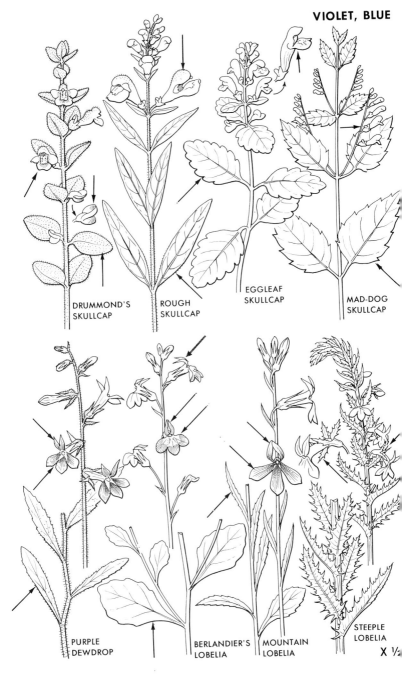

DRUMMOND'S SKULLCAP

ROUGH SKULLCAP

EGGLEAF SKULLCAP

MAD-DOG SKULLCAP

PURPLE DEWDROP

BERLANDIER'S LOBELIA

MOUNTAIN LOBELIA

STEEPLE LOBELIA

X ½

5 PETALS; BILATERAL SYMMETRY: VIOLETS

Violet Family (Violaceae) See also pp. W 50; Y 170.

WALTER'S VIOLET *Viola walteri*
Stem leafy, but prostrate. Leaves round to somewhat kidney-shaped, *whitish* with dark green veins. Flowers violet, *lower lip rectangular* with darker lines. The 2 lower side petals are as long as, or half as long as, lower lip. Upper 2 side petals *folded backward.* Long, running stems; 1–10 cm. Hardwood forests, river bottoms. E. Tex. FEB.–APRIL

WESTERN DOG VIOLET *Viola adunca*
Long erect stem. Rounded to heart-shaped leaves with *lance-like bracts* just below the petiole base. Flowers deep to pale violet. 2–20 cm. Pine forests. Northern S.W., R. Mts.
JUNE–JULY

KIDNEYLEAF VIOLET *Viola nephrophylla*
Stemless plant. Leaves broad, *kidney-shaped to heart-shaped.* Petals deep blue-violet with white hairs at base. 3 *lower petals veined,* well-bearded. 5–15 cm. Shady mountain forests. S.W., ne. Tex., R. Mts. MARCH–MAY

BAYOU VIOLET *Viola langloisii*
Stemless plant. Leaf blade *triangular, with 10 or more teeth* on upper third of blade. Pale blue-violet flowers above the leaves. Lip petal *narrow;* both pairs of side petals in same plane as lip petal. 5–15 cm. Hardwood forests near rivers. Cen. and e. Tex., S.E. MARCH–APRIL

MISSOURI VIOLET *Viola missouriensis*
Triangular leaf blade with *none to 6 teeth* on upper third of blade. Flowers light blue. 5–15 cm. Common in woods. Cen. and ne. Tex., N.M., Pl. Sts. MARCH–MAY

WOOLLY SISTER VIOLET *Viola sororia*
Wide, heart-shaped leaves and stems; covered with *downy or woolly hairs.* Side petals bearded at base. 5–15 cm. Woods. Eastern half of Tex., Pl. Sts. MARCH–APRIL

TRILOBE VIOLET *Viola triloba*
Stemless plant. Each leaf blade divided into 5 *broad lobes from 3 basal divisions,* outer pair of lobes *partly re-divided.* Flowers violet. Both lip petal and lower side petals *short, stubby.* 10–15 cm. Hardwood bottomlands. E. Tex., Pl. Sts., S.E.
MARCH–APRIL

BIRDFOOT VIOLET *Viola pedata*
Stemless plant. Leaf blade *divided into narrow lobes* (usually 5–7). Flower pale blue, pansylike, with a large, *broad lip petal.* Lower side petals *narrow, slightly twisted.* 10–15 cm. Sandy woods, open fields. E. Tex., Pl. Sts. MARCH–APRIL

ARROWLEAF VIOLET *Viola sagittata*
Stemless plant. Leaf blade slightly divided at base, *large central portion arrow-shaped.* Flowers deep violet. 5–8 cm. Dry woods. E. Tex., Pl. Sts., S.E. MARCH–APRIL

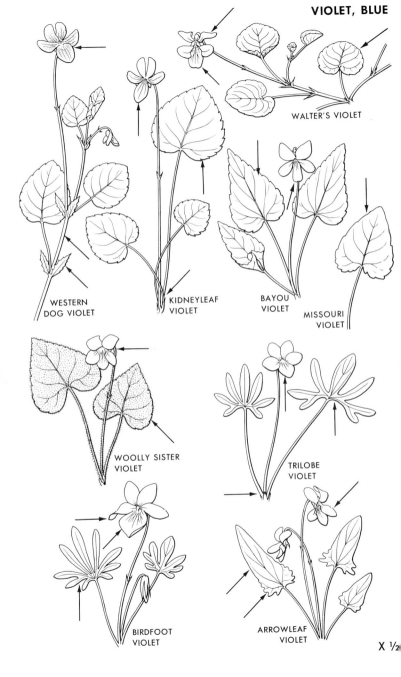

VIOLET, BLUE

WALTER'S VIOLET

WESTERN DOG VIOLET

KIDNEYLEAF VIOLET

BAYOU VIOLET

MISSOURI VIOLET

WOOLLY SISTER VIOLET

TRILOBE VIOLET

BIRDFOOT VIOLET

ARROWLEAF VIOLET

X ½

PEALIKE FLOWERS; 3 OR 5 LEAFLETS

Pea Family (Leguminosae)
See also pp. W 94–96; Y 190–196;
R 320–328; B 346–348, 382.

ALFALFA Alien *Medicago sativa*
Leaves *trifoliate*. Small (5 mm) violet to purple flowers in a *dense raceme*. Stipules at leaf petiole base *lancelike*. Seedpod tightly curled 2–3 times. 30–90 cm. Very common as an escape; also a crop plant. S.W., Tex., R. Mts., Pl. Sts. APRIL–JULY

PIGEONWINGS *Clitoria mariana*
Stem erect to trailing, but *never twining*. Large purplish banner petal *vertically oval, with a dark purple* (occasionally white) *splotch* at center. Leaves mostly trifoliate. *Seedpods beaded.* Often found with Butterfly Pea in Tex. 20–90 cm. Common. Eastern half of Tex., mountains of se. Ariz. MAY–SEPT.

BUTTERFLY PEA *Centrosema virginianum*
A trailing or upright *twining vine*. Large purplish banner petal *horizontally rounded, with a white central spot.* Leaves *pinnately trifoliate. Seedpods smooth.* Often found with Pigeonwings. 20 cm–1.5 m. Woods. Eastern half of Tex.
MARCH–NOV.

SKUNKTOP SCURFPEA *Psoralea mephitica*
Each palmate compound leaf consists of 5 flat, *wedge-shaped leaflets.* Stemless plant. Thick spikes of dark purple flowers with fuzzy-haired bracts. Skunklike odor if handled. 10–30 cm. Juniper zone and lower. N. Ariz., s. Ut. APRIL–JUNE

WHITERIM SCURFPEA *Psoralea subulata*
Palmate compound leaves with 5 *slightly cupped,* lancelike leaflets that have *white-haired margins.* Stemless plant with many leaves nearly *hiding the thick flower spikes.* 2–20 cm. Openings in woods. Eastern half of Tex. MARCH–MAY

SLIMLEAF SCURFPEA *Psoralea linearifolia*
Tall, *wandlike* stems with *very long-peduncled* flower racemes. *Short, linear, trifoliate leaves.* Flowers purplish. 20 cm–1 m. Rocky places on plains. Ne. N.M., n. Tex., Pl. Sts.
MAY–JUNE

WEDGELEAF SCURFPEA *Psoralea tenuiflora*
Similar to Slimleaf Scurfpea. Leaflets *wedge-shaped.* 20–90 cm. Dry open plains, pine forests. S.W., western half of Tex., Pl. Sts. MAY–SEPT.

SILVERY SOPHORA *Sophora stenophylla*
Note the *silvery-haired,* linear leaflets of the long, pinnate leaves. Dense *terminal brush of royal purple,* pealike flowers. 30–60 cm. Red sandy places. Very poisonous to sheep. N. Ariz., nw. N.M., adjacent Ut. and Colo. MAY–JUNE

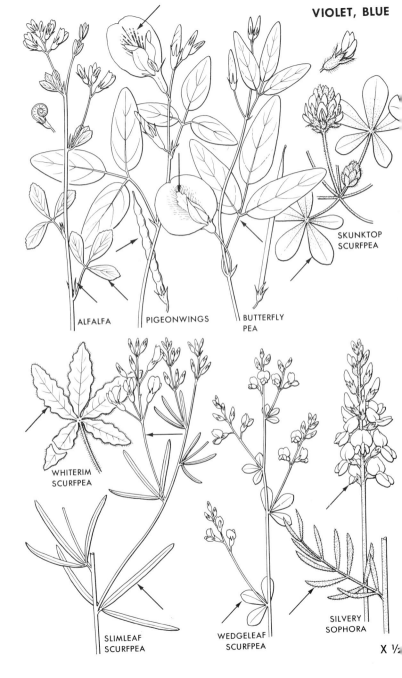

SKUNKTOP
SCURFPEA

ALFALFA

PIGEONWINGS

BUTTERFLY
PEA

WHITERIM
SCURFPEA

SLIMLEAF
SCURFPEA

WEDGELEAF
SCURFPEA

SILVERY
SOPHORA

X ½

PEALIKE FLOWERS; LOCOWEEDS

Pea Family (Leguminosae)
See also pp. W 94–96; Y 190–196; R 320–328; B 346–348, 380.

NUTTALL'S LOCOWEED *Astragalus nuttallianus*
Sprawling stems with *long, bare intervals;* petioles and flower stalks long. A few purple and white flowers in a *very short terminal cluster.* Tiny, narrow, troughlike leaflets with bristly hairs. *Curving, bananalike seedpods* in terminal spreading clusters; pod grooved on underside. A highly variable species. 20–30 cm. S.W., western two-thirds of Tex., R. Mts., Pl. Sts.   FEB.–MAY

SILVERLINE LOCOWEED *Astragalus tephrodes*
Blue to red-purple and white flowers in a broad terminal cylinder on a naked flower stem. Dark green *oblong* leaflets, often *strongly rolled up and inward;* dense hairs on underside make *leaf margins look silvery.* Seedpods *oblong, slightly curved.* Plant 15 cm tall. Pine forest, open plains. S.W., w. Tex.   APRIL–JULY

HALFMOON LOCOWEED *Astragalus allochorus*
Dense, *low, broad* clusters of *reddish stems.* Dull blue-green leaflets with *sharp points at both ends.* Flowers blue to red-purple, with *white-tipped wing petals.* Seedpods *inflated, egglike.* 10–30 cm. Common. S.W., w. Tex.   MARCH–MAY

GROUND PLUM *Astragalus crassicarpus*
Purple, pink, cream, or greenish flowers; elongated, with a *long, curving banner petal.* Leaflet tips rounded. Large, *plumlike seedpods.* 10–30 cm. Plains, prairies. E. Ariz. to Tex., Pl. Sts.
MARCH–JULY

ALPINE LOCOWEED *Astragalus alpinus*
Note the long stems with a cluster of whitish flowers that have dark purple tips. 13–23 bright yellow-green leaflets with *rounded tips.* Plant hairless, but *seedpods* covered with *black hairs.* 5–30 cm. Subalpine forests. Northern N.M., R. Mts.   JUNE–JULY

MISSOURI LOCOWEED *Astragalus missouriensis*
Blue-purple to violet flowers in *short terminal heads.* Wing petals *cupped and turned horizontally.* Elliptical leaflets with *silvery white hairs.* Seedpods are *elongated cylinders.* 10–60 cm. Plains. Eastern N.M., western quarter of Tex., Pl. Sts.   MARCH–JUNE

LINDHEIMER'S LOCOWEED *Astragalus lindheimeri*
A few large *bicolored* purple to violet flowers with *white veins and a white "eye"* in the center of the banner petal. Few flowers in a short terminal cluster. Oblong leaflets *bright light green,* with small notched tips. Seedpods resemble *lima bean pods.* 20–40 cm. Cen. and e. Tex., Pl. Sts.   APRIL–MAY

BENTPOD LOCOWEED *Astragalus distortus*
Note the *purple-striped white "eye"* on the banner petal, within a solid outer margin of purple; wing petals *white-tipped.* Sometimes petals are entirely white. Bright yellow-green, oblong leaflets with *nearly square tips.* Seedpods resemble lima bean pods, but are slightly bent. 5–15 cm. Prairies, woodland openings. Eastern third of Tex., Pl. Sts.   MARCH–JUNE

382

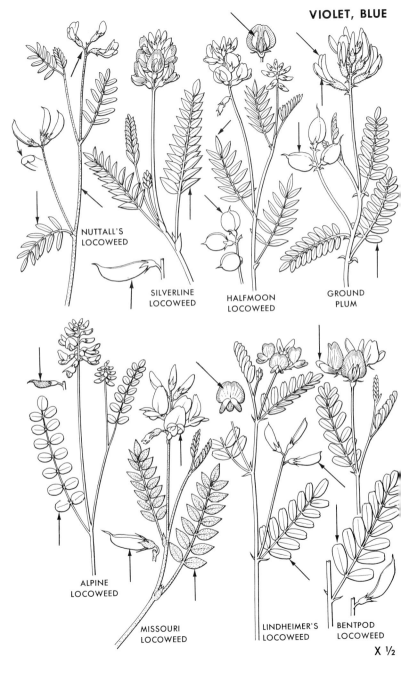

NUTTALL'S
LOCOWEED

SILVERLINE
LOCOWEED

HALFMOON
LOCOWEED

GROUND
PLUM

ALPINE
LOCOWEED

MISSOURI
LOCOWEED

LINDHEIMER'S
LOCOWEED

BENTPOD
LOCOWEED

X ½

SUNFLOWERS, ASTERS, THISTLES

Sunflower Family (Compositae)
See also pp. W 98–110; Y 198–222;
O 234; R 330–334; B 384–386; G 402.

Chicory Tribe: Cichorieae

BLUE SAILORS Alien   *Cichorium intybus*
Large, flat, *pale blue, windmill-like* flowerheads on well-branched,
leafless stems. Basal leaves dandelionlike. Milky sap. 30 cm–1 m.
S.W., northern half of Tex., R. Mts., Pl. Sts.   JUNE–OCT.

SALSIFY Alien   *Tragopogon porrifolius*
Flowerhead has *only* purple ray flowers; no disk flowers. Milky sap.
Waxy-blue, linear leaves and stem. Flowerheads become *round
brown balls* of seeds with parachutes. 30 cm–1 m. Scattered localities. S.W., western half of Tex., Pl. Sts., R. Mts.   MAY–JUNE

Thistle Tribe: Cynareae

BACHELOR'S BUTTONS Alien   *Centaurea cyanus*
Slender, erect stems with *fluffy* heads of blue, purple, pink, or white
disk flowers only. Broad, shinglelike flowerhead bracts. Leaves *linear, with light gray hairs.* 30 cm–1 m. S.W., Tex., Pl. Sts.

                                          APRIL–JUNE

Aster Tribe: Astereae

STICKY SPINE ASTER   *Machaeranthera bigelovii*
Erect stem. Bright green, *straplike leaves* with *short, sharp-pointed
lobes.* Curled flowerhead *bracts with sticky hairs.* Showy ray flowers, bright purple to violet. 20 cm–1 m. Plains to mountains. S.W.,
R. Mts.   MARCH–NOV.

TANSYLEAF SPINE ASTER   *Machaeranthera tanacetifolia*
Note the *highly divided, pinnate* leaves with tiny *spiny tips.* Many
broad, blue-purple to red-purple ray flowers around yellow disk
flowers. 10–50 cm. S.W., western third of Tex., Pl. Sts.
                                          JUNE–OCT.

SOUTHERN DAISY   *Erigeron speciosus*
Lower and upper stem leaves *similar,* lancelike. *Many very narrow,*
blue ray flowers. 10–90 cm. Mountain meadows. N.M., R. Mts.
                                          AUG.–OCT.

REGAL DAISY   *Erigeron superbus*
Basal leaves *spoonlike.* Upper stem leaves *elliptical, clasping.*
Many semi-narrow blue or rose-purple ray flowers around yellow disk flowers. 10–60 cm. Mountains. Eastern half of Ariz. to
sw. Tex.   JULY–SEPT.

PRINCELY DAISY   *Erigeron formosissimus*
Lower leaves *narrowly spatula-like,* becoming much smaller up the
stem. 10–60 cm. Common in mountain meadows, at edges of aspen-
spruce forests. S.W., R. Mts.   JULY–SEPT.

MOJAVE DESERT STAR   *Monoptilon bellioides*
A small mound of *asterlike* flowers above hairy linear leaves.
Both bright blue and white flowers. 1–10 cm. Common in sandy
deserts. Western half of Ariz., s. Ut.   FEB.–APRIL

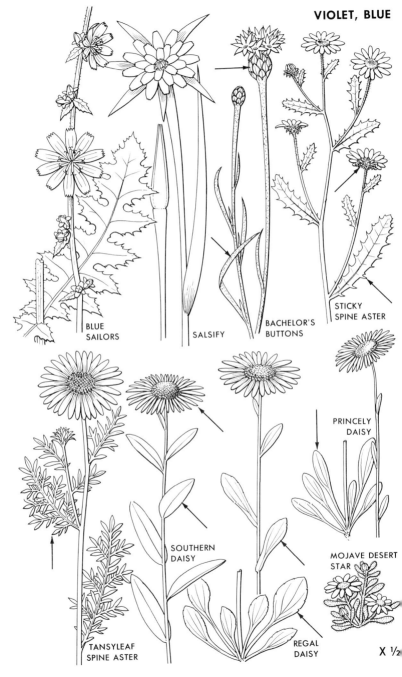

VIOLET, BLUE

BLUE SAILORS

SALSIFY

BACHELOR'S BUTTONS

STICKY SPINE ASTER

TANSYLEAF SPINE ASTER

SOUTHERN DAISY

REGAL DAISY

PRINCELY DAISY

MOJAVE DESERT STAR

X ½

ASTERS, DAISIES

Sunflower Family (Compositae)
See also pp. W 98–110; Y 198–222;
O 234; R 330–334; B 384–386; G 402.

Aster Tribe: Astereae

LEAFYHEAD ASTER *Aster foliaceus*
Note the *many leafy bracts immediately around the flower-head.* Broad, arrow-shaped leaves with clasping bases. Flower-heads blue, rose-purple, or violet, with 15–50 flowers. 10–90 cm. Mountain woods. S.W., R. Mts. AUG.–SEPT.

GRAND ASTER *Aster glaucodes*
Broad, yellow-green, straplike leaves with *minute* cut lobes; bases *clasp the dark red stems. Very broad,* all violet or all white ray flowers in one layer on each flowerhead. 30–50 cm. Mountains. N. Ariz. JULY–AUG.

LAYERED DAISY *Erigeron divergens*
Each flowerhead of *numerous* light blue, pink, or white ray flowers in *several layers.* Spreading, erect stems and leaves covered with *many erect, stiff hairs.* Upper stem leaves narrow, *straplike;* lowermost leaves *pinnate.* 10–70 cm. Very common in open dry places from lowest deserts to higher mountains. S.W., w. Tex., R. Mts., Pl. Sts. FEB.–OCT.

GEYER'S ASTER *Aster laevis*
Note the *crowded, tiny, lancelike* leaves only on the upper flower branches. Lowermost stem leaves broad, with a tapering petiole and sawtoothed margins. Ray flowers blue. 30 cm–1 m. Frequent in dry places at lower elevations. N.M., R. Mts., Pl. Sts. JULY–SEPT.

SILKY ASTER *Aster sericeus*
Note the many *silky, gray-haired* (chalky colored) *lancelike leaves up the entire stem,* becoming *similar* flowerhead bracts. Broad, dark blue-purple ray flowers and yellow central disk flowers. 30–60 cm. Plains, ne. N.M., Tex., Pl. Sts. OCT.–DEC.

AWLLEAF ASTER *Aster subulatus*
Note the *narrow, awl-like leaves* and *broad, triangular* flower-head bracts. *Few* broad ray flowers blue–purple to pinkish. Many-branched stems. 10 cm–1 m. Very common in wet places. S.W., Tex., Pl. Sts. JULY–OCT.

SKYDROP ASTER *Aster patens*
Note the *broad, short, spatula-like leaves crowded* on the flower stems, contrasted by much larger, similar leaves on the middle and lower main stem. Blue to violet ray flowers. 40–80 cm. Common in open *dry places.* Eastern two-thirds of Tex., Pl. Sts. AUG.–NOV.

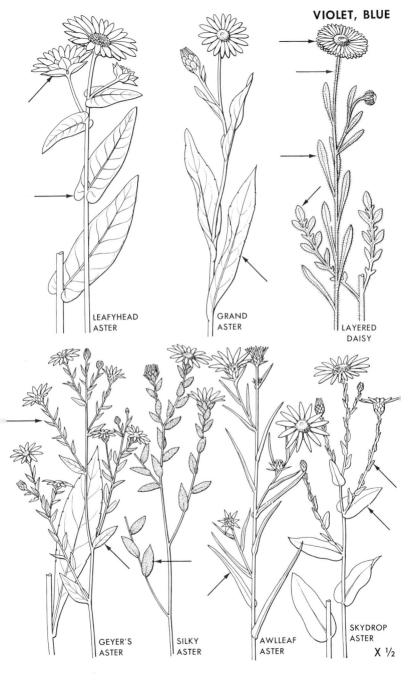

VIOLET, BLUE

LEAFYHEAD
ASTER

GRAND
ASTER

LAYERED
DAISY

GEYER'S
ASTER

SILKY
ASTER

AWLLEAF
ASTER

SKYDROP
ASTER

X ½

Brown and Green Flowers

Brown, red-brown, and green flowers are included in this section. Some are 2-colored flowers; if in doubt also check the other color. When possible, the group characteristics given in the text page titles are repeated in each color section, and in the same order. Where the flowers on a page look nearly the same but your sample does not fit, use the cross references given for other colors.

3 OR 6 PETALS; LILIES, ORCHIDS

Lily Family (Liliaceae)
See also pp. W 8–14; Y 114; O 226; R 272; B 338.

MOUNTAIN BELLS *Fritillaria atropurpurea*
7–14 broadly linear leaves on *upper stem; lower stem naked.*
1–4 nodding, bell-like flowers are brown-purple with *thin,
windowlike spots* of white and yellow. 10–60 cm. Mountain
meadows. Northern S.W., R. Mts.   APRIL–JUNE

Orchid Family (Orchidaceae)
See also pp. W 18–20; Y 114; O 228–230; G 390–394.

BROWNIE LADY'S-SLIPPER *Cypripedium fasciculatum*
Only *2 large, opposite,* oval leaves. *Slipper-lipped flowers,*
greenish yellow with brown veins. 1–8 flowers in a cluster above
the leaves. 5–30 em. Rare; under firs in subalpine zone. Northern S.W., R. Mts.   JUNE–JULY

WHORLED POGONIA *Isotria verticillata*
Note the *umbrellalike whorl* of 5–6 elliptical leaves and a
single yellow-green flower. Purple-streaked lip petal; *3 very
long, madder-purple sepals.* 10–30 cm. Beech forest bottoms.
E. Tex., S.E.   APRIL–JULY

SHADOW WITCH *Ponthieva racemosa*
Note the *V-pointed, channeled, upward-pointing* lip petal. 2
pairs of broadly triangular petals and sepals; flowers greenish
white. Fragrant. Leaves in a basal cluster. 10–50 cm. Shady
streams. E. Tex., S.E.   SEPT.–NOV.

LITTLE CLUB ORCHID *Habenaria clavellata*
Note the *short, blunt lip petal;* spur with a *swollen, clublike tip.*
Relatively naked stem, usually with only 1 well-developed leaf.
Flowers oblique, greenish or yellowish white. 10–50 cm. Wet
slopes in woods. E. Tex., S.E.   JUNE–AUG.

SOUTHERN REIN ORCHID *Habenaria flava*
Leafy bracts. Note the roundish petals and *broad lip,* usually
with a small *tooth* on each side. 10–60 cm. Muddy swamp bottoms, prairies. E. Tex.   APRIL–AUG.

RAGGED FRINGED ORCHID *Habenaria lacera*
Note the *deeply fringed, highly variable, 3-parted* lip petal,
creamy to yellowish green. 20–90 cm. Open woods along
streams, open sedge meadows, marshes. Ne. Tex.   MAY–AUG.

LONGHORN ORCHID *Habenaria quinqueseta*
Similar to Water Spider Orchid, but *spur much longer than*
inferior ovary. 30–90 cm. Swamps, margins of wet places.
Se. Tex. and along coast to S.E.   JULY–NOV.

WATER SPIDER ORCHID *Habenaria repens*
Note the 4 *thin petal lobes* that resemble *spider legs* (actually, each petal has 2 lobes). *Spur about as long* as inferior
ovary. 30–90 cm. Edges of ponds, on floating debris in lakes.
Eastern half of Tex.   MAY–NOV.

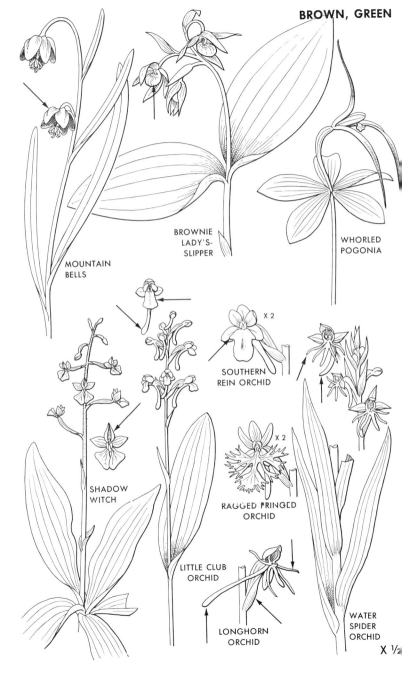

MOUNTAIN
BELLS

BROWNIE
LADY'S-
SLIPPER

WHORLED
POGONIA

SOUTHERN
REIN ORCHID

X 2

SHADOW
WITCH

RAGGED FRINGED
ORCHID

X 2

LITTLE CLUB
ORCHID

LONGHORN
ORCHID

WATER
SPIDER
ORCHID

X ½

3 IRREGULAR PETALS; ORCHIDS

Orchid Family (Orchidaceae)
See also pp. W 18–20; Y 114; O 228–230; G 390–394.
Habenaria species of Arizona and New Mexico.

SPARSE REIN ORCHID *Habenaria sparsiflora*
Spur slender, *as long as or longer than* lip petal. Spike sparsely
flowered. 30–60 cm. Wet boggy places in midmountains. Northern half of Ariz., western two-thirds of N.M., R. Mts.

JUNE–OCT.

MALE ORCHID *Habenaria saccata*
Spur petal a *broad sac, shorter than* the lip petal. Flowers in a
spike above lancelike leaves. 10–60 cm. Boggy places in higher
mountains. E. Ariz., cen. N.M., R. Mts. MAY–SEPT.

NORTHERN REIN ORCHID *Habenaria hyperborea*
Spur petal *shorter than* lip petal. Leaves lancelike. 10–60 cm.
Very common. Boggy meadows, streamsides in mountains.
E. Ariz., cen. N.M., R. Mts. JULY–AUG.

ALASKA ORCHID *Habenaria unalascensis*
Single, quite slender stem with *tiny* green flowers scattered up a
long, slender flower spike. Spur petal *shorter than ovary.*
Leaves dry up by flowering time. 30–90 cm. Dry conifer woods.
Uncommon. S.W., R. Mts. JUNE–JULY

THURBER'S BOG ORCHID *Habenaria limosa*
Note the *very long spurs* on yellow-green flowers, usually *twice
as long or longer* than the *tapering* lip petal. *Very long,
crowded flower spikes* above alternate, linear leaves. 50 cm–
1 m. Damp streamsides in higher mountains. S. Ariz. and
sw. N.M. JUNE–SEPT.

EARED ORCHID *Habenaria brevifolia*
Note the *short, earlike, green* leaf bracts, as long as each flower.
Spurs about 2 times longer than the *triangular lip petal. Short,
earlike* stem leaves. 10–50 cm. Damp to dry pine woods. Mountains. Sw. N.M. JUNE–SEPT.

SATYR ORCHID *Habenaria viridis*
Note the *broad, rectangular* lip petal with *2–3 lobes* at the *tip.*
Flower leaf bracts *much longer* than each flower. Stem leaves
medium large, clasping. 10–60 cm. Openings in aspen woods.
Mountains. N.M., R. Mts. JUNE–SEPT.

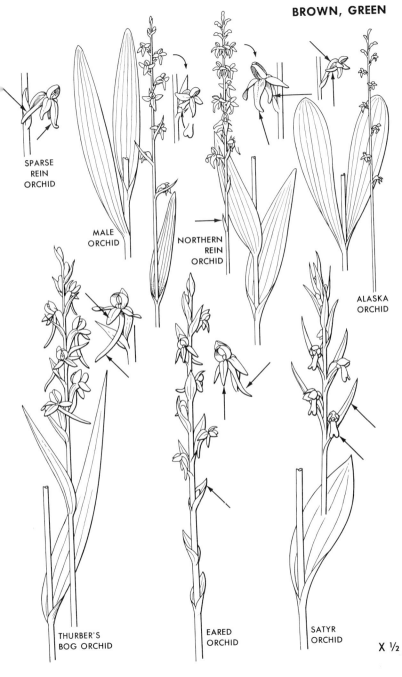

SPARSE
REIN
ORCHID

MALE
ORCHID

NORTHERN
REIN
ORCHID

ALASKA
ORCHID

THURBER'S
BOG ORCHID

EARED
ORCHID

SATYR
ORCHID

X ½

3 IRREGULAR PETALS; ORCHIDS

Orchid Family (Orchidaceae)
See also pp. W 18–20; Y 114; O 228–230; G 390–394.

Note: *Listera* species have a single opposite pair of leaves.

HEARTLEAF TWAYBLADE *Listera cordata*
Long lower lip petal *narrow, with a short forked tip* and *moustache-like* lobes on upper portion. 10–20 cm. Dense, shrubby subalpine forests. Northern N.M., R. Mts. JULY–AUG.

BROADLIP TWAYBLADE *Listera convallarioides*
Lower lip petal *broadly wedge-shaped, notched.* 10–20 cm. *Edges of shaded, mossy springs.* Mountains. S. Ariz., R. Mts.

JULY–SEPT.

NORTHERN TWAYBLADE *Listera borealis*
Greenish blue lip petal *broadly oblong,* with base end *as wide as tip.* Other petals and sepals narrow, swept backward. 5–25 cm. Moist, mossy conifer forests. Northern S.W., R. Mts. JUNE–JULY

SOUTHERN TWAYBLADE *Listera australis*
Greenish to maroon lower lip petal with *very long* lobes that resemble a *snake's forked tongue.* Note the *tiny bearded spot* at upper (basal) end of lip petals. 10–20 cm. Moist woods near wet places. E. Tex. FEB.–MAY

Note: *Malaxis* species have a single, clasping leaf at midstem.

HEADED ADDER'S-MOUTH *Malaxis corymbosa*
Note the *short, headlike cluster* of greenish flowers on a long, naked spike. Upper and lower petals triangular. 10–40 cm. Moist mountain slopes. S. Ariz., sw. N.M. JULY–AUG.

RATTAIL ADDER'S-MOUTH *Malaxis macrostachya*
Very small (5 mm), yellow-green flowers *tightly hug* the long, slender flower spike that resembles a *rat's tail.* Upper petal broad, *bilobed.* 10–50 cm. Common on moist flats in mountain conifer forests. Mogollon Rim of n. Ariz. and southward; also east to sw. Tex. JULY–OCT.

EHRENBERG'S ADDER'S-MOUTH *Malaxis ehrenbergii*
Maroon (red-brown) to greenish flowers *project out on tiny pedicels,* forming a *long, brushlike spike.* Upper petal *narrow,* lower petal *arrow-shaped.* 20–60 cm. Among deep grass and flowers on steep mountain slopes. Southern S.W. to Chisos Mts. in sw. Tex.

AUG.–SEPT.

BOTTLEBRUSH ADDER'S-MOUTH *Malaxis tenuis*
Yellow-green flowers in a *very loose* raceme, held *stiffly at right angles.* Flower pedicels half as long or longer than flowers. Upper petal *triangular.* 10–30 cm. Shady woods near streams in mountains. Southern S.W. JULY–AUG.

GREEN ADDER'S-MOUTH *Malaxis unifolia*
Greenish flowers in a *long, loose cluster,* held stiffly at right angles. Lip petal variable, *heart-shaped to rectangular* with 2–3 lower points, *pointing upward.* Lower petals *narrow, linear.* 10–50 cm. Moist hardwood slopes near streams. E. Tex., S.E.

MARCH–JULY

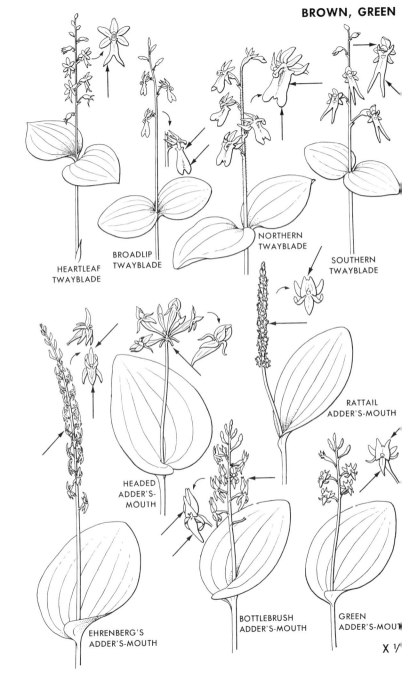

HEARTLEAF
TWAYBLADE

BROADLIP
TWAYBLADE

NORTHERN
TWAYBLADE

SOUTHERN
TWAYBLADE

RATTAIL
ADDER'S-MOUTH

HEADED
ADDER'S-
MOUTH

EHRENBERG'S
ADDER'S-MOUTH

BOTTLEBRUSH
ADDER'S-MOUTH

GREEN
ADDER'S-MOUT

X 1/

TINY FLOWERS IN SPIKES

Plantain Family (Plantaginaceae)

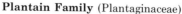

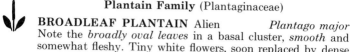

BROADLEAF PLANTAIN Alien   *Plantago major*
Note the *broadly oval leaves* in a basal cluster, *smooth* and somewhat fleshy. Tiny white flowers, soon replaced by dense brown seed spikes. 50 cm–4 m. Lawns, disturbed places. Common. S.W., Tex., R. Mts., Pl. Sts.   ALL YEAR

PATAGONIA PLANTAIN Alien   *Plantago patagonica*
Note the dense, *long silky hairs* on both the *slender* leaves and flower stem. 5–20 cm. Tex.   MARCH–JUNE

ENGLISH PLANTAIN Alien   *Plantago lanceolata*
Long, lancelike leaves in a basal cluster below dense brown flower spikes. 10–90 cm. A familiar plant in home yards. S.W., Tex.   ALL YEAR

HOOKER'S DWARF PLANTAIN   *Plantago hookeriana*
A diminutive plantain with *softly downy-haired,* linear leaves. *Thick, long, cylindrical* flower spikes on long stems. *Hairs lie flat* on leaves. 1–15 cm. Eastern two-thirds of Tex.
          MARCH–JUNE

DESERT PLANTAIN   *Plantago insularis*
A diminutive plantain with *hairs at right angles* on the broadly linear leaves and flower stem. Flower spike *fat, short.* 1–15 cm. Deserts. S.W., western third of Tex.   JAN.–MAY

PALESEED PLANTAIN   *Plantago virginica*
Shiny green leaves and flower stems with *well-spaced stiff hairs at right angles.* Leaf margins slightly toothed at wide intervals, or smooth. Flower spike *well above* leaves. Seeds *dull pale brown or blackish.* 10–30 cm. Eastern third of Tex., Pl. Sts.
          MARCH–JUNE

REDSEED PLANTAIN   *Plantago rhodosperma*
Dull green leaves, strongly toothed along margins. Somewhat dense, semi-silky hairs at right angles on leaves and stem. Slender flower spikes *barely above* the basal leaves. Seeds *bright red to bright red-black.* 10–30 cm. Rocky brushlands. Western half of Tex., Pl. Sts.   MARCH–MAY

Buttercup Family (Ranunculaceae)
See also pp. W 42–44; Y 162–164; R 236, 286;
B 344, 356–358; G 406.

SOUTHWESTERN MOUSETAIL   *Myosurus minimus*
Note the *tapering, pointed, mouse-tail-like spike* with many *smooth, green, triangular seeds* and the series of *papery bracts* at base of spike. Long, linear, *smooth succulent* leaves, in a basal cluster. 5–20 cm. Frequent in rocky places in juniper woodlands. S.W. and Tex., Pl. Sts.   MARCH–JULY

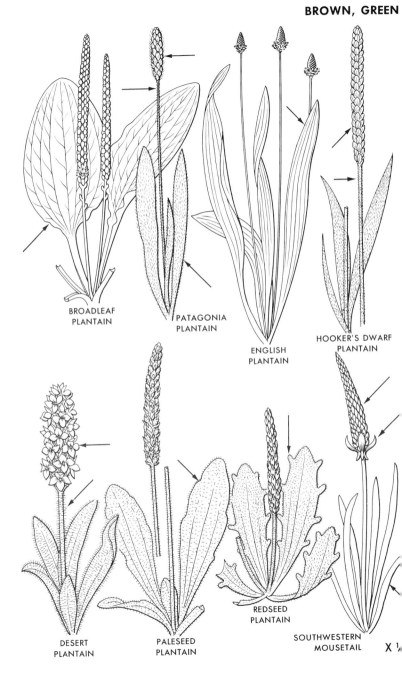

BROADLEAF
PLANTAIN

PATAGONIA
PLANTAIN

ENGLISH
PLANTAIN

HOOKER'S DWARF
PLANTAIN

DESERT
PLANTAIN

PALESEED
PLANTAIN

REDSEED
PLANTAIN

SOUTHWESTERN
MOUSETAIL

X 1

AERIAL PARASITES, EPIPHYTES;
MILKY-SAPPED GROUND PLANTS

Pineapple Family (Bromeliaceae)

SPANISH MOSS *Tillandsia usneoides*
Long, curly strands of *grayish* linear leaves, often in gracefully *drooping masses*. Flower *long, tubular,* yellow-green. An epiphyte, this plant uses the tree it grows on for support only, obtaining water and food from passing specks in the air. Eastern and s. Tex., S.E. FEB.–JUNE

BALL MOSS *Tillandsia recurvata*
Gray leaves in a *tangled ball* around a tree branch. *Long, wiry,* spiderlike green stems with terminal, tubular yellow-green flowers. An epiphyte. Southernmost Ariz., Big Bend region east to Gulf Coast of Tex. MOST OF YEAR

Mistletoe Family (Loranthaceae)

GREENLEAF MISTLETOE *Phoradendron tomentosum*
Note the *thick, leathery, green leaves* in opposite pairs on brittle, woody twigs that hang from the host tree in large, shrubby masses. Berries white or pink. A parasite on oaks, walnuts and other trees. 10–30 cm. S.W., Tex., Pl. Sts. ALL YEAR

JUNIPER MISTLETOE *Phoradendron juniperinum*
Shiny green, leafless stems in clusters; a parasite on branches of juniper (cedar) trees. 10–60 cm. S.W., w. Tex., R. Mts. ALL YEAR

MESQUITE MISTLETOE *Phoradendron californicum*
Leafless, twiggy stems in large clusters. Berries red. A common parasite on mesquite and other pea family shrubs. 10–60 cm. Lower deserts. Southern and w. Ariz., s. Ut. ALL YEAR

WESTERN DWARF MISTLETOE
Arceuthobium campylopodum
Dwarf, yellow-green stems in small clusters. Leaves reduced to tiny bracts. The pink berries *explode* when touched and shoot their sticky seeds a considerable distance. 5–60 cm. A parasite on conifer branches. S.W., R. Mts. ALL YEAR

Spurge Family (Euphorbiaceae) See also pp. W 74; R 314.

PETTY SPURGE Alien *Euphorbia peplus*
Oval stem leaves in opposite pairs, with *short petioles*. Flower gland has *2 slender horns*. Plant yellow-green throughout. Milky sap. 10–30 cm. Common in yards. S.W., Tex.
ALL YEAR

THREADED SPURGE *Euphorbia eriantha*
Long, slender, *threadlike floral leaves* from the central flower clusters. Barrel-like female flower parts on a *curving side branch*. Stem leaves long, slender. 10–60 cm. Common in dry places. Lower deserts. Southern S.W., sw. Tex. JAN.–OCT.

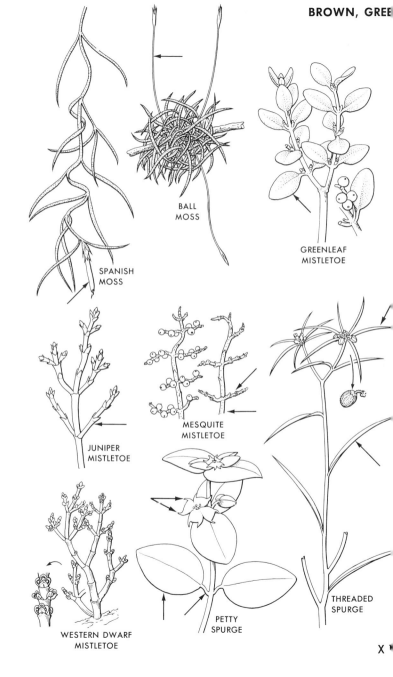

SPANISH
MOSS

BALL
MOSS

GREENLEAF
MISTLETOE

JUNIPER
MISTLETOE

MESQUITE
MISTLETOE

WESTERN DWARF
MISTLETOE

PETTY
SPURGE

THREADED
SPURGE

X ¹

DUTCHMAN'S-PIPES
GREEN GENTIANS

Birthwort Family (Aristolochiaceae)

WATSON'S DUTCHMAN'S-PIPE *Aristolochia watsonii*
Flower resembles a *gaping baby bird's mouth*, rimmed with red-brown and spotted within. A low, ground-hugging vine with *long, narrow, arrow-shaped* leaves. Near or in seasonally wet gullies. Southern half of Ariz., sw. N.M., possibly sw. Tex.
APRIL–OCT.

WRIGHT'S DUTCHMAN'S-PIPE *Aristolochia wrightii*
Flower erect, with a *long, tapering "tail;"* upper part of flower (including rim around tree-holelike opening) *red-brown.* Short vines with broad, heart-shaped leaves. 5–60 cm. Among boulders, rocks. Big Bend region of Tex. MARCH–JUNE

CORY'S DUTCHMAN'S-PIPE *Aristolochia coryi*
Upper end of flower *shaped like the collar of a horse's harness;* mostly pure white with a rich, red-brown edge and inner spots. Vines; 5–30 cm. Central lobe of each leaf *sharply pointed, triangular;* 2 side lobes *round, hooked* at base. Among shrubs. Rocky brushlands. W.-cen. Tex. to Big Bend region of Tex.
APRIL–SEPT.

SWANFLOWER *Aristolochia longiflora*
Vaselike flower with a *long, slender neck* below an upper lobe that is *curved,* like a swan's neck and head. Short vines; 5–30 cm. Leaves *long, linear.* Very common on grassy flats. S. Tex. MARCH–NOV.

Gentian Family (Gentianaceae)
See also pp. W 78; Y 174; R 242; B 342.

MONUMENT PLANT *Frasera speciosa*
Each green-white petal has *a pair of hairy gland spots.* Single, *tall, monumentlike stem* with linear leaves *in whorls.* Leaf margins green, *not white.* 1–2 m. Open mountain slopes, forests. Ariz., northern N.M., R. Mts. MAY–AUG.

PARRY'S FRASERA *Frasera parryi*
Greenish white petals with black dots; each has a *single, U-shaped* hairy gland spot. Smooth, triangular leaves in opposite pairs with *white margins.* A single, stout stem. 50 cm–1 m. Ariz. MAY–SEPT.

DESERT FRASERA *Frasera albomarginata*
Each green-white petal has a *single, oblong, fringed* gland spot, which is open for $\frac{4}{5}$ of its length. Well-branched stem with *white-margined leaves in whorls* of 3–4. Plant smooth. 10–40 cm. Rocky places, juniper woodlands. N. Ariz., nw. N.M., R. Mts. MAY–SEPT.

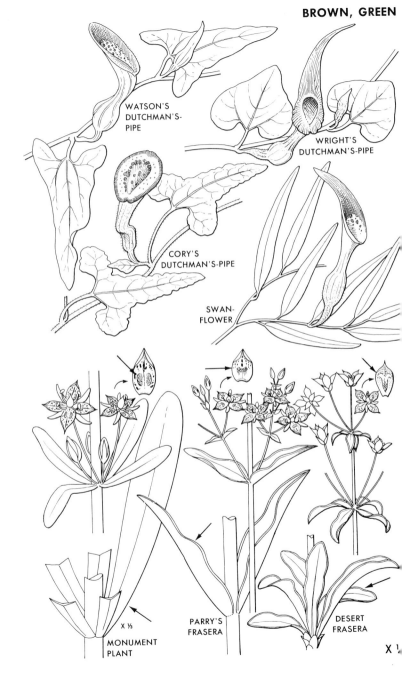

WATSON'S
DUTCHMAN'S-
PIPE

WRIGHT'S
DUTCHMAN'S-PIPE

CORY'S
DUTCHMAN'S-PIPE

SWAN-
FLOWER

X ⅓

MONUMENT
PLANT

PARRY'S
FRASERA

DESERT
FRASERA

X 1

TINY, BARELY VISIBLE, GREEN FLOWERS

Goosefoot Family (Chenopodiaceae)
See also p. G 406.

LAMB'S QUARTER Alien *Chenopodium album*
Triangular leaves with a white granular covering. Tiny flowers
in thick spikes. 30 cm–1 m. Common. S.W., Tex., R. Mts.,
Pl. Sts. APRIL–SEPT.

RUSSIAN TUMBLEWEED Alien *Salsola kali*
Note the short, bractlike leaves with spiny tips; seed capsules
look like pink or orange flowers. Multiple-branching stems form
a *very large, bushy ball,* which when blown about is the familiar tumbleweed. 10 cm–1 m. Very common. S.W., Tex., R. Mts.,
Pl. Sts. JULY–OCT.

Nettle Family (Urticaceae)

STINGING NETTLE *Urtica* species
Flowers in *loose, stringy clusters* above each pair of velvety
leaves. Watch out for *stinging hairs.* 50 cm–1.5 m. Moist fields,
thickets. S.W., Tex., R. Mts., Pl. Sts. FEB.–SEPT.

Amaranth Family (Amaranthaceae) See also p. W 38.

PROSTRATE AMARANTH *Amaranthus blitoides*
Stem nearly *prostrate,* with *intermittent clusters* of small green
flowers mixed with long bristles. Leaves pale green, oval. May
become a tumbleweed. 10 cm–1.5 m. Common in disturbed
places. S.W., Tex., R. Mts., Pl. Sts. JULY–OCT.

GREEN AMARANTH *Amaranthus retroflexus*
Plant erect, with dense terminal spikes of chaffy green flowers
mixed with long, *bristlelike bracts.* Leaves oval, gray-green.
30 cm–1 m. Common. S.W., Tex., R. Mts. JUNE–OCT.

Sunflower Family (Compositae)
See also pp. W 98–110; Y 198–222;
O 234; R 330–334; B 384–386.

COCKLEBUR *Xanthium strumarium*
Note the *large, oblong burs* with numerous *stiff, hooked hairs.*
Leaves broadly triangular. Flowers minute. Disturbed places.
20–90 cm. S.W., Tex., R. Mts. JUNE–OCT.

MARSH ELDER *Iva annua*
Note the many half-open spikes of tiny, heart-shaped flower
bracts with *spiny margins.* Large, oval to heart-shaped leaves
in opposite pairs. 10–90 cm. Very common in open fields.
Eastern half of Tex. JULY–DEC.

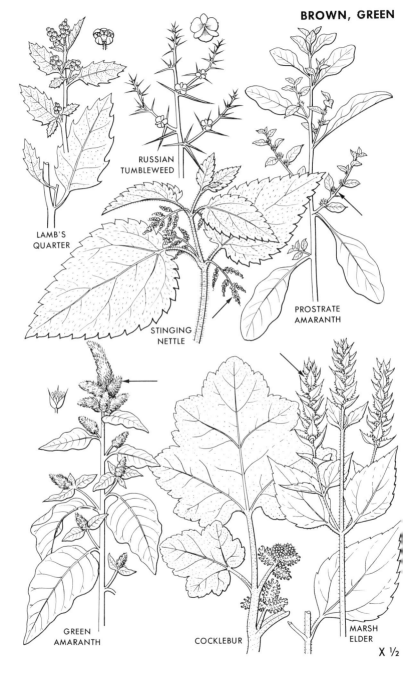

LAMB'S QUARTER

RUSSIAN TUMBLEWEED

STINGING NETTLE

PROSTRATE AMARANTH

GREEN AMARANTH

COCKLEBUR

MARSH ELDER

X 1/2

PLANTS OF MOIST SHADY WOODS

Arum or Calla Family (Araceae)

JACK-IN-THE-PULPIT *Arisaema triphyllum*
Flaplike spathe curves gracefully over the *club-shaped spadix*
(the "Jack" is a preacher in his canopied pulpit). Flowers tiny,
at base of spadix. Flower all yellow-green, or striped green and
purplish brown. 3 broadly lancelike leaflets. Fruit (not shown) a
cluster of scarlet berries. 30–90 cm. Soggy bottomlands in hardwood forests with rich soil. E. Tex., Pl. Sts.   MARCH–MAY

GREEN DRAGON *Arisaema dracontium*
Very long, whitish spadix (dragon's tongue) extends from the
green yellow spathe (dragon's head). Each leaf divided into
many pointed leaflets. 20 cm–1 m. Deep soil of thickets, hard-
woods. Eastern half of Tex., Pl. Sts.   MARCH–JUNE

TUCKAHOE *Peltandra virginica*
Note the *huge, arrow-shaped* leaf blades. *Long, white, spikelike flowers* with the spadix barely emerging, hidden among the
leaves. 1–2 m. Swamps, bogs. E. Tex., Pl. Sts., S.E.
APRIL–MAY

Saxifrage Family (Saxifragaceae)
See also pp. W 52–54; Y 170; R 236.

FIVEPOINT BISHOP'S CAP *Mitella pentandra*
Each threadlike petal consists of a central shaft and 6–10 side
branches; *each petal set opposite a stamen.* Elongate, maplelike leaves. 10–60 cm. Wet streambanks and damp, shady
woods. Mountains. Northern N.M., R. Mts.   JUNE–AUG.

Milkweed Family (Asclepiadaceae)
See also pp. W 66–72; O 234; R 302–304.

NETTED MILKVINE *Matelea reticulata*
Note the *flat, starlike* green petal lobes with *netlike* markings
and the *shiny, pearly white central dome.* Long, twining vines
with heart-shaped leaves. Very common in shady woods, along
fencerows, etc. Se. N.M., Tex.   APRIL–OCT.

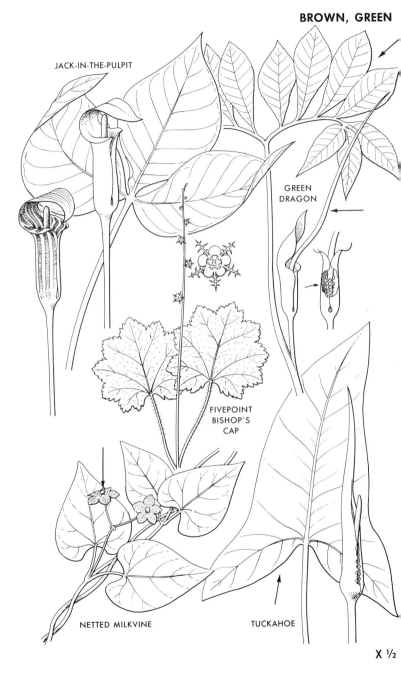

BROWN, GREEN

JACK-IN-THE-PULPIT

GREEN DRAGON

FIVEPOINT BISHOP'S CAP

NETTED MILKVINE

TUCKAHOE

X ½

MARSH AND POND PLANTS

Water Lily Family (Nymphaeaceae)
See also pp. W 6; Y 186; B 344.

WATERSHIELD *Brasenia schreberi*
Note the *floating,* oval to semi-round leaves with uncleft margins. Flowers with many long, *red-brown stamens* and 3–4 petals. Underwater plant surfaces coated with a *thick, jellylike* substance. Ponds, sluggish streams. E. Tex., R. Mts. MARCH–MAY

Goosefoot Family (Chenopodiaceae) See also p. G 402.

SLENDER PICKLEWEED *Salicornia europaea*
Succulent, erect stem *jointed, cylindrical.* Leaves minute. Flowers minute, sunk into the stem joints. 30–60 cm. Alkali and salt marshes. S.W., Tex. ALL YEAR

Arrow-weed Family (Juncaginaceae)

SALTMARSH ARROWGRASS *Triglochin maritimum*
Tall, arrowlike stem with numerous tiny flowers above a tuft of fleshy, grasslike leaves. Poisonous to cattle. 30–60 cm. Salt and alkali marshes. Nw. Ariz., N.M., R. Mts. ALL YEAR

Buttercup Family (Ranunculaceae)
See also pp. W 42–44; Y 162–164;
R 236, 286; B 344, 356–358; G 396.

FENDLER'S MEADOW RUE *Thalictrum fendleri*
Note the numerous pendulous, yellow-green flowers *without petals.* Any one plant has either *all male flowers* (stamens only) or *all female flowers* (pistils only). 1–1.5 m. Common in moist places near streams, in woods. S.W., w. Tex., R. Mts. APRIL–SEPT.

Cattail Family (Typhaceae)

NARROWLEAF CATTAIL *Typha angustifolia*
Flower stems stiff, with a thick, brown, *sausagelike "cat"* of numerous female flowers and a *slender "cat's tail"* of male flowers above it. Note the *bare interval* between the 2 flower areas. Narrow (5–15 mm wide), erect, straplike leaves, deep green and *taller than* the flower spikes. Tall plants growing in dense clumps in freshwater marshes. S.W., Tex., Pl. Sts. ALL YEAR

TULE CATTAIL (not shown) *Typha domingensis*
Similar to Narrowleaf Cattail, but pale green leaves *broad* (15–30 mm wide). Tops of leaves usually reach same height as the fat, smooth female flowers (fat, sausagelike portion), but *rarely* grow taller than the entire flower spike. 2–3 m. Common in fresh water or slightly brackish, subalkaline tidal water. S.W., Tex. APRIL–MAY

BROADLEAF CATTAIL *Typha latifolia*
Note the thick, sausagelike female flowers below the slender "tail" of male flowers, with *no space between* them. Leaves broad (3–5 cm wide). 1–2 m. Freshwater marshes. S.W., Pl. Sts. APRIL–JULY

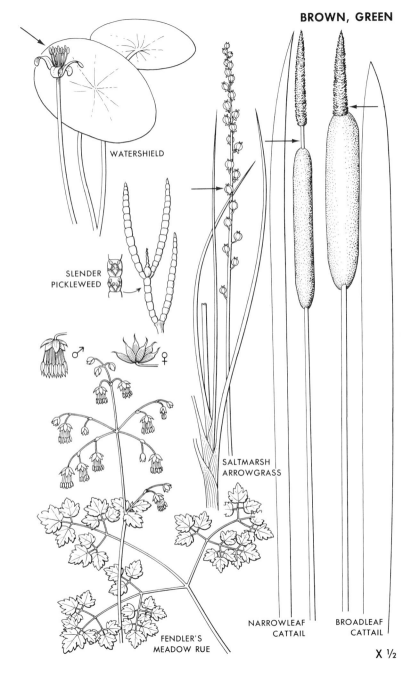

WATERSHIELD

SLENDER
PICKLEWEED

♂ ♀

FENDLER'S
MEADOW RUE

SALTMARSH
ARROWGRASS

NARROWLEAF
CATTAIL

BROADLEAF
CATTAIL

X ½

Family Descriptions and Key

A plant family is a large group of species that share the same general traits. The key given here immediately enables you to narrow down the number of families to which an unidentified plant could belong to a few possibilities, based on such characteristics such as the number of flower petals. The portion of the key found on any given page leads only to families found on that same page or the facing pages, so page turning is unnecessary. At the end of each family description are inclusive ranges of page numbers where the species in that family are treated in this *Field Guide*.

The family descriptions state the visual characteristics necessary for quick field identification of a plant family. Remember that the page headings in this key summarize more briefly some of those family characters. The family symbol is a visual representation of the most distinctive features. If you learn to recognize the family traits on sight, you will be able to identify an unknown species much more rapidly.

How to Use the Key. By following these four steps, you will be led to the name of any wildflower you wish to identify.

1. Learn the names of the plant parts shown on the endpapers.
2. Look at the flower and note its shape, color, arrangement, and so on. How many petals does it have? Are they free from each other or fused? Are they arranged regularly or irregularly? Is the ovary in a superior or inferior position? What shape is each flower part?
3. The key consists of numbered pairs of contrasting statements. Choose the alternative that best describes the flower part in question.
4. At the end of the statement chosen, note the *See* reference, which guides you to the next pair of statements. Continue until you reach the name of the appropriate plant family. Note the family symbol and the pages where that family is covered in the text. Look on the plates in that section for your flower.

Key to Families

1a. Flowers without petals, or petals not apparent. See 5 on p. 409.
1b. Flowers with petals. See 2 (below).

2a. Petals 3 or 6. See 15 on p. 411.
2b. Petals 4 or 5, or numerous. See 3 (below).

3a. Petals numerous. See 102 on p. 426.
3b. Petals 4 or 5. See 4.

4a. Petals 4. See 32 on p. 414.
4b. Petals 5. See 44 on p. 416.

Petals Absent or Not Apparent
(Families keyed below are described on this page.)

5a. Plants of marshes or ponds. See 6.
5b. Plants of dry land, or parasitic. See 10 on p. 410.

6a. Flowers in a white torch or tail. **Saururaceae.**
6b. Flowers *not* in a torch or tail arrangement. See 7.

7a. Flowers in a brown, sausagelike cylinder. **Typhaceae.**
7b. Flowers in various arrangements, not as above. See 8.

8a. Flower stem triangular. Brownish, rattlelike flower clusters.
Cyperaceae.
8b. Flower stem round. Flowers in balls or with a spathe. See 9.

9a. Flowers in round balls; pond plant. **Sparganiaceae.**
9b. Flowers surrounded by a spathe. **Araceae.**

LIZARD-TAIL FAMILY (Saururaceae). Leaves simple and alternately arranged. Flowers in a dense spike or raceme. Flower parts free. Sepals and petals absent. Stamens 6–8, pistils 3–4, free or fused. White, p. 6.

CATTAIL FAMILY (Typhaceae). Tall marsh plants in dense stands. Leaves straplike. Stem stiff and rodlike, with a thick, cylindrical (sausagelike) brown spike of numerous minute female flowers tightly packed together. A slender tail of paler male flowers above. Brown, p. 406.

SEDGE FAMILY (Cyperaceae). Grasslike marsh plants. Linear, grasslike leaves. Erect, naked, *solid-cored* flower stems, often *triangular in cross-section*. Several leaves in a *terminal, umbel-like cluster* just below the rattlelike flower clusters. Flower parts in 2's and 3's. White, p. 6.

BUR-REED FAMILY (Sparganiaceae). Pond plants. Flowers in *round, globelike heads*. Heads unisexual — the lower female, the upper male. Individual flowers on plan of 3's. No petals present. Leaves linear, grasslike. White, p. 6.

ARUM or CALLA FAMILY (Araceae). A specialized, large, colored leaf *(spathe)* partly surrounds a spikelike stem *(spadix),* on which numerous tiny flowers are crowded. Brown, p. 404.

Petals Absent or Not Apparent (*contd.*)
(Families keyed below are described on this page.)

10a. Plant with copious milky juice. Ovary hangs to one side of flower. **Euphorbiaceae.**
10b. Plants without milky juice. Ovary erect. See 11.

11a. Plants parasitic; stems orange or green. See 12.
11b. Plants not parasitic. See 13.

12a. Plants parasitic; stems orange, threadlike. **Cuscutaceae.**
12b. Parasitic; stems orange or green, twiggy. **Loranthaceae.**

13a. Tiny green flowers on short strings beneath leaves. Severe sting if plant is touched. **Urticaceae.**
13b. Tiny green or reddish flowers in clusters. See 14.

14a. Plant surface scurfy or mealy. Flower bracts rounded. **Chenopodiaceae.**
14b. Plant surface smooth. Flower bracts pointed. **Amaranthaceae.**

 SPURGE FAMILY (Euphorbiaceae). Usually with thick, milky sap. Flower consists of (1) *colored bracts* that appear to be petals (the red bracts of the familiar Poinsettia are an example); (2) a central cluster of stamens and glands; and (3) a *3-lobed ovary,* next to the stamens but *hanging to one side.* White, p. 74; Red, p. 314; Brown, p. 398.

 DODDER FAMILY (Cuscutaceae). *Yellow* or *orange,* parasitic, twining vines. Leaves reduced to minute scales. Flowers tiny; waxy-white, bell- or urn-shaped, with 4 or 5 petal lobes. Related to the Morning Glory Family. Orange, p. 234.

 MISTLETOE FAMILY (Loranthaceae). Twiggy stems in parasitic clusters on host plant. Stems with or without leaves. Flowers minute. Fleshy pink berries. Green, p. 398.

 NETTLE FAMILY (Urticaceae). In our area, most have stinging hairs. Leaves opposite. Tiny greenish flowers without petals, in small stringy clusters. Calyx with 4 parts; stamens 4. Green, p. 402.

 GOOSEFOOT FAMILY (Chenopodiaceae). Weedy herbs, often with *mealy, scurfy-white, dandrufflike* surfaces. Greenish flowers, very small; no petals. Flowers in dense spikelike clusters. Green, p. 402, 406.

AMARANTH FAMILY (Amaranthaceae). Weedy herbs; inconspicuous flowers in spikes or clusters. *Each flower* arises from *3 sterile, membranous bracts* that are spiny. Plants not mealy as in the Goosefoot Family. White, p. 38; Green, p. 402.

Petals 3, 6, or 9

15a. Ovary in inferior position. See 16.
15b. Ovary in superior position. See 20 on p. 412.

Petals 3 or 6; Ovary Inferior

(Families keyed below are described on this page.)

16a. Petals in irregular arrangement. **Orchidaceae.**
16b. Petals in regular arrangement. See 17.

17a. Leaves with parallel veins. See 18.
17b. Leaves with netlike veins. See 19.

18a. Flowers in racemes, stem usually leafy. **Iridaceae.**
18b. Flowers in umbel on a leafless stem. **Amaryllidaceae.**

19a. Flowers reddish brown. **Aristolochiaceae.**
19b. Flowers red-purple, in long spikes. **Lythraceae.**

 ORCHID FAMILY (Orchidaceae). Flowers *irregularly shaped;* sepals similar in shape. Petals 3; 2 are similarly shaped side petals, the 3rd petal — the *lip petal* — is lower and larger. Ovary *inferior.* Leaves entire, with parallel veins. White, pp. 18–20; Yellow, p. 114; Orange and Red, pp. 228–230; Green, pp. 390–394.

 IRIS FAMILY (Iridaceae). Leaves flat, *swordlike,* and *flatly* packed edge-to-edge (equitant). Flowers regularly shaped. Parts in 3's. 2 flower plans: (1) 3 broad, petal-like sepals and 3 narrow, erect petals *(Iris)*; and (2) both sepals and petals equal-sized and colored, in flat circle of 6. Ovary *inferior.* Yellow, p. 116; Red, p. 272; Blue, p. 340.

 AMARYLLIS FAMILY (Amaryllidaceae). Sepals and petals in 3's, that often look like 6 similarly colored petals. Flowers arranged on *leafless stalks* (scapes) in a *terminal umbel* with *papery bracts at base.* (Compare with Lily Family in which plants have leafy flower stems and flowers never in umbels.) White, pp. 14–16; Yellow, p. 116; Red, p. 274; Blue, p. 338.

 BIRTHWORT FAMILY (Aristolochiaceae). Leaves variously heart-shaped. Flowers reddish brown, either shaped like a fused Dutchman's Pipe (of various shapes) or cuplike, with *3 petal-like sepals* that flare out from a swollen, cuplike (semi-inferior) ovary. No petals. Stamens 12. Brown, p. 400.

 LOOSESTRIFE FAMILY (Lythraceae). Flowers regularly shaped. Sepals and petals 4 or 6, free. Ovary within a *6-ribbed, cylindrical* calyx that looks like an inferior ovary. Style 1; stigma 2-lobed. Steeplelike racemens. Red, p. 280.

Petals 3 or 6 or 9; Ovary Superior
(Families keyed below are described on this page.)

20a. Petals in irregular arrangement. See 21.
20b. Petals in regular arrangement. See 22.

21a. Large petals. Marsh or pond plants. **Pontederiaceae.**
21b. Tiny or small petals. Dry land plants. **Polygalaceae.**

22a. Ball-like or hanging plants on tree limbs. **Bromeliaceae.**
22b. Plants grow at ground level, rooted in earth. See 23.

23a. Flower of 6–9 waxy petals in a nodding bell between 2 large leaves. **Berberidaceae.**
23b. Flower petals not waxy. See 24.

24a. Stamens numerous; milky sap. **Papaveraceae.**
24b. Stamens 3, 6, or 9. See 25.

25a. Scaly knob with yellow flowers, wiry stem. **Xyridaceae.**
25b. Flowers not on a scaly knob. See 26 on p. 413.

 PICKEREL WEED FAMILY (Pontederiaceae). Marsh plants. Flowers on a plan of 3's. Flower spike arises from a spathe. 6 large, violet petals fused in a tube only near base, *uppermost petal with a yellow center.* Blue, p. 356.

 MILKWORT FAMILY (Polygalaceae). Calyx (5 sepals) irregularly arranged, 2 often winglike and petal-like at the sides, and a *boatlike central tube.* 3 (or 5) petals; middle petals sometimes *fringed.* Stamens 8. White, p. 92.

 PINEAPPLE FAMILY (Bromeliaceae). Clustered or hanging, strandlike, aerial stems attached to trees (epiphytes); or agave-like land plants with sawtoothed leaves that form a distinct *spiral cup.* Sepals and petals in 3's. Stamens 6. Brown, p. 398.

 BARBERRY FAMILY (Berberidaceae). Flowers regular, tiny, without petals, in a pencil-sized spike *or* with 6 separate petals in 2 circles; petals bent (reflexed) backward. Stamens 6. Ovary superior. Leaves pinnate. White, p. 24.

 POPPY FAMILY (Papaveraceae). Flowers regular; parts free. *Sepals 2 or 3 and caducous* (fall off when flower opens). Showy petals, 4 or 6. *Stamens numerous.* Ovary superior. Yellowish *milky sap.* White, p. 22; Yellow, p. 122; Orange, p. 232.

 YELLOW-EYED GRASS FAMILY (Xyridaceae). Marsh plants with grasslike leaves. *Long, wiry, naked* flower stems topped by a *scaly knob* with yellow, 3-petaled flowers. Yellow, p. 116.

Petals 3 or 6; Ovary Superior (*contd.*)

(Families keyed below are described on this page,
except as noted.)

26a. Flowers arranged in umbel. **Amaryllidaceae.** See p. 411.
26b. Flowers not arranged in an umbel. See 27.

27a. Calyx a 6-ribbed cylinder. **Lythraceae.** See p. 411.
27b. Calyx smooth or various, not 6-ribbed. See 28.

28a. Leaves variously net-veined. **Polygonaceae.**
28b. Leaves parallel-veined. See 29.

29a. Leaves linear, spongy. Tiny green flowers on a spike.
Juncaginaceae.
29b. Leaves not spongy. Larger, normal-sized flowers. See 30.

30a. Both sepals and petals nearly or same color. **Liliaceae.**
30b. Dissimilar green sepals and 3 colored petals. See 31.

31a. Leaf base sheathes the stem. **Commelinaceae.**
31b. Leaf with petiole, not sheathing stem. **Alismataceae.**

 BUCKWHEAT FAMILY (Polygonaceae). Leaves alternate with a papery sheath (ocrea) around the swollen node ("knots"). *Or* if ocreae absent (as in *Eriogonum*), flowers in involucrate (invol) clusters. Numerous small flowers, each consisting of 4, 5, or 6 green or colored, petal-like sepals. No true petals. Stamens 6 or 9. Ovary superior, with a 2- or 3-parted style. Fruit a 3-sided achene, often with 3 papery, winglike margins. White, pp. 38–40; Yellow, pp. 158–160; Red, pp. 282–284.

 ARROW-WEED FAMILY (Juncaginaceae). Salt-marsh plants. Fleshy, grasslike leaves. Flowers in *dense, elongated spikes.* Flowers with 3 or 6 greenish sepal or petal-like segments. Fruits cylindrical. Green, p. 406.

 LILY FAMILY (Liliaceae). Sepals and petals in 3's and *similarly colored.* Stamens 3 or 6. Ovary superior. Flowers arranged in racemes, panicles, or spikes. White, pp. 8–14; Yellow, p. 114; Orange, p. 226; Red, p. 272; Blue, p. 338; Green, p. 390.

 SPIDERWORT FAMILY (Commelinaceae). Leaf bases clasp the stem. Linear, alternately arranged leaves. Flower clusters emerge from a *large, closed, sheathing,* leaflike bract. 3 small green sepals. 3 colored petals. Red, p. 272; Blue, p. 338.

 WATER PLANTAIN FAMILY (Alismataceae). Freshwater marsh plants. Sepals 3. *3 large white petals, free.* 6 or more stamens. Fruit a collection of single-seeded achenes. White, p. 6.

Petals 4

(Families keyed below are described on this
or the facing page.)

32a. Ovary in superior position. See 33.
32b. Ovary in inferior position. See 42.

33a. Petals free from each other. See 34.
33b. Petals fused, at least near base. See 40.

34a. Leaves and stem thick, succulent. **Crassulaceae.**
See p. 419.
34b. Leaves and stems thin, not succulent. See 35.

35a. Sepals 2 (falling off early in 1 family). See 36.
35b. Sepals 4. See 37.

36a. Flower regularly shaped; stamens numerous, milky sap.
Papaveraceae. See p. 412.
36b. Flower irregularly shaped and flattened; stamens 4 or 6.
Fumariaceae.

37a. Leaves opposite. Anthers release pollen through terminal
pores. **Melastomataceae.**
37b. Leaves alternate. Anthers open lengthwide to release pollen. See 38.

38a. Petals in a Maltese cross. See 39.
38b. Petals in tiny urns. Fruits are angled achenes.
Polygonaceae. See p. 413.

39a. Leaves palmate compound. Skunky odor.
Capparidaceae.
39b. Leaves various, not palmate compound. **Cruciferae.**

40a. Flowers papery brown, in spikes. **Plantaginaceae.**
40b. Flowers green, red, or blue. See 41.

41a. Stamens alternate to petals. Corolla without a constriction. **Gentianaceae.**
41b. Stamens often long and protruding, opposite petal lobes.
Corolla tube constricted near base. **Nyctaginaceae.**

42a. Ovary of 2 rounded, spiny lobes. **Rubiaceae.**
42b. Ovary elongated or of 1 round lobe. See 43.

43a. 4 petals large or small; no central tiny flowers. Conspicuous, elongated inferior ovary. **Onagraceae.**
43b. 4 large, white "petals" with a center of tiny yellow flowers.
Cornaceae.

 BLEEDING HEART FAMILY (Fumariaceae). Leaves
highly divided into lacy segments. Sepals 2, small and falling off
early. Petals 4, *flattened* into an elongated, heart-shaped or
spurred sac. Stamens 4 and individually free; or stamens 6,
united in 2 sets. Ovary superior. Yellow, p. 174; Red, p. 298.

Petals 4 (*contd.*)

 CAPER FAMILY (Capparidaceae). Similar to Mustard Family (Cruciferae, below), but note the following differences. Leaves usually *palmate compound.* Ovary *bananalike,* with a *long, thin, pedicel-like* base that is attached to a very long pedicel. Skunklike odor when handled. White, p. 32; Yellow, p. 152; Red, p. 236.

 MUSTARD FAMILY (Cruciferae). Leaves alternate. Urnlike flowers in a regular Maltese-cross shape of 4 sepals and petals of equal length. Stamens 6 (2 are attached at a lower level). The seedpod is a *silique* or *sicile* (found only in this family). A few genera have a cylindrical, non-opening seedpod. White, pp. 26–32; Yellow, pp. 144–152; Orange, p. 232; Red, p. 276.

 MEADOW BEAUTY FAMILY (Melastomataceae). Leaves opposite. Petals 4 or 5, twice as many stamens. Anthers release pollen through *terminal pores.* Ovary superior in our species. Red, p. 280.

 PLANTAIN FAMILY (Plantaginaceae). Numerous brownish flowers in a dense, *thumblike spike* on a long, *leafless stalk.* Each flower has 4 sepals; 4 united, tiny brown petals (corolla semi-transparent, dry and papery); and 2 stamens. Leaves in a basal rosette. Brown. p. 396.

 GENTIAN FAMILY (Gentianaceae). Sepals 4 or 5, united. Petals 4 or 5, fused at base; bowl-like or tubular flower (corolla). Stamens 4 or 5, fused to corolla wall and alternate to petals. Ovary superior, style 1, entire. Leaves opposite. White, p. 78; Yellow, p. 174; Red, p. 242; Blue, p. 342; Brown, p. 400.

 FOUR O'CLOCK FAMILY (Nyctaginaceae). Flowers in *umbels* or solitary. Leafy bracts below each umbel are free or fused into large, calyxlike cups. Funnel-like corollas (actually colored sepals) with 4 or 5 petal lobes; *tube constricted at base.* No true petals. Ovary superior. Pistil 1. White, p. 64; Red, p. 306.

 BEDSTRAW or MADDER FAMILY (Rubiaceae). 4 minute sepals. Petals 4, in a *tiny cross.* Stamens 4 and alternate to petals. Ovary *inferior,* becoming *twin* rounded seeds. Stems square. Leaves in whorls or pairs. White, p. 24; Red, p. 280.

 EVENING PRIMROSE FAMILY (Onagraceae). Flower parts in 4's, free. *Long, slender inferior ovary.* Style 1, the stigma either a 4-branched cross or bulblike. *Pollen enmeshed in cobwebby threads.* White, pp. 34–36; Yellow, pp. 154–158; Red, pp. 278–280.

 DOGWOOD FAMILY (Cornaceae). *4 large, showy, white bracts* (often mistaken for petals) surround a cluster of tiny yellow flowers with inferior ovaries. Style 1. White, p. 24.

Petals 5

44a. Each petal *completely free* from others. See 45.
44b. Petals fused slightly at base, or fused more. See 46.

45a. Free petals in an irregular arrangement. See 48.
45b. Free petals in a regular arrangement. See 51 on p. 417.

46a. Ovary in superior position. See 47.
46b. Ovary in inferior position. See 95 on p. 424.

47a. Flowers 2-lipped (irregularly shaped). See 72 on p. 421.
47b. Flowers round (regularly shaped). See 78 on p. 422.

5 Petals, Completely Free
Irregular Arrangement

(Families keyed below are all described on this page.)

48a. Sap red to orange. Flowers orange. **Cochlospermaceae.**
48b. Sap clear. Flowers yellow, red, or blue. See 49.

49a. Easily seen glands on lower 2 petals. **Krameriaceae.**
49b. No glands on petal bases. See 50.

50a. Flowers pealike. Leaves compound. **Leguminosae.**
50b. Flowers violet-like. Leaves mostly entire. **Violaceae.**

 COCHLOSPERMUM FAMILY (Cochlospermaceae). Palmate compound leaves. *Numerous* stamens in 2 sets. Anthers release pollen through *terminal pores.* Sap red-orange. Orange, p. 232.

 RATANY FAMILY (Krameriaceae). 5 free, *unequally arranged,* reddish purple petals. 3 large upper petals, 2 tiny *glandlike lower petals.* Stamens 4. 1-seeded fruit. Red, p. 328.

 PEA FAMILY (Leguminosae). *Pealike* flower shape and *peapod* (legume capsule) found only in this family. Flowers irregularly shaped. 5 petals: 1 large, broad upper petal *(banner petal);* 2 similarly shaped side petals *(wing petals);* 2 lower petals joined to form a canoelike keel *(keel petals).* Leaves usually alternately arranged and compound, with *stipules* at the petiole base. Terminal leaflet replaced by a tendril in some genera. White, pp. 94–96; Yellow, pp. 190–196; Red, pp. 320–328; Blue, pp. 346–348, 380–382.

 VIOLET FAMILY (Violaceae). Flower parts on a plan of 5's. Irregularly shaped. *Violet-like* flowers each consist of 2 upper petals, 2 side petals, and a single lower lip petal. Ovary superior. The pistil has a distinctive thickened head and a short beak. White, p. 50; Yellow, p. 170; Blue, p. 378.

Petals 5, Completely Free
Regular Shape, Ovary Superior

(Families keyed below are all described on this page. Also, more families with characters listed in this heading follow on the next 2 pages.)

51a. Sepals 2. **Protulacaceae.**
51b. Sepals more than 2. See 52.

52a. Leaf tubular, or leaf blades flat with red glandular hairs. See 53.
52b. Leaf *not* as in 52a. See 54.

53a. Leaf long and tubular, with hood. **Sarraceniaceae.**
53b. Leaf flat with red glandular hairs. **Droseraceae.**

54a. Leaf and stem white or red. **Pyrolaceae.**
54b. Leaves green. See 55.

55a. Ovary in superior position. See 56.
55b. Ovary semi-inferior or in inferior position. See 68 on p. 420.

56a. Style and stigma beaklike and elongated; *or* stamens in an elongated, fused column. See 57 on p. 418.
56b. Style *not* beaklike or stamens *not* fused. See 59 on p. 418.

PURSLANE FAMILY (Portulacaceae). *Sepals 2.* Leaves entire, often linear, *thick and fleshy* with a *smooth yellow-green* or dark green surface. Petals 5 or many (3–16). Stamens 5 to many. Ovary superior. Orange, p. 238; Red, pp. 294–296.

PITCHER-PLANT FAMILY (Sarraceniaceae). Insect-eating plants that grow in bogs. Leaves tubular and hollow; erect with a caplike lid. Flower nodding on a leafless stem. Sepals and petals 5, free. Stamens many. Yellow, p. 174.

SUNDEW FAMILY (Droseraceae). Insect-eating herbs that grow in bogs. Leaves in a flat rosette; upper surfaces covered with *sticky, red, club-shaped glands*. Sepals and petals 5, free. Leafless flower stems (scapes). Red, p. 298.

WINTERGREEN FAMILY (Pyrolaceae). Low evergreen plants or saprophytes (red or white). Sepals and petals 5, petals distinct or united near bases. 10 elongated, *sausagelike anthers* open to release pollen through terminal pores or by lengthwise slits. Style 1 with a *caplike stigma.* Flowers regularly shaped. Ovary superior. The distinct subfamily Montropoideae consists of fleshy, white to red saprophytes. Petals 4, 5, or 6 (usually 5), forming an *urnlike corolla.* White, p. 76; Red, p. 314.

5 Petals, Completely Free
Regular Shape, Ovary Superior

(Families keyed below are described on this page or facing page, except as noted.)

57a. Stamens 5–10, free from each other. See 58.
57b. Stamens numerous, fused into a column. **Malvaceae.**

58a. Leaf base without stipules. **Geraniaceae.**
58b. Leaf base with stipules. Flowers yellow. **Zygophyllaceae.**

59a. Stem joints swollen, covered with a papery sheath. Flowers greenish; stamens 3–9. **Polygonaceae.** See p. 413.
59b. Stem joints bare; flowers colored (not green). See 60.

60a. Stamens numerous. See 61.
60b. Stamens 5, 10, or 20. See 62.

61a. Leaves in distinct opposite pairs, to top of stem. Stamens in 3 or 4 fused bundles. **Hypericaceae.**
61b. Leaves usually alternate or basal only. All stamens completely distinct to base. **Ranunculaceae.**

62a. Pistils 5, each with 1 style; nearly separate. Leaves thick, succulent. **Crassulaceae.**
62b. Pistils 1 or 2 (stigma may have 1–5 lobes. See 63.

63a. Pistils 2, forming 2 divergent beaks (rarely 3 or 4). **Saxifragaceae.** See p. 420.
63b. Pistil 1 or many, but not 2. See 64.

64a. Each leaf petiole has a pair of stipules at base. **Rosaceae.** See p. 420.
64b. No stipules at base of leaf petiole. See 65.

65a. Stigma caplike. **Pyrolaceae.** See p. 417.
65b. Stigma with 1–5 linear lobes, never caplike. See 66.

66a. Leaves opposite or whorled, often sticky-haired. See 67.
66b. Leaves alternate, surfaces smooth. **Linaceae.**

67a. Stamens 10 or fewer. **Carophyllaceae.**
67b. Stamens more than 10. **Aizoaceae.**

 MALLOW FAMILY (Malvaceae). Flowers regular. Leaves often *maplelike*. Showy, *hollyhock-like* flowers with 5 broad petals, free or slightly fused. Filaments (basal threadlike portion) of the *numerous stamens fused into a column* around the elongated styles. Blunt style tips protrude above the cluster of *free anthers*. Fruit *separates* into *nutlike carpels*. White, p. 44; Yellow, p. 166; Orange, p. 238; Red, pp. 288–290.

5 Petals, Completely Free
Regular Shape, Ovary Superior (*contd.*)

 GERANIUM FAMILY (Geraniaceae). Flower parts in 5's, free. Stamens 10. Ovary superior. *Styles elongated and beaklike.* When the 5 seeds mature, both the seed and the elongated style separate as one unit, with the style portion *coiling.* White, p. 50; Red, p. 292.

 CALTROP FAMILY (Zygophyllaceae). Leaves *pinnate,* with a pair of *stipules* at base of petioles. Flowers on a plan of 5's, stamens 10. Styles in a *short, erect column.* Ovary superior. Yellow, p. 124; Orange, p. 232.

 ST. JOHN'S WORT FAMILY (Hypericaceae). Leaves in *opposite pairs to top of stem,* often with dark or translucent dots. Flowers regular. Sepals and petals 5, free. *Stamens numerous,* united at bases into *bunches.* Yellow, p. 166.

 BUTTERCUP FAMILY (Ranunculaceae). Flowers regular or irregular in shape, with a spur or spurs in *Delphinium, Aconitum,* and *Aquilegia.* Flower parts free. Sepals and petals usually 5 to many. Sepals petal-like, but no true petals in *Thalictrum* and *Trautvettaria.* Stamens usually *numerous.* Fruits often a cluster of 1-celled achenes or a follicle pod *(Delphinium),* occasionally a berry. White, p. 42–44; Yellow, pp. 162–164; Red, pp. 236–286; Blue, pp. 344, 356–358; Green, pp. 396, 406.

 SEDUM FAMILY (Crassulaceae). Leaves and stems fleshy. Sepals and petals 5. Stamens 5 or 10. In some species, all parts in 3's or 4's. Petals often fused to form an *elongated urn.* Ovary segments barely adhere to each other. White, p. 78; Yellow, p. 180; Red, p. 286.

 PINK FAMILY (Caryophyllaceae). Leaves mostly opposite. *Joints of stem often swollen.* Flowers regularly shaped. Sepals 4 or 5, free or united. Petals 4 or 5, very small or larger, often *notched or deeply divided.* Stamens 10 or fewer. White, pp. 46–48; Yellow, pp. 158–160; Red, p. 296.

 FLAX FAMILY (Linaceae). Slender-stemmed plants, often with short, threadlike, linear leaves in alternate arrangement. Flower on a plan of 5's, parts free. Stamens set alternate to petals. Yellow, p. 122; Blue, p. 356.

 CARPETWEED FAMILY (Aizoaceae). Variable, mainly fleshy, sprawling plants. Sepals 4 or 5, green or *pink to reddish* and *petal-like.* No true petals. Stamens 3–10 or *numerous.* Red, p. 296.

5 Petals, Completely Free
Regular Shape, Ovary Inferior

(Families keyed below are described on this page.)

68a. Flowers in racemes, panicles, or spikes. See 69.
68b. Flowers in umbels. See 71.

69a. Styles 2, forming 2 divergent beaks (occasionally 3 or 4). **Saxifragaceae.**
69b. Style 1 or numerous, but not 2. See 70.

70a. Leaf petiole base with a pair of stipules. **Rosaceae.**
70b. Leaf petiole base without stipules. **Loasaceae.**

71a. Styles 2, the base swollen into humps. **Umbelliferae.**
71b. Style 1 or 5, base not swollen. **Araliaceae.**

 SAXIFRAGE FAMILY (Saxifragaceae). Flowers regular. Sepals and petals 5, often *dainty or threadlike*. Stamens 5 or 10. Semi-inferior ovary of *2 carpels* that are barely fused to each other, giving a *forked, hornlike* appearance. Leaves often *maplelike,* with *scattered, erect hairs*. White, pp. 52–54; Yellow, p. 170; Red, p. 236; Green, p. 404.

 ROSE FAMILY (Rosaceae). Flowers regular. Sepals and petals 5, free. *Stamens numerous.* Ovary semi-inferior, usually *saucerlike or cuplike* with upper surface often *shiny or glassy.* Fruit a group of achenes, a pome (apple), a drupe (prune), or an aggregate of tiny drupelets (raspberry). Leaves often compound. A *pair of prominent stipules* usually present at base of leaf petiole. White, p. 50; Yellow, p. 172; Red, p. 298.

 LOASA FAMILY (Loasaceae). Sepals 5, petals 5–10, *stamens numerous.* Flower parts attached on top of the *long, inferior ovary.* Leaves covered with short, barbed hairs that can *cling tightly* to passersby. Yellow, p. 168.

 CARROT FAMILY (Umbelliferae). Herbs with umbrella-like clusters (umbels) of numerous *tiny, 5-petaled flowers.* Leaves often compound. Flowers small, of 5 free petals and 5 stamens. Ovary inferior, with *2 styles. Style bases swollen,* forming a stylopodium. Fruit a dry schizocarp of 2 halves, found only in this family. White, pp. 58–62; Yellow, p. 176; Red, p. 286.

 GINSENG FAMILY (Araliaceae). Our species is an immense herb that grows in shady places. Tiny flowers in round umbels. Each flower of 5 tiny, free petals; stamens 5, set alternate to petals. Ovary more or less inferior with *1 or 5 styles* (base not swollen). Fruit a small fleshy berry. White, p. 58.

5 United Petals, Irregular Shape
Ovary Superior

(Families keyed below are described on this page).

72a. Stems square, ovary of 4 nutlets. See 73.
72b. Stems rounded, ovary a capsule. See 74.
73a. Ovary clearly 4-lobed. Strong mint odor. **Labiatae.**
73b. Ovary not lobed. No mint odor. **Verbenaceae.**
74a. Stems with green foliage. See 75.
74b. Stems *without* green foliage. **Orobanchaceae.**
75a. 1 spurred flower on a leafless stem. **Lentibulariaceae.**
75b. Flowers never single. Stems leafy. See 76.
76a. Stems and flowers in distinct pairs. **Acanthaceae.**
76b. Stems not branching in pairs. See 77.
77a. Sticky-haired plant. Ovary 1-chambered. **Martyniaceae.**
77b. Not sticky-haired. Ovary 2-chambered. **Scrophularia-ceae.**

 MINT FAMILY (Labiatae). Stems *square;* leaves *opposite.* Petals 5, in a 2-lipped corolla. Stamens 4 or 2. Style 1, tip unequally bilobed. Ovary of *4 nutlets.* Often a mintlike odor. White, p. 90; Yellow, p. 188; Red, 318; Blue, pp. 374–376.

 VERVAIN FAMILY (Verbenaceae). Resembles Mint Family (above), but no mintlike odor. Flowers *slightly 2-lipped.* Ovary *slightly 4-lobed.* Style 1 with *tip entire.* Orange, p. 238; Blue, p. 372.

 BROOMRAPE FAMILY (Orobanchaceae). Similar to Snapdragon Family (below). Low, fleshy herbs *without chlorophyll;* parasitic on roots of other plants. Yellow, p. 188; Red, p. 316.

 BLADDERWORT FAMILY (Lentibulariaceae). Plants grow in ponds or mud. Sepals 5, united. 5 united petals in a 2-lipped corolla with a spur. Stamens 2. White, p. 92; Yellow, p. 188; Red, p. 298.

 ACANTHUS FAMILY (Acanthaceae). Stems *streaked.* 2-lipped flowers, stems in mirrorlike pairs. Red, p. 316; Blue, p. 372.

DEVIL'S-CLAW FAMILY (Martyniaceae). *Sticky-haired* plant. Large, showy, 2-lipped flowers. Stamens 4. Very large, 2-hooked, clawlike seed capsule. Yellow, p. 122; Red, p. 316.

SNAPDRAGON FAMILY (Scrophulariaceae). Petals 4 or 5, fused in a *2-lipped corolla.* Stamens 4 (sometimes 5 or 2) with a sterile remnant of a 5th stamen present. *Fruit a capsule.* Various corolla shapes: (1) a wide tube with 2 distinct lips; (2) a narrow, pipelike tube with an upper lip that forms an arched, pointed snout; (3) nearly regularly shaped. *Stems round.* White, p. 88; Yellow, pp. 118–122; Red, pp. 244–250; Blue, pp. 350–354.

5 United Petals, Regular Shape
Ovary Superior

(Families keyed below are described
on the facing page, except as noted.)

78a. Stamens 10 or more. See 79.
78b. Stamens 5–8. See 82.

79a. Fused column of many stamens. **Malvaceae.** See p. 418.
79b. Stamens 10 (never in a fused column). See 80.

80a. Fleshy leaves, pistils 5. **Crassulaceae.** See p. 419.
80b. Leaves usually thin. Ovary a capsule. See 81.

81a. Each leaf of 3 heart-shaped leaflets. **Oxalidaceae.**
81b. Leaf of 1 blade of scale. **Pyrolaceae.** See p. 417.

82a. Plant tissue with thick, milky sap. See 83.
82b. Plant tissue with ordinary, watery sap. See 84.

83a. Flowers starlike, in umbels. **Asclepiadaceae.**
83b. Flowers in racemes, panicles, or solitary. **Apocynaceae.**

84a. Stems and leaves yellow-green or white. See 85.
84b. Stems and leaves green. See 86.

85a. Trailing yellow-orange stems. **Cuscutaceae.** See p. 410.
85b. Round or cone-shaped clusters of purple flowers.
     Lennoaceae.

86a. Corolla base constricted. **Nyctaginaceae.** See p. 415.
86b. Corolla tube not constructed at base. See 87.

87a. Stamens 5, opposite the 5 petal lobes. See 88.
87b. Stamens 5, set alternate to the 5 petal lobes. See 89.

88a. Flowers resemble pinwheels or shooting stars.
     Primulaceae.
88b. Tubular flowers in a headlike cluster. **Plumbaginaceae.**

89a. Flowers usually in 1-sided clusters. See 91.
89b. Flowers arranged in racemes, panicles, or spikes. See 90.

90a. Leaf petiole base with stipules. Leaves opposite.
     Loganiaceae.
90b. Leaf petiole without stipules. Leaves alternate. See 92.

91a. Fruit 2 or 4 distinct nutlets. Style 1. **Boraginaceae.**
91b. Fruit a capsule. Style 2-lobed. **Hydrophyllaceae.**

92a. Styles 3, cleft; ovary 3-celled. **Polemoniaceae.**
92b. Style 1 or 2; ovary with 1 or 2 cells. See 93.

93a. Style 1, tip entire. See 94.
93b. Style 1, tip 2-lobed. Stems vinelike. **Convolvulaceae.**

94a. Leaves in opposite pairs. **Gentianaceae.** See p. 415.
94b. Leaves in alternate arrangement. **Solanaceae.**

5 United Petals, Regular Shape
Ovary Superior (*contd.*)

 WOOD SORREL FAMILY (Oxalidaceae). Compound, *clover-like leaves.* Flowers funnel-like, stamens 10. Fruit an elongated, *explosive* capsule. Yellow, p. 170; Red, p. 298.

 MILKWEED FAMILY (Asclepiadaceae). Thick *milky sap.* 5 backswept petals, 5 cups (hoods) around a central column, each with a curving horn. Flowers in *umbels.* White, pp. 66–72; Yellow, p. 178; Orange, p. 234; Red, pp. 302–304; Green, p. 404.

 DOGBANE FAMILY (Apocynaceae). Thick *milky sap.* Corolla urnlike. White, p. 72; Red, p. 314; Blue, p. 356.

 LENNOA FAMILY (Lennoaceae). Petals 5–8 in a purplish, tubular corolla. Stamens 5–8. Stigmas caplike. Blue, p. 356.

 PRIMROSE FAMILY (Primulaceae). Flowers on a plan of 5's. Stamens *opposite* petals. Style 1. Flower shaped like a pinwheel or shooting star. White, p. 78; Yellow, p. 170; Red, p. 300.

 LEADWORT FAMILY (Plumbaginaceae). Sepals 5, fused and *folded like a fan.* Petals 5, fused or nearly free; stamens 5, opposite petals. Styles 5, free or united. Red, p. 286.

 LOGANIA FAMILY (Loganiaceae). Leaves opposite. Long, tubular corollas. Flowers in a *1-sided spike.* Red, p. 236.

 FORGET-ME-NOT FAMILY (Boraginaceae). Corolla trumpetlike. Stamens alternate to petals. Style 1, with *1–2 lobes.* Fruit *4 hard nutlets.* Flowers in a *1-sided coil.* White, p. 84; Yellow, p. 182; Orange, p. 234; Red, p. 314; Blue, pp. 344, 366.

 WATERLEAF FAMILY (Hydrophyllaceae). Flowers on a plan of 5's. Small, *bell-like* corollas. Stamens whiskerlike. Style 1; *2 caplike stigmas.* Flowers in a *coiled* cyme. White, p. 82; Yellow, p. 182; Red, p. 312; Blue, p. 364.

 PHLOX FAMILY (Polemoniaceae). Corolla trumpetlike. Stamens alternate to petals. *Style 1, with 3 clefts.* White, p. 88; Yellow, p. 180; Orange, p. 234; Red, pp. 308–312; Blue, pp. 360–362.

 MORNING-GLORY FAMILY (Convolvulaceae). Flowers on a plan of 5's. Corolla *bell-like, twisted* in bud. Stamens alternate to petals. Stigmas 2. White, p. 80; Red, p. 240; Blue, p. 362.

 NIGHTSHADE FAMILY (Solanaceae). Flower a trumpet or flat star. Stamens beaklike, alternate to petals. Style 1. White, p. 86; Yellow, p. 184; Red, p. 312; Blue, p. 368.

5 United Petals, Ovary Inferior

(Families keyed below are described on this or facing page.)

95a.   Corolla regularly shaped. See 96

95b.   Corolla irregularly shaped (2-lipped or flat). See 98.

96a.   Vines with tendrils. **Cucurbitaceae.**

96b.   Stem erect or prostrate, without tendrils. See 97.

97a.   Flowers in racemes, spikes, or solitary. See 99.

97b.   Numerous tiny disk flowers in heads, as in sunflowers. Each disk flower tubular (sometimes surrounded by ray flowers). **Compositae.**

98a.   Flowers pink, in twin pairs. **Caprifoliaceae.**

98b.   Flowers white or blue. **Campanulaceae.**

99a.   Flowers in racemes, panicles, or loose spikes. See 100.

99b.   Many tiny flowers in a flat or cone-shaped head. See 101.

100a.   Corolla base spurred; stamens 1–3. **Valerianaceae.**

100b.   Corolla not spurred; stamens 5. **Campanulaceae.**

101a.   Flowerhead a spiny cone; stamens free. **Dipsacaceae.**

101b.   Flowerhead of numerous ray flowers with flat, straplike corollas (inner disk flowers with tubular corollas often present). **Compositae.**

CUCUMBER FAMILY (Cucurbitaceae). Vines with or without tendrils. Flowers unisexual — female flower with an *inferior ovary*. Melonlike fruits. Flowers on a plan of 5's. Stamens often in a fused column. White, p. 56; Yellow, p. 124.

HONEYSUCKLE FAMILY (Caprifoliaceae). Regular shape. Sepals 5. Long, *funnel-like* flowers in *twin pairs*. Stamens 4. Ovary *inferior*. Leaves opposite. Red, p. 316.

BLUEBELL FAMILY (Campanulaceae). Regular *or* irregular in shape. (1) Bluebell subfamily — Campanuloideae. Sepals 5; petals 5, united as bowls or tubes. Stamens 5, fused into a distinctive *baseball-bat* structure. Ovary *inferior*. (2) Lobelia subfamily — Lobelioideae. Similar to Bluebell subfamily, but corolla has 2 distinct lips. White, p. 92; Red, p. 236; Blue, pp. 370, 376.

VALERIAN FAMILY (Valerianaceae). Irregularly shaped. Sepals obscure. Corolla tubelike, often with a *spur or inflated bulge at base*. Stamens 3 or 1. Ovary *inferior*. Fruit naked. Leaves opposite. White, p. 92; Red, p. 316.

TEASEL FAMILY (Dipsacaceae). Tiny flowers in a *dense head*. Calyx cuplike, with lobes ending in bristlelike tips. Irregular corolla with 4 or 5 lobes. Stamens 4. Ovary *inferior*. Blue, p. 370.

5 United Petals, Ovary Inferior: Sunflowers

SUNFLOWER FAMILY (Compositae). A sunflower is a *tightly packed head of numerous small flowers*. The individual flowers are of two types: (1) **ray flowers** with a *flattened, straplike* corolla; and (2) **disk flowers** with a *round, tubular* corolla. Within a head, 3 combinations of these 2 flower types are possible: all ray, all disk, or both outer ray and inner disk flowers. An individual flower consists of an *inferior,* single-seeded ovary *(achene);* an outer set of awns, feathery bristles, or scalelike *pappus* (sepals); a tubular corolla (disk flowers) or straplike corolla (ray flowers) of fused petals; a column of stamens (filaments free, but anther portion fused into a tube); and a 2-lobed style. Below the head are leafy bracts *(phyllaries).* The family is subdivided into tribes (subfamilies); see key below. White, pp. 98–110; Yellow, pp. 198–222; Orange, p. 234; Red, pp. 330–334; Blue, pp. 384–386; Brown, p. 402.

Key to Compositae Tribes

1a. Flowerhead composed *only of straplike ray flowers*. Each ray corolla tipped by *5 teeth. Milky sap.* Chicory Tribe: Cichorieae. White, p. 106; Yellow, pp. 218–222; Orange, p. 234; Red, p. 330; Blue, p. 384.
1b. Flowerhead of all disk flowers, or a combination of disk and ray flowers (each ray corolla tipped by *3 teeth*). See 2.

2a. Plants spiny, *thistlelike.* Flowerhead consists *only of disk flowers.* Each corolla *deeply divided* into narrow lobes. Thistle Tribe: Cynareae. White, p. 108; Yellow, p. 218; Red, p. 332; Blue, p. 384.
2b. Plant rarely spiny. Head of disk flowers only, *or* of disk and ray flowers. Corolla not deeply cleft. See 3.

3a. Flowerhead bracts (phyllaries) greenish. See 4.
3b. Flowerhead bracts papery or translucent. Plants white, woolly; or if green, they have a disagreeable odor. See 8.

4a. Papery scale around *some or all* flowers in head and attached *below achene* (seed-ovary) base. See 5.
4b. Papery scales *absent* from all flowers in head. See 6.

5a. 1 papery scale *below all disk flowers* in head. Each ray flower subtended by a bract but not enclosed. Sunflower Tribe: Heliantheae. White, p. 98; Yellow, p. 198–204; Red, p. 330.
5b. Papery scales *only in 1 circle* between the outer row of ray flowers and the inner zone of disk flowers. Each ray flower *enclosed* by an outer green bract. Plants often have unpleasant, resinous, *sticky hairs.* Tarweed Tribe: Madiinae. White, p. 98.

6a. Pappus (sepals) at tops of achene (seed) of bristles, awns, scales; or often without pappus. See 7.

6b. Pappus (sepals) at top of achene (seed) of *soft, spiderweb-like* or feathery (plumose) bristles. Flowerhead phyllaries (bracts) usually in *1 row;* if more than 1 row, the outer row very short. Senecio Tribe: Senecioneae. White, p. 110; Yellow, pp. 212–214.

7a. Flowerhead phyllaries (bracts) in 1 or 2 rows of equal lengths, *never overlapping* like shingles (imbricate). Woolly Sunflower Tribe: Helenieae. White, p. 100; Yellow, pp. 206–210; Red, pp. 330, 334.

7b. Flowerhead phyllaries (bracts) in several to many rows of graduated lengths, *overlapping like shingles* (imbricate). Aster Tribe: Astereae. White, pp. 102–104; Yellow, p. 216; Red, p. 334; Blue, pp. 384–386.

8a. Plants *white, woolly.* Flowerheads of *numerous* rows of *papery, translucent* phyllaries (bracts). Heads *only* of tiny disk flowers. Anther-sac bases *tailed* (see front endpapers). Everlasting Tribe: Inuleae. White, p. 110; Red, p. 334.

8b. Plants green. Leaves lacy, with a *strong, disagreeable odor.* Flowerhead with or without a few rows of thin, papery bracts. Anther-sac bases blunt. Mayweed Tribe: Anthemideae. White, p. 108; Yellow, p. 218.

Petals Numerous, Regular Shape
(Families keyed below are described on this page.)

102a. Pond plants. **Nymphaeaceae.**

102b. Land plants. See 103.

103a. Threadlike petals in a wheel; vines. **Passifloraceae.**

103b. Broad petals. Stem usually not vinelike. See 104.

104a. Leaves ordinary, flat. **Ranunculaceae.** See p. 419.

104b. Leaves absent; plant cactuslike with spines. **Cactaceae.**

WATER LILY FAMILY (Nymphaeaceae). Pond plants with large, floating leaves. Large, showy flowers. All flower parts numerous. White, p. 6; Yellow, p. 186; Blue, p. 344; Brown, p. 406.

PASSION FLOWER FAMILY (Passifloraceae). Vines. Wheel-like flowers with *many-colored, threadlike spokes.* Stamens *split into arches.* Yellow, p. 186; Red, p. 236; Blue, p. 344.

CACTUS FAMILY (Cactaceae). Thick, spiny plants; leafless. Cuplike flowers of numerous petals and stamens. Ovary inferior. Identity often based on *number and arrangement of spines in each spine cluster.* White, pp. 2–4; Yellow, pp. 126–142; Red, pp. 252–270.

Index

Smooth

Glandular

Haired

Starlike
hairs

Mealy

Rasplike

SURFACE TRAITS OF STEMS, LEAVES, ETC.

Capsule

Follicle

Legume
(peapod)

Nutlets

Achenes
(1-seeded units)

(opened)

Schizocarp
(Umbelliferae only)

Berry

Aggregate
fruit

Silique
(has central partition;
Cruciferae Family only)

Silicle
(small round
silique)

FRUIT TYPES

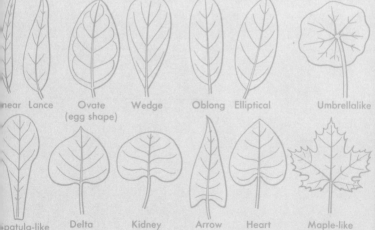

Linear Lance Ovate
(egg shape) Wedge Oblong Elliptical Umbrellalike

Spatula-like
(spoon shape) Delta Kidney Arrow Heart Maple-like

PLANT SHAPES—LEAVES USED AS EXAMPLES